WAITING for the UNICORN

CHINESE LITERATURE IN TRANSLATION
Editors
Irving Yucheng Lo
Joseph S. M. Lau
Leo Ou-fan Lee
Eugene Chen Eoyang
Poems and Lyrics of China's
INDIANA UNIVERSITY PRESS
鄭板橋

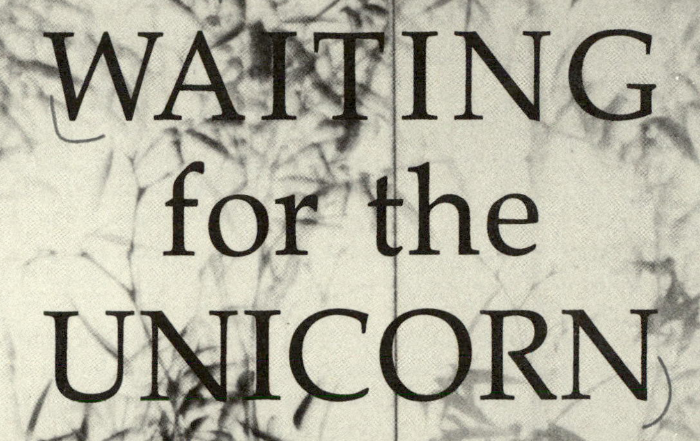

WAITING for the UNICORN

Last Dynasty,
1644–1911

EDITED BY
Irving Yucheng Lo
and
William Schultz

BLOOMINGTON & INDIANAPOLIS

This book has been published with the assistance
of a grant from the Pacific Cultural Foundation of Taiwan.

Manufactured in the United States of America

Library of Congress Cataloging-in-Publication Data

Waiting for the unicorn.
(Chinese literature in translations)
Bibliography: p.
Includes index.
1. Chinese poetry—Ch'ing dynasty, 1644–1912.
I. Lo, Irving Yucheng, 1922– . II. Schultz,
William, 1923– . III. Series.
PL2537.W28 1986 895.1'14'08 85-42816
ISBN 0-253-36321-7

1 2 3 4 5 90 89 88 87 86

For

Lena Dunn Lo

and

Darline L. Schultz

whose unsung labors of love
went into the making of this book.

CONTENTS

HUANG TSUNG-HSI (1610–1695)

KU YEN-WU (1613–1682)

SUNG WAN (1614–1673)

YU T'UNG (1618–1704)

WU CHIA-CHI (1618–1684)

LIU SHIH (1618–1664)

HSÜ TS'AN (fl. 1650)

SHIH JUN-CHANG (1619–1683)

WANG FU-CHIH (1619–1692)

CH'EN WEI-SUNG (1626–1682)

CHU YI-TSUN (1629–1709)

CH'Ü TA-CHÜN (1630–1696)

P'ENG SUN-YÜ (1631–1700)

YÜN SHOU-P'ING (1633–1690)

WANG SHIH-CHEN (1634–1711)

TS'AO CHEN-CHI (1634–?)

WU WEN (1644–1704)

HUNG SHENG (1645–1704)

CHA SHEN-HSING (1650–1727)

CHAO YI (1727–1814)

YAO NAI (1732–1815)

HUNG LIANG-CHI (1746–1809)

WU HSI-CH'I (1746–1818)

LI CHIEN (1747–1799)

HUANG CHING-JEN (1749–1783)

WANG TS'AI-WEI (1753–1776)

SUNG HSIANG (1756?–1826)

CHANG HUI-YEN (1761–1802)

CHANG WEN-T'AO (1764–1814)

SHU WEI (1765–1816)

PART III
Poets of the Nineteenth Century

KUNG TZU-CHEN (1792–1841)

WEI YÜAN (1794–1857)

HSIANG HUNG-TSO (1798–1835)

HO SHAO-CHI (1799–1873)

KU T'AI-CH'ING (1799–1876?)

WU TSAO (fl. 1840)

CHENG CHEN (1806–1864)

CHIANG CH'UN-LIN (1818–1868)

CHIN HO (1819–1885)

CHIANG SHIH (fl. ca. 1861)

LI TZ'U-MING (1830–1894)

WANG K'AI-YÜN (1833–1916)

CHUANG YÜ (? –1878)

FAN TSENG-HSIANG (1846–1931)

HUANG TSUN-HSIEN (1848–1905)

CH'EN PAO-SHEN (1848–1935)

WANG P'ENG-YÜN (1849–1904)

CHING AN (1851–1912)

CH'EN SAN-LI (1852–1937)

WEN T'ING-SHIH (1856–1904)

CHENG WEN-CHO (1856–1918)

CHU HSIAO-TSANG (1857–1931)

K'ANG YU-WEI (1858–1927)

YI SHUN-TING (1858–1920)

K'UANG CHOU-YI (1859–1926)

CHENG HSIAO-HSÜ (1860–1938)

T'AN SSU-T'UNG (1865–1898)

HSÜEH SHAO-HUI (1866–1911)

LIANG CH'I-CH'AO (1873–1929)

CH'IU CHIN (1877–1907)

WANG KUO-WEI (1877–1927)

ILLUSTRATIONS

PREFACE

When we first contemplated the idea of compiling an anthology of Ch'ing dynasty poetry, we agreed that it should be something more than a Cook's tour of what is a vast, relatively unknown, and often difficult terrain. In a manner of speaking, the question was whether to stop briefly at almost every station along the way, or whether to plan extended visits to only a few scenic spots of recognized acclaim. Because the territory had not been well charted, we decided to strike a balance between the two extremes. Thus, rather than translating only one or two poems by a large number of poets or translating a large number of poems by only a few poets, we have selected seventy-two poets who, we believe, best exemplify the substantial riches and enormous diversity of that era. The amount of space we have assigned to each poet varies substantially and represents our view of their respective importance and place in the context of their times, as well as our judgment of their poetry. Actually, we made some last-minute additions to the anthology with poems by Chin Jen-jui, Sung Hsiang, Wu Tsao, Chiang Shih, Cheng Hsiao-hsü, and Hsüeh Shao-hui when we discovered that their poetry still has considerable appeal for modern readers. On the whole, while some poets are represented by only two or three poems in translation, all major poets have been accorded a much larger representation.

The overall arrangement of the anthology is chronological; however, we have made no attempt to arrange the poems of a given poet in a similar fashion, for there are too many instances where we lack adequate data to do so.

In the introduction, we have sought to identify some of the primary historical and literary factors that helped shape the Ch'ing dynasty, and particularly those ideas and events that held special significance for the poet engaged in the act of creation. Although many matters concerning the history of Ch'ing dynasty poetry remain to be studied and clarified, our findings, while tentative in nature, are intended to provide some background against which the reader can measure the accomplishments of the poets represented in this volume. And, in a similar way, the short essays which precede the works of each poet are intended to assist the reader, particularly the nonspecialist, in gaining a deeper appreciation of the life and work of the individual writer.

These essays contain essential biographical and bibliographical information, and many include general comments on the literary and stylistic features of the poets concerned. Taken as a whole, these essays supplement and give specific meaning to many of the ideas expressed in the introduction.

The translations which comprise the centerpiece of this volume are almost entirely new. Only a very small percentage of the total are new versions of earlier translations into English or other Western languages. In some instances, modern annotated editions of a poet's work may exist in Chinese, in which case problems of understanding and interpretation are made less difficult. In other cases, previous translations into Japanese have proved helpful. However, in most instances our translators have had to sort out the problems themselves.

Although the editors are responsible for selecting the individual poets to represent their times, the choice of which poems to translate for a given poet has been left to the individual translator. Similarly, no attempt was made to impose a uniform style on our collaborators, for we believe that no single standard or method of translation is inherently superior to all others. On the other hand, it is vital that the integrity of the original poem be preserved with respect to meaning, structure, and informing spirit. Therefore, we have compared every translation to the original text, and have made such changes in the English as we deemed necessary to assure accuracy.

There are some features of this volume that require explanation. All Chinese words and names cited herein have been romanized according to the modified Wade-Giles system of transcription. Exceptions to this general rule are the use of the circumflex above the *e*, *en* and *eng* and the breve above *u*, both of which have been omitted, and the replacement of the letter *i* by *yi* so as to avoid unnecessary confusion. The spelling of Chinese place names also follows this same system, except in those instances where other spellings have long been standard, such as the names of major cities and the provinces; e.g., Hangchow instead of Hang-chou or Hangzhou, and Kiangsu instead of Chiang-su or Jiangsu.

Chinese personal names can be confusing at times, primarily because the individual often has more than two or three by which he or she is known. Throughout the narrative sections of this book, we have employed the formal names (*ming*) of individuals instead of their courtesy (*tzu*) or style (*hao*) names, unless otherwise indicated. The various personal names of an individual are listed at the beginning of the prefatory essays, where an author's courtesy name is given in italics and his or her style name is given in small capital letters. However, some men of letters adopted many different style names during the course of their careers, and in those instances there has been no attempt made to be exhaustive.

For those readers who may wish to consult the poems in their original texts, citations are provided for each poem indicating its location in a standard edition. For reasons of convenience, the titles of the Chinese texts are abbreviated. Most often, these are simple acronyms derived from the full title of the text in question. For example, the original texts of the poems translated for Ch'ien Ch'ien-yi are to be found in the *Mu-chai ch'u-hsüeh chi* and the *Mu-chai yu-hsüeh chi,* which have been abbreviated as MCCHC and MCYHC respectively. The collected works of some poets are, however, difficult to find outside China. Consequently, there are times when the reference is to an anthology or general collection, which is indicated by the surname of the compiler. Those references, along with a small number of other abbreviations used in the text, are identified in a list of abbreviations following the introduction. The citations also indicate volume (*chüan*) and page number. Modern texts require only page number listings; however, for old-style Chinese texts, Arabic numerals are used to indicate *chüan* numbers, and the letters *A* and *B* are employed when necessary to distinguish between *shang* and *hsia* ("upper" and "lower") sections of a single *chüan*. Page numbers follow the virgule, and there the letters *a* and *b* signify recto and verso sides of the page, respectively.

The primary materials for each poet—prefatory essay, translations, and footnotes—appear in that order in the text. Generally speaking, we have attempted to keep the annotation to a minimum; however, where a figure of speech or an allusion is central to the meaning of a line or poem, explanations are given in the appended notes. Some poems abound in historical and literary allusions, and in those cases the annotation has had to be quite extensive to clarify for the reader the full meaning of the poem.

The *tz'u* (lyrics) enjoyed a notable revival in Ch'ing times, and thus this kind of poetry is well represented in this volume. The various *tz'u* tune titles are cited in transliteration at the head of each lyric, and on their first occurrence translations of these tune titles in parentheses follow immediately below. Whenever a *tz'u* is provided with a "subject title," as increasingly is the practice in the Ch'ing dynasty (with the exceptions of Singde and Wang Kuo-wei in most instances), this subject title is given as the title of that lyric.

ACKNOWLEDGMENTS

This work was published with a Pacific Cultural Foundation subsidy, and we wish to acknowledge with gratitude this publication subsidy from the Pacific Cultural Foundation of Taiwan. Additionally, we gratefully acknowledge the several grants made to us at various stages of the editing and production process by both the Office of Research and Graduate Development and the International Programs Office of Indiana University.

We also thank Mr. Sung Lung-fei, editor-in-chief, *The National Palace Museum Monthly of Chinese Art* of Taiwan, for his technical help, especially in the preparation of the Chinese-language edition, *Tai-lin chi.* We also would like to thank Dr. Hsiao Ch'ing-sung, University of Arizona Library, for supplying us with the Chinese calligraphy found on the title page of the Chinese edition.

We wish to thank three of our friends—Professors Joseph S. M. Lau, University of Wisconsin; Jing-shen Tao, University of Arizona; Hung-i Wu, National Taiwan University—for reading through the introduction to the Chinese edition and suggesting a number of stylistic improvements on the translation.

We are also grateful to Professor Chu-tsing Li, University of Kansas, and to Dr. Julia K. Murray, The Art Museum, Princeton University, for their assistance in identifying the paintings of Cheng Hsieh and Yün Shou-p'ing used in this volume; and to the curatorial staffs of the National Palace Museum of Taiwan, The Art Museum of Princeton University, and the Shanghai Museum in the People's Republic of China for their courtesy and their kind permission to reproduce from their respective collections the rare calligraphy by some of the Ch'ing poets included in our anthology.

We also are grateful to the curatorial staffs of Shanghai Museum in the People's Republic of China and of the National Palace Museum of Taiwan for their permission to reproduce illustrations used on the jacket and in the book, and to our friends in the United States for the use of similar material from their private collections. Acknowledgements are also gratefully made to Random House, Inc. for permission to reprint three poems by Emperor K'ang-hsi from Professor Jonathan Spence's *Emperor of China: Self-Portrait of K'ang-hsi,* copyright © 1974 by Jonathan D. Spence; and to Doubleday Inc. for permission to reproduce two lyrics by Wang Kuo-wei in Ching-i Tu's translation and an excerpt from a poem by Li Po in Joseph J. Lee's translation, all from *Sunflower Splendor: Three Thousand Years of Chinese Poetry,* copyright © 1975 by Wu-chi Liu and Irving Lo.

For the inception and the completion of this project, we are also indebted to many colleagues in the field and former students for their encouragement and support. At an early stage, Professor Frederick W. Mote of Princeton University and the late Professor James J. Y. Liu of Stanford University generously provided helpful advice in reading over our list of individual poets represented in this volume. More recently, we have benefited from a careful reading of our manuscript by Professor Liu and by Professor Hans Frankel of Yale, both of whom have made invaluable suggestions for improvement and saved us from many errors; from an earlier discussion of the coverage with Professor Ch'ien Chung-lien of Kiangsu Normal University, Soochow, China; and from stylistic improvements of the Chinese version of the Introduction by Professor Joseph S. M. Lau of the University of Wisconsin. We also would like to acknowledge the help of two project assistants, Renée McCurdy and John D. Coleman, for their assistance in the preparation of the manuscript over a long period of time.

We owe the largest debt to our contributors, without whom this anthology would not have been possible. In their patience and understanding, and in the scholarly concern they have shown in their translations and short critical essays, all entered into the spirit of a collaborative effort with enthusiasm and graciousness. At the final editing stage, some of our collaborators very kindly offered helpful suggestions for refining translations other than their own, sometimes giving rise to fruitful exchanges, and in such instances, it was our privilege to serve as a conduit of advice and consultation. The spirit of cooperation extended to all aspects of the project, and this fact encourages us to believe that this anthology may be more of a beginning than an end to shared goals and interests. A very large share of any credit accruing from this undertaking must therefore go to all of those like-minded individuals who have contributed to its completion, all of whom have a deep interest in Ch'ing dynasty literary studies and are committed to good translation of Chinese poetry. Responsibility for any shortcomings or deficiencies in the final work are, of course, our own.

Finally, we wish to thank John Gallman, director of Indiana University Press, for his unfailing good humor and courtesy at all times and his staunch support of the project from its inception, and his editorial staff for their careful assistance in the production of this book.

IRVING YUCHENG LO
WILLIAM SCHULTZ

WAITING
for the
UNICORN

INTRODUCTION

> I desire to select and transmit the old,
> So that its splendor will last a thousand ages
> If I could succeed in emulating the Sage,
> I'd stop writing as though a unicorn had been captured.
>
> —Li Po (701–762)[1]

> Caged birds, too, know excitement and joy;
> Literature should flourish with the capture of a unicorn.
>
> —Tu Fu (712–770)[2]

In 481 B.C., or two years before the death of Confucius, it was recorded that a certain wagoner in the employ of the Shu-sun family in the state of Lu, found a *lin*, or female Chinese unicorn.[3] The animal had its left foreleg broken by the wagoner, who carried it home in a carriage. His master, deeming the matter inauspicious, sent word to Confucius, asking "What is it? Is it an antelope with a horn?" Confucius went to see it and said, "It is a *lin*. Why has it come? Why has it come?" Then he took the back of his sleeve to wipe away his tears which had dampened the lapel of his coat. Asked by his disciple why he had wept, Confucius replied, "The *lin* comes only when there is a wise ruler. It has now appeared when it is not the time, and it has been injured. That is why I am much grieved."[4]

Ch'i-lin, the name given by the Chinese to this fabled animal, finds its first mention in the book *Ch'un-ch'iu* (Spring and Autumn Annals), attributed to Confucius. Although the story may have been only apocryphal, the animal is said "to have the body of an antelope, the tail of an ox, and one horn," according to the *Shuo-wen*, the earliest Chinese dictionary published in 100 A.D. Writers of the other *Ch'un-ch'iu* commentaries, such as the *Kung-yang* and the *Ku-liang*, described it as "an animal of auspicious omen"; and from these accounts has emerged the legend that Confucius abandoned the writing of the annals of his native state after the capture of this unicorn. For millenia since, Chinese scholars have kept alive the metaphor about the reappearance of the unicorn as an omen of a world at peace.

This yearning for stability is no less intensely evoked in a poem by the T'ang poet Tu Fu—probably written during the years 742–744 or soon after the poet's sojourn in the Eastern Capital of Loyang and its vicinity—than what might have been expressed by a Ch'ing dynasty poet a thousand years later. Tu Fu's poem, in thirty couplets, was addressed to a "man in the mountain," the hermit Chang Piao, renowned for his filial piety and his accomplishments in calligraphy and verse. The last sixteen lines[5] of this poem read as follows:

> Nothing but remorse and sorrow since time began,
> A drifting life knows only to bend or stretch.
> This nation even now is glorifying conquests;
> Where can I find a place that still clings to humanity?
> Drums and pipes have usurped the music of the heavens;
> Mountain passes and hills, precarious beneath the wheel of a moon.
> The official arena: a network of garrison stations;
> Rebel flames: approaching the T'ao and Min rivers.[6]
> Desolate: the places of military council;
> Perplexed: the days of squabbling generals.
> Huge armies have been deployed everywhere;
> Remnant rebels are still numerous and disorderly.
> Caged birds, too, know excitement and joy;
> Literature should flourish with the capture of a unicorn.
> Late autumn is the time for plants to wither and die;
> I turn my head and gaze toward the pine groves.

Here, the sentiments expressed may be said to be identical with those found in the ancient *Shih-ching* (Book of Songs), or in some of the *yüeh-fu* poetry of later times, but the language and the feelings behind those images are distinctly Tu Fu's own.

Similarly, one can be intrigued by the same kind of continuity that exists between Tu Fu's verse and what was written by many Ch'ing dynasty poets. The voice might have been that of a Ming loyalist, like Ku Yen-wu,[7] couched with greater circumspection (by means of an allegorical bird), in lamenting the defeat of his emperor at the hands of the Manchus:

> The world is full of iniquities,
> Why do you struggle so in vain,
> Always urging on that tiny body,
> Forever carrying sticks and stones?

Or, it might have been that of a woman revolutionary, Ch'iu Chin, martyred in 1907, crying out:

> The sun and the moon lusterless, heaven and earth grow dark;
> Submerged womankind—who will rescue them?

Regardless of the differing circumstances, and the nature of a given poet's anguish, Chinese *classical* poetry (i.e., poems [*shih*] or lyrics [*tz'u*] written in classical meters; henceforth *poetry*) is what it always has been through the millenia—a tool of moral suasion on the one hand and on the other a means of self-expression for the educated class.

Despite the commonality of their basic assumptions about poetry, poets and critics sometimes differ on "what" dimensions of the self can or should be accommodated in verse and "how" this expression can best take place, and to what end. And, precisely because the art of poetry in China represents such an old tradition, the yearnings of later poets to break free from the constraints of the past appear especially strong among Ch'ing dynasty poets. They not only had the advantage of surveying the entire tradition but also frequently felt compelled to declare their preference on which aspects of the past they wished to emulate or reject. The poetry of the entire Ch'ing period, therefore, reflects a notable vitality deriving from a great heterogeneity of interests and ideas, a wide catholicity of tastes, continuity in certain things and discontinuity in others.

PROBLEMS OF PERIODIZATION

The arts, both literary and plastic, seldom go hand in glove with politics. Early T'ang poetry, for instance, represents in virtually all essential details a continuation of late Six Dynasties' verse. What is taken to be the characteristic voice of the T'ang era, the poetry of the "High T'ang" as represented by such figures as Wang Wei (701–761), Li Po, and Tu Fu, emerged only many decades after the founding of the dynasty. Our concern here, however, is not the often intractable problem of historical periodization per se, but rather merely to note that when we decided there was a need for an anthology of late imperial poetry in translation, we were conscious then, as now, that the literary record, like that of institutional or intellectual developments, seldom coincides precisely with political history. Our decision to follow established practices and preserve the dynastic framework was therefore based on matters of convenience more than anything else. Furthermore, also as a matter of convenience, we have divided the main section of the text into three divisions: the seventeenth, eighteenth, and nineteenth centuries. It would therefore be useful to indicate where the literary boundaries might lie, were we to be guided by literary considerations alone.

We are still at a relatively primitive stage in the formal study of Ch'ing dynasty classical verse; at present there are only three monographic studies in English on the poets of that era, and few more than that in Chinese or Japanese. The present evidence does seem to suggest, however, that there is little if any discontinuity in literary values and practice between the late Ming and the early Ch'ing. The point at which significant change seems to have occurred is the late sixteenth century, when Li Chih (1527–1602) and the iconoclastic Kung-an School of the Yüan brothers—Yüan Tsung-tao (1560–1600), Yüan Hung-tao (1568–1610) and Yüan Chung-tao (1570–1623)—raised aloft the banner of revolt against the rigid and restrictive classicism which had long dominated the literary scene. That liberation of the creative spirit, which tended to coincide with the onset of changes in the intellectual world at large, continued into the early Ch'ing era, with important consequences for the history of Chinese poetry. And it is for this reason that we have felt justified in beginning our selection of poets with the so-called Ming loyalists (*yi-min*), such as Huang Tsung-hsi, Ku Yen-wu, Wu Chia-chi, and Wang Fu-chih. Moreover, the term *yi-min* is primarily a political concept, and only by extension a literary one.

At the other end of the Ch'ing political continuum, starting perhaps as early as the late eighteenth century, there are once again indications of a change in literary sensibilities. What these early stirrings actually mean is certainly arguable, but there is a hearkening back to Kung-an School arguments that each age must speak in its own voice. A growing awareness of external social realities also becomes evident in the poems of Cheng Hsieh, Chao Yi, and Chang Wen-t'ao. Other poets of the time, such as Wei Yüan, Cheng Chen, and Li Chien, also show an independence of spirit and a consciousness of the social relevance of the poetic act. Later, the little known but significant poet Chin Ho demonstrated even greater independence from the received tradition by adopting a remarkably free style, a semivernacular diction, and folk themes in his long narrative verse. Toward the close of the nineteenth century, the poet-diplomat Huang Tsun-hsien publicly declared his intention to write as he spoke, manifested a modernist interest in new and foreign themes and vocabulary, and consciously sought to make his poetry relevant to the times. These several poets were not alone in voicing a claim to independence: even a political conservative like K'ang Yu-wei, who founded the Society for the Preservation of the Emperor (Pao-huang hui) declared, "My meaning, my experiences have nothing to do with Li Po or Tu Fu." In fact, political and literary sensibilities do not always neatly coincide: an arch royalist like K'ang found life tolerable only as a teacher after the fall of the empire, while a scholar thoroughly trained in Western philosophy and research methodologies like Wang Kuo-wei was similarly antirepublican in spirit (both men died in the same year). Besides, there are modernist elements in the poetry of Chin Ho, Huang Tsun-hsien, Ch'iu Chin, and others that are entirely indigenous or only partly foreign derived. Taken all together, such evidence seems to suggest that by the late Ch'ing poetry had already entered a period of transition, thus supporting the thesis advanced by Milena Doleželová-Velingerová for drama and fiction that the rise of modern Chinese literature should be viewed as "part of a continuous process into which even the most discontinuous periods and strongest foreign influences have to be integrated,"[8] and perhaps also for poetry.

THE HISTORICAL SETTING

When the Manchus, a small nomadic tribe of Jurched peoples which had been united and welded into a disciplined, cohesive paramilitary society early in the seventeenth century, invaded the vast and populous Chinese world several decades later (they were ably assisted in this enterprise by Chinese and other allies), their avowed purposes were to avenge the Ming emperor who had committed suicide prior to the capture of Peking by the rebel armies of Li Tzu-ch'eng (1605?–1645), and to preserve native Chinese culture. They had prepared themselves well for their self-appointed task, and for at least the first 150 years of their 260-year reign, they proved to be vigorous, remarkably able, and firm-minded autocrats. Under their guidance and supervision, the Ming form of government was revived largely intact, and the basic social, economic, and cultural patterns of life were little disturbed.

Once the initial conquest and consolidation of power was completed, a long era of relative peace and stability was ushered in. During the reigns of the emperors K'ang-hsi (*reg.* 1662–1722), Yung-cheng (*reg.* 1723–1735), and Ch'ien-lung (*reg.* 1736–1795), which spanned the latter half of the seventeenth and nearly the entire eighteenth century, the Ch'ing empire achieved an almost unprecedented level of splendor and influence in East and Southeast Asia. Its armies extended its borders to embrace an area surpassed only by the Yüan (Mongol) dynasty of the fourteenth century. Agricultural production increased significantly as new lands were brought under cultivation and new crops and quick-ripening strains of rice were introduced. Production in the nonagricultural sector also showed important gains, and there was substantial growth in domestic commerce and foreign trade. These impressive gains in the economic life of the nation were offset however by a rapid growth in population. According to Leo A. Orleans's study of China's population growth, between 1651 and 1734 "more reasonable estimates seem to range from about seventy to eighty million early in the period and 130 and 140 million during the later years."[9] Chinese sources cited by Orleans indicate an increase "from 143 million in 1741 to 432 million in 1851,"[10] but the author of this study finds these figures "undoubtedly excessive." He adds, however, that despite questionable variations in the annual figures, "the long-range trend of increase is reasonable." He also finds evidence to show a decline from a "high of over 430 million just prior to the Taiping Rebellion to a figure usually estimated at between 375 and 400 million when the empire fell in 1911."[11] This enormous growth in population created heavy pressures on the land, which led to large scale migrations into marginal regions, but this did little to alleviate the problem. In time, these tensions gave rise to widespread social disorder and violence.

The final years of the Ch'ien-lung era were marked by the outbreak of rebellion among Miao tribal peoples in Kweichow province and nearby areas, which was followed by the White Lotus sectarian rebellion in the Shensi-Hupeh-Szechwan region. Widespread corruption in government at this time also limited its ability to respond effectively to these threats to its existence. Although both rebellions were ultimately suppressed by its military forces, the cost in human lives and government fiscal resources was enormous. By mid-nineteenth century, the Manchu government found itself beset by still more serious challenges: new and dangerous pressures along its coastal borders exerted by the intrusive Western powers, worsening economic and social conditions within its borders, spreading corruption in its understaffed, overstrained bureaucracy, and widening domestic discontent. Ultimately, rebellions erupted across the land: the Taiping Rebellion in the southern and central provinces, the Nien Rebellion in the central and north-central provinces, Muslim rebellions in both southwest and northwest China, another in the long line of Miao rebellions, and numerous other disturbances of a more localized nature. Without the vital aid of local Chinese leaders and the militias they raised in defense of the dynasty, it is unlikely it could have survived these events. Eventually, however, a semblance of order was restored, although the underlying causes of unrest remained largely unresolved, and thus the old order persisted amid a darkening storm raised by internal decay and foreign aggression. A rethinking about a whole range of topics, including poetry, became imperative.

SOCIOECONOMIC ASPECTS OF CH'ING POETRY

The literature of any age is subject most of all to its own inner dynamics, and less directly to the various intellectual, political, and socioeconomic currents of its time. Readers of Chinese poetry in translation must reckon with the fact that classical poetry served a multiplicity of functions in traditional Chinese society. Members of the literate class, both men and women, received their training in the art of versification from early childhood. All were expected to be able to compose poems extemporaneously on a variety of social occasions. A poem could be sent, in lieu of a letter, to one's family or friends while traveling. Or, poems could be demanded of participants at a gathering of friends on an outing, on important occasions such as birthdays, homecomings, or leave takings, or to celebrate festivals, or as a parlor game (such examples can be seen in the novel *Hung-lou meng*, in which art truly imitates life in every detail). And, as literacy spread rapidly among the newly wealthy merchant class, private academies flourished (accepting more and more students from humble backgrounds), and both the printing and the collecting of books became more widespread, poetry became less and less the exclusive preserve of aristocrats, officials, and scholars, as was largely true of earlier dynasties (although, to be sure, the scholar/gentry class retained its dominance in this sphere, as in others relating generally to the polite arts). The first effect on literature of all this was the vast number of men and women who actively cultivated the art (and the relative ease with which their works could get published), resulting in a prodigious outpouring of poetry. The modern anthology *Ch'ing shih hui* (A Collection of Ch'ing Poetry),[12] compiled under the sponsorship of Hsü Shih-ch'ang (1855–1939) and published in 1929, contains representative selections from the works of more than six thousand poets—about three times the number of poets anthologized in the *Ch'üan T'ang shih* (Complete T'ang Poetry)—and literally tens of thousands of poems. The recently founded Ming-Ch'ing Literature Institute, which is based at Kiangsu Normal University (under the directorship of Professor Ch'ien Chung-lien), has since 1982 published two volumes of articles and essays on Ming and Ch'ing authors. It is currently surveying the extant literature, and it reports that the individual collected works of Ch'ing *tz'u* poets alone number over five thousand titles. These figures can provide some indication of the immensity of the extant literature, and our coverage of only seventy-two poets must therefore be considered very modest, indeed.

The wide diversity of background of the poets included in this volume, their social provenance, and even their places of birth, is also

Geographical Distribution of the Place of Origin of the Seventy-two Poets Included in This Volume

		Kiangnan		Central Plain				Northern Provinces			Remote Provinces				
Number of Poets		*K.*	*Ch.*	*A.*	*Ki.*	*Hn.*	*Hp.*	*Hop.*	*Stg.*	*Shi.*	*Sn.*	*Kw.*	*Kg.*	*Kgi.*	*Fn.*
Part I:	25	10	5	1	0	1	0	2(M)	4	1	0	0	1	0	0
Part II:	16	9	4	1	0	0	0	0	0	0	1	0	1	0	0
Part III:	31	4	8	0	2	6	1	1(M?)	1	0	0	1	3	1	3
Total	72	23	17	2	2	7	1	3	5	1	1	1	5	1	3
Total by regions:		40 (55%)		12 (17%)				9 (13%)			11 (15%)				

Abbreviations: *K.*: Kiangsu; *Ch.*: Chekiang; *A.*: Anhwei; *Ki.*: Kiangsi; *Hn.*: Hunan; *Hp.*: Hupeh; *Hop.*: the modern-day province of Hopei (i.e., Chihli, with *M.* in parenthesis following the numeral used to indicate Manchu origin); *Stg.*: Shantung; *Shi.*: Shansi; *Sn.*: Szechwan; *Kw.*: Kweichow; *Kg.*: Kwangtung; *Kgi.*: Kwangsi; *Fn.*: Fukien.

characteristic of the times. It is to be expected that since the Kiangnan region, roughly corresponding to the present-day provinces of Kiangsu and Chekiang (i.e., the lower Yangtze delta) was the wealthiest and most culturally advanced region in the empire, the representation of poets from this area would be consistently high for all three periods. Such is indeed the case, totaling forty of seventy-two poets, or 55 percent. As the tabulation (see above) will also show, Southerners outnumber Northerners, and only toward the second half of the nineteenth century, as the high culture spread further south and west, did outlying provinces like Kwangtung or Fukien begin to assume greater importance, with Fukien continuing as an important book-publishing center.

An even more interesting revelation than geographical distribution is perhaps the professional orientation of these poets. While the majority can be regarded as "professionals" in the sense that they were seriously devoted to their craft—many of them edited and published their own works, and were prolific writers of "remarks on poetry" books as well as annotators and compilers—they were in another sense "amateurs" since they were involved in other types of work and also made important contributions to other branches of learning. The scholarly annotations of Tu Fu's works by Ch'ien Ch'ien-yi and Su Shih's (1037–1101) works by Shih Jun-chang are still admired today. Scores of other poets like Wang Shih-chen, Chu Yi-tsun, Shen Te-ch'ien, Chang Hui-yen, and Chu Hsiao-tsang have left us massive anthologies and collectanea, which are still in use. On the other hand, there were poets who were primarily political thinkers and philosophers (Ku Yen-wu, Huang Tsung-hsi, etc.) or historians (Chao Yi), essayists (Yao Nai and Li Tz'u-ming), literary historians (Wang Kuo-wei), bibliophiles (Ch'ien

Ch'ien-yi, etc.), playwrights (Hung Sheng, Chiang Shih-ch'üan, etc.), calligraphers (Ho Shao-chi, etc.), painters (Cheng Hsieh, Yün Shou-p'ing, etc.), political activists (Chin Jen-jui, Ch'iu Chin, etc.), reformers (Liang Ch'i-ch'ao, etc.), diplomats (Huang Tsun-hsien), geographers (Wei Yüan), emperors (K'ang-hsi), or Buddhist monks (Ching An). There are also quite a few commoners and social failures like Wu Chia-chi, Huang Ching-jen, Chiang Ch'un-lin, and Chiang Shih. There are also well-bred, educated women from both scholar and merchant families (Wu Tsao, Hsüeh Shao-hui, etc.) as well as talented courtesans who married well (Liu Shih, Ku T'ai-ch'ing). That so many of these men and women were not only committed poets but also actually "engaged" in one kind of work or another (besides merely serving in the state bureaucracy after passing the civil service examinations for men) testifies to the pervasiveness of poetry among the educated and also helps to differentiate the poets of the Ch'ing dynasty from those of earlier periods. And that so many of the better poets of the age also had developed interests in classical scholarship is a reflection of the immense vitality of that field of endeavor in Ch'ing times.[13] This fact also accounts in part for the scholarly tone we find in the verse of many of these people. But since poetry represented both the exercise of acquired literary skills and, as it had always been so regarded by Confucianists, the highest form of the literary arts, Ch'ing poets and critics had to reconcile the highest human aspirations with life in the real world as they found it. How to make the noblest of ideals relevant to their own times became the all-engrossing task for those writers who felt the need, perhaps, to define and defend poetry before a world growing more distant and more disenchanting as the era drew to its close.

SOME CHARACTERISTICS OF CH'ING POETRY

Ch'ing dynasty poets did not invent new genres as did the poets of the T'ang, Sung, and Yüan periods; their assertive role, however, can be seen in their attempts to accommodate, to transform, and at times to enrich the old traditions. As material conditions altered, the poets of different periods and of divergent background, training, and temperament naturally responded to the outside world in differing ways. Nevertheless, a few dominant modes of thinking may be pointed to as characteristic of the poetry of this dynasty as a whole. The first is the intensity of its patriotic fervor, particularly at the beginning of the period and toward the end, with grief and indignation being replaced by intense pessimism and despair. The second is a constant awareness of the conflicting demands of "imitation" versus "originality," creating a plethora of critical theories, and accompanied by an ongoing debate on the relative merits of T'ang versus Sung poetry. A third quality is the greater degree of historical-mindedness and preference for dealing with the concrete, as evidenced by the growth of realism and popularity of both narrative and *yung-wu* poetry (poems on objects). And finally, paradoxical though it may seem, there is a pronounced retreat into the allegorical mode, especially in connection with the revival of the *tz'u*, under the rallying cry of the Ch'ang-chou school of criticism, whose purpose was no more and no less than to justify the obscure as relevant and also to make the relevant obscure.

POETRY AND POLITICS

The most enduring concept in Chinese poetic criticism, from the "Great Preface" to the *Shih-ching*, teaches that poetry has the power "to express grievances" (*yüan*) and to enable the poet to acquit himself as a member of an organized social group or community" (*ch'ün*). This dictum more than points to an ideal, as if to say: "In the beginning there is the Word." In this instance, the Word is actually made tangible when one remembers that the earliest known poet in China is the historical figure, Ch'ü Yüan (343?–278 B.C.), a minister of the state of Ch'u whose career ended in suicide by drowning and whose grievances against the corruptions of his time were couched in the elegant allegorical language of the autobiographical poem *Li Sao*, beloved by nearly all Chinese poets ever since. Hence, following the fall of each dynasty in China, there was always an attempt to collect and publish the works of eminent men of letters from the ancien régime, who were always euphemistically referred to as *yi-min*, or "remnant people," denoting that they were not only "surviving" exemplars from the past, but also, perhaps, in the Arnoldian sense, "saving remnants" to the present. Ch'ien Ch'ien-yi, Huang Tsung-hsi, Ku Yen-wu, and Wang Fu-chih are considered among the luminaries of this group at the beginning of the Ch'ing era, just as people like Cheng Hsiao-hsü, Chu Hsiao-tsang, and many others would be similarly classified in Republican times. That their poetic oeuvres contain a heavy outpouring of melancholy and despair should therefore come as no surprise.

The despondent voices of these men and women gain greater poignancy when one recalls that many of them were actively engaged in the political life of the nation, either resisting the new Manchu court, or defending it against rebel forces. This kind of involvement stemmed from the popularity of organized societies, such as the Fu-she (Renewal

Society) founded by Chang P'u (1602–1647) and Wu Wei-yeh. Its 1639 "Nanking Manifesto" ("Liu-tu fang-luan kung chieh," or "A Public Proclamation Against Disorder for Those Remaining at the Capital"), regarded by historians as the first "direct interference in politics on the part of students" in China, was signed by Huang Tsung-hsi, for instance. Other similar organizations flourished in the Kiangnan region, the hotbed of resistance against the invading Manchu armies, and were later banned by the court.

Nevertheless, this type of politico-literary club survived until the very end of the Ch'ing dynasty. The Nan-she (The Southern Society) was founded by three poets: Ch'en Ch'ao-nan (1874–1933), Kao T'ien-mei (1877—1925), and Liu Ya-tzu (1887–1964). It had its first meeting on 13 November 1909, at Tiger Hill (Hu-ch'iu) in Soochow, the site of a Fu-she meeting in 1633. Many of those modern poets became revolutionaries, and the story of Liu Ya-tzu's friendship with Mao Tse-tung (1893–1976) is especially well known to students of modern Chinese history. The picture of Liu Ya-tzu, with his gaunt, esthetic face and his flowing white beard, standing behind the chairman on a platform in front of T'ien-an-men to celebrate the Communist victory in 1949, may be said to epitomize a kind of siren's song, a spell which politics has cast over poetry in China from ancient times to the present. As a matter of fact, toward the end of the dynasty, there was a strong interest in reviving the loyalist sentiments through the publication of the writings of such men as Ku Yen-wu and Huang Tsung-hsi, as in the attempt by Liang Ch'i-ch'ao to popularize the latter's *Ming-yi tai-fang-lu*, (translated by Wm. Theodore de Bary as "A Plan for the Prince," unpublished doctoral dissertation, Columbia University, 1953). And it may be more than a matter of stylistic coincidence that, while the 1629 Fu-she Oath consists of "Seven Don't's" ("Don't follow that which is contrary to established norms," "Don't ignore the classics," etc.), the battle-cry of the May Fourth Movement—Hu Shih's (1891–1962)"A Humble Proposal For Reforming Literature" (*Wen-hseüh kai-liang ch'u-yi*), published in January 1917—is also couched in the similar "Eight Don't's" ("Write only when you have something to say," "Don't imitate the ancients," etc.).[14] Indeed, whether or not the beginnings of modern Chinese literature can be assigned to the late Ch'ing era, an indisputable element of continuity is the strong note of patriotism, which colors both periods. In classical Chinese poetry at least, only a thin line divides a "poet" and a "patriot" in that tradition. From Ku Yen-wu and Wang Fu-chih to K'ang Yu-wei and Ch'iu Chin, their poetic works visibly reflect subtle changes in the political and social temper of the times, as for instance when the modern sense of nationhood gradually dawns in the Chinese consciousness and ultimately replaces the concept of loyalty to the emperor, which Confucianists regarded as the chief duty of a subject.

POETRY IN AN AGE OF PATRONAGE, CONTROVERSY, AND PARTISANSHIP

A system of rewards and punishments, resulting in several celebrated instances of patronage and persecution of literature, is characteristic of any dictatorial rule, imperial or proletarian. It is widely known, for example, that during the height of the Great Proletarian Cultural Revolution, which nearly decimated the Chinese intellectual class in this century (1965–1975), many of the leading scholars in the People's Republic of China were shielded from physical harm by the late Premier Chou En-lai (1898–1976), who assigned them to the huge task of editing and punctuating the *Twenty-five Dynastic Histories.* The initial Manchu distrust of Chinese intellectuals at the beginning of the Ch'ing dynasty was also destructive of the intellectual life of the time. It led to the persecution, trial, and execution of seventy scholars in 1663, as documented by the excellent study *The Literary Inquisition of Ch'ien-lung* by Luther Carrington Goodrich. A scholar from Chekiang by the name of Chuang T'ing-lung, who aspired to edit a history of the Ming dynasty and who was said to have used "improper" language, such as mentioning the Ch'ing emperors by their personal names, perished in prison around 1660. His body was disinterred and burned, and his family and colleagues were all executed or exiled. Between 1741 and 1788, as many as sixty-three cases of such literary inquisition were perpetrated. The 1769 edict against the poet Ch'ien Ch'ien-yi, then dead for over a century, reads as follows:

> Now Ch'ien Ch'ien-i is already dead, and his bones have long since rotted away. We will let him be. But his books remain, an insult to right doctrines, and a violation of [the principles of] loyalty. How can we permit them to exist and be handed down any longer. They must early be done away with. Now therefore let every governor-general and governor see to it that all the bookshops and private libraries in his jurisdiction produce and send [to the yamen] his *Ch'u Hsüeh Chi* and *Yu Hsüeh Chi.* In addition let orders be despatched to small villages, country hamlets, and out of the way regions in mountain fastnesses for the same purpose. The time limit for this operation is two years. Not a volume must escape the burning.[15]

Such harsh measures of suppression were intended, of course, to silence opposition, imagined or real. The other side of the coin was rewards and patronage. In addition to the regular civil service examinations, for example, the Ch'ing court convened a special examination to seek out men of talent in private life. This was the *po-hsüeh hung-tz'u*, or "Extensive Learning and Superior Literary Arts" examination offered in 1678 and again in 1771, whereby hundreds of scholars, regardless of age, were invited, on recommendation, to participate. To be sure, some of those invited to do so declined the honor. In 1771, as many as 267 candidates were recommended to the emperor, but only 220 actually showed up for the examination. In time, special styles of rhetoric, in the writing of both prose and verse, were encouraged and expected of examination candidates, with style invariably being assigned greater value than content. This practice stifled creativity, and many scholars such as Chin Jen-jui, Cheng Hsieh, and later progressive thinkers protested against the excessive rigidity of the so-called eight-legged (*pa-ku*) essay style. While success in passing the civil service examinations usually led to high office for the individual, conformity to the official orthodoxy was the price exacted by the system.

Perhaps the greatest contribution to knowledge made by the Ch'ing government was the assiduous and often valuable patronage of large scale literary undertakings. Wealthy officials and merchants, following the lead of the government, also supported the arts and letters.[16] However, the government suspended its patronage of scholarship after the eighteenth century. Among the more notable results of such officially sponsored scholarship were the still standard *K'ang-hsi tzu-tien* (K'ang-hsi Dictionary), completed in 1716; the widely-used phrase dictionary, the *P'ei-wen yün-fu*, in 106 *chüan*, which was commissioned in 1704 and completed in 1711 (the printing was supervised by Ts'ao Yin, 1658–1712, the grandfather of the novelist Ts'ao Chan); the *Ming-shih* (History of the Ming Dynasty), one of the finest works of historical scholarship of its kind, which was authored by an imperial commission during the K'ang-hsi reign; the *P'ei-wen-chai yung-wu shih* (P'ei-wen Collection of Poems-on-Objects), compiled by a group of scholars including Cha Shen-hsing and printed in 1706; the *Ch'üan T'ang shih* (Complete T'ang Poetry), consisting of more than 48,900 poems by more than 2,200 authors, in 900 *chüan*, was printed in 1713; the *T'ang-Sung shih-chun* (The Best Poetry of T'ang and Sung), printed in 1751–1760; the *Ku-chin t'u-shu chi-ch'eng* (The Complete Collection of Writings and Illustrations, Past and Present), a vast collectanea of data in 10,000 *chüan*, intended as a guide for the emperor and his officials in the conduct of government affairs and presented to the throne in 1725; and, of course, the *pièce de resistance*, the *Ssu-k'u ch'üan-shu* (The Complete Collection of the Four Treasuries), the largest compilation of classical and literary tests ever undertaken by the Chinese state, was the product of years of labor by a panel of 361 distinguished scholars who were convened and supported by the Ch'ien-lung emperor. These scholars selected and edited for publication in a common format 3,461 individual works deemed worthy of preservation, totaling 78,000 *chüan*. The final collection was so large that only seven copies were produced for deposit at designated locations in the empire. The *Ssu-k'u ch'üan-shu tsung-mu t'i-yao* (An Annotated Index to the Complete Collection of the Four Treasuries), containing descriptive and critical notes on these 3,461 works and another 6,793 works not copied into the *Ssu-k'u*, was printed in 100 *ts'e* by means of movable-type block-print in 1782. No other Chinese or foreign government ever sponsored textual and emendation scholarship on such a massive scale. The closest parallel may be the Académie Francaise, under King Louis XIV, when one recalls that the first dictionary of the French language, published by the Académie—in four volumes (admittedly, a Chinese *chüan* corresponds to a "chapter" rather than a "volume" in the Western sense)—was offered to the public only in 1694, nearly sixty years after the founding of the Académie!

But the objectives of the Ch'ien-lung emperor in sponsoring the last-mentioned project were not wholly benign. For the survey of all extant literature and scholarship which the *Ssu-k'u* project entailed was a convenient mechanism for ferreting out all subversive, anti-Manchu sentiments, real and imagined. As a result, many invaluable texts were ordered destroyed and their authors, if still living, subjected to extremely harsh reprisal. The inquisitorial spirit which infected some of these compilation projects quite naturally generated a mood of nervous caution among the scholarly community. On the other hand, this kind of patronage, public and private, did provide employment for degree holders who could not find positions in the state bureaucracy.

Many scholars themselves were attracted to this kind of endeavor, and the compilation of large anthologies or collectanea became, if not the rage, at least a common enough activity since the beginning of the Ch'ing dynasty. To cite just a few of the outstanding compilations, there were Ch'ien Ch'ien-yi's *Lieh-ch'ao shih-chi* (Anthology of Ming Poetry), 1649; Ku Ssu-li's (1669–1772) *Yüan-shih hsüan* (Selected Poems of the Yüan), published in three series in 1694, 1702, and 1720 with the fourth series coming out circa 1810); and Li E's *Sung-shih chi-shih* (Records of Sung Poetry), 1746—not to mention the widely influential *T'ang shih san-pai shou* (Three Hundred T'ang Poems), compiled by an anonymous scholar during the Ch'ien-lung era, known as *Heng-t'ang t'ui-shih* (The Retired Scholar of Heng-t'ang), later conjecturally identified as Sun Chu.[17] Because of its compactness and the depth of insight that governs the selection, this small anthology achieved a place comparable to Palgraves's *Golden Treasury* in China, thus becoming a primer for school children for generations to come. Many other poets of the era, from Wang Shih-chen to Shen Te-ch'ien and Chu Hsiao-tsang were avid anthologists; and several resorted to the task of compiling anthologies in order to advance their own critical views on poetry. The impact on poetry of all this kind of scholarship was to encourage greater introspection, a deeper awareness of the past, and sometimes a heavier reliance on the use of allusions, as is true in the case of Ch'ien Ch'ien-yi.

This tendency also translated into a devotion to textual criticism and a fascination with historical personages, as with the sage minister Chu-ko Liang and the assassin Ching K'o. The past was inescapable. And because the present was so bound up with the past, the comparison of contemporary poetry with the works of the great masters, most often those of the T'ang and Sung eras, became unavoidable. Indeed, the perception that the monumental achievements of such great poets as Ch'ü Yüan, T'ao Ch'ien (365–437), Li Po, or Tu Fu could not be matched, let alone surpassed, was common. This belief, although apparently less pervasive in Ch'ing than in Ming times, nevertheless laid heavily on all fledgling poets. Those who took their craft seriously had to struggle constantly with the most difficult problem of coming to terms with long established norms and values without losing their identity in the process. Especially when it came to the question of what kind of poetry prior to their own age was worthy of emulation, most Ch'ing poets sooner or later found themselves embroiled in a debate on the relative merits and limitations of the poetry of the two eras: T'ang and Sung. Comparisons led to claims and counterclaims, charges and countercharges, and schools of poetry proliferated. For the study of Chinese poetry, the Ch'ing period, from Ch'ien Ch'ien-yi to Wang Kuo-wei, looms larger than any other historical period as an age of criticism.

THE PROLIFERATION OF THEORIES OF POETRY

The proliferation of schools of poetry in the Ch'ing era is an extraordinary phenomenon, but considerations of space limit us to giving only a capsule summary in this introduction. "Of all successive dynasties," Professor James J. Y. Liu wrote in 1964, "the more systematic discussion of poetics was undertaken by the several major poets of the Ch'ing dynasty. Those of us who study Ch'ing poetics will actually be engaged in studying the sum total of the different schools of poetics of successive dynasties."[18] The florescence of poetic criticism in this age[19] is actually a continuation of the battle waged in the Ming dynasty between the Archaic school of poetry, under the leadership of Li Meng-yang (1472–1528) and others, and the more independent-minded Kung-an and Ching-ling poets. The controversy stems from a seminal anthology of T'ang verse known as the *T'ang shih p'in-hui* (A Collection of Tang Poetry in Ranked Order of Excellence), compiled by Kao Ping (1350–1423), preface dated 1392, which argues for the emulation of only the poetry of the High T'ang (713–756). Against such strict prescriptions of orthodoxy, the importance of *hsing-ling* (native sensibilities) as the bedrock of poetry was championed by the Kung-an and Ching-ling critics, the latter under the leadership of Chung Hsing (1574–1624) and T'an Yüan-ch'un (1586–1631)—who jointly compiled the *Ku-shih kuei* (Fountainhead of Ancient Poetry) and the *T'ang-shih kuei* (Fountainhead of T'ang Poetry), both printed in 1617. This overthrowing of authority finds a strong parallel in the Classical-Romantic debate in England in the eighteenth century. For example, just as Alexander Pope (1688–1744) had written, in 1711, in *An Essay on Criticism* (note that by "Nature" Pope means "human nature"):

> Those Rules of old discover'd, not devis'd,
> Are Nature still, but Nature methodiz'd. . . .
> When first young Maro in his boundless mind
> At work t' outlast immortal Rome design'd. . . .
> Nature and Homer were, he found, the same. . . .
> To copy nature is to copy them.[20]

Li Meng-yang wrote in his "Letter to Master Chou" (published in 1530) the following words of wisdom:

> Words must have methods and rules before they can fit and harmonize with musical laws, just as circles and squares must fit with compasses and rulers. The ancients used rules, which were not invented by them but really created by Nature. Now, when we imitate the ancients, we are not imitating them but really imitating the natural laws of things.[21]

This famous credo became the central teaching of the Archaic (*fu-ku*, literally "return to the ancients") school of critics who believed that to imitate Tu Fu was the surest way of mastering harmony and all the natural laws of the universe.

Though neither Chung Hsing nor T'an Yüan-ch'un wrote any inspired poetry, many of their critical ideas were echoed in the writings of several early Ch'ing poets, such as Ch'ien Ch'ien-yi, Ku Yen-wu, and Wang Fu-chih. In the preface to *Ku-shih kuei*, for example, Chung Hsing writes, "Genuine poetry is the product of a writer's spirit (*ching-*

shen), to make manifest his hidden emotions and singular thoughts."[22] In a similar vein, T'an Yüan-ch'un insists that "In everyone there is what he uniquely understands . . . and that is the stuff of poetry."[23] Ch'ien Ch'ien-yi, the founder of the Yü-shan school of poetry, also condemns plagiarism (*p'iao*) and slavish imitation (*nu*), although he openly castigates the Ching-ling poets for "burrowing in ratholes" or, even worse, for being "gobblins and monsters." Being a friend of the youngest of the Yüan brothers, however, he was more sympathetic to the goals of the Kung-an school and shared their view on the importance of emotion (*ch'ing*) as the sine qua non of genuine poetry. In the matter of emulation, Ch'ien advocated a broader outlook favoring, as he said, the method of "learning from several masters," a dictum he borrowed from a quatrain on poetry, by Tu Fu, whose supremacy he nonetheless upheld all his life.

Another important advance in the critical approach of the Kung-an school is the idea that every age should speak in its own voice, that change (*pien*) is a natural law. An early defender of this "evolutionary" view of literature is Ku Yen-wu, who in his *Diaries* (*Jih-chih lu*) argues this point as follows:

> If people writing poetry today were to imitate the ancients who lived over a thousand years ago, could that be really possible? One of two things is sure to happen: If the work does not succeed in resembling the ancients, then it fails in the very purpose for which it was written as a poem; if the work succeeds in resembling the ancients, it fails also, because there is no longer the "I" who wrote it.[24]

The other poet-critic whose ideas anticipated not only Wang Shih-chen but also Wang Kuo-wei is Wang Fu-chih. Wang Fu-chih is best remembered today for his original theory on the fusion in poetry of *ch'ing* (emotion) and *ching* (scene), referring to the poet's "inner experience" and the "exterior reality" described in a poem. These elements he regarded not as separate entities, but as "two only in name . . . inseparable in reality" (as transformed by the poet's consciousness).[25] While Wang Fu-chih shows a strong affinity for the intuitionist view of poetry advocated by the Sung critic Yen Yü (fl. 1180–1235) and later by Wang Shih-chen, he also recognizes the importance of the principles (*li*) of things. He believes that the only way "to experience things and capture the spirit" (*ti-wu erh te-shen*) is through "what one sees with his own eyes and what one experiences himself." And he considers the presence of talent (*ts'ai*), learning (*hsüeh*), and thought (*ssu*) as important as emotion, thus revealing a catholicity of taste which anticipates nearly all the major poetic theories of the Ch'ing era.

The appreciation for T'ang poetry during the Ch'ing reign reached a peak with the critical writings of Wang Shih-chen, the major voice whose theory on the spirit and personal tone (*shen-yün*) of poetry caused prolonged controversy. Indebted to the T'ang critic Ssu-k'ung T'u (837–908) and to Yen Yü, Wang used the term *shen-yün* to mean "an ineffable personal tone or flavor in one's poetry."[26] And, to illustrate this quality, Wang anthologized the poems of forty-three T'ang poets, dominated by Wang Wei and Meng Hao-jan (689–740), without including a single poem by Li Po or Tu Fu, under the title of *T'ang-hsien san-mei chi,* (Samadhi Collection of T'ang Worthies), 1668. In the preface of this work, Wang writes:

> Yen Ts'ang-lang [Yen Yü] discussed poetry and said, "The people of the High T'ang were only concerned with inspired interest (*hsing-ch'ü,* or inspired gusto). They were antelopes who hung by their horns leaving no traces by which they could be found. Their marvelousness lies in being as clear as crystal and being free from blocking. Like a sound in the void, color in appearance, like the moon reflected in water or an image in a mirror—their words came to an end, but their ideas are limitless." Ssu-k'ung Piao-sheng [Ssu-k'ung T'u] discussed poetry and said, "It's the flavor beyond sourness and saltiness. . . ."[27]

Wang Shih-chen implies by this statement that the essence of poetry is spiritual enlightenment, or a sudden awakening, as taught by the Ch'an (Zen) school of Buddhism. Opposing this metaphysical view of poetry is Wang's kinsman and contemporary poet Chao Chih-hsin, who argues that poetry must be based on the rules of prosody and deal with concrete events.

QUALITIES OF T'ANG AND SUNG VERSE CONTRASTED

It may be useful at this point to illustrate these rather abstruse ideas about the nature of poetry with a comparison of some T'ang and Sung poems, especially since the debate between the admirers and followers of the two respective styles was kept alive throughout most of the Ch'ing dynasty. At the risk of oversimplification, one may say that the communication of emotion (*ch'ing*) is paramount with T'ang poets while, with Sung poets, the attention is shifted to what has been called the event (*shih*) or principle (*li*). Take, for instance, a familiar quatrain by Meng Hao-jan:

> Asleep in Spring, I missed the dawn.
> Now I hear everywhere the sound of birds.

In the night there was wind and rain,
I wonder how many blossoms fell?[28]

and contrast it with "Spring Day" by Su Shih:

Cooing pigeons, nursling swallows, all quiet without a sound;
Sunlight pierces western windows, splashes my eyes sparkle.
Awakened from noontime torpor, I find nothing to do
Except in spring sleep to enjoy a sunny spring.[29]

Or, contrast this Sung poem with "A Quatrain" by Tu Fu:

Late sun, the stream and the hills: the beauty
Spring breeze, flowers and grasses; the fragrance
Steaming mudflat, swallows flying.
Warm sand, and mated ducks, asleep.[30]

One can see that the qualities the Chinese critics found and prized in T'ang poetry included what Wang Shih-chen would call "inspiration encounters" (*hsing-hui*), while a Sung poet like Su Shih focused on the "event" or the core of an experience, that is, the "principle" of things. The latter manner involves a more orderly, logical development—so much so that much of Sung poetry is said to be "discursive," and a poet like Su Shih is sometimes accused of being too prosaic. His poem, too, seems much more labored, and those critics who emphasize the technical approach will probably praise Su's imaginative use of "pierces" (*she*), an archery term, and "splashes" (*p'o*) which literally means "splashing water." There is wit in his poem, for the last word of the poem, *ch'ing*, "a sunny day," is homophonous with *ch'ing*, meaning "emotion." A number of Ch'ing poets, such as Li E, Chiang Shih, Ch'en San-li, and Cheng Hsiao-hsü, attempted to write in this manner. Like a pendulum swinging back and forth, the elevation of Sung over T'ang poetry engaged many critics of the eighteenth and nineteenth centuries, compensating somewhat for the excessive veneration for the works of Wang Wei, Li Po, or Tu Fu earlier in the dynasty.

THE LATER CRITICS

The most moralistic critic of the Ch'ing era is undoubtedly Shen Te-ch'ien, who believed that poetry owed its exalted position to its power "to modulate human nature and emotions, to improve human relationships, to assist in the affairs of governing a nation, and to move the gods."[31] He hoped to inculcate through poetry the virtues of *wen* (moderation), *jou* (gentleness), *tun* (sincerity), and *hou* (depth). Although he also advocated the imitation of the ancients, he maintained that imitation should not be so slavish as to exclude the possibility of change (*pien*).[32] Shen even discoursed on the formal elements of poetry, as when he said, "One practical manifestation of poetry is the sound quality . . . [and] by means of controlled breathing . . . [a good reader] will come to experience what has never before been expressed by writers, and to catch the subtlety of the extra message beyond the sound."[33] Shen's approach, therefore, though basically didactic, is an admixture of ideas embracing both the intuitionistic and the technical.

Shen Te-ch'ien's emphasis of formal elements of style led to Weng Fang-kang's (1733–1818) theory of *ko-tiao*, two words implying either a standard of excellence (as in *p'in-ko*, which is said of one's character) or rules (as in *ko-lü*, prosodic rules), or both. To reinforce this idea of a formal (as opposed to personal) style, Weng proposed a theory of "flesh texture" (*chi-li*, literally "muscles" and "veins"), which, he insisted, was the same thing as Wang Shih-chen's *shen-yün* but which had been misinterpreted by Wang to emphasize only the abstract and the abstruse. According to Weng, poetry "is concerned with self, concerned with the times, concerned with the events, with each and every thing based on reality before it is transformed [by the poet's consciousness]."[34] Therefore, he directs our attention to the text itself and to the need for learning (*hsüeh*) as a prerequisite for the writing and understanding of poetry. In an obvious reference to the words of Chuang Tzu made famous by Wang Shih-chen about "forgetting the trammel after catching the fish," Weng wrote: "An archer must subject himself to rules before he can forget about the use of his hands or mind; he who sets up nets for fish or trammels for rabbits must first obtain the net and trammels before he can forget them."[35]

Rebelling against such close attention to the formal aspects of poetry, Yüan Mei became an ardent advocate of the *hsing-ling* or "native sensibilities" theory. Of course, such early Ch'ing poets as Chin Jen-jui, Huang Tsung-hsi, Yu T'ung, and others had maintained that the primary function of poetry is to describe one's human nature and emotions (*hsing-ch'ing*). But it was this popular literatus of Hangchow who took up the cudgel in challenging the views of such a redoubtable scholar of his time as Shen Te-ch'ien (both Yüan and Shen passed the *chin-shih* examination in the same year [1739], when Yüan was merely twenty-three years of age and Shen was already sixty-six). In two letters Yüan addressed to Shen, the youthful critic accused Shen of "having given his approbation to a change of style from Han and Wei times to T'ang, and yet refusing to sanction a change of style from T'ang to Sung."[36] He went on to declare that "in what is encountered by one's human nature and sensibilities, in everyone there is this 'I.' "[37] He even accused Shen of esthetic blindness and moral inconsistency by leaving out some love poems from an anthology Shen had edited. Yüan may be guilty of self-contradiction, as some modern scholars have charged, or of occasional flippancy, but his defense of originality and of everything that is "fresh," "new," or "alive" must be seen as a bold stance, representing a crystalization of more advanced and more refined ideas on individuality than those held by the Kung-an and Ching-ling critics two hundred years earlier. It may be instructive to note that an analogous battle between conventionality and individualism took place in the field of Chinese painting at a slightly earlier date. In *The Compelling Image*, a recent work of deep insight and understanding, James Cahill describes seventeenth-century China as "a great age of individualism . . . [though fragmented by local and personal styles]."[38] "The expressionism," he wrote, "that inspired [artists] was attained, like all types of expressionism, by limiting artistic means, emphasizing and exaggerating some elements of style at the cost of others."[39] The same dilemma was true of Chinese poetry also. Like so many Chinese individualist poets, the great painter Tao-chi (also known as Shih-t'ao, 1642–1708), a royal Ming dynasty prince who became a Buddhist monk before taking up painting, wrote "Long ago I saw the four-word phrase *wo yung wo fa* [I use my own method] and was delighted with it. Painters of recent times have all appropriated the styles of the old masters, and the critics accordingly say then, 'So-and-so's style resembles [the old masters], so-and-so's style does not.' I could spit on them."[40] Even Yüan Mei could not have been less civil or more direct.

THE RISE OF REALISM IN CH'ING POETRY

The stresses and strains in the body politic also found reflection in the poetry of the times. In an age of peace and tranquility, it was often enough to celebrate the scenic beauty and bucolic delights of an idealized natural world, the pleasures of human companionship, and the interrelationship of heaven, earth, and man. However, when the times were out of joint, these conventional themes gradually gave way to those of a more pressing concern. To be sure, social protest verse is as old as Chinese poetry itself, dating back to the *Shih-ching* and *yüeh-fu* style verse, and it was sanctioned by Confucian literary and political theories which urged the public to voice injustice and the educated elite to be responsible for the well-being of the lower classes. As early as the T'ang era, the ballads of Tu Fu, and later those of Po Chü-yi (772–846), which pointed the way for poets to satirize harsh government taxation measures and conscription practices, won universal admiration for their powerful imagery and humanitarian spirit. It was always necessary, of course, that the voicing of complaints against political injustices be couched in circumspect and allusive terms lest the poet run the risk of being charged with lèse majesté.

Poems depicting the inhumanity and suffering of war, the hardships caused by excessive taxation, the devastation of rural areas by natural disasters, and other social and economic ills increase with the passage from early to late Ch'ing times, and they constitute one of the elements which give that poetry its distinctive flavor and vitality. As the crisis in Chinese society deepened, reflections of this fact assumed a sharper, more distinct image in the poetry of the times, and this may also account for the revival of interest in Sung-style poetry among some poets. In this respect, these poets represent the poet engagé calling public attention to the darker side of life; they were also "poet-historians" (*shih-shih*) recording the cataclysmic events of the day in poetic form, in the time-honored tradition of a Ch'ü Yüan or a Tu Fu. Thus, Cheng Hsieh describes in moving terms the plight of the peasantry being driven from the land by famine and migrating great distances in search of a new livelihood, while Wei Yüan writes of the malaise and economic dislocation caused by the insidious opium trade. In the mid-nineteenth century, Cheng Chen chronicled in verse the horrors and savagery of the so-called Miao Rebellion in Kweichow province, where for more than a decade the conflict raged between and within ethnic and sectarian groups in a maelstrom of violence. Chin Ho drew on his own personal experiences to capture as few others did the human side of the Taiping Rebellion. Later, Huang Tsun-hsien and others recorded China's struggle against the foreign powers which sought to profit from her weakness, and reflected the inner conflicts of intellectuals confronted for the first time with an awareness of the outside, alien world. This period of vitality failed to survive the early 1900s, however, as the rapidly developing political events of the time engulfed the old culture. Classical poetry proved to be too fragile a craft, too specialized a training, to compete in attention and popularity with advances in journalism or popular fiction, or with the new, experimental forms of verse, derived mainly from the West and written in the vernacular (*pai-hua*) language.

THE REVIVAL OF THE TZ'U

There were good reasons for the resurgence of *tz'u* poetry in the Ch'ing era. *Tz'u*, lyric poems, were originally songs set to fixed tune patterns and meant to be sung. The new poetic form emerged in the late T'ang era and achieved a high level of sophistication during the Northern and Southern Sung periods.[41] Then, with its musical origins largely forgotten or ignored, *tz'u* poetry became a powerful vehicle for many purposes, including narration and intellectual discussion. Under the Ming dynasty, lyric poetry was not totally neglected, but was unable to compete successfully with other literary genres, such as fiction and the dramatic and nondramatic verse (*hsi-ch'ü* and *san-ch'ü*) that gained ascendency. After a long period of relative disuse, *tz'u* poetry found favor again with many Ch'ing poets: initially with Ch'en Wei-sung and Chu Yi-tsun—the authors of a joint *tz'u* anthology entitled *Ch'u-Ch'en ts'un-tz'u*—who succeeded in popularizing this genre before the end of the seventeenth century; in the second phase, with the rise of the Ch'ang-chou school, under Chang Hui-yen, just a century later; and, finally near the end of the nineteenth century, with a group of talented *tz'u* writers that includes Wang P'eng-yün, Cheng Wen-cho, Chu Hsiao-tsang, and others.

With the fall of the Ming, the new cultural and political milieu must have suggested to many poets that a China under Manchu rule was not much different from the society of the Southern Sung, precarious under the constant threat of occupation by the Chin rulers to the north. There was at the time a strong sense of the close connection between *tz'u* poetry as a literary genre and key historical events. In a recent study of the origins of lyric poetry by the eminent scholar Jen Pan-t'ang (Jen Erh-pei), he reports that over twenty of the T'ang *chiao-fang* (Palace Music School) tune titles were either directly or indirectly descriptive of royal entertainments, and that the emperor Hsüan-tsung, the great patron of poetry and music, himself once performed a dance to the music of "Ch'ang-ming nu" (Maid of Longevity).[42] Jen also suggests that the poets who cultivated this type of poetry, which depicted life either in the palace or at military outposts, could qualify to be called poet-historians or music-historians (*yüeh-shih*).[43] We also know that in the winter of 1278, when the tombs of the Sung emperors were said to have been plundered and the corpses desecrated, a group of fourteen scholar-poets met to compose highly allusive lyrics to express their sorrow and rage.[44] Over six hundred years later, a group of late Ch'ing lyricists, under the leadership of Wang P'eng-yün, gathered to write a series of lyrics published under the title of *Keng-tzu ch'iu tz'u* (Lyrics of the Autumn of 1900), to register their outrage and sorrow over China's defeat by the Western powers in the Boxer Rebellion. Similar historical parallels could not have escaped such early lyricists as Wu Wei-yeh, Wang Fu-chih, or Ch'en Wei-sung (whose father was a signer of the "Nanking Manifesto" and whose grandfather was a member of the Tung-lin Party). With or without Chang Hui-yen's allegorical theory, the historicity of the lyric tradition must have exercised a strong appeal among the empirical-minded Ch'ing poets.

Of the many poets who composed lyrics during the seventeenth century, two emerged as leaders: Ch'en Wei-sung as the founder of the Yang-hsien school (Yang-hsien being the ancient name of Ch'en's hometown, Yi-hsing, Kiangsu), and Chu Yi-tsun as the founder of the more successful Che-hsi (West Chekiang) school. The former sought to emulate Su Shih and Hsin Ch'i-chi (1140–1207) by writing in a bold and vigorous style; the latter set out to emulate Chang Yen (1248–1320?) and Chiang K'uei (ca. 1155–ca. 1221) by writing in a more elegant and refined manner. But the greatest lyric poet of the century, and perhaps the entire age, was Singde, a member of the Manchu ruling class, the naturalness and immediacy of whose verse was believed by Wang Kuo-wei, the modern *tz'u* critic and himself a lyricist par excellence, to represent the supreme achievement in that form. In his *Jen-chien tz'u-hua* (Remarks on Lyric Poetry in the Human World), Wang has written, "*Tz'u* writers can be considered among those who have not lost their childlike heart."[45] Thus, we again encounter the Ming philosopher Li Chih's famous assertion that the "childlike heart" is the "true heart," and whoever retains it will be able to produce great literature.[46] Time and again in his critical writings, Wang also insists on the importance of authenticity (*chen*) as the touchstone of lyric poetry.

But such authentic voices among poets are of course rare, and Singde founded no school of poetry. Thereafter, the lyric came under the influence of Chang Hui-yen. In 1797—just a year before two English poets, Wordsworth and Coleridge, wrote their famous Preface to the epochal *Lyrical Ballads* (no two books published so close together in time, though admittedly the products of two worlds, could be more dissimilar)—Chang Hui-yen and his brother Chang Ch'i (1765–1833) compiled a slim volume of 116 lyrics by forty-four T'ang, Five Dynasties, and Sung poets, for the edification of their pupils. And it is from this collection that we date the beginning of the influential Ch'ang-chou school of lyric poetry.[47]

In an attempt to elevate the lyric above the charges of frivolity and eroticism, Chang Hui-yen insists that a lyric must always express a covert meaning through the devices of *pi* (comparison) and *hsing* (analogy), two terms borrowed from the ancient *Shih-ching* criticism. Essentially moralistic and old-fashioned, Chang surprisingly found in even the most straightforward of occasional love lyrics deeper, hidden meanings of an allegorical nature. One cannot but wonder: was someone like Chang Hui-yen an effective advocate of *tz'u* poetry, or its own terrible nemesis?

To be fair to this school, it must be pointed out, as other scholars have done, that the inflexible position of its founder was transformed by its later, more able leaders, such as Chou Chi (1781–1839) and T'an Hsien. For example, Chou Chi admits, "Whatever inspiration moves a man to write does not necessarily have to be serious or proper. . . . The words [of a lyric] will not cause any harm to the intent (*chih*) of a reader; therefore, the reader must not reject the work on any account."[48] And this from T'an Hsien: "To the same extent that a writer's meaning may never be known, the reader is free to interpret a work of literature in whatever way he pleases."[49] This unbiased approach to literary interpretation, when sanctioned for lyric poetry, represents a far cry from the narrow, didactic views of its founder, and a significant advance in Chinese poetic criticism.

It may be helpful here to inquire into another aspect of *tz'u* poetry which became more and more pronounced during the Ch'ing era. The lyric, originally a short, subjective statement deriving from personal experiences, often involved the use of material objects (*wu*) or scenes (*ching*) to objectify the poet's feelings. The majority of T'ang and Five Dynasties lyrics do *not* have subject titles; only tune titles are given (and this is also true of Northern Sung lyrics to a large extent). The use of subject titles, and even long prose prefaces, started in the Southern Sung era. But when poets felt the need to become more secretive and private, they resorted to a subgenre of Chinese poetry known as the *yung-wu shih* (or *tz'u*); that is to say, poems written on objects. A large number of our selections, especially of the *tz'u* variety, are poems of this type. To be sure, *yung-wu shih* is nearly as old as the Chinese poetic tradition itself, dating back at least to the Six Dynasties period; but, ever since Su Shih's *tz'u* on willow-catkins, a lyric written in response to another person's on the same subject,[50] won the wide praise of many readers, this mode of composition inspired much of the finest poetry in China, and became a favorite with many Ch'ing poets.

In his study of the lyric tradition of the Southern Sung period, and particularly Chiang K'uei's contributions to *yung-wu* poetry, Shuen-fu Lin states, "In writing a *yung-wu* song, the poet shrinks from the vast world of his lived experience and concentrates his creative vision on one tangible object. . . . The poet retreats from a position in which his own perception of a given poetic situation constitutes the lyric center of a poem, into another position in which the poet himself becomes a mere observer of that lyric center."[51] Thus, he finds, "[t]he experiential world of a lyric poet is reduced to one single point of view, one moment, or a series of moments of feeling, vision, or awareness of the lyrical self."[52] Whether or not this refinement of technique exemplifies "new forms of eremitism" which, Professor Lin believes, also crystalized in the paintings of Southern Sung artists like Ma Yüan and Hsia Kuei[53]—is another matter. But there is no question that this subgenre of *yung-wu* poetry enjoyed a great vogue among Ch'ing lyric poets.

CONCLUSION

Our anthology includes examples of the poetry of men and women who held a wide variety of political and esthetic views. There were as many who retreated to a contemplation of the "lyric center" in a *yung-wu* lyric as there were others who expressed in verse a candid, passionate protest against social injustices. There were as many who, like Yüan Mei, preferred the bucolic delights and sensual pleasures as there were others who involved themselves in the mainstream of political activities and struggled to alleviate existing social problems.

Of all the *fin de siècle* writers who kept alive the lyric tradition after Chang Hui-yen—including Hsiang Hung-tso and Chiang Ch'un-lin in the first half of the nineteenth century and T'an Hsien, Cheng Wen-cho, Chu Hsiao-tsang, K'uang Chou-yi, and others toward the end of the dynasty—none were able to match the greatness of Wang Kuo-wei, a tragic genius whose suicide in 1927 truly marked the end of an era. An attractive, though still undocumented, theory advanced by Professor Chow Tse-tsung, of the University of Wisconsin, has suggested that there exists a special affinity between the propensity of *tz'u* to record a darker, more deterministic, view of the universe and the life and philosophy of this scholar-poet-critic.[54] As this quality defies easy definition, Professor Chow also resorts to the traditional interpretation; namely, that it comprises two characteristics: "nothing to be done" (*wu-k'o-nai-ho*) and "seems-to-have-known" (*ssu-ts'eng hsiang-shih*), two phrases taken from a *tz'u* by Yen Shu (991–1055).[55] These two phrases were made even more famous by an apocryphal story and still later by an anecdote involving Wang Shih-chen. According to the apocryphal story, found in the works of the Sung critic Hu Tzu (fl. ca. 1147), these two lines were said to represent a perfect illustration of parallelism and were the result of collaboration between the author and another poet, Wang Ch'i (fl. ca. 1056).[56] In the later anecdote, taken from Wang Shih-chen's own account, when Wang was asked by his students to describe the differences between *shih* and *tz'u* (or *ch'ü*), he quoted these two lines as an apt illustration of the quality of lyric poetry.[57] Another attempt at defining *tz'u*, by K'uang Chou-yi, has been quoted by Chow: "Whenever I listen to the wind and rain, whenever I view the mountains and rivers, I often feel that beyond the wind and rain, beyond the mountains and rivers, there is something like 'it-cannot-be-otherwise' [*wan-pu-te-yi*] that endures. This is the heart of *tz'u* poetry."[58]

Whatever the subtle characteristics of lyric poetry may be, no other poet understood them better than Wang Kuo-wei. He was familiar not only with his native traditions but also with Western literature and thought. Between 1903 and 1907, he studied Kant, Schopenhauer, and Nietzsche intensely, and only later returned to literature, abandoning the study of philosophy. "By 1907," according to Adele Austin Rickett, "he had become disillusioned with Schopenhauer, whom he felt failed to answer the question of universal salvation."[59] According to Chow, Wang's own philosophical writings are replete with references to "will" and "freedom," both of which were eventually dismissed by Wang as illusionary.[60] Perhaps, it is Wang's constant awareness of the contradiction between the concept of social responsibility on the one hand and individual feelings of regret or remorse on the other that gave rise to some of the best Chinese lyrics ever written.

Perhaps, also, it was just as characteristic of Wang Kuo-wei to adopt the title *Jen-chien tz'u* (*Lyrics of the Human World*) for the collection of his own *tz'u* poetry, and the title *Jen-chien tz'u-hua* for the book containing his remarks on lyric poetry. Professor Chow has pointed out that the phrase *jen-chien* appears thirty-eight times in Wang's 115 lyrics.[61] At any rate, an awareness of the human condition was paramount in Wang Kuo-wei's mind. In this respect, Chow finds Wang Kuo-wei to have been heavily indebted to the German poet Friedrich Schiller (1759–1805), who believed that poetry must always be concerned with human life.[62] Another German thinker who influenced Wang's theory of esthetics, Professor Chow suggests, was Johann Gottfried von Herder (1744–1803), whose doctrine of *humanität* was fundamental to German Neoclassicism and who was hailed by Goethe as a "philosopher of the sublime and beautiful in humanity."[63] Another contemporary critic, Ch'ien Chung-shu (b. 1910) finds Wang Kuo-wei's poetry to be imbued not only with the idea of *Sehnsucht* (yearning) from German Romanticism, but also with the ideas of Plato and Protagoras.[64] When the scope of Chinese lyric poetry could be so enlarged as to accommodate such diverse strands of thought and expression in addition to those of the Buddha, Confucius, or Lao Tzu, it should be clear that Ch'ing poetry, *tz'u* and *shih*, was not fatally impaired by derivativeness or stagnation, as many critics have heretofore believed.[65]

In the realm of *shih* poetry, the curtain was brought down on the Ch'ing era perhaps less dramatically, but with equally clear signs of a greater realism and a more candid espousal of expressionism. From Ku Yen-wu and Wang Fu-chih at the beginning of the era to Kung Tzu-chen, Huang Tsun-hsien, and K'ang Yu-wei, we have seen that even the staunchest of the Confucianists recognized that emulation of any sort must not stifle self-expression. The revival of interest in Sung poetry, signaling a more intense preoccupation with the real world, actually started in the eighteenth century, with poets like Cha Shen-hsing, Li E, and Chao Yi. But the cause was pursued with greater boldness and vigor by poets of the nineteenth century, such as Ho Shao-chi, Ch'en San-li, and Cheng Hsiao-hsü, leading to a lessening of the influence exerted by the poetry of the High T'ang. And among the great T'ang poets, the influence of other masters, such as Han Yü, Liu Tsung-yüan, Po Chü-yi, Yüan Chen, Meng Chiao, and Li Shang-yin, also began successively to be felt. The poetry of Han, Wei, and the Six Dynasties period, too, found staunch admirers, especially in Wang K'ai-yün. Throughout the period, an unusually strong interest in the narrative, satiric tradition can be detected; witness the selections by Cheng Hsieh, Chiang Shih-ch'üan, Chin Ho, and others—not to mention the two historical, epic-like poems on Yüan-yüan by Wu Wei-yeh and on the Yüan-ming Imperial Park by Wang K'ai-yün. As recently as 1982, it was reported in *Chinese Literature*, a monthly journal in English published in Peking, that "[t]wo long [Ch'ing] poems of more than two thousand lines each have been discovered in Wuxi and Wujiang in Kiangsu by folk literature researchers," both being tragic love stories.[66] It is obvious that not all the extant literature of the Ch'ing era has been studied even by scholars in China.

It may be said that Ch'ing dynasty poets labored, on the one hand, under the heavy constraints of a long, rigid tradition and, on the other, had to contend with a rapidly changing reality, especially after the middle of the nineteenth century. There were those, like Wei Yüan, Huang Tsun-hsien, and K'ang Yu-wei, who were eager to experiment with new vocabulary and modern concepts and to assimilate them into classical verse forms. And there were others who looked exclusively to the past for inspiration. A good example is Ho Shao-chi's poem "Samantabhadra Facing Westward," in which the tone of moral indignation, the condemnation of superstitious faith, is straight out of Han Yü, the famous opponent of Buddhism of another era. (Similar poems may be found in the works of Chiang Shih-ch'üan and Chin Ho.) This poem by Ho Shao-chi also employs lines of unequal length—a clear sign that perhaps some poets, including Sung Hsiang and Chang Wen-t'ao were already growing restive with the constraints of the prevailing five- and seven-word meters. As a matter of fact, erudite poetry in China was constantly invigorated by folk poetry. Many Ch'ing poets, beginning with Chu Yi-tsun and including Kung Tzu-chen, Wei Yüan, and Huang Tsun-hsien, collected or wrote their own "Bamboo-Branch" and other folk songs of their respective regions.[67] The commingling of these two traditions of vocabulary and style never really ended, even after the rise of the vernacular (*pai-hua*) poetry in the 1920s.

With the advent of the modern era, what was fast disappearing from the scene was really the values and mores of traditional China. For it can be assumed that even in such trivial matters as travel, life in eighteenth-century China was not much different from what it had been a thousand years before—not to mention the same imperial form of government and a similar social and family structure. But with the coming of the railway, steamboat, and airplane (which made its first appearance in classical poetry in a poem by Cheng Hsiao-hsü that is translated in the main body of the text), and the disintegration of the old society, life was irretrievably altered; and it became more and more difficult to keep alive a dying tradition. In a recent article "In Search of an American Muse," a contemporary poet, Robert Bly, laments the difficulties of being a poet in America, of having to spend much of the time alone. Perhaps in tongue-in-cheek fashion, he asks: "To be a poet in the United States is more difficult than to be a poet in Ireland. If poetry is a harnessed horse, we can say that in Ireland one finds harnesses still hanging in a barn. In the United States one has to kill a cow, skin it, dry the hide, cure it, cut the hide into straps, make buckles by hand, measure all the straps on a horse that won't stand still and then buy a riveter from some old man, get a box of rivets, rivet the straps together, make reins. And then what about the bridle? What about the collar? And what do you hitch it to?"[68] Indeed, as Mr. Bly says, "to be a poet . . . one . . . has to find some way back to the nourishment of the ancestors."[69] And these "nourishments" certainly will include more than a bridle or a rein. As modernism spreads in China, both the "singing whip" (*yin-pien*) and the "carved saddle" (*tiao-an*) will become as rare as the Chinese say, as "the phoenix's feathers or the unicorn's horn." But the poet's yearning for a world at peace remains a universally shared dream.

IRVING YUCHENG LO
WILLIAM SCHULTZ

NOTES

1. "Ancient Airs, No. 1," translation by Joseph J. Lee, reprinted (with modification) from Wu-chi Liu and Irving Yucheng Lo, eds., *Sunflower Splendor:*

Three Thousand Years of Chinese Poetry (Bloomington: Indiana University Press, 1975; New York: Doubleday/Anchor, 1983), p. 114.

2. "Thirty Rhymes Addressed to Hermit Chang Piao, Chang the Twelfth," *A Concordance to the Poems of Tu Fu* (Cambridge: Harvard-Yenching Institute Sinological Index Series, supplement no. 14; 1966), p. 338.

3. The compound designating a Chinese unicorn is usually given as *ch'i-lin,* with *ch'i* referring to the male of the species and *lin,* the female.

4. The translation of this passage from *Ch'un-ch'iu* and *Tso-chuan* follows that of James Legge's, with minor modifications; see *The Chinese Classics,* 5 vols. (Hong Kong: 1960 reprint of the 1894–1896 Oxford University Press edition), 5:833–835.

5. Translation by Irving Lo.

6. Major tributaries, respectively, of the Yellow River and the Yangtze.

7. Dates are not provided in the introduction for poets represented in the text that follows, where they are cited in the short bio-critical essays which precede each poet's selections.

8. "The Origins of Modern Chinese Literature," in Merle Goldman, ed., *Modern Chinese Literature in the May Fourth Era* (Cambridge: Harvard University Press, 1977), p. 17. Ms. Doleželová-Velingerová discusses these matters with reference to the novel and drama but also notes that "these new poets," like Huang Tsun-hsien, K'ang Yu-wei, etc., "emphasized the necessity for authentic emotions," in order to break out of "ossified patterns" of the past (p. 27).

9. Leo A. Orleans, *Every Fifth Child* (Palo Alto: Stanford University Press, 1972), p. 20.

10. Ibid., p. 24.

11. Ibid.

12. The full title of this anthology is *Wan-ch'ing-yi* [*Ch'ing*] *shih hui,* with the first three words being the name of Hsü's studio inside the presidential palace. Hsü Shih-ch'ang was the only civilian in modern Chinese history to hold the presidency of China, 10 October 1918–1922. Within the palace, Hsü established a society for the study and writing of classical poetry, and a bureau for sponsoring other literary projects, including the compilation of the *Ch'ing-ju hsüeh-an,* modeled after Huang Tsung-hsi's *Ming-ju hsüeh-an* and *Sung-Yüan hsüeh-an.* Hsü was awarded a D. Litt. degree by the University of Paris.

13. The history of Ch'ing dynasty scholarship is a complex subject and therefore beyond the purview of this introduction. For a recent study of the major schools and individual scholars and their works, see Benjamin A. Elman, *From Philosophy to Philology: Intellectual and Social Aspects of Change in Late Imperial China* (Cambridge: Harvard University Press, 1984). See also the seminal article "Some Preliminary Observations on the Rise of Ch'ing Confucian Intellectualism," by Ying-shih Yü in *Tsing Hua Journal of Chinese Studies,* 2:105–146 (December, 1975).

14. *Hsin ch'ing-nien* (*La jeunesse*), January 1917 issue; in *Hu Shih wen-ts'un* (Shanghai, 1921), 1:7–23.

15. Luther Carrington Goodrich, *The Literary Inquisition of Ch'ien-lung* (New York: The American Council of Learned Societies, 1935; Paragon Book Reprint, 1960), pp. 102–103.

16. See, for instance, Ping-ti Ho, "The Salt Merchants of Yang-chou: A Study of Commercial Capitalism in Eighteenth-Century China," *Harvard Journal of Asiatic Studies,* 17:130–168 (1954); and Lynn Struve, "The Hsü Brothers

and Semiofficial Patronage of Scholars in the K'ang-hsi Period," *Harvard Journal of Asiatic Studies,* 42.1:231–266 (1982).

17. This anthology has several English translations, the most popular being *The Jade Mountain,* translated by Witter Bynner from the texts of Kiang Kang-hu (New York: Knopf, 1929) and reprinted by Doubleday/Anchor, 1964.

18. "Ch'ing-tai shih-shuo lun-yao," ("On the Essentials of Ch'ing Dynasty Poetic Criticism"), *Hsiang-kang ta-hsüeh wu-shih chou-nien chi-nien lun-wen chi* [Hong Kong University Fiftieth Anniversary Symposium Volume], (Hong Kong: Hong Kong University, 1964), p. 32. The "several major poets" whose views on poetry are discussed by Liu in this article are: Shen Te-ch'ien, as representative of the didactic school; Chin Jen-jui and Yüan Mei, of the individualistic school; Wang Fu-chih, Wang Shih-chen, and Wang Kuo-wei, of the intuitionist school. Compare his *The Art of Chinese Poetry* (Chicago: Chicago University Press, 1962) for a definition of these terms.

19. See Wu Hung-yi, *Ch'ing-tai shih-hsüeh ch'u-t'an* [An Exploratory Study of Ch'ing Poetics], (Taipei: Mu-t'ung ch'u-pan she, 1977).

20. Pope, *An Essay on Criticism,* lines 88–140, in Gay Wilson Allen and Harry Hayden Clark, eds., *Literary Criticism: Pope to Croce* (New York: American Book Company, 1941), pp. 6–7.

21. Yeh Ch'ing-ping and Shao Hung, eds., *Ming-tai wen-hsüeh p'i-p'ing tzu-liao hui-pien,* 2 vols. [A Collection of Ming Dynasty Literary Criticism Materials], (Taipei: Ch'eng-wen chu-pan she, 1979), 1:295. Translation by James J. Y. Liu, in *The Art of Chinese Poetry,* p. 80.

22. Ibid., 2:744.

23. Ibid., 2:777.

24. *Jih-chih-lu chi-hsi, chüan* 21; 2:70.

25. See Siu-kit Wong, "*Ch'ing* and *Ching* in the Critical Writings of Wang Fu-chih," in Adele Austin Rickett, ed., *Chinese Approaches to Literature from Confucious to Liang Ch'i-ch'ao* (Princeton: Princeton University Press, 1978), pp. 121–150.

26. James J. Y. Liu, *Chinese Theories of Literature* (Chicago: Chicago University Press, 1975), p. 45.

27. Translation by Richard Lynn. See Richard John Lynn, "Orthodoxy and Enlightenment: Wang Shih-chen's Theory of Poetry and Its Antecedents," in Wm. Theodore de Bary, ed., *The Unfolding of Neo-Confucianism* (New York: Columbia University Press, 1975), pp. 218–257. The translation appears on p. 240.

28. Unpublished translation by Eugene C. Eoyang.

29. Translation by Irving Lo, *Sunflower Splendor,* p. 345.

30. Translation by Jerome P. Seaton, *Sunflower Splendor,* p. 142.

31. "Second Preface" to *T'ang-shih pieh-ts'ai.*

32. *Shuo-shih ts'ui-yü,* item 10; *Ch'ing shih-hua,* 2:525.

33. Ibid., item 3; 2:524.

34. "Shen-yün lun, II," in Yeh Ch'ing-ping and Wu Hung-yi, eds., *Ch'ing-tai wen-hsüeh p'i-p'ing tzu-liao hui-pien,* 2 vols. [A Collection of Ch'ing Dynasty Literary Criticism Materials], (Taipei: Ch'eng-wen chu-pan she, 1979), 2:536.

35. Ibid.

36. Ibid., p. 451.

37. Ibid.

38. James Cahill, *The Compelling Image: Nature and Style in Seventeenth-Century Chinese Painting* (The Charles Eliot Norton Lectures at Harvard University, 1979), (Cambridge: Harvard University Press, 1982), p. 225.

39. Ibid.

40. *Ta-ti-tzu t'i-hua shih pa,* quoted by Cahill, p. 185.

41. For background information on the *tz'u,* see James J. Y. Liu, *Major Lyricists of the Northern Sung* (Princeton: Princeton University Press, 1974); Irving Yucheng Lo, *Hsin Ch'i-chi* (New York: Twayne, 1971); Lin Shuen-fu, *The Transformation of the Chinese Lyrical Tradition* (Princeton: Princeton University Press, 1978); Kang-i Sun Chang, *The Evolution of Chinese Tz'u Poetry* (Princeton: Princeton University Press, 1980); Lois Fusek, *Among the Flowers: Hua Chien Chi* (New York: Columbia University Press, 1982); and Marsha Wagner, *The Lotus Boat: The Origins of Chinese Tz'u Poetry in T'ang Popular Culture* (New York: Columbia University Press, 1984).

42. Jen Pan-t'ang, *T'ang-sheng shih* [Poetry in the T'ang Voice], 2 vols. (Shanghai: Ku-chi chu-pan she, 1982), 2:28.

43. Ibid., p. 11.

44. Thirty-six lyrics by Chou Mi (1232–ca. 1310) and others, written on such preselected subjects as "the dragon's saliva," "the crab," etc., collected and published under the title of *Yüeh-fu pu-t'i.* See Lin Shuen-fu, pp. 191–193, for a fuller account of this episode.

45. *Jen-chien tz'u-hua,* item 16; p. 94 in the new annotated edition by Teng Hsien-hui, *Jen-chien tz'u-hua hsin-chu* (Jinan: Ch'i-lu ch'u-pan-she, 1981). The translation is that of Adele Austin Rickett in her "Wang Kuo-wei's *Jen-chien tz'u-hua:* A Study in Chinese Literary Criticism" (Hong Kong: Hong Kong University Press, 1977), p. 46.

46. Liu, *Chinese Theories of Literature,* p. 78.

47. See Chia-ying Yeh Chao, "The Ch'ang-chou School of *Tz'u* Criticism," in *Chinese Approaches to Literature from Confucius to Liang Ch'i-ch'ao,* pp. 151–188. Chao offers the following evaluation: "Through the remainder of the Ch'ing dynasty and into the early years of the Republic scarcely a *tz'u* writer or critic escaped the enveloping influence of the Ch'ang-chou School" (p. 152). And some revealing statistics: a collection of Ch'ing *tz'u* written in the Ch'ang-chou style, published toward the end of the nineteenth century, included 3,110 selections by 498 poets.

48. Quoted in Chao, p. 183 (translation slightly modified).

49. Ibid. (translation slightly modified).

50. See James J. Y. Liu, *Major Lyricists of the Northern Sung,* pp. 145–160. About this poem, Liu writes: "It is difficult to imagine a more striking example of how genius triumphs over technical restraints. . . . It is as if someone had written another 'Ode to a Nightingale' using the same meter and rhyming words as Keats yet successfully expressing his own thoughts and feelings" (p. 150).

51. Lin, *The Transformation of the Chinese Lyrical Tradition,* p. 11.

52. Ibid., p. 143.

53. Ibid., pp. 36–43.

54. Chow Tse-tsung, *Lun Wang Kuo-wei Jen-chien Tz'u* (Hong Kong: Wan-yu t'u-shu kung-ssu, 1972).

55. See Liu, *Major Lyricists of the Northern Sung,* pp. 18–19. Liu's translation of this lyric is as follows [italics ours]:

> A song with newly written words: of wine, a cup.
> Last year's weather, the same pavilion and towers.
> The sun is setting in the west: when will it return?

Nothing to be done about the flowers' falling away.
Seeming acquaintances—the swallows coming back.
A little garden, a fragrant path: alone pacing to and fro.

56. *T'iao-ch'i yü-yin ts'ung-hua,* 20:5a.
57. *Hua-ts'ao meng-shih,* in vol. 2 of *Tz'u-hua ts'ung-pien,* p. 7a.
58. Chow, *Lun Wang Kuo-wei Jen-chien Tz'u,* p. 3.
59. Rickett, *Wang Kuo-wei's Jen-chien Tz'u-hua,* p. 18.
60. Chow, *Lun Wang Kuo-wei Jen-chien Tz'u,* p. 10.
61. Ibid., p. 40.
62. Ibid.
63. Ibid., p. 41.
64. Ch'ien Chung-shu, *T'an-yi lu* (Hong Kong: Lungmen, 1965 reprint of the 1931 edition), p. 30.
65. This mistaken belief finds expression for instance in John Scott, *Love and Protest: Chinese Poems from the Sixth Century* B.C. *to the Seventeenth Century,* A.D. (New York: Harper & Row reprint, 1972), p. 23, where the author dismisses the poetry of the entire Ch'ing era as being "relatively undynamic," a point of view now being dramatically revised by the research of contemporary scholars.
66. "Cultural News," *Chinese Literature* (September 1982), p. 125.
67. We regret that space considerations compell us to exclude *san-ch'ü,* or the nondramatic song-poems, by known authors, from our anthology. Actually, quite a few of the poets included in this volume are also writers of *ch'ü,* notably Chu Yi-tsun, Wu Hsi-ch'i, Li E, Hung Sheng, etc. Regrettably, for reasons of space, we were also unable to include translations of folksongs submitted to us by several scholars.
68. *The New York Times Book Review* (22 January 1984), p. 29.
69. Ibid.

LIST OF ABBREVIATIONS

The following abbreviations are used in the text and in the bibliography below.

COMPILATIONS AND GENERAL COLLECTIONS

BDRC	See Boorman in the bibliography.
Ch'en	See Ch'en Yen in the bibliography.
Ch'ien	See Ch'ien Chung-lien in the bibliography.
Chou	See Chou Fa-kao in the bibliography.
CMCT	See Ch'en Nai-ch'ien in the bibliography.
CTCKSLTK	*Chin-tai Chung-kuo shih-liao ts'ung-k'an*
ECCP	See Hummel in the bibliography.
HHSC	*Hu-hai shih-chuan,* see Wang Ch'ang in the bibliography.
Hsü	See Hsü Shih-ch'ang in the bibliography.
KHCPTS	*Kuo-hsüeh chi-pen ts'ung-shu.*
PPTSCC	*Pai-pu ts'ung-shu chi-ch'eng.*
SKCSCP	*Ssu-k'u ch'üan-shu chen-pen.*
SPPY	*Ssu-pu pei-yao.*
SPTK	*Ssu-pu ts'ung-k'an.*
Wang	See Wang Wen-ju in the bibliography.
WCSSCSC	See Wu K'ai-sheng in the bibliography.
Wu	See Wu Tun-sheng in the bibliography.
Yeh	See Yeh Kung-ch'o in the bibliography.

INDIVIDUAL WORKS

AYTWKK	See under Sung Wan.
CCC	See under Ch'iu Chin.
CCCSC	See under Cheng Chen.
CCYSC	See under Hsü Ts'an.
CCYSY	See under Hsü Ts'an.
CFYF	See under Cheng Wen-cho.
CLKC	See under Wang Ts'ai-wei.

CLTCC	See under Ch'en Wei-sung.
CPCC	See under Cheng Hsieh.
CPT	See under Chuang Yü.
CSSTH	See under Chang Wen-t'ao.
CTYY	See under Chu Hsiao-tsang.
CYLSH	See under Chin Jen-jui.
CYTSC	See under Cha Shen-hsing or under Chiang Shih-ch'üan.
CYTSHC	See under Cha Shen-hsing.
FHSFC	See under Li E.
FHSFHC	See under Li E.
HCLSC	See under Wang K'ai-yün.
HFT	See under K'uang Chou-yi.
HHSFYK	See under Sung Hsiang.
HPCSWC	See under Hung Liang-chi.
HPHSC	See under Yao Nai.
HTCML	See under Yu T'ung.
HTHT	See under Yu T'ung.
HTLS	See under Cheng Hsiao-hsü.
HTSFSC	See under Yüan Mei.
HYTSC	See under Shih Jun-chang.
JCL	See under Huang Tsun-hsien.
KHT	See under Ts'ao Chen-chi.
KHTYCWC	See under Hsüan-yeh.
KNHHSCC	See under K'ang Yu-wei.
KTCCC	See under Kung Tzu-chen.
KTLSCHC	See under Ku Yen-wu.
LTHC	See under Huang Ching-jen.
LYC	See under Wu Wen.
MCCHC	See under Ch'ien Ch'ien-yi.
MCMKH	See under P'u Ch'uan.
MCYHC	See under Ch'ien Ch'ien-yi.
MKT	See under Chang Hui-yen.
NLSL	See under Huang Tsung-hsi.
NLT	See under Singde.
NSHP	See under Wang Chieh-t'ang.
OHKC	See under Yün Shou-p'ing.
OPSC	See under Chao Yi.
PCHC	See under Hung Shen.
PCTTSC	See under Ching An.
PHYY	See under Hua Kuang-sheng.
PSCSC	See under Shu Wei.
PSTC	See under Chu Yi-tsun.

PTTK	See under Wang P'eng-yün.
SYCSHC	See under Ch'en San-li.
SYCSS	See under Ch'en San-li.
SYLT	See under Chiang Ch'un-lin.
SYTCC	See under P'eng Sun-yü.
TCLSC	See under Ch'en Pao-shen.
THCK	See under Ku T'ai-ch'ing.
THYK	See under Ku T'ai-ch'ing.
TSTCC	See under T'an Ssu-t'ung.
TYLSC	See under Hsüeh Shao-hui.
TYLTC	See under Hsüeh Shao-hui.
WCCSCC	See under Wu Chia-chi.
WCSSWC	See under Wang Fu-chih.
WKTHSCC	See under Wang Kuo-wei.
WPSFTTSC	See under Li Chien.
WSCL	See under Wu Wei-yeh.
WSSC	See under Ch'ü Ta-chün.
WSSW	See under Ch'ü Ta-chün.
WTSCC	See under Wen T'ing-shih.
WTT	See under Wu Tsao.
WYC	See under Wei Yüan.
YCHT	See under Wen T'ing-shih.
YCWCT	See under Wu Hsi-ch'i.
YLT	See under P'eng Sun-yü.
YPSHC	See under Liang Ch'i-ch'ao.
YSSC	See under Chao Chih-hsin or under Singde.
YYSJCHL	See under Wang Shih-chen.
YYT	See under Hsiang Hung-tso.

PART I

Poets of the Seventeenth Century

CH'IEN CH'IEN-YI

(22 OCTOBER 1582–17 JUNE 1664)[1]

Ch'ien Ch'ien-yi (*Shou-chih;* MU-CHAI, MU-WENG, YÜ-SHAN MENG-SHOU, and TUNG-CHIEN YI-LAO) was an official, scholar, bibliophile, and poet whose controversial career spanned the two dynasties of Ming and Ch'ing. A native of Ch'ang-shu, Kiangsu, and scion of a scholarly family, he passed his *chin-shih* examination in 1610 and rose through the Hanlin Academy to become vice-president of the Board of Ceremonies. In 1629, amid bribery charges, he retired to his native place, where he had to face the additional disgrace of imprisonment as a result of a lawsuit involving a kinsman. Not long after his release from prison, however, Ch'ien was able to indulge his twin passions—beautiful women and rare books—neither of which he found a hindrance to the spread of his poetic fame.

As a bibliophile, Ch'ien was said to have amassed a magnificent collection containing many Sung and Yüan editions, which he housed in his Purple Clouds Pavilion (Chiang-yün lou) on his country estate. Though his collection was partly destroyed in a fire that engulfed the building in 1650, five years after it was built, a catalog of his collection is still extant, known as the *Chiang-yün lou shu-mu* (in series 9 of the *Yüeh-ya-t'ang ts'ung-shu*). He shared the use of his villa and library with a celebrated singing girl to whom he gave the name of Liu Shih (q.v.), who was then much admired for her literary talents as well as for her beauty among the courtesans frequented by the poets of his day. He met her in 1640 and a year later officially married her as a concubine (she was then in her early twenties). Among the many accounts of this romantic affair, it is said that when she asked Ch'ien why he favored her, he answered, "I love you for your raven-black

1. L. Carrington Goodrich and J. C. Yang, ECCP, 1:148–150.

hair and your snow-white complexion." To this reply, she gave the rejoinder (for choosing him above others): "Then I love you for your snow-white hair and your dark-as-lacquer complexion." The two of them shared literary tasks, as in the editing of an anthology of Ming poetry, and wrote poems in "response" (by using the same rhyme words) to each other's works. (These poems were separately published as the *Tung-shan ch'ou-ho chi,* now included in Ch'ien's *Mu-chai Ch'u-hsüeh chi, chüan* 18–19).

Unfortunately, the poet's luck in love did not spill over into politics: a series of frustrations dogged his political career. His advancement in the Ming court was cut short by his alleged activities as a member of the Tung-lin party. Then, out of loyalty to the Ming royal house, he even served briefly as president of the Board of Ceremonies (1644–1645) after Peking had fallen and the Prince of Fu, Chu Yu-sung (1607–1646), had set up his temporary court in Nanking. When the Manchu forces entered Nanking, however, Ch'ien was said to have rejected his concubine's suggestion that they commit suicide together, and he was among the first to declare allegiance to the new dynasty. Under the new regime, he was again given high posts in Peking, but was soon dismissed and imprisoned on charges of aiding some Ming loyalists. Worse still, during the long Ch'ien-lung reign (1736–1796), all his writings were condemned as disloyal to the new dynasty and placed on the proscribed list (and the printing blocks were ordered to be burned).[2] His unsavory reputation as "someone who has served two masters" (*erh-ch'en*) persisted for the next two hundred years, and this was sufficient to account for his lack of influence among later Ch'ing poets. It was not until the twentieth century that a fresh appraisal of Ch'ien as a poet began to appear.[3]

There should be, however, no dispute as to Ch'ien's stature as a scholar or as a poetic genius. At the time of his death, he was mourned by the fiercely independent Huang Tsung-hsi (q.v.) as a "leader of all poets in the empire for fifty years" (*ssu-hai tsung-meng*). This indeed is high praise. Ch'ien Ch'ien-yi's reputation now rests on three large works: 1) his oeuvres, in two collections, known as *Mu-chai Ch'u-hsüeh chi* (110 *chüan*) and *Mu-chai yu-hsüeh chi* (50 *chüan*), published re-

2. See especially Luthur C. Goodrich, *The Literary Inquisition of Ch'ien-lung* (American Council of Learned Societies, 1935), pp. 100–107.

3. Notably Chou Fa-kao's annotated edition of Ch'ien's poetry, the *Mu-chai shih-chu chiao-ch'ien* (Taipei, 1978) and his separate volume *Ch'ien Mu-chai/Liu Ju-shih yi-shih chi: Liu Ju-shih yu-kuan tzu-liao* (The Lost Poems of Ch'ien Ch'ien-yi and Liu Ju-shih and Materials for Research related to Liu Ju-shih), published in the same year. Also see the three-volume *Liu Ju-shih pieh-chuan* by the eminent historian Ch'en Yin-k'o (1890–1969), published posthumously in Shanghai (Ku-chi, 1980).

spectively in 1643 and 1644; 2) his anthology of Ming poetry, *Lieh-ch'ao shih-chi* (81 *chüan*), published in 1649; and 3) his annotated edition of Tu Fu's (712–770) poetic works, published three years after his death. His own poetry is characterized by a wealth of allusions and gives evidence of his catholic tastes. He was highly critical of the Archaic School of Ming poets, the "Former Seven Masters," and he declared his admiration not only for Tu Fu but also for poets of the Sung and Yüan dynasties. His scholarly interests ranged from history and the Confucian classics to the travel diaries of Hsü Hsia-k'o (1586–1641); a convert to Buddhism in his later life, he also wrote on Nestorian Christianity and Manichaeism under the T'ang. Ch'ien was a man for all seasons, it seems. That he could transform, for example, "boudoir poetry" into a kind of veiled political criticism or personal allegory is a mark of his true genius. (Additional selections from Ch'ien Ch'ien-yi's poetry will be included under Liu Shih in this volume.)

(Irving Lo)

Two Quatrains on the "Awash-in-Springtime Garden" Album by Hsiao Po-yü of T'ai-ho:[1]

I
Willow Creek

Mist clings to bank upon bank of willows,
Clouds rise from pool upon pool in the creek.
Try to find a place to drop a line?
One can get lost in the space of a foot.

(No. 1 from a series of 14, MCCHC, 7:15b–16a) *(Tr. Irving Lo)*

II
Lotus Pond

Lotus leaves, how plump and full,
Flowery scent drifts on the water's filigree;
Wistful, the mood of lotus pickers:
Their echoed songs haunt the autumn stream.

(No. 2 from a series of 14, MCCHC, 7:16a–16b) *(Tr. Ronald Miao)*

Watching a Game of Chess:[2] Second Series

In hushed silence come the hollow echoes
of chessmen from the board—
Sobbings of the cold tide on the Ch'in-huai River
when autumn is gone.
A white head beneath the shadow of a lamp
on a cold night
Espies the fate of the Six Dynasties[3]
in a dying game of chess.

(No. 3 from a series of 6; MCYHC, 1:9b) *(Tr. Irving Lo)*

Written in Prison

I ward off lance-sharp tongues and lips of steel,
Sitting, resting on a wheel blown by wind and fire.
But I don't crave the fate of the Guest of Chung-shan[4] drunk for three thousand days,
Unless I can return from death in six, like the prisoner beheaded at Chiang marketplace.[5]
A purplish jacket and hempen sandals[6] do not proclaim me disease-ridden;
Between broad earth and high heaven, there's some life in this body still.
With old age, what's so becoming as a man's rank or title?
From now on, let me just call myself "The Unrepentent One."

(No. 1 from a series of 30; MCCHC, 12:2b) *(Tr. Irving Lo)*

Upon Reading the Boudoir Poem of Mei-ts'un:[7] Impressions

The Milky Way still warns of the fate of the Clear One;[8]
In the royal chamber, the incense-stick is ashes, the mana-gathering plate fallen.[9]
As silent as the stone stelle, who can talk when one's mouth must be sealed?
A chessboard naturally groans from defeat, with beatings of an unquiet heart.
Donning a new robe for court audience: an affair of long ago;
Being cast aside like the Round Fan in autumn:[10] my predestined fate.

Only on such a night when the imperial consort weeps her fate by
the window,[11]
Can such a feeling be known to a dying lamp and evening rain.

(No. 4 from a series of 4; MCYHC, 4:3a–3b) *(Tr. Irving Lo)*

Drinking Wine: Second Series

The oars stop. I go to buy dark brew.
They say that only the wine from the Sun family's good.
The old woman selling wine says to me:
"Too bad, Sir, you didn't come earlier,
This year the price of wine is double. 5
My wine storage is nearly swept clean,
Only six tall jugs remain.
Their flavor is sweet and color, clear;
I saved them to marry off a pretty daughter,
And buy mutton to treat the neighbors. 10
I don't mind making a special present, sir,
You'll not suffer for want of dalliance!"

We trek through heavy rain, wet and slippery mud,
The servant boy's teeth are tightly clamped.
Carefully, we lay up store in the ship's cabin: 15
Here's a burst of wealth—just like finding a treasure.
Bright lamps emit fresh blossoms,
Night rain echoes from the autumn grass.
"If you don't hurry up and drink,
We'll fail the old wineshop woman!" 20

(No. 1 from a series of 7, MCCHC, 12b–13a) *(Tr. Ronald Miao)*

NOTES

1. Po-yü was the courtesy-name of Ming scholar-painter Hsiao Shih-wei (1585–?), a native of T'ai-ho, modern-day Lu-ling, Kiangsi province. Hsiao's collected works were published under the title of *Ch'un-fo yüan pieh-chi.*

2. The game of *go,* or *wei-ch'i,* is meant here.

3. The term "Six Dynasties" refers to the Kingdom of Wu (222–80) during the Three Kingdoms period in Chinese History, and the five later dynasties of Eastern Tsin (317–420), Liu Sung (420–477), Southern Ch'i (477–502), Liang (502–557) and Ch'en (557–581), ruling over southern China, all of which had their capital in present-day Nanking. The river Ch'in-huai flows by this city

to join the Yangtze, and the area along both banks of this tributary was famous in the old days as a bustling entertainment district.

4. According to an apocryphal story preserved in *Po-wu chih*, a man named Liu Hsüan-shih once drank a wine that put him to sleep for 3,000 days because the winemaker, a man of Chung-shan, forgot to warn him of the strength of his brew. At the end of this period, he suddenly remembered and found out Liu had been buried. When the coffin was opened, Liu came back to life.

5. A story from the *Tso-chuan*. A spy caught by the state of Tsin and beheaded at the marketplace of Chiang came to life six days later.

6. I.e., the traditional garb of a prisoner.

7. The poet Wu Wei-yeh (q.v.). Referring to the four "Without Title" *lü-shih* poems found in volume 12b, *Wu-shih chi-lan*.

8. According to legend, the T'ai-po Star once stole the waiting maid of the Weaving Girl, who was named Liang Yü-ch'ing (Jade-Bright) and together they disappeared into a cave for sixteen days. Yü-ch'ing was later banished to the moon, where she became the person who pounds rice with a pestle.

9. Signs of imperial decay, alluding to the bronze pillars of Chien-chang Palace of Han times, each holding a plate to gather manna from heaven, which was believed to confer immortality on those who drank it.

10. Alluding to the story of Pan Chieh-yü (ca.48–ca.6 B.C.), who is reputed to be the author of the poem "Round Fan," which tells of her fate when she fell out of favor with a Han emperor.

11. Alluding to the story of another imperial consort of the Han dynasty, Chao Fei-yen (Flying Swallow; ?–1 B.C.), who was said to have told her life's story to a confidant. She was made an empress by Emperor Ch'eng (reg. 32–7 B.C.), but she took her own life after being demoted to the rank of commoner under Emperor P'ing (reg. A.D. 1–5). Her biography later found its way into unofficial histories.

WU WEI-YEH

(21 JUNE 1609–23 JANUARY 1672)[1]

Wu Wei-yeh (*Chün-kung*; MEI-TS'UN), along with Ch'ien Ch'ien-yi (q.v.), is one of the foremost poets of the early Ch'ing. A native of T'ai-ts'ang, Kiangsu province, his talent for literature became evident while he was still a boy. He became a student of Chang P'u (1602–1641), one of the founders of the Fu-she party. Taking the *chin-shih* degree with high honors in 1631, Wu became a compiler in the Hanlin Academy. In 1639 he was appointed a tutor in the Imperial Academy in Nanking. When the rebel Li Tzu-ch'eng (1605?–1645) captured Peking and the last Ming emperor committed suicide in 1644, Wu attempted to take his own life but was prevented from doing so by his relatives. The following year he accepted a position on the staff of the prince of Fu, Chu Yu-sung, only to resign after a short time. For almost ten years, between 1645 and 1653, he lived in seclusion. He completed a historical account of the last years of the Ming dynasty, the *Sui-k'ou chi-lüeh,* in 1652. The following year he capitulated to official pressure and family urging and accepted a post under the new dynasty. He rose to the rank of rector of the Imperial Academy. Four years later his mother's death furnished him with a reason to resign from public office. Around 1660 he was involved in a tax evasion charge which resulted in a heavy fine and the stripping of his official rank. Until his death in 1672, Wu Wei-yeh remained haunted by his imagined betrayal of the imperial house of Ming; just before his death he was supposed to have instructed his family to bury him in a simple monk's habit. They were also forbidden to erect a shrine or to commission an epitaph in his name. His grave was to have a simple round tablet that read, "The Poet, Wu Mei-ts'un."

1. Lien-che Tu, ECCP, 2:882–883.

The fall of the Ming dynasty and his own ensuing dilemma also resulted in a perceptible change in Wu Wei-yeh's poetic style. If his early verse is marked by extreme elegance and surface refinement, the later works are imbued with a sense of nostalgia, desolation, and loss which makes them some of the greatest poetic works of the early Ch'ing period. He excelled in historical narrative poems, such as the "Yüan-yüan ch'ü" (see below) and the "Yung-ho kung-tz'u" (A Song of Yung-ho Palace), which his contemporaries called "poetic histories" (*shih-shih*). In narrative power and emotional depth (*ch'ing-yün*), these poems compare favorably with the best of Po Chü-yi's historical ballads. In the slightly more overblown language of poetic encomium by Emperor K'ang-hsi (q.v.), the style of Wu Wei-yeh was said to combine the allusiveness of Li Shang-yin with the melancholiness of Tu Fu (*Hsi-k'un yu-ssu Tu-ling ch'ou*).

The earliest edition of Wu Wei-yeh's poems and essays was published under the title *Mei-ts'un chi* (Mei-ts'un's Collection) in 1668–69. In the eighteenth century, three separate annotated editions of his poetry were printed. The one cited here is the *Wu-shih chi-lan* (A Collection of the Poetic Works of [Mr.] Wu), annotated by Chin Jung-fan (*chin-shih,* 1748), and published in 1775.

(Marie Chan)

The Song of Yüan-yüan

When the Emperor had departed from the world of men,[1]
General Wu[2] destroyed the enemy and took the capital, descending
  through Jade Pass.[3]
With grievous sobbing, all six Armies dressed in mourning;
But bristling with anger, their general was enraged about a beauty.[4]

This beauty, stranded and alone, should not be my concern; 5
The rebels, doomed by Heaven, still indulged in wild debauchery.
Swiftly General Wu wiped out the Yellow Turbans and pacified
  Black Mountain;[5]
When the mourning ended, Lord and Lady met again.

They had first met at the homes of T'ien and Tou;[6]
In a marquis' mansion, with song and dance, she came forth like a
  flower. 10
Thus the palace lute girl was promised to the general,
As soon as he could fetch her in a lacquered carriage.

She came originally from Wan-hua Village in Ku-su;[7]
Yüan-yüan was her nickname; she was lovely and refined.
She dreamt that she would journey to the gardens of Fu-ch'ai,[8] 15
And that when she entered with the throngs of palace ladies, the
Emperor would rise.
In a former life she must have been a lotus picker,[9]
Before whose gate the waters of Heng Pond stretched out.[10]

Across Heng Pond a pair of oars came flying;
A certain mighty lord abducted her by force. 20
At that instant could she know that she was not ill-fated?
At that moment she could only soak her robe with tears.

This lord's vaunted power reached into the palace chambers,
But Yüan-yüan's sparkling eyes and pearly teeth went unnoticed by
the Emperor:
Back they dragged her to Eternal Lane, then shut her up within the
mansion,[11] 25
And taught her some new songs to entrance her guests.

The guests drank on and on; the red sun set;
Her mournful song—for whom intended?
The fair-complected one, of T'ung-hou rank, was youngest of the
guests;[12]
In choosing from among the flowers, repeatedly he looked
her way. 30
Soon from its cage he freed this lovely bird,
But when could they cross the Milky Way to join each other?[13]
How sad that military orders rushed him away,
How bitter that the meeting they had pledged was thwarted!

They had pledged each other deep devotion, but for them to meet
was hard: 35
One morning hordes of rebels swarmed like ants, engulfed
Ch'ang-an.[14]
How sad that to the wistful wife the willows near her tower
Seemed like catkins at horizon's edge.
Then, searching the environs for Green Pearl, the general besieged
the inner mansion,[15]
And loudly called for Scarlet Tree to come forth from the
ornamented portals. 40

Had he not been a hero, all-victorious,
Could he have won his mounted moth-browed beauty back?
Calling out, they led the moth-browed beauty in on horseback;

Her cloudy locks were disarrayed; her startled soul had barely settled.
The torches blazing on the battlefield to greet her 45
Revealed her makeup, marred by crimson streaks.

Then with pipes and drums they marched off for Ch'in River;[16]
Upon Gold Oxen Road a thousand chariots advanced.
Where the clouds within Hsieh Valley deepened, painted towers rose;
As the moon went down behind San Pass, she opened up her mirrors. 50

By the time that Yüan-yüan's fame had spread throughout the river district,
Ten times the tallow's scarlet flowers had seen the frost.
Yüan-yüan was pleased her singing teacher still lived there;
She recalled when she had been among the girls who laundered silk.
To the old nest all these swallows had borne mud together, 55
But one alighted on a branch and was transformed into a phoenix.
While her friends gazed at their goblets and lamented growing old,
Yüan-yüan's husband was aspiring to be king.

At that time she was entangled only by her fame;
The noble and the powerful vied with each other to invite her. 60
One peck of bright pearls: ten thousand pecks of sorrow;
Adrift amidst mountains and passes, her waist grew thin.
She unjustly blamed the violent wind for buffeting the falling blossoms;
But then spring's boundless beauty came again to earth and heaven.

We have often heard of beauties who could bring down towns and kingdoms,[17] 65
But, more than this, she even made her Chou Lang famous.[18]
How can a woman heed great plans of state,
Or a hero help but be a man of passion?

Now, as the bleached bones of his whole family turn to dust,
She illumines history's record as the beauty of the age. 70
For don't you see:
The Kuan-wa Palace beauty rose from a love-bird's nest;[19]
The girl of Yüeh was like a flower; never could he tire of looking.
Now dust accumulates on Fragrant Path and birds call out alone;
From Echo Corridor all have vanished and moss grows undisturbed.

From "do" to "la," ten thousand miles of sorrow; 75
Songs like pearls, kingfisher dances as in old Liang Province.[20]
Now I have sung for you a different song about Wu Palace,
The waters of the Han flow southeast night and day.[21]

(WSCL, 7A:5a–9a) *(Tr. John D. Coleman and Gloria Shen)*

Leaving T'u-sung at Dawn[22]

A lonely moon beside the village,
The chilly tide comes and goes.
Voices emerge from the low awnings,
Ropes sink by the creek's bridge and trees.
Braving the frost, I leave in my light skiff, 5
Donning my clothes, I hear the cock at dawn.
Bamboo weirs sound like roaring rapids,
Rushes on islets seem like precipitous rain.
Fishermen call as they enter the estuary,
Farmers in fear shout from their gates. 10
Unexpected is the sight of torch fires,
Market sounds: voices of sires and dames.
The tide turns, village shops move,
A single sail have I seen so far.
Livelihood is asking about sedges and rushes, 15
Worldly affairs are cut off by the marshland.
'Tis fitting at last to part from friend and kin,
To pole my boat and live here evermore.

(WSCL, 1A:3a–b) *(Tr. Marie Chan)*

Blocked by Snow

The mountain pass is magnificent, yet the road is arduous.
The team of horses harnessed and just as soon unharnessed.
Yellow dust fills a hundred feet, snow a thousand,
And you know that this is not south of the river.

(WSCL, 17B:10b–11a) *(Tr. Marie Chan)*

Ancient Sentiments

My love is like the silk on the loom,
To be woven into a Tree of Longing.

I'm like blossoms on your cloth coat
Which no spring wind can deflower.

(WSCL, 17A:6a–6b) *(Tr. Irving Lo)*

Written in Jest: On "The Old Man Who Rolled with the Punch"[23]

He nods his head, leads a floating life[24]—
half the weight of a sheet of paper;
Sealed/enfeoffed in a ball of clay,[25]
he lets himself be kicked every which way.
No harm at all if he should lose his footing—
it's all a game he craves.
Can't stand sleeping quietly in bed—
just a bit rash, immature.
Long used to being pushed and shoved,
he is at times most obdurate.
Would he trouble to ask for a hand or a staff?
no, he's proud of standing by himself.
Pity that he should meet the sere stem of a peach tree[26]
sneering at him as no more than "pretty skin":[27]
"In my tummy's empty hollow," he replies,
"there's lots of room, renowned all over the world."[28]

(WSCL, 14A:12b–13a) *(Tr. Irving Lo)*

NOTES

1. The text reads *Ting-hu* (Tripod Lake), reported to be the place where the mythical Yellow Emperor ascended to Heaven, but here alluding to the suicide of Emperor Ch'ung-chen (1628–44), who hanged himself from a tree on Coal Hill behind the palace when the Ming dynasty collapsed.

2. General Wu San-kuei (1612–78). Cf. the notes below.

3. Like other geographical and proper names used in this poem, "Jade Pass" does not refer to the actual, strategic Yü-kuan in Kansu province, but refers to Shan-hai-kuan, just outside Peking, where a fierce battle took place on 27 May 1644, leading to the defeat of the rebel leader Li Tzu-ch'eng by the combined forces of the Manchu troops and the army of Wu San-kuei.

4. According to a contemporary account by Lu Tz'u-yün (fl. 1662), Yüan-yüan, or Ch'en Yüan, was a courtesan of peerless beauty and the concubine of a man named T'ien Wan, the father of one of Emperor Ch'ung-chen's consorts. As a result of internal weaknesses, the last reign of the Ming dynasty was troubled by a series of peasant rebellions, and the greatest rebel leader

was the self-proclaimed "Dashing King" Li Tzu-ch'eng, whose forces were so powerful that they briefly occupied Peking in the summer of 1644 and founded the short-lived Shun dynasty. At this time, the Chinese general Wu San-kuei, who was supposed to guard the commandery of Liao-tung against the Manchus, was about to surrender to Li Tzu-ch'eng. In desperation, the court of Emperor Ch'ung-chen turned to T'ien Wan and asked him to give this "beauty," Yüan-yüan, to the general to win his support. General Wu immediately succumbed to this lure, but was slow to deploy his troops in defense of Peking. Li Tzu-ch'eng soon took General Wu's father as hostage, but the general, on hearing the news, expressed confidence that his father would win release once the rebels were correctly informed of the size and worth of his fighting men. Then, when the news reached him that his favorite concubine Yüan-yüan had been taken hostage by Li, General Wu immediately decided to join forces with the Manchus to bring about the defeat of Li. (Wu San-kuei was later enfeoffed as a prince and as "The Generalissimo Who Pacifies the West" by the Manchu court; but later, along with two other Chinese generals in their employ, Wu rebelled against the Ch'ing government. Only in 1681 was the so-called War of the Three Feudatories concluded when Wu's grandson was defeated.) The concubine Yüan-yüan was said to have accompanied General Wu to Yunnan, where in later years she became a nun.

5. The Yellow Turbans were a group of Taoist-inspired rebels during the Eastern Han dynasty (25–220). Another group of rebels during the Han dynasty was known as the Black Mountain rebels. Here both allusions refer to Li Tzu-ch'eng.

6. The original Chinese of this line reads, "They first met through the T'ien and Tou families." Both of these families were related by marriage to the imperial family during the Han dynasty.

7. Wan-hua village is located in Ch'eng-tu prefecture, Szechwan province. This place is associated with a famous T'ang dynasty woman poet, Hsüeh T'ao (768–831), which is why it is mentioned here. Ku-su is the modern-day Wu prefecture in Kiangsu province.

8. Fu-ch'ai (?–473 B.C.), king of the ancient kingdom of Wu, defeated the neighboring kingdom of Yüeh. Desiring peace, the king of Yüeh offered Fu-ch'ai the beautiful Hsi-shih, who had been a silk-washing girl before she was abducted because of her great beauty.

9. Hsi-shih was also known as a lotus picker.

10. Heng Pond, also translated as Heng Dike, is the scenic spot Heng-t'ang in Wu prefecture, Kiangsu province, celebrated in many love poems.

11. Eternal Lane (Yung-hsiang) was that part of the royal palace during Han times where those concubines were kept who had committed some offense or had, for some other reason, lost the Emperor's favor.

12. The T'ung-hou rank was one of the highest ranks during the Ch'in (221–206 B.C.) and Han dynasties.

13. Crossing the Milky Way (Yin-ho) alludes to the myth of the two stars Weaver Girl and Herd Boy, a pair of celestial lovers who can meet only once a year on the seventh evening of the seventh month. Myriads of magpies fly together to make a bridge for the lovers to cross the Milky Way.

14. Ch'ang-an was the capital of several Chinese dynasties, most notably of the T'ang. Here and elsewhere, it stands for Peking.

15. Green Pearl (Lü-chu), in this line, and Scarlet Tree (Chiang-shu), in the next, were paragons of female beauty, talent, and virtue.

16. The names in this stanza are all places associated with the journey to Szechwan.

17. A Han dynasty song which celebrated a beauty so stunning that with one glance she could bring down a city and, with two glances, a whole kingdom.

18. Chou Lang, or "Young Chou," refers to Chou Yü, a young general who defeated the superior forces of Ts'ao Ts'ao in 208 A.D. at the famous battle of the Red Cliff.

19. Kuan-wa was the name of a palace in the ancient kingdom of Wu, and by extension, became a term used to refer to palace beauties. The other place names in this stanza refer to parts of the palace of the king of Wu.

20. Liang Province was one of the nine provinces into which ancient China was divided. It included Yunnan province, where Yüan-yüan spent the last few years of her life.

21. The Han River is a tributary of the Yangtze.

22. T'u-sung is a city north of T'ai-ch'ang in Kiangsu province.

23. I.e., *pu-tao-weng*, a popular Chinese toy in the shape of a human figure, corresponding to what is known in the West as the "tumbler" or "roly-poly," which always manages to stand erect, no matter how it is knocked around, because of the weight contained in its base. In political jargon, used even today, someone able to withstand fortune's buffeting and come out always on top is frequently referred to as a *pu-tao-weng*.

24. Also alluding to a passage from the *Chuang-tzu*: a sparrow just nods its head and remarks, "I know nothing about a floating life."

25. *Feng* in this line means both "to seal" and "to enfeoff." The quotation alludes to a story in the *Hou-Han shu*, about the official Wang Yüan, who jokingly asked for a ball of clay "to seal off/to be enfeoffed at the Han-ku Pass."

26. Alluding to a debate in the *Chan-kuo ts'e*, arising from an encounter between a clay figurine and a sere peach-tree stem, with the latter boasting to the former, "You are made of clay from the western bank; when the Tzu River floods, you will be deformed."

27. Alluding to an ancient saying, "Pretty skin is not used to wrap silly bones."

28. Alluding to the witticism exchanged between Wang Tao (276–339), statesman of the Eastern Chin dynasty, and Chou Yi (269–322), an aristocrat and bon vivant, as recorded in the *Shih-shuo hsin-yü*. Wang pointed to Chou's stomach and asked, "What do you have in there?" And Chou retorted, "Just an empty hollow, but big enough to hold several hundreds of people like you."

CHIN JEN-JUI

(1610?–7 AUGUST 1661)[1]

Chin Jen-Jui (*Sheng-t'an*), scholar, literary critic and theorist, and poet was a native of Wu-hsien (Soochow), Kiangsu province. Little is known of his immediate forebearers, or for that matter, of the actual details of his own life. His father was apparently a learned man, but we known nothing of his degree status or of precisely how he earned a living. There are indications that the Chin family was living in straitened circumstances during Chin Sheng-t'an's youth (he is usually known by his *tzu*, Sheng-t'an), and he was sent to the village school for his education, rather than being tutored at home as was then common among the well-to-do. He is said to have shown considerable intelligence as a student, and sometime during his late teens or early twenties he succeeded in earning the first or *hsiu-ts'ai* examination degree. Independent of mind and somewhat unconventional in behavior, he may well have decided not to pursue the traditionally accepted route to social status and financial rewards, the examination career and subsequent appointment to public office for the successful. Instead, he chose to devote himself to a life of scholarship, but with an important difference. The disciplined philological analysis of the Confucian classics was then coming into vogue, but Chin Sheng-t'an's inclinations were more strictly literary. Thus it was that he undertook to produce several major works of textual emendation and commentary that have justly earned him a secure place in Chinese letters as a literary critic of unique sensibility and lasting influence.

During a time when the new Manchu government was still heavily engaged in the task of completing the conquest of China proper, and when it was anxious to impose its authority on the prosperous Chiang-

1. Chao-ying Fang, ECCP, 1:164–66.

nan region, a major center of loyalist sympathies, Chin Sheng-t'an, perhaps somewhat impulsively, joined a student protest demonstration against the harsh methods then being employed by local and regional officials to enforce the payment of delinquent taxes. As a result, he became involved in the famous *k'u-miao* (Lamenting in the Temple) incident and this eventually led to his arrest, his trial for "disturbing the peace of the lately deceased emperor," and his execution by decapitation, along with seventeen other defendents in the case. Moreover, the family property was confiscated and his survivors transported to Manchuria.[2]

As a result of his endeavors as a literary scholar, Chin Sheng-t'an was instrumental in enhancing the critical standing of two major works of the popular tradition; namely, the novel *Shui-hu chuan* (Water Margin Story, better known as *Tales of the Marsh,* also translated as *All Men are Brothers*) and the celebrated play *Hsi-hsiang chi* (Romance of the Western Chamber). In this respect, he was perpetuating critical concepts recently given voice by Li Chih and the so-called Kung-an School, who advocated an evolutionary view of literature and championed popular literary forms. Chin Sheng-t'an, however, went beyond his predecessors in converting theory into practice with his careful analysis and critical emendations of these two works, which, like Li Chih and Yüan Hung-tao, he placed on a par with such venerated classical texts as the *Shih-ching* (Book of Songs) and the *Tso-chuan* (Tso Commentary). He designated the two above-mentioned literary works, along with the *Chuang-tzu,* the *Shih-chi* (Records of the Historian), and the works of the ancient poet Ch'ü Yüan (the *Li Sao*) and those of the great T'ang poet Tu Fu, the "Six Works by and for Men of Genius." For Chin Sheng-t'an, great literature is preeminently an expression, spontaneously and sincerely voiced, of personal emotions. At the same time, the expressive element is moderated by the learned values of moderation (*wen*), gentleness (*jou*), sincerity (*tun*), and profundity (*hou*). As a practicing critic, he was the first to undertake an extensive critical analysis of popular literary works. However, in addition to the writing of prefatory and interlinear critical comments on the *Shui-hu chuan* and the *Hsi-hsiang chi,* he also made extensive emendations in the texts themselves. In the case of the former, he dropped most of the last fifty chapters which he believed to be artistically inferior. The seventy-chapter version of the novel which resulted from his labors is generally speaking a more coherent, dramatic, and readable work than the complete 120-chapter original. Although he also took unusual liberties with the text of the *Hsi-hsiang chi,* once again the result was a tighter, more

2. Ibid., p. 165.

consistent work. When he met his untimely death, Chin Sheng-t'an was engaged in a third major critical study, namely, a detailed examination of the poetic works of Tu Fu.

Ching Sheng-t'an is little remarked today as a poet, quite possibly because his eminence as a practicing critic has tended to overshadow his own works of a creative nature. Whatever the reason for his neglect in this regard, his poetry merits serious consideration for its clear and precise diction, its congenial and temperate manner, and its occasional flashes of humor. Radical though he was as a critic-scholar, as a poet he was apparently content to conform to the established boundaries of form and genre.

(William Schultz)

The Tiniest of Lives

Beneath the leaf a green insect, and frost upon the leaf;
The tiniest of lives, having come to this, is most to be pitied.
Had I the strength of high heaven and rotund earth,
I'd make you live a thousand autumns, ten thousand years.

(CYLSH, p. 61) *(Tr. Irving Lo)*

Capriciousness[1]

Capricious was the guest of another day;
Now hungry and cold is this six-foot man.
People today make heroes of thieves and robbers;
I alone am fit to weep for a unicorn.[2]
Days grow so long that they never seem to dusk,
My wicket gate is facing an empty spring.
Night after night the fish-dragon[3] frolics;
Who are those surfeited of wine and meat?

(CYLSH, p. 37) *(Tr. Irving Lo)*

Don't Ask

Don't ask what it has been like in my old garden:
The blooming season for flowers has passed.
The intruding bees[4] devoured clean all the young insects;

Stupefied rats brazenly seized the swallow's nest at the altar.
No longer does the warm breeze come to my window,
Nor is there a secluded place to sit and sing.
What use is there in writing petitions to Heaven?
So bidding farewell to the God of Spring, I weep my tears.

(CYLSH, pp. 100–101) *(Tr. Irving Lo)*

Last Word: For My Son Yung[5]

The miraculous part of our relationship is being apart;[6]
Like Form following Shadow[7]—this is found only in books.
After today, "being apart" means we can never again be parted;[8]
Unattached either to Heaven or to parents[9] is true happiness.

(No. 2 from a series of 3; CYLSH, p. 92) *(Tr. Irving Lo)*

NOTES

1. The title of this poem—*hao-tang*—is taken from Ch'ü Yüan's (343?–278 B.C.) poem, *Li Sao,* line 44. David Hawkes translates it as "waywardness" ("What I do resent is the Fair One's waywardness:/Because he will never look to see what is in men's hearts." *The Songs of the South,* p. 24). Originally applied to water, the term has a broad connotation in referring to the qualities of being indiscriminate and heedless.

2. That is, to lament its absence. The unicorn (*ch'i-lin*), a mythical animal even in ancient times, is considered by the Chinese as a symbol of universal peace. According to the *Lun-yü,* Confucius once remarked that he would stop writing when a unicorn appeared.

3. Fish-dragon Game (*yü-lung hsi*) is kind of a magic diversion according to the "Account of the Western Regions" in the *Han-shu.* It was performed by a large animal, also called *man-yen,* said to be from India, which would first frolic in the courtyard before jumping into the water. Then it would be transformed first into a paired-eyed fish (*pi-mu yü*) and finally into a sixty-foot-long dragon of dazzling brightness. The term "Fish-dragon" could also be alluding to a line by Tu Fu, from the fourth of the series of eight poems entitled "Autumn Meditation": "While the fish and the dragons fall asleep and the autumn river turns cold" (translation by A. C. Graham).

4. The word translated as "intruding" here is *hu,* which denotes a "barbarian from the north of China," and often occurs as a prefix to designate anything of foreign origin, as in *hu-ch'in* (a string instrument), hence "intruding." The first word in the next line, exactly parallel to it, is *hun,* which also means "evening." Double entendre is clearly intended in the use of both words.

5. This series, entitled "Chüeh-ming tz'u" ("Songs Sung as Life Comes to an End"), was composed in 1661, before the poet was led off to the execution ground to be decapitated on a charge of sedition. This is the second of three

quatrains, and it alone carries a subtitle. It reads as follows: "My son Yung [born 1632] is not only the seedling of a true scholar [*tu-shu chung-tzu*], but also an authentic student of the Tao [*pen-se hsüeh-tao-jen*]."

6. This line contains two unusual words in describing a father-son relationship. "Miraculous," or *miao,* is a word Chin frequently used in his literary criticism to indicate approval or admiration, meaning "wonderful, miraculous." "Apart" or "distant" (*shu*), in describing human relationships, means "not frequently together, distant, or aloof." This does not necessarily mean that the father and son in this case were distant from each other. In Wang Yi's (ca. 89–ca. 158) commentary on the *Li Sao,* line 44, (see Chin's poem "Hao-tang" above), there occurs this passage (following a quotation from the *Meng-tzu*): "When a parent has glaring faults, and the son does not utter his grievance (*yüan*), this is known as growing more 'distant.' "

7. "To cling together like one's form and shadow" (*hsing-yin hsiang yi*) is a common Chinese expression.

8. Literally, the last five words of this line may be translated as: "Being apart has now reached the land where there will be no more 'separation.' "

9. The first four words of this line—*Wu-cho t'ien-ch'in*—very probably conceal a pun in that Wu-cho (and) T'ien-ch'in (literally, "heaven" and "parent") are also the transliterated names of two Buddhist saints of the fifth century A.D., two brothers who were the founders of the Fa-hsiang or Dharmalaksara Sect. *Wu-cho,* according to W. E. Soothill, means "unattached" (*A Dictionary of Chinese Buddhist Terms* [London: Kegan Paul, 1937], p. 382) and is the name of Asaṅga, the brother of Vasubandhu, or T'ien-ch'in, by whom he was converted to the School of Mahāyāna. These two names occurred in a poem by Wang Wei entitled "Kuo Ch'eng-ju Ch'an-shih Hsiao-chü-shih Sung-ch'iu lan-jo" (*Wang Yu-ch'eng chi ch'ien-chu* [Shanghai: Chung-hua, 1961], 1:188). We are indebted to Professor Hans Frankel, Yale University, for elucidating this line and calling our attention to the poem by Wang Wei.

HUANG TSUNG-HSI

(24 SEPTEMBER 1610–12 AUGUST 1695)[1]

Huang Tsung-hsi (*T'ai-ch'ung*; NAN-LEI, LI-CHOU HSIEN-SHENG) was witness to nearly a century of political and military tumult. His father, Huang Tsun-su (1584–1626), a Ming censorial official and prominent member of the Tung-lin politico-literary society, was among several courageous statesmen who lost their lives for opposing eunuch rule in 1626. At the age of only nineteen, Huang Tsung-hsi traveled from his home in Yü-yao, Chekiang, to the capital in Peking, where he engaged in bold acts of vengeance against figures whom he held responsible for his father's persecution. Throughout his life Huang's spirit of resistance to all forms of tyranny, injustice, and absurdity was sharpened by the memory of this calamity in his youth.

When Peking fell to rebel siege and North China subsequently was overtaken by invading Manchu-Ch'ing forces in 1644, Huang declined to serve the first Southern Ming resistance regime in Nanking because of enmities generated previously during his active participation in the Fu-she (Restoration Society), a reformist group which succeeded the Tung-lin. However, when Nanking fell in 1645, Huang joined directly in defense of the Ming Prince of Lu, Chu Yi-hai (1618–1662) and his temporary court in south-central Chekiang. He continued to resist Ch'ing forces after the Lu regime was routed from the mainland in 1646, dividing his efforts between the Ssu-ming Mountains in southern Chekiang and the Chu-shan Islands off the coast near Hangchow Bay. In order to protect his family, Huang returned home in 1650, but for at least another decade conditions continued to be hazardous for him, as Chekiang became the scene of campaigns and counter-campaigns between Ch'ing contingents on one hand and Ming resistance

1. Lien-che Tu, ECCP, 1:351–354.

forces penetrating from the southeastern coastal area. These were led most notably by Cheng Ch'eng-kung (i.e., Koxinga, 1624–1662) and Huang's compatriot, Chang Huang-yen (1620–1664).

After the Ming cause finally was lost, Huang devoted himself entirely to scholarship and teaching and refused to have any association with the Ch'ing government. When pressed to participate in compiling the official Ming dynastic history, Huang sent a student, Wan Ssu-t'ung (1638–1702), in his stead to labor on this project without official stipend or recognition. Huang was renowned as one of the most broadly learned men of his time. He was best known as a historian (especially of recent centuries) and as a philosopher who carried on the teachings of Liu Tsung-chou (1578–1645), a conservative but original interpreter of Wang Yang-ming's (1472–1529) thought. Huang's most substantial extant work is an intellectual history, the *Ming-ju hsüeh-an* (Philosophical Teachings of Ming Confucianists).

In belles lettres, Huang contributed more as a critic and anthologist than as a literary stylist. His *Ming-wen an* (Anthology of Ming Literature) survives in 207 *chüan*, and his comments on literature are scattered among his collected writings, chiefly the *Nan-lei wen-ting* and *Nan-lei wen-an*. Although Huang strongly advocated thorough study of the classics and histories for all writers, his view of literary creativity was expressionistic, stressing the importance of heightened genuine emotion. He was opposed to slavish imitation but also criticized the Kung-an and Ching-ling schools for their pettiness. Among poets of the late Ming and his own day, Huang most admired Kuei Yu-kuang (1507–1571), Ai Nan-ying (1583–1646) and his teacher in belles lettres, Ch'ien Ch'ien-yi (q.v.). However, consistent with his spirit of intellectual independence, Huang maintained no allegiances in literary theory or practice. A stern critic even of his own work, Huang preserved only about three hundred (20 percent) of his own poems, which constitute the *Nan-lei shih-li*, in four *chüan*.

(Lynn Struve)

Rising Early with My Son Chih to Leave Tung-ming Ch'an Monastery

Bell sounds penetrate the mountain mist,
A rope bed rolls up lingering dreams.
Fog twists far down the monkeys' path,
A rippling spring turns fishes' hearts to caprice.

Severed rainbows vie with the sun,
Spring birds play with scraps of things.
Ashes warm the terraced fields,
Trees broaden a poor man's roof.
The world in chaos–only now my heart at rest;
How could I be spared the jeers of rocks and springs?

(NLSL, 1:1a) *(Tr. Lynn Struve)*

Miscellaneous Songs from Living in the Mountains[1]

I

Who says that in the mountains everything is grand?
Quiet nights in the mountains I especially loathe.
Old men cough and cackle to the chase of hornless deer;
Widows moan and groan to the yowls of tigers and owls.
The moon goes down on a thousand dreary strands of white hair;
Jumbled grave mounds surround one green lamp.
I don't know what evening this is in my life's time;
Life and death, after all, are not separate tiers.

II

For fifty years I followed an "overturned cart,"[2]
But lately I've come to enjoy being like people of the hills.
Windy days I go to gather pine cones for fuel;
After frost I come to seek wild mum for tea;
A pair of leather shoes wear through the stone road;
Three squat rooms cap over the rush flowers.
Who says we must force ourselves to get a place in rank?
I'm proud to take the wind and sunshine as my lot.

III

I've come again to Yen Bend and built a hut of thatch;
Leave or stay awhile—never very long.
All the farmers at Twin Peak presented me some food;
An eighty-year-old man even offered poems.
Then I knew that Earth and Sky, in dire collapse,
Still lean on such hill village dullards for support.

But I can't stand up to the ways of this world.
This feeling brings me shame, but I've no apology.

(Nos. 2, 3, and 5 from a series of 6; NLSL, 1:10a–10b) *(Tr. Lynn Struve)*

Cold-night Moon—In the Manner of Meng Tung-yeh[3]

Frost lustre washes the winter moon—
The scene passes before me in great clarity.
But I can only gaze from my pillow,
Unable to stand in the center courtyard.
On the pillow, one foot of light— 5
From the courtyard a thousand miles wide.
A thousand miles—so much despair
One foot—enough challenge for me.
Sickly and poor, I view the bright moon;
Not a sound, much less that of pipes or strings. 10
Just to say, "This night is nice,"
Brings my moon-watching mood to a close.
And I begin to see that Heaven's moon is there
Not just to shine bright for the sickly and poor.

(NLSL, 1:5a) *(Tr. Lynn Struve)*

Hearing the Cuckoo on the Nineteenth Day of the Third Month [1646]

Silent river village, bamboo wet with rain;
The cuckoo—up and down—has a bitter sound.
This bird comes to the Cold Food Feast every year;
Why only now so heartrending to hear?
Of old, men said it was an ancient emperor's soul, 5
So now I bow twice, not daring to forget a former lord.
Year before last, third month, nineteenth day,
A mountain peak's collapse grieved the ground below.[4]
Now jumbled flowers have grown up, and orioles fly again,
But the flesh of rebel leaders still escapes the axe. 10
In the Yen Hills,[5] pipe tunes of mourning too far away to hear;
While south of the Yangtze River, bells and drums lie languishing.[6]
King T'ai's intent was nurtured, and sages were thus acclaimed.[7]
In the central hall their truth is known and deeds recalled.
High ministers conduct affairs of state, 15

But poisonous rancor still burns within our gates.
As I listen in stillness, the bird's cry seems to say:
It's hard, even for a coward, to find peace as a swampland destitute.
Why don't I shout in anguish from the sacred altar?
Instead, I simply let my tears spot the grassy land. 20

(NLSL, 1:1b) *(Tr. Lynn Struve)*

Encountering Fire in Early Spring, 1662

Tall pines enveloped my thatched roof
Where jumbled stones faced my southward room.
At midnight there was candleglow;
By noonday no more cooking smoke.
Three years I'd worn the hoe head smooth; 5
Flowers, herbs filled the early spring.
Life entered pitfalls, then flowed again,[8]
Mind by itself discerning square and round.
To escape a bad year's brigands and marauders,
I'd gone back awhile to my former home. 10
Spring winds bellowed a field fire;
Red flames roiled up to the sky.
New poems were scorched on the plaster wall;
Old trees died young after long years.
Now tumbled walls give echo to a cold cascade, 15
And rustic tools lie idle in the moonlight
So I'm led to plan a long journey forth—
For ne'er-do-wells it's hard to be steadfast.
An old book snatched from midst the blaze,
Page upon page like lotus leaves. 20
I feel pity at this, then good fortune at it,
While abandoning neither food nor sleep.
Once I censured [Yüan] Yi-shan,[9]
Who sold his books for a bower.

(NLSL, 1:15b) *(Tr. Lynn Struve)*

Encountering Fire Again in the Fifth Month

Ill at ease, I returned to my old dwelling,
With dogs and chickens to share a single room.
Head tucked under bedding from the rain;
Eyes blinded by smoke from the stove.

A south wind strangely issued forth; 5
It happened just before midnight.
Scaled the wall to save my mortal life;
Bowed repeatedly to tell my ancestors.
This servant's years already five times ten—
No reversal from this nadir of Decline.[10] 10
The words I say all risk ill will from men;
With every step more alien to God.
Halfway through life, ten times I'd seen death's shore;
Now two fires in the space of this one year.
Don't say that my thatched hut's too low: 15
My guests are not the common run of men.
Demon's eyes don't peer about;
Though it's not so sturdy as a splendid hall.
Its principle cannot be understood;
All speculations are idle and tedious. 20
Lately there's Liu Po-sheng,[11]
Who sleeps uneasily on my account.
But I'm really from beyond this realm;
How could I ever care about a homestead?

(NLSL, 1:15b) *(Tr. Lynn Struve)*

NOTES

1. The Ssu-ming Mountains in Chekiang, where Huang had led a fruitless anti-Ch'ing resistance effort ten years earlier. The fortifications built by Huang and his surviving followers were torn down by the local people who feared Ch'ing retaliation.

2. I.e., to fail to learn from one's experience.

3. I.e., the T'ang poet, Meng Chiao (751–814), who, having failed in the civil examinations, wrote bitterly of suffering and poverty in his poems.

4. A reference to the death of emperors generally, and here it refers to the suicide of the Ming Ch'ung-chen emperor, as rebels overtook Peking on 25 April 1644.

5. I.e., Hopei.

6. Large temple musical instruments: a metonomy for capable men of the empire.

7. T'ai Wang, progenitor of the ancient Chou, moved his people southward (in present-day Shensi) rather than fight with an intruding barbaric tribe, and to avoid exposing his people to the tribe's uncivilized ways. His line of descent subsequently produced the sage rulers King Wen and King Wu, who established the idealized Chou state.

8. A reference to the twenty-ninth hexagram, *K'an,* in the *Yi-ching.*

9. Yüan Hao-wen (1190–1257) refused to serve in government after the Mongol (Yüan) conquest of North China, devoting himself entirely to literary pursuits.

10. A reference to the twelfth hexagram, *P'i*, in the *Yi-ching*.

11. Liu Shao (1613–1664), son of Huang's deceased mentor, Liu Tsung-chou.

KU YEN-WU

(15 JULY 1613–15 FEBRUARY 1682)[1]

Ku Yen-wu (*Ning-jen;* T'ING-LIN, CHIANG-SHAN-YUNG), a native of K'un-shan, Kiangsu province, was a leading intellectual as well as an accomplished poet of the early Ch'ing. He was adopted by an uncle who soon died, and raised by his uncle's intended wife. She was devoted to Ku's upbringing and education, and he later celebrated her life in a well-known essay.

Though most of Ku Yen-wu's adult life was lived under Manchu rule, and though his philosophical and scholarly works were among the most influential of the dynasty, Ku remained a Ming loyalist, refusing to serve in the government in any capacity. He was officially celebrated in the late Ch'ing as an exemplar of Confucian loyalty.

Ku served briefly in minor positions at two Ming princely courts after the fall of Peking. Deeply devoted to his foster mother, née Wang, Ku honored her deathbed wish that he refuse service to the Ch'ing court. The exercise of this filial duty must have given considerable support to his devotion to the virtue of loyalty—one honored in the breach by the majority of his contemporaries.

Ku spent the years following the fall of the Ming in travel and study, settling first in Shantung province as a farm manager, and then in Shansi, where he promoted the improvement of the banking system, agricultural technology, and mining operations. There is some conjecture that his travels and his practical improvements were centered in the vain hope of organizing popular rebellion against the Manchus. He was accused of consorting with Cheng Ch'eng-kung and of helping in the publication of seditious works, but he escaped with minimal punishment.

---

1. Chao-ying Fang, ECCP, 1:421–426.

Ku Yen-wu is not merely, or even primarily, famous for his exemplary loyalty or his practical patriotism. He was one of the foremost scholars of his time, and the originator of the major Ch'ing branch of Confucianism, the "School of Han Learning." In addition, he was a major geographer, a historical phonetician, and an important commentator on his times. In the course of his reaction against the Neo-Confucianism of the late Ming, which he held to be responsible for the fall of the dynasty, Ku delineated disciplined methods of historical scholarship. His investigations of the language of the *Shih-ching* and of the *Yi-ching* led him to a clear definition of internal and external evidence, and the insistence on the formation and testing of hypotheses as the essential elements of true scholarship.

Ku Yen-wu's poetry might be regarded as the least of his myriad accomplishments. Nonetheless, it reflects the power of a multifaceted personality, always erudite, and at times surprisingly original through a controlled use of allusions. The emphatic role of allusion in his poems may be accounted for as much by his vulnerable position as by his personal commitment to the literary tradition.

(J.P. Seaton)

Ching-wei[1]

The world is full of iniquities,
Why do you struggle so in vain,
Always urging on that tiny body,
Forever carrying sticks and stones?
"I will fill up the Eastern Sea.
My body may fail; my aim won't change.
Until the great sea's filled
My heart can't know surcease."
Alas, don't you see
The many birds with sticks and stones among the Western Hills?
Magpies come, swallows go, all building their own nests.

(TLSWC, 1:14a) *(Tr. J.P. Seaton)*

Eight Feet[2]

Eight feet tall, the lonely sail on one leaflet skiff,
Together with wind and water, has carried me to this autumn.

We've been to White Emperor city to search for our late ruler,[3]
Thence east of the river to ask about Chung-mou.[4]
In the sea the fish and dragons should know our anguish;
Among the hills the trees and plants pour forth their grief.
I trust you'll speak no more of "rise and fall";
The boatman of another year is white-haired now.

(TLSWC, 1:20b–21a) *(Tr. J.P. Seaton)*

Mocking Myself

I mock myself: another year and I'm still unable to return;
A goblet of wine, a book of poems—to whom could I turn?
I call the boy at dawn to saddle up the horse;
I must find an old woman before winter comes to mend my gown.
No "Yellow Ear"[5] has come with letters from home;
White-haired, I've come to ponder the mountain ferns of old.[6]
Without cause I've become a goose that follows the sun;
Riding the west wind, I fly to Reed Marsh.[7]

(TLSWC, 3:6a) *(Tr. J.P. Seaton)*

Po-hsia[8]

Fallen leaves, driven by the wind, invade Po-hsia;
Again I've come to this place, climbed up for a view.
A reed pipe clear, the moon bright—autumn lingers on the ramparts;
The wilds ablaze, cold stars emerge from the forest at night.
These ancient hills and streams must have a master,
But for years, with spears and armor, we've searched hard and long.
Let each of us fill our hands with New Pavilion tears[9]
And make the river rise at once ten fathoms full.

(TLSWC, 3:15b) *(Tr. J.P. Seaton)*

NOTES

1. Ch'ing-wei, a mythical bird, believed to be an incarnation of the daughter of Shen Nung (the god of agriculture), who died while travelling the Eastern Sea. The bird supposedly carries sticks and stones to fill in the sea. The poem is unusual in its use of the myth and the extended development of the metaphor, implying perhaps the lack of rebellious spirit among the people.

2. This poem is unusual not only in its title but also in the fact that the first three words of the first line *pa-ch'ih ku* ("eight-foot long") contain a curious figure because the word *ku* also means "orphan." In a chronological biography of the poet by Chang Mu (1805–1849), printed in 1843, the author rejects the possibility that this *Pa-ch'ih* could be a place name on the Wu River. The three words, therefore, can also be taken as a paraphrase of the term "six-foot orphan" (*liu-ch'ih ku*) from *Lun-yü,* referring to a "six-foot-tall fatherless one," usually meaning a boy under fifteen years of age and also a young ruler who has not yet attained his majority (a Chinese foot is about 20 percent shorter than a foot in the English system). This phrase gains added poignancy from the famous "Proclamation Remonstrating Against Empress Wu" penned by the poet Lo Pin-wang (fl. 680) on behalf of Prime Minister Hsü Ching-yeh (?–691), the leader of the court faction opposing the usurpation of the throne by Empress Wu Tse-t'ien (624–705). It is said that when she read the passage, "Before even one cup of earth on the grave mound (of the deceased emperor) is dry, how can one forget the six-foot orphan (i.e., the heir-apparent)," she was so moved by the elegance of Lo's language that she ordered his life be spared.

3. Pai-ti ch'eng (White Emperor City), situated along the gorge of the Yangtze River, in Szechwan, is where Liu Pei (162–233), the ruler of the Shu Kingdom, died and entrusted the care and guidance of his son to the wise and devoted councillor Chu-ko Liang (181–234).

4. Chung-mou is the courtesy name of Sun Ch'üan (182–252) of the Three Kingdoms period, the Ruler of Wu and rival of Liu Pei; it is also the courtesy name of P'eng Sun-yi (1615–1673), son of the Ming martyr P'eng Ch'i-sheng (1584–1646). The young P'eng, a poet and historian, was the author of the well-known work *P'ing-k'ou chih* (Record of the Pacification of Bandits), which records the rise and fall of various rebel groups during the years 1628–1661. Hence, the "rise and fall" of line 7.

5. The messenger dog of Lu Chi (261–303), a poet of the Tsin dynasty.

6. An allusion to the story about the legendary brothers Po-yi and Shu-ch'i of Shang times who fled to the mountains, refusing to eat the grains of the new Chou dynasty, and determined to eat only mountain ferns (they eventually perished).

7. Li-tse (Reed Marsh), located in Kiangsu province, is the site of a battle between the ancient states of Wu and Yüeh.

8. An important garrison town near the ancient Chien-k'ang, modern-day Nanking.

9. I.e., Hsin-t'ing, located in a suburb of Chien-k'ang, where the literati often gathered in the Six Dynasties period to lament the loss of North China to non-Chinese tribal peoples.

SUNG WAN

(1614–1673)[1]

Sung Wan (*Yü-shu;* LI-SHANG, MAN-SHAN-JEN) was a native of Lai-yang, Shantung province. Like his father and elder brother before him, Sung Wan received the *chin-shih* degree in 1647 and was subsequently appointed to public office, first in the capital and later to a succession of provincial posts.

About 1660, Sung Wan was implicated by a fellow clansman in a rebellion in his native district. He was imprisoned for several years before being cleared of the charge and returned to office.

Although he is remembered chiefly as a leading poet of his times, Sung Wan led a full and active creative life. He was a calligrapher of some repute, and he turned his hand on one occasion to the writing of a play. When he was posted to Yung-p'ing, Chihli province, as the circuit intendent, he compiled the local gazeteer of that area.

The famous critic Wang Shih-chen (q.v.) spoke highly of Sung Wan's talents as a poet, and later writers have remarked on the vigorous northern manner of his verse, the excellence of his poems in the heptasyllabic "regulated verse" and "old-style" forms, and the tone of realism that is encountered in some of his best poems. His collected works reveal a penchant for experimentation with various verse forms. For instance, several dozen lyrics are cast in the hexasyllabic quatrain pattern, a form not commonly used, and he made interesting use of the long narrative poem, also a genre not commonly cultivated by Chinese poets. Sometimes serious in manner, sometimes humorous, even at the most difficult of times, his verse explores a wise range of human sentiment and emotion from a gentle, humanitarian point of view.

(William Schultz)

---

1. Lien-che Tu, ECCP, 2:690.

On Hearing a Cricket[1] in the Boat

The blossoms of water reeds take wing like willow floss;
I am surprised that it is again time to put on more clothing.
Who knows from where the busy weaver comes,
Bringing with him autumn's sounds to fill the painted boat!

(AYTWKK, 5:7b) *(Tr. William Schultz)*

Songs Composed in Prison

I
A Piece of Rush Matting

A grieving heart can't be rolled up like a mat;
This mat is good enough for a brief nap.
Don't be disgusted because it is cheap,
For it could still produce a Fan Sui.[2]

II
An Earthen *K'ang*[3]

An ivory, bamboo, and kingfisher bed
Compared to this is coarse and ugly!
The butterfly and Master Chuang-chou,[4]
Sir, can you tell them apart?

III
A Stool with a Broken Leg

When the morning warmth enters the window,
I bare my back and go to sleep.
No telling when the Spirit of Poverty will leave me,
I invite him to take this seat for honored guests.

IV
An Earthen Stove

A solitary lamp glows in the dark room;
My old servant, his head drooping, sleeps.

I get up to heat some water in the pot
And put my underpants on upside down!

(Nos. 1,2,3, and 6 from a series of 8, AYTWKK, 5:3a–b) *(Tr. William Schultz)*

A Song of a Fisherman

South of Nan-yang, north of Yi Mountain,
The man doesn't till, the woman doesn't weave.
They cut rushes, built a hut in marsh lands;
Heaven provided fish and shrimp for them to sow and reap.
The young wife can steer the small skiff; 5
Black as a cormorant is their small son.
No rain this autumn, and the lake is drying up;
Large fish strand and die, loach and dace grow weak.
Buyers for the market stay away, fish are cheap as mud;
But the tax collector comes with a power that binds. 10
They boil him fish, serve him wine, pray he won't be angry,
And crying, to the village they go to sell their woven nets.

(AYTWKK, II:24a–b) *(Tr. William Schultz)*

A Ballad of the Righteous Tiger

In Fen-shui there once lived a woodsman,
Who climbed lofty ridges to cut firewood.
There the forest was thick, the chasms slick,
And down he plunged beside a tiger's lair,
Where tiger cubs, still not weaned, 5
In fang and claw lacked the lance's point.
Panic-stricken, hastily he looked about,
Where sheer cliffs stood like garden walls.
Before long, White Brow itself appeared,
With a wind that rattled in a myriad ravines. 10
In its mouth it carried half a carcass,
Deer or roebuck, one couldn't tell.
Rending and tearing, it fed its young;
What need for hulled, dried grain?
Turning about, it eyed the newcomer, 15
Its angry eyes flashing lightning bolts.
But soon it ceased its angry roars,
As if pondering some weighty matter;
And then, tossing over scraps of meat,

It received the woodsman with food to eat. 20
As a guest, he dared not eat his fill,
So cautious was he, lest he still land in the pot.
Mother and cubs at last fell sound asleep;
The moon shone and upland birds did sing.
In his mind, the woodsman weighed his fate: 25
"At breakfast, surely I'll be their plate!"
Who would have thought that, heedlessly,
With one leap the tiger would plunge into the bush?
Returning every day just at noon,
Regularly it supplied him sustenance. 30
Morning and evening he got his fill,
Drank blood as though it were the finest wine.
At month's end, out the tiger went with cubs in tow,
To teach them stalking and headlong attack.
The woodsman, left to guard an empty den, 35
Grieved long, cried out to the gods above:
"Why did it not finish its virtuous deed?
And why, suddenly, has my host abandoned me?
Should bear or leopard come here to bide,
Would they also be so compassionate? 40
If not, then I will starve to death,
And here they will make my grave!"
But soon the tiger carried him out of the lair,
Their only path the scent of pine and fir,
Where the forest was so dense no birds would fly, 45
Where the color of the sun was dark as dusk.
Limping along, the tiger he beseeched:
"With reverent bow, I beg to speak, Great King:
This humble servant, whose name is thus and so,
Who makes his home in the southern suburbs, 50
Who cuts wood to feed eight starving mouths,
Lost his footing, stumbled into your domain.
With reverance, I thank you for not eating me,
For graciously feeding and succoring me besides.
In a former life, you must have known me, 55
Have been my father, my elder brother perhaps.
Long has it been since I left my home,
My parents waiting by the village gate;
If you can understand my speech,
See me back to my native place." 60
His entreaty ended, off the tiger led him,
And thus they came upon a path.

On they walked, until about to part
Host and guest set to pacing back and forth.
The woodsman said, "Grateful am I for my life, 65
And in some small ways, your virtue I'll repay.
Upon my return, I'll buy a woodsman's axe,
And a fat lamb to fill your belly.
Outside the town is an ancient temple ruin,
And two white poplars by a narrow lane; 70
There, next month when the moon is full,
South of the pavilion, I will dine you."
The tiger twice nodded its head,
And in parting, both wept copious tears.
Crawling, to his thatched hut he returned, 75
Startling his family, who into hiding went.
He called and beckoned to his wife,
"I'm a man; how could I be a were-tiger?"[5]
Turning up the lamp, he ate his simple fare,
And with remorse, in detail told his tale. 80
His neighbors half-doubted, half-believed him.
For he was as thin as the Shamaness Wang.[6]
Impoverished, lacking fodder for his animals,
He pawned his short cotton jacket.
Before the sacrificial knife he could apply— 85
Fierce animals mostly roam by night—
Because of its promise to share a meal,
Switching its tail, the tiger entered the village gate.
In a flurry, the villagers raised a hue and cry,
Beat the gong, clambered up on ridgepoles. 90
They wielded neither hook nor shield,
For there they'd already spread a net.
In a flash, fast the tiger was bound;
To show their catch, they climbed the yamen steps.
The magistrate declared, "Kill it!" 95
Thus we shall punish this unlucky thing!"
Hearing this verdict, the woodsman
Beat the gong, brought forth the the shackles,
And kneeling, reported to the magistrate in full,
"Consider its great mercy; how can you take its life?" 100
Turning to the tiger, he spoke of former times,
While the yamen steps grew as crowded as a market:
"This great Lord, now snugly tied and bound,
Received these wounds because of me.
To gods and sovereign, I beg for its life; 105

Let me, useless as I am, take its place."
Praising his intent, the magistrate declared:
"Release its bonds! tend to its wounds!"
Then they went to the appointed place,
Upon an altar was laid a sacrificial sheep. 110
By nibble and bite, quickly it was consumed;
Then the tiger departed, and how it leaped and raced!
Crowding streets and lanes, bystanders,
Young and old alike, all abustle rushed about;
For a shrine to be named "Righteous Tiger," 115
A stone was cut to proclaim the event to the suburbs.
The state of Ch'u was suckled by a tiger,
To this the records, undistorted, do attest.[7]
I write this poem to tell of this strange event, 120
To put to shame all Wolves of Chung-shan.[8]

(AYTWKK, I:1a–2b) *(Tr. William Schultz)*

Random Poem on the Lake

Of mountain scenery, the Southern Screen is best:[9]
Its atmosphere misty, half is hidden, half is there.
A small skiff moors in the winding pond;
Pelicans rest under withered willow trees.
Clouds rise up and a thousand peaks are thrown together;
The sky clears and a single pagoda stands alone.
With inspiration come thoughts of distant views;
Melodies from a Tartar flute fill West Lake.

(No. 3 from a series of 10; AYTWKK, 3:3b) *(Tr. Yin-nan Chang)*

A Miscellany on the Garden of Autumn Clouds: Peach-Blossom Pond

Green water reflects scales of bright red;
Weeds and algae appear as clear as in a mirror.
When the fisherman rapped on his boat,
I thought it was petals falling.

(No. 5 from a series of 15; AYTWKK, 5:1b–2a) *(Tr. Yin-nan Chang)*

NOTES

1. Crickets are also known as *ch'u-chi* ("busy weavers," l. 3) since their cries, heard in the autumn, are said to urge people to prepare their winter clothing. Cf. "In the Seventh Month," a poem from the *Shih ching* (Ode no. 154).

2. Fan Sui (fl. 3rd century B.C.) rose to high office in the state of Ch'in after he had been beaten and thrown into a toilet when taken for dead.

3. A raised and heated platform bed made of bricks which is common in north China.

4. The ancient Taoist philosopher Chuang-tzu.

5. The ghost or spirit of a person who has been killed and eaten by a tiger, after which it becomes an agent of the tiger in luring other people to a similar end.

6. According to commentaries in the *Tso-chuan,* Shamaness Wang, who was responsible for a great drought, was sickly and emaciated in appearance.

7. According to the *Tso-chuan,* Tou Ku-yu-t'u, or Tou Who-was-nourished-by-a-tiger, was a man of the Spring and Autumn era, who was abandoned in the wilds when still a baby. A tiger found him there, nursed him, and raised him to manhood, after which he served the state of Ch'u with great skill and fidelity.

8. "The Wolf of Chung-shan" is the title of a Ming dynasty short story. This tale was also dramatized twice during the same era. For a translation of the short story, see Ma, Y. W., and Lau, Joseph S. M., eds., *Traditional Chinese Stories, Themes and Variations* (New York: Columbia University Press, 1978), pp. 117–121. In this story, a Mohist philosopher rescues a wolf from some hunters, after which the ungrateful wolf turns on him. The philosopher is eventually saved only after the wolf is tricked by a clever old man.

9. The Southern Screen, or Nan-p'ing, hills are located southwest of Hangchow; the lake in the title refers to the famous West Lake.

YU T'UNG

(16 JUNE 1618–? JULY 1704)[1]

Yu T'ung (*T'ung-jen, Chan-ch'eng;* HUI-AN, KEN-CHAI, HSI-T'ANG LAO-JEN), a native of Ch'ang-chou, Kiangsu, enjoyed a long and successful life as a distinguished scholar and sometime official during the early Ch'ing period. Widely known for his literary abilities while still an uncapped youth, he later served for four years (1652–1656) as police magistrate of Yung-p'ing *fu* in Chihli province. He then returned home to a life of ease, devoting himself to his literary pursuits, until in 1678 he was put up, at the age of sixty, to take the special *po-hsüeh hung-tz'u* examination. He passed the examination the following year and was appointed to a post in the Hanlin Academy where he assisted in compiling the *Ming shih*. In 1683 he retired once more to his home near Soochow and lived out his remaining years as a respected literatus whose friendship was eagerly sought by younger scholars.

Yu was a prolific writer of both prose and poetry, and produced admired compositions in all major verse forms, including dramatic lyrics. His works were extremely popular and had wide currency during his lifetime, even being read at the imperial palace where his talents were praised by both the Shun-chih (*reg.* 1644–1662) and K'ang-hsi emperors. His best poems often exhibit playful turns of phrase or surprising conceits handled in an easy and natural manner.

(Paul W. Kroll)

---

1. Lien-che Tu, ECCP, 2:935–936.

Burning Incense

A storm of wind and rain suddenly whips up, autumn talking with itself;
In an empty chamber still and calm I myself seem a stranger.
Ducklings sleeping quietly are not yet aware of the cold;
The heart of the incense is nearly gone, and threads of fragrance rise.
They allure me with their dark shadows like the folds of a gauze robe,
Almost becoming smoke but not, almost becoming clouds but not.
Now the embers of the snuff are quenched, yet the fumes still remain—
A clear breath that wafts its odor to one who sits in silence.

(No. 1 in a series of 2; HTCML, 1:15b) *(Tr. Paul W. Kroll)*

Desultory Thoughts on My Old Home

With a whip as my staff I've come home under autumn's evening sky;
The sunbright things of my old garden still are richly green.
White nuphar, with no one to tend it, floats on the water of the brook;
Yellow sparrows, always active, contend over the wild fields.
Sunlight slanting down sinks away at last, in the wake of withering leaves;
The distant hills suffer no shifting along with the unruly clouds.
And the lotus blossoms as before flaunt their colorful hues,
By the west wind swung and scattered about for who knows how many years.

(HTHT, 1:6b) *(Tr. Paul W. Kroll)*

On Hearing the Chukar

Within the chukar's call the twilight sun moves westward,
Upon the footpath travelers, all with heads bowed down.
Over this earth's passes and mountains their journeys never done.
—Are your cries so full of feeling for their bitter misery?

(SHEN, 11:13b–14a) *(Tr. Paul W. Kroll)*

Bananas

Leaf upon leaf dancing in the western window,
Their voices increasing the solitude of the nighttime rain.
They are water sprites waving bamboo fans,
Or mountain demons in sheared-off singlets of gauze.
Or paper unfolded by the wind and written on by a monk,
A portrait set flying by snow, on which is drawn a visitor.
—In my house there are such autumn dreams;
Those chasing the deer[1] may laugh at a poor woodcutter.

(HTCML, 1:18b) *(Tr. Paul W. Kroll)*

An Autumn Night

The air at night an unbroken whistling wail,
But my dreams are as deep as an entire year.
The failing lamplight glistens on shadows of teardrops,
And falling leaves stir mournful zither strings.
I mark the dots of time, like a traveler writing on the void,
Grow thin as a monk in meditation facing the wall.
A bell at daybreak reaches me from somewhere—
And a hundred deep feelings are gone utterly into vagueness.

(HTCML, 1:16a) *(Tr. Paul W. Kroll)*

NOTE

1. "Chasing the deer" here implies the pursuit of official position. The poet pictures himself in the figure of the simple woodcutter.

WU CHIA-CHI

(8 NOVEMBER 1618–? JUNE 1684)

Wu Chia-chi (*Pin-hsien*; YEH-JEN)—native of An-feng-ch'ang, T'ai-chou prefecture of Yangchow, Kiangsu—was a commoner. He lived a secluded life in the salt-producing region of the lower Yangtze, exchanging visits and poems with a few friends, and eventually died of consumption. He may have on occasion supported himself as a merchant or fortune-teller. In 1663 his works came to the attention of the famous poet Wang Shih-chen (q.v.) who, along with another prominent scholar-official Chou Liang-kung (1612–1672), lauded Wu as an extraordinary genius. Both Chou and Wang contributed prefaces to his collected works, in which the "simplicity" (*tan*) and "loftiness" (*kao*) of Wu's verse were singled out for praise as reminiscent of the T'ang poets Meng Chiao and Chia Tao (779–849). The majority of his poems mirror some common experience of his generation in the dislocation of the Ming-Ch'ing transition, moving from a more or less active Ming loyalist resistance to an ambivalent acceptance of the new order. They describe survival in poetry and express sympathy for the poor and the downtrodden. Collected under the title of *Lou-hsüan shih-chi* (Poems from a Dilapidated Studio), his works were printed frequently in his own lifetime and down to 1902. A modern annotated edition, by Yang Chi-ch'ing, was issued in Shanghai in 1980. It contains over one thousand poems, including those that had appeared in the supplement (*hsü-chi*) and the addendum (*shih-pu*) volumes published after the poet's death.

(John E. Wills, Jr.)

Miscellaneous Poems

I

Beside the road the *wu-t'ung* tree,
Bent, crippled, and ghastly pale.
Together we exist between earth and sky;
Yet alone it's tortured by dust storm and gale.
Coming and going are many "overturned carts";[1]
All around, nothing grows but thorns and brambles.
When the roots can find no proper place,
Trunk and branches stretch out in vain.
Beneath the frigid sky, the vermillion phoenix is far away;
Common birds swirl and fight for a place to rest.

II

I have beaten my sword into an axe,
And must get along as a woodcutter.
Who says my zeal has been smoothed away?
I still have a sharp tool in my hands.
Going into the mountains, I weep among pines and cypresses;
To catch a tiger, I want to be the first among peers.
At sunset we would return home singing,
Our voices echoing back and forth.
Yellowing war clouds hang over the city;
Face flushed, again and again I glance back.

(Nos. 1 and 2 from a series of 8; WCCSCC, pp. 2–3) *(Tr. John E. Wills, Jr.)*

On the Ninth Day of the Month, Thinking of Ch'eng Yi-shih at Soochow

Itinerant trade is the business of petty men,
Laboring their minds and bodies over carats and ounces,
Intimate with the grubby and the unkempt,
Consorting with the stinking foul.
Alas, in the midst of wild grasses,
A proud wild swan among skinhead cranes!
Companions in thirst and hunger,
The young and strong make light of the road;
While the many are glad you share their interests,

But who would know that your heart keeps its distance?
The Soochow moon rises amid pines and junipers;
The startled deer call out to each other.
Thoughts of home may make you sad;
Deep, deep is your longing there beside Lake T'ai.[2]

(No. 2 from a series of 2; WCCSCC, p. 165) *(Tr. John E. Wills, Jr.).*

Ten Miscellaneous Poems on Tung-t'ao:[3] At the Ch'ang Family Well

A salt worker always eats salty food.
A milder taste, he would think it strange!
I sigh that this cold and pure spring
Is found amid these briny wastes.
Even the marshes aren't dry in a drought;
On a moonlit night, the water's fit for tea.
Desolate here among the rambling grasses,
I draw the water but who'd come to join me from afar?

(No. 8 from a series of 10; WCCSCC, p. 198) *(Tr. John E. Wills, Jr.)*

Passing the Retreat of Hsü Ching-po[4]

A grassy road with few passersby,
A bramble door, a wild unkempt view.
You chant poems to while away the long blank day,
You escape from the world to keep the ruddy look of youth.
Few books on your shelves—Fu Hsi's[5] earnest thoughts;
The old wine lees—an amber's deep glow.
Everything invites me to get drunk with you
And take a nap in the bamboo shade.

(No. 1 from a series of 2; WCCSCC, p. 131) *(Tr. John E. Wills, Jr.)*

On Virtuous Government—For His Excellency Wang Fu-ssu,[6] Salt Subcontroller of T'ai-chou

Flowering plums from the southern passes, fresh and pure,
Their fragrance can move the mind of man.
The black-haired masses, though dull witted,
Long for virtuous government, in their heart.

Desolate are these ocean shores!
Harried, the saltern workers!
All year they work to pay their taxes,
Their bodies deformed by salt-village life.
Starving children lie in the grasses;
Crickets join in their woeful cries.
If no good shepherd had come along,
How could the people find consolation?
He daily toils at nurturing and comforting them;
He daily soothes the wearied and the sick.
Their prayers will turn the salt marsh sweet,
As the sounds of singing rise across the fields.

(No. 1 from a series of 5; WCCSCC, p. 185) *(Tr. John E. Wills, Jr.)*

Falling Leaves

How many days do they live on the branch
Before death comes one night in autumn?
They, too, conform to the mind of heaven and earth
To fall helter-skelter on the courtyard below—
Creating tumult where the moon slants,
Calculated to startle a white-headed old man.
Who needs to complain of quavering and faltering?
The busybody culprit is the spring wind.

(WCCSCC, p. 11) *(Tr. Irving Lo)*

NOTES

1. See Huang Tsung-hsi, note 2.
2. The text gives "Chü-chü," which was called Cheng-tse in ancient times, alluding to the story about Fan Li, a trader-turned-statesman of the Warring States period who spurned a king's reward and sailed off on a boat on Lake T'ai.
3. Tung-t'ao, another name of An-feng-ch'ang, is the poet's native place. Wu claimed spiritual kinship with a fellow villager, the Ming Neo-Confucianist philosopher Wang Ken (1483–1541) who advocated the self-cultivation of common men and women and was later regarded as the leader of the "leftist" wing of the Wang Yang-ming School of Neo-Confucianism.
4. Not identified.
5. Reputed author of the *Yi-ching*.
6. Courtesy name of Wang Chao-chang (fl. 1667), an official known for his integrity.

LIU SHIH

(1618–21 JULY 1664)[1]

Liu Shih (*Ju-shih;* HO-TUNG-CHÜN, MI-WU, and WO-WEN CHÜ-SHIH), a native of Wu-chiang, Kiangsu, was one of those rare Chinese women who, despite her humble origin (her profession was that of a singing girl, or courtesan, in the entertainment quarter), managed to acquire an education. Before she met Ch'ien Ch'ien-yi (q.v.), in 1640, she was probably known as Yang Yi (the character *yang,* a common surname, also means "poplar tree," which is usually associated with the character *liu,* "willow"). Under that name, she won fame not only for her beauty but also for her talents as a poet and calligrapher; and many men of letters of her time were her friends, including the late Ming poet Ch'en Tzu-lung (1608–1647), who was also her lover. After becoming Ch'ien's concubine on 14 July 1641, Ch'ien gave her the new name of Liu Shih, or Liu Ju-shih (with the two characters of her given name being taken from a conventional Buddhist scriptural phrase (*ju-shih wo-wen,* meaning "and so I have heard").

The couple shared many a literary interest: in addition to composing poems together, Liu also helped him compile a highly reputable anthology of Ming poetry, assuming responsibility for the section on women poets. She remained faithful and loyal to Ch'ien for the rest of her life, often bringing on herself unwelcome tasks in order to shelter him from one kind of crisis or another in his stormy career. After a fire destroyed their library, the Chiang-yün lou, she took up Buddhist studies and became a nun a year before the poet's death. After Ch'ien died in 1663, some of his kinsmen pressed her for money and treasures and, finally, in order to shame her blackmailers, she hanged herself,

---

1. Chao-ying Fang, ECCP, 1:529–530.

leaving a request to the authorities that justice be done. (A settlement was eventually worked out whereby a modest income was settled on Ch'ien's son by his first marriage and on the daughter she had borne with Ch'ien.) Liu Shih's poetic output was not large—barely two slim volumes included in her husband's collected works—but it reflects an intensity of feeling reminiscent of the best poetry of the Sung lyricist Ch'in Kuan (1049–1100).[2]

(Irving Lo)

Poem on a Sleeping Butterfly

Flitting to and fro, by winding paths and sparse fence,
Quietly, done with dancing, it settles down, pillowing on a branch.
With perfume stolen from the handsome young clerk,[1] but less
nimble-limbed;
With the soul of the philosopher,[2] but dreaming of darker mysteries;
As if lying in a thousand-day stupor from the nectar it drinks;[3]
And the sun's shadow idles on the moss, to lock up all grief within
a curtain.
Alas, awakened by the rascally east wind blowing,
It joins the silly bees in disturbing a lady's chamber.

(Chou, p. 54) *(Tr. Irving Lo)*

A *Tz'u-yün* Poem Written in Response:[4] Tiger Hill [Original Poem by Ch'ien Ch'ien-yi]

In a little house on Western Hill, undisturbed by crowd or clamor,
I watch a gentle snowfall through a thin curtain, a brazier in front.
A girl pretty as jade keeps me company in an abbot's room;
From a bed of gold, I can still view flowers rain down from a
paradisal sky.[5]
In the light chill, her face wears makeup fresher than early spring;
The notes of her song, rising from the flute, twirl as round as the
moon.
Tomorrow when the city of Soochow gets wind of this affair,
From a thousand homes, who won't make way for such
exquisiteness?

2. Ibid., p. 530.

[Poem in Response by Liu Shih]

As the flute and strings cease playing, there's only laughter and clamor;
Cozy, we sit before goblets of wine, a railing in front.
Already I suspect the moon has fled from the lantern-lit night;
But it's more like flowers yielding their place to snowflakes in the sky.
Pistils of jade which spring keeps from budding are as thin as I am;
From the silver lamp tonight, the flame burns for you as round as the moon.
New verses, lusty and strong, should quicken peach and plum trees into flower;
Let not the rampaging wind and rain[6] cast envious eyes on such exquisiteness.

(Chou, pp. 151–52; MCCHC, 18:7a–7b) *(Tr. Irving Lo)*

Tune: *T'a so hsing* (Treading the Sedge)
Title: Sending a Letter

A trace of flowers, a streak of moonlight,
Tip of sorrow, tail end of remorse:
Not many tears were left when I started this letter;
Now finished, it is suddenly scattered by the wily wind.
May the wily wind smash my feelings to smithereens!
By a half-rolled-up curtain, the dying lamp
Turns everything into dream, into water.
My soul dissolves as I seem to catch sight of him,
Wresting from me for a moment my total devotion;
But because it's a little dream, he's nowhere to be found.

(Chou, pp. 63–64) *(Tr. Irving Lo)*

NOTES

1. The text reads "Han Ch'üan," the name of a handsome young man in the Tsin dynasty who eloped with the daughter of his employer, Chia Ch'iung. When Han first presented himself for an interview with her father, she secretly peeked at him and quickly fell in love with this handsome young clerk. They successfully arranged to have an affair, and the father learned about it when he first detected on the young man's clothing the scent of a rare perfume he had given her.

2. The text reads "Chuang Chou," alluding to the famous parable in the *Chuang-tzu* where the Taoist philosopher discoursed on how he had dreamed about turning into a butterfly and, in that state, not knowing if he was really Chuang Chou. Upon waking, he had no assurance that he wasn't in fact a butterfly dreaming that he was Chuang Chou.

3. See Ch'ien Ch'ien-yi, note 4.

4. A Regulated Poem (*lü-shih*) requires rhyme at the end of the first, second, fourth, sixth, and eighth lines; i.e., *t'ien* ("fullness" and "loud noise"); *ch'ien* ("front"); *t'ien* ("sky"); *yüan* ("round"); and *yen* ("exquisiteness"). A *tz'u-yün* type of "harmonizing" (*ho*) poem, written in response to a particular poem, must use the same rhyme words. The full title of this set of poems reads: "On the Night of the Lantern Festival, Together with Prince Ho-tung, Mooring Our Boat at West Creek of Tiger Hill [in Soochow] and Stopping at the Studio of Shen Pi-fu for a Drink."

5. *Yü-hua t'ien* (rain-flowers sky), a Buddhist term, said of a moving sermon by a monk of the Liang dynasty which caused the sky to rain down flowers.

6. Possibly containing a pun on the two words *liu-feng*, which, if written in reverse order, would describe a person of romantic temperament and great charm.

HSÜ TS'AN
(FL. 1650)

Hsü Ts'an (*Ming-shen,* HSIANG-P'ING and MAO-YÜAN), a native of Soochow, Kiangsu, married Ch'en Chih-lin (1605–1666, Yen-sheng, SU-AN) of Hai-ning, Chekiang province. Ch'en obtained the *chin-shih* degree in 1637 and received official appointment. After the collapse of the Ming dynasty, he served the Ch'ing dynasty, twice reaching the position of Grand Secretary. He was also named Junior Guardian of the Heir-Apparent. Entangled in factional struggles at court, he was banished to Liao-yang in Manchuria for a time, but was later summoned back to Peking. Soon he was accused of attempting to bribe a eunuch and sent into exile from which he was never allowed to return. Hsü Ts'an accompanied her husband to Peking and twice followed him into exile. She therefore led a colorful and eventful life, at one moment the wife of a senior official, and the next that of a criminal. Banishment took her beyond the frontiers and to a life in the wilderness. After the death of her husband, she was pardoned and allowed to return home. There she devoted her remaining years to copying Buddhist sutras.

Hsü Ts'an was skilled in calligraphy, painting, and poetry. Her *tz'u* (lyric) poems are in the Northern Sung style; they are lucid in expression and tinged with melancholy. Her poetry was highly rated by her contemporaries and later critics, such as Ch'en Wei-sung (q.v.).

(Pao Chia-lin)

Headwaters of the Lung River[1]

Westward, the gloom of the remote wilds;
Eastward, the grief of my native land.
One heart tugged at by two places,
Two rows of tears fall separately.
Autumn's military summons allow for no delay,
War chariots roll all night without rest.
Brave soldiers make light of crossing the frontier
Before they reach the top of the Lung Mountains.[2]

(CCYSC, 1:16b) *(Tr. Pao Chia-lin)*

Moon over the Mountain Pass

In the dead of winter, crossing the mountain pass—
The short jacket feels as cold as iron.
Two or three sounds of the Tartar flute
Blow down the moon from the winter sky.

(CCYSC, 2:3a) *(Tr. Pao Chia-lin)*

Tune: *Hsi-chiang yüeh* (West River Moon)
Title: Rain on the Night of the Full Moon

It isn't that we are deprived of a bright moon:
The moon has done wrong to a pleasant evening.
Otherwise why must it drizzle, drizzle on the fifteenth?
It only helps the dense grass and grief to multiply.

Clouds roll in a gentle chill at the approaching dusk;
By a single lamp, a gaunt shadow, an agitated heart—
For my dream to reach home, the night is short, the road long;
So tonight I must begin early my dream of going home.

(CCYSY, 1:2b–3a) *(Tr. Irving Lo)*

Tune: *Lin-chiang hsien* (Immortal at the River)
Title: Boudoir Feeling

I hardly recognize that autumn has entered my mirror;
How often tears stain my makeup.
Clear dew over the green wave is distressing to pink fragrance.

The shy heart of the lotus has formed,
But in most the pods are empty.

Hanging willows by the low pavilion are done with dancing;
Returning geese in the formation peep into my room.
My soul is wafted to the home of water and clouds;
Here soft wind and rain,
And a night by the chilling creek.

(CCYSY, 2:1a–2b) *(Tr. Irving Lo)*

NOTES

1. A major river in Kansu province.
2. Located northwest of Lung county in Shensi province, a strategic mountain west of the pass which extends into Kansu province.

SHIH JUN-CHANG

(6 JANUARY 1619—5 AUGUST 1683)[1]

Shih Jun-Chang (*Shang-pai* and *Ch'i-yün*; *YÜ-SHAN*, CHÜ-CHAI, HUO-CHAI), a native of Hsüan-ch'eng, Anhwei province, was orphaned at an early age and raised by a paternal uncle. He is said to have been an industrious student, and to have begun the writing of poetry while still young. He obtained the coveted *chin-shih* degree in 1649, and he was later appointed to several posts in the provinces, including that of circuit intendant of Hu-hsi, Kiangsi. There he was confronted with the solving of social problems arising from depressed economic conditions and widespread bandit activities. These experiences were recorded in some of his most memorable verse. Later he was invited to participate in the *po-hsüeh hung-ju* examinations of 1679, after which he was posted to the Hanlin Academy and named to the editorial board of the Ming Dynasty history project.

Shih Jun-chang was acclaimed by his contemporaries as one of the leading poets of the day. The famous scholar Ch'ien Ch'ien-yi (q.v.) described his poetry as being "as resonant as golden bells, comparable to the beauty of jade chimes." The distinguished poet Wang Shih-chen (q.v.) observed in his *Yü-yang shih-hua* (Poetry Talks of the Recluse of Yü-yang) that, "when I speak of contemporary poets, the best may be said to be Shih of the south [i.e., Shih Jun-chang] and Sung of the north [i.e., Sung Wan, q.v.]," thus giving rise to the popular saying "Shih of the south and Sung of the north." Wang Shih-chen especially admired Shih Jun-chang's mastery of the pentasyllabic line.

A prolific and versatile poet, Shih Jun-chang dedicated himself with conscious seriousness to the perfection of his craft. In the *Hu-chai shih-hua* (Poetry Talks of the Hu-chai Studio), he observed that "Tu

1. Martin C. Wilbur, ECCP, 2:651.

Fu did not imitate the old *yüeh-fu* songs; instead he employed new titles and recorded contemporary events." This remark reveals a not unexpected admiration for the great poet Tu Fu; also, it indicates that he did not feel bound by the tradition, and that he believed in the social and historical values of poetry. Imbued by a Confucian sense of humanitarian idealism, he viewed poetry as one of several means to record natural and human events as he witnessed them, and he expressed critical judgments on what he observed. Shih Jun-chang was not, however, insensitive to the importance of compositional values. In this respect, his poetry reveals a somewhat spare and economical style, a preference for simplicity of diction rather than rhetorical embellishment. Wang Shih-chen has recorded a conversation between Shih Jun-chang and the celebrated poet-dramatist Hung Sheng (q.v.), in which the former remarked: "If one is building a house, the tiles, bricks, timbers, and stones must be erected one by one on level ground." In this way, he metaphorically stated his belief that the rules of composition are fundamental to the poet's craft. The themes which find expression in his verse are for the most part traditional, although he uses them to portray his times, and this he does in a realistic manner and with a deep sense of compassion for and understanding of the diversity and hazards of life as he experienced it.

(William Schultz)

Songs on Accompanying the Governor-General

I

Drums and horns rouse the river town;
Army banners advance in the falling rain.
Alas, fragrant grasses turning green
Barely survive the horses' trampling hooves.

II

On the battlefield, the spring wind is harsh;
In deserted villages, ruined houses lean askew.
Once again swallows return, two by two,
But whose house will provide them shelter?

(Nos. 1 and 2 from a series of 4; HYTSC, 46:2b) *(Tr. William Schultz)*

A Random Song on Approaching a River

Red oranges, white bamboo shoots, don't mention the cost!
Sincere, simple mountain and river folk, truly they're to be pitied.
One acre for the official tax, three acres for grain—
And yet, the farmers grow tired of saying "It's been a good year."

(No. 5 from a series of 9; HYTSC, 48:5a) *(Tr. William Schultz)*

A Ballad of Hu-hsi

In the *hsin-ch'ou* year [1661], I was sent to administer the circuit of Hu-hsi [Kiangsi Province], where the land is infertile and there is annual famine. The administrative officials responsible for the collection of delinquent taxes were derelict in their duties and looked to me for help. I had received instructions to set things right and to enforce the law. At that time, the military was engaged in the southwest, and before long three or four documents arrived, stating that petty officials and people in violation of the law would not be excused. Alas, one official was censured and did not dare deny the charges. But what remedy was there for the people? With pain and anguish, I could only notify and admonish them, and thus I wrote "A Ballad of Hu-hsi."

As an imperial officer, I collect the taxes,
A matter I have never attended to before.
Day and night, pressure for army rations;
How dare I any longer hesitate, delay?
Yesterday's orders just now received 5
Are by today already long overdue.
Seizing the reins, I hasten into the field:
All is desolate, few people remain.
Brambles and thorns cover the stricken villages;
How all the fields are overgrown! 10
An aged rustic kneels to speak at length:
"This year there's been both flood and drought;
Crumbled walls, what else remains?
Willingly I'd part forever from wife and child,
But in these hard times it's hard to find a buyer." 15
Tears stain his tattered jacket.
Grieved at heart to hear these words,
I can only sigh in alarm, cover my face.
I am ashamed of this duty of whip and lash,
In this manner to win honor for my worthless self. 20
The State's grace should be truly generous;

Already it should have excused unpaid taxes.
Officers and men wait for their morning rations,
So who can hesitate for even a moment?
Chanting this poem, again I weep; 25
My tears run dry in this empty mountain nook.

(HYTSC, 6:14a–b) *(Tr. William Schultz)*

A Ballad of One Hundred Fathoms

"At Eighteen Cataracts, the rocks are jagged teeth;[1]
A hundred fathoms of green rope, pitiable are we.
Barefooted, short jackets tied at the waist,
Rice grains we swallow cold, scoop river water to drink.
From the north, heavy cavalry crowds on board; 5
In rapids and steeps, the boat rushes past boulders, pierces deeps.
Chickens, pigs, oxen, wine—no telling their numbers;
Tied to the mast, the hawser moves, a thousand trackers hauling.
District officials, fearful of blame and zealous as fire,
Counting up our numbers, sit facing the river. 10
Detained in an ancient temple and treated like prisoners,
Told when to come and go, we starve while they make us wait.
Along sand and gravel banks, endless crumbling cliffs,
Stretching our arms like apes, we quarrel and shout.
Autumn and winter the water is sluggish, surging and rushing in
spring; 15
Flood dragons lie in pools and caverns, tigers and leopards are on
shore.
Beating the drums, sounding the cymbals, the morning boat flies;
Yang-hou stands erect in the waves, Chiang-o laughs.[2]
Don't speak of bitter toil, of working for the master:
Harried by cudgel and whip, we are half dead, half alive. 20
Sir, look at those who have died, fallen by the shore.
Mates, which one of you dares to cry out?
Once flat on the waves, down you go to southern lands.
How much human blood flows into barbarian rivers?
The hundred fathoms rope won't break, but our guts surely will! 25
Even the flowing waters are heartless, though they sob and wail."

(HYTSC, 18:4a–b) *(Tr. William Schultz)*

Falling Teeth

Try to detain joy, and alas, it will not remain;
Worry about old age, and suddenly it arrives.
Without knowing, one's strength begins to fade,
But first, one's teeth begin to come out.
Leaves fall, but with spring they grow again; 5
The sun sets, but at dawn it rises from the ground.
I sense time's passing like the flowing river:
Once departed, all things are cast aside.
Both wife and child cry out in alarm
Because I look so worn and haggard. 10
Petty officials dine on one another;
Sharp teeth are thus a moral trap.
If they're few, what harm in that?
I whistle this song to please myself.
Thrice Master Chuang of Meng declared,[3] 15
In nourishing life, there's a bit of shame.

(HYTSC, 6:17b–18a) *(Tr. William Schultz)*

Upper Garrison Farm:[4] A Ballad
A Lament for a Woman Killed by the Soldiery

In the village there is a crying child;
Wail upon wail, it calls for its mother.
Its mother is dead; blood soaks her clothing,
But still she clasps it to her breast to suckle.

(HYTSC, 2:5a) *(Tr. William Schultz)*

NOTES

1. The Eighteen Cataracts are located near the confluence of the Chang and the Kan rivers in Kiangsi province.
2. Yang-hou and Chiang-o: a river god and goddess, respectively.
3. Master Chuang: the ancient philosopher Chuang-tzu, or Chuang Chou.
4. "Upper Garrison Farm" (Shang-liu-t'ien) is a popular northern *yüeh-fu* ballad title from the Six Dynasties period.

WANG FU-CHIH

(7 OCTOBER 1619–18 FEBRUARY 1692)[1]

Wang Fu-chih (*Erh-nung;* CHIANG-CHAI, CH'UAN-SHAN, YI-HU TAO-JEN, and HSI-T'ANG)— a classical scholar, philosopher, literary critic, anthologist, and poet—was a native of Heng-yang, Hunan province. Both his father, Wang Ch'ao-p'in (1570–1647), and an elder brother had achieved fame as scholars, and Wang Fu-chih followed in that tradition. He passed the provincial examination in 1642, but rapidly changing political conditions prevented his taking the final degree. When the Ming fell to the rebel armies of Li Tzu-ch'eng, he fled from Peking with his father. An ardent patriot, he joined the loyalist forces opposing the Manchu conquest, but the factionalism which plagued the southern Ming courts ultimately caused him to return to private life. For the next forty years, he secluded himself in his native place, where he cut himself off from national politics and devoted himself to his many scholarly pursuits. He was a prodigiously productive scholar and writer, but he had little influence on his own times, owing to the fact that most of his writings, which contained seditious ideas, remained in manuscript form until late in the Ch'ing era.

In breadth and profundity, Wang Fu-chih's learning is no less impressive than his productivity and includes a valuable historical account of one of the Ming loyalist courts, a critique of traditional political and economic institutions, several short expositions of his political philosophy, and numerous studies of classical texts. He wrote commentaries on the works of the Sung dynasty Neo-Confucianist Chang Tsai (1020–1077), whose philosophical views he generally shared, and on the *Chuang-tzu* and several Buddhist sutras. In all of his historical and

---

1. S. H. Ch'i, ECCP, 2:817–819.

classical scholarship, he reflected the growing concern of his age for verifiable data and precise philological methods.

In addition to his philosophical writings, Wang Fu-chih was deeply concerned with the theory and practice of the literary arts. He compiled seven separate anthologies of poetry, which collectively span the entire range from ancient times to his own day, and he was a critic of remarkable perception. Especially celebrated was his theory on the fusion of *ch'ing* (emotion; i.e., inner experience) and *ching* (scene; i.e., externality) as a kind of "touchstone" for poetry. He considered them "inseperable" though "called by two different names"; and he insisted that in all good poetry "emotion" must reside in the external world being described and that all externality explored in a poem constitutes a poet's inner experience. Directing all this is what Wang speaks of as the "mind" (*yi*) of the poet, or "thought," which he considers as essential to a poem as "a general for the army, without whom the army is not an army but an inchoate mass of men." Though anticipating the theory of "spirit and tone" (*shen-yün*) of Wang Shih-chen (q.v.) and later that of "worlds" (*ching-chieh*) of Wang Kuo-wei (q.v.), Wang Fu-chih was essentially a Confucianist in his literary outlook. Yet he was never one-sided or partial; rather, he considered *shih* (events), *li* (principle of things), *ch'ing* (emotion), and *chih* (what is desired by the mind or heart) as the necessary complements of all good poetry. (For further discussion of his views, see Siu-kit Wong's informative essay "*Ch'ing* and *Ching* in the Critical Writing of Wang Fu-chih" in Adele Austin Rickett, ed., *Chinese Approaches to Literature From Confucious to Liang Ch'i-Ch'ao*.) Also a prolific poet, Wang left fifteen collection of *shih* poetry and three separate collections of *tz'u*, or lyrics, in which genre he is still much admired as a master. Chu Hsiao-tsang (q.v.), for instance, regarded the patriotic sentiments and elements of personal pathos in the poetry of Wang Fu-chih as belonging to the grand tradition of the *Li Sao* by Ch'ü Yüan, the archtypal Chinese poet.

(Irving Lo and William Schultz)

A Miscellany

Sad winds rise in the middle of the night,
War horses on the border whinny in fright.
A stalwart fellow is a precious sword in a box
Which on stormy nights sings a mournful tune.
No brave general has as yet appeared; 5

The desolate road north is forever blocked.
Mountain passes and rivers recede from view;
Helter-skelter, the vision of tall grasses in the mist.
I put on my coat, go out to view the placid sky;
The Milky Way is already sinking in the west. 10
I can't stop worrying over the nation's fate.
Why bother to console myself in this life?

(No. 4 from a series of 4; WCSSWC, p. 137) *(Tr. Irving Lo)*

Bamboo Branch Song[1]

Lotus flowers will one day burst out in golden whiskers;
Lotus leaves set no store on pendant watery beads.
When waves beat duckweed apart, how you annoy me!
Waves depart but the duckweed remains, how I pity you!

(No. 7 from a series of 10; WCSSWC, p. 180) *(Tr. Irving Lo)*

An Autumn Song

The level lake brings news of wild geese returning,
By winding steps crickets are already singing.
A short oar: dreams of clear waves;
A dark window: wind among fallen leaves.
Life persists in today's affairs;
Autumn grows old in clumps of trees.
"Questioning Heaven"[2]—but who's to provide answers?
Clouds over the creek obscure a broken rainbow.

(No. 6 from a series of 6; WCSSWC, p. 255) *(Tr. Irving Lo)*

Tune: *Tieh lien hua* (Butterflies Love Flowers)
Title: Withered Willows

Ask the west wind why it keeps up its lament—
        Endlessly swirling, turning,
    Determined to break the thread of love?
Drifting down leaf after leaf, all so callously!
The winding creek appeared long ago as far as the world's end!

Chaotic shadows of winter crows, row upon row,
        Always latching onto a setting sun—

Who is still willing to linger?
In a dream, the buds were sprouting soft yellow brocade threads,
But how hard it is to summon spring light with cicadas' cries!

(WCSSWC, p. 592) *(Tr. Irving Lo)*

Tune: *Fen tieh-erh* (White Butterflies)
Title: On Frost

Ask even at the world's end
How much more is there of cold love, empty feelings?
I dread springtime when wandering catkins, flying floss,
All carried by the wind,
Attach themselves to
River, sky, and crimson trees;
Flirting gracefully,
They entice the wind to set them flying.

Quietly, unbeknownst, west of the small bridge,
A rooster's cry hurries the dawn;
When the slanting moon is still up
In the sky, everywhere, crushed pearls of dew
Fall with naught to restrain them but the sour wind.
Let all this desolation
Be confided in soft whispers to winter crows!

(WCSSWC, p. 592) *(Tr. Irving Lo)*

NOTES

1. The poet's own headnote to the title *Chu-chih tz'u* reads roughly as follows: "When Yang Lien-fu [the Ming poet Yang Wei-chen (1296–1370), known for his *T'ieh-ya yüeh-fu,* which was a collection of lyrics often treating of contemporary subjects but employing a style akin to folk songs] composed his 'Bamboo Branch Songs,' he had many followers. The style, however, is not true to the original, which was first invented in the Ch'ang-ch'ing reign of the T'ang dynasty but evolved from it. In this type of song, the contemporaneous is employed to express hidden, obscure meanings—to approximate the ideal of the ancient *feng* [referring to the 'Airs of States' from the *Shih-ching*] poetry. Here I try my hand at it."

2. "T'ien-wen" (Questioning Heaven) is the title of a poem from the ancient collection of verses known as the *Ch'u Tzu,* attributed to Ch'ü Yüan. This poem deals largely with philosophical and mythological speculations.

CH'EN WEI-SUNG

(3 JANUARY 1626–12 JUNE 1682)[1]

Ch'en Wei-sung (*Ch'i-nien, Chia-ling*), a native of Yi-hsing, Kiangsu province, was born into a prominent family, and his father, Ch'en Chen-hui (1605–1656), played an active leadership role in the Fu-she political party in late Ming times. When young, Ch'en Wei-sung received a traditional education, and early in life won a name for himself as a master of Parallel Prose. Those literary skills notwithstanding, he repeatedly failed the civil service examinations. In his early fifties he was invited to participate in the *po-hsüeh hung-tz'u* examinations, and he finally gained the success that had so long eluded him. He was subsequently appointed to the Hanlin Academy and then assigned to the board of scholars engaged in compiling the official history of the Ming dynasty. Ch'en spent the remainder of his life in Peking, where he associated with the leading literary figures of the time, such as Chu Yi-tsun (q.v.), whom he had known for many years as a fellow poet, and Singde (q.v.).

During the years of his youth and early manhood, Ch'en Wei-sung cultivated the various *shih* forms of poetry, and he had already achieved a reputation as a promising poet when he began to explore the *tz'u* genre, which was then undergoing a modest revival after a long period of relative neglect. He soon found this form of poetry to be especially congenial, and over the next several decades he devoted much of his time and energy to the cultivation of that form, thus becoming ultimately the most prolific *tz'u* poet in all of Chinese literary history. The *Hu-hai lou tz'u-chi* (The *Tz'u* Collection of the Pavilion of Lakes and Seas) contains over 1,600 lyrics, the majority of which employ the longer modes which had come into fashion in Sung times. In

---

1. Lien-che Tu, ECCP, 1:103.

matters of theme, diction, and general style, the influence of such great Sung dynasty masters as Su Shih (1037–1101) and Hsin Ch'i-chi (1140–1207) is apparent in his poetry. Like those poets, Ch'en Wei-sung refused to be bound by the belief that the *tz'u* form was best suited to the treatment of delicate boudoir sentiments, of love between the sexes. Instead, he made no distinction between the *shih* and *tz'u* forms with respect to subject matter, and thus his lyric poetry treats of such diverse subjects as parting, a wide range of individual emotional states of mind, recollections of the past, natural physical scenes, contemporary affairs, and so forth. In rejecting the *tz'u* poetics of the *Hua-chien* school, he also favored a freer, more natural diction over the richly embellished line associated with the early history of the form. In this way, his poetry in this form manifests a vigorous, masculine manner, but one no less lyrical in spirit.

As a vigorous advocate for *tz'u* poetry and one of its most noted practitioners during the time of its revival in the seventeenth century, Ch'en Wei-sung's influence on future developments in the form was considerable. He is regarded as the founder of the Yang-hsien school of lyric verse.

(William Schultz)

Tune: *Fa-chia tao-yin* (A Taoist Nun's Song)
Title: The Hungry Crow

The hungry crow caws,
The hungry crow caws,
Down and feathers terribly tattered and torn.
At home, the harvest already covered with frost and snow;
Abroad, I mistakenly believed the rice and grain to be fat.
Twilight deepens, but I must keep on flying, flying.

(CLTCC, 1:6a) *(Tr. Madeline Chu)*

Tune: *Hao-shih chin* (Happy Events Approaching)
Title: One summer day, invited by Mr. Shih Chü-an[1] to have a drink, I wrote a poem to the same rhyme as the one he wrote to celebrate my return from Wu-ch'ang.

When we parted, it was willow blossom season,
Like snow whirling toward a sunny window.

In a trice, hollyhocks begin to bloom,
Again reddening the corner of the curved rail.

Since our parting, once more things are renewed,
Only we are the same as yesterday.
When we talk of heroes who have lost their way,
Suddenly a chill wind comes up soughing.

(CLTCC, 3:1b) *(Tr. Madeline Chu)*

Tune: *Yü mei-jen* (The Beautiful Lady Yü)
Title: Listlessness

Smiling listlessly, I finger a spray of blossoms and say:
"Everywhere the cuckoos are weeping blood;
Fine flowers should open beside a fine pavilion,
Not by the frontiers of Ch'in or the steep roads of Shu:
not on the battlefield."

Leaning on the terrace, gazing afar enhances my melancholy;
Again, to the east wind I say,
"Fine wind, do not unfurl the war flag red,
But quickly blow the snow-white shad eastward across the river."

(CLTCC, 5:7a–7b) *(Tr. Madeline Chu)*

Tune: *Ho hsin-lang* (Congratulating the Bridegroom)
Title: The Song of the Boat Trackers

Battle ships arrayed by the estuary—
On the far horizon,
The True Sovereign grants the seal
Carved with coils and twists of a scaly dragon,
To recruit boat haulers, a hundred thousand men. 5
Every district plunged into a maelstrom,
I grieve for the eastern village,
Where chickens and dogs are thrown into turmoil;
Elders of the front ward hurry the rear tithing.
All in lashings,
Chained and bound behind an empty storehouse;
To be dragged away,
Who dares to raise a hand? 10

Rice flowers are now forming ears under a frosty sky.
    There, a conscript,
    At a fork in the road, bids farewell
    To his sick wife lying among the weeds;
"From here I go to Three Rivers to haul at the thousand-foot hawser—
Where snowy billows splash on the mast, roar in the night. 15
    Can my back endure
    The bullwhips or not?
Better that you return to the maple trees in the rear garden.
    Face the deserted temple,
  And urge the shamans to pour the libation;
    Ask for a blessing from the gods 20
    To let me return to the fields."

(CLTCC, 27:3b–4a) *(Tr. Madeline Chu)*

Tune: *Ho hsin-lang*

Title: Written on Yün-lang's Nuptial Day[2]

  Slowly sip the sweet thick brew;
    Joyful is today:
    Hairpins aglitter, their shadows on the mat,
    Cast a dazzling pattern before the lamp.
Beyond the screen, amid loud laughter and talk,
  Comes a report the headdress has just been put on. 5
    Once more I peer at
    This handsome young man;
Puzzled, unable to distinguish male from female.
    Furtively,
  I take the measure of the shoes he wears,[3]
    Escort him away,
    And raise the bridal curtain. 10

My sole companion for six years in my hostel—
    Most unforgettable:
    By flowery pillows
    Tears gently shed.
Today, your marriage rites will be fulfilled,
Tenderly the wife will comply with her husband. 15
    Attentively,
  Let the husband comport himself in decency.
But alone, under a gauze quilt cold as iron,

I'll hold the peachwood pipes,
Waiting for dawn by the gauze window.
But don't, for me, 20
Feel the least sad.

(CLTCC, 26:3a–3b) *(Tr. Madeline Chu)*

NOTES

1. An unidentified friend of the poet.

2. This poem was written on the occasion of Yün-lang's marriage. Yün-lang is Hsü Tzu-yün, formerly a boy actor in the singing troupe in Mao Hsiang's (1611–1693) household. Mao Hsiang gave Hsü Tzu-yün to Ch'en Wei-sung as a gift. Hsü then became Ch'en Wei-sung's intimate companion. This poem, with its obvious overtones of homosexual love, created quite a sensation in literati circles at the time.

3. The meaning of this line is somewhat obscure, perhaps intentionally so.

CHU YI-TSUN

(7 OCTOBER 1629–14 NOVEMBER 1709)[1]

Chu Yi-tsun (*Hsi-ch'ang;* CHU-CH'A), a native of Hsiu-shui (present-day Kashing), Chekiang, was an extraordinary poet, scholar, compiler, and bibliophile who rose from a commoner to become a Hanlin academician and one of the most celebrated men of letters in the empire. Born into an impoverished scholar's family, Chu was too poor to pursue an educational career through the regular channels; instead, he spent his youthful years seeking employment as a teacher or secretary in the families of high government officials, many of whom were provincial governors or commissioners. The positions he held during this period provided him with the chance to travel to many remote parts of China (where he befriended many poets including Ch'ü Ta-chün, Sung Wan [qq.v.], etc.) and to accumulate enough money to buy a villa in 1669 in his native district. The poet named his villa Chu-ch'a (Bamboo Knoll).

In 1678, at the age of fifty, Chu became one of the 188 scholars of the empire summoned to compete in a special examination known as the *po-hsüeh hung-tz'u,* and he emerged as one of the fifty winners. After passing this examination, he was showered with many imperial favors, including an appointment as an editor of the official history of the Ming dynasty. But, concurrently with his official duties, Chu was also able to pursue his own interests. He edited and published two works containing his own prose and poetry, respectively, in 1672 and 1674. Several other titles—local histories, works on archaeology, and philological studies of the classics—followed; and in 1705 he completed a large anthology of Ming poets (*Ming-shih tsung*) in one hundred

1. Chao-ying Fang, ECCP, 1:182–185.

volumes. In 1698 he retired to Kashing where he built a pavilion which at one time housed a large library of over 80,000 *chüan* and which he named P'u-shu t'ing (Sunning Books Pavilion).

In his own lifetime, Chu enjoyed a reputation as the leading poet of the South, rivaling Wang Shih-chen (q.v.) as the leading poet of the North. A contemporary poetry-critic Chao Chih-hsin (q.v.) once remarked, "Wang labors to produce better poetry while Chu is a more voluminous poet." This remark was probably directed at Chu's natural and easy style as well as at the quantity of his output, which was indeed prodigious. An inventive poet, Chu often took great pains with metrical variations (by combining lines of varying lengths) even in his *shih* poetry, or tried to say something new by utilizing some bits of familiar vocabulary from the works of earlier poets. While he acknowledged T'ang poetry to be superior to that of the Sung dynasty, Chu disdained imitation and always strove for originality of expression. And, unlike Wang, Chu also distinguished himself as a writer of lyric poems. His lyrics, preserved in four separate collections, were molded in the tradition of Chang Yen (1248–ca.1320) and Chiang K'uei (ca.1155–ca.1221) of the Southern Sung period. Immensely popular, they established a vogue later identified as the Chekiang School of poetry. He also compiled an anthology of *tz'u* containing selections from T'ang, Sung, Chin, and Yüan dynasty poets, the *Tz'u-tsung*, which was printed in 1678. His influence as a lyric poet lasted for nearly a century, until his position was challenged by the rise of the Ch'ang-chou School (see Chang Hui-yen).

(Irving Lo)

Two Quatrains on Yung-chia[1]

I
Pine Pavilion Hill

Green, green the pine trees on the hill,
Sa-sa, the rain beats at pine tree roots.
Pine nuts fall on the deserted mountain,
When morning comes, no one knows where.

II
Southern Pavilion

Light clouds at the first clearing after rain;
Reflecting sunlight upon the Southern Pavilion at dusk.
If I should encounter autumn tides rising,
I, too, am a guest going home in the West.

(Nos. 1 and 7 from a series of 20; PSTC, 6:2a–2b) *(Tr. Irving Lo)*

Two Quatrains on Peking's Western Suburb

I
Brown Oxen Knoll

Jumbled rocks push up through flowers' roots;
Rushing sands gather around the roots of trees.
Above Brown Oxen Knoll is the moon;
But the transverse flute has already passed before the village.

II
Chia Mountain Monastery

On a Ch'an branch cries a valley bird;
Arhat grasses[2] guard the pine gate.
By chance I enter a woodcutter's trail,
Peach blossoms and another mountain.

(Nos. 6,8 from a series of 9; PSTC; 15:5b–6b) *(Tr. Irving Lo)*

Sent to My Beloved Far Away

The south wind blows day and night across rivers and lakes;
A traveler's dream bound for home is unfamiliar with the road.
I send word: "Send no winter clothes to remind me of you;
Neither frost nor snow has come to southern skies."

(PSTC, 3:12a) *(Tr. Irving Lo)*

Evening View from P'eng-lai Pavilion[3]

Where the river springs: peach blossoms, tree after tree;

When spring winds blow, fledgling swallows in home after home;
Where my view is cut off: thoughts of return to the south;
Whom do I worry about: the one not here at the world's edge.

(PSTC, 3:6a) *(Tr. Irving Lo)*

Crossing Ta-yü Mountain Ridge[4]

Straight up against the clouds above the ridge, stands the awesome pass alone;
Along the post road, plum blossoms tell of months and years long gone.
A temple to the Prime Minister[5] keeps company with solitude;
The palace of the King of Yüeh is forever rank with weeds.
From days of yore, no wild geese from the north ever come here;
From this time forth, flying south, only the cuckoo birds.[6]
I turn away in sorrow from a second look at my native land;
Jumbled hills and a setting sun obscure my long way home.

(PSTC, 3:11a) *(Tr. Irving Lo)*

Mallard Lake Boating Songs: Two Selections[7]

I

Sandbar egrets, sleeping, nestle close to my boat;
Startled crows, beyond the willows, cry from the other shore.
Because I love autumn, I've come to admire the bright moon,
I no longer live east of the lake but have moved to the west.

II

The wind above Long River spreads the scent of lotus, leaf after leaf;
Accustomed to spending the night at Crooked Pond are the untamed mallards.
"Your boat just loves to head for Crooked Pond;
But, for me, how I pity that Long River is so long!"

(Nos. 2 and 31 from a series of 100; PSTC, 9:2b, 9:5b) *(Tr. Irving Lo)*

Tune: *Sheng-ch'a tzu* (A Song of Mountain Hawthorns)
Title: Walking to Mou-chou[8] at Dawn

Thick woods lead to a long embankment;
Heavy dew in tiny drops drips down.
Only the clucking of shore birds can be heard
As I slowly take my place in a column of travelers.

In the distance I catch sight of the tall city wall;
The road winds out of the tall city gate.
Before my cloak feels the warmth of the early sun,
Its light first flashes on the backs of shivering crows.

(PSTC, 26:11a) *(Tr. Chang Yin-nan)*

Tune: *Chieh-p'ei ling* (Untying A Jade Pendant: A Song)
Title: A Self-Portrait: Inscribed upon My
Own Collection of Lyrics

Ten years of honing my sword,
And roaming the capital[9] in fine company—
I've done with shedding a lifetime's tears.
Since my old age, to "fill in" the words
For old tunes, 5
I have half a mind to express vain regrets.
Too often have I been
Around the elegantly coiffured ladies!
I've never copied the style of Ch'in Kuan,[10]
Nor aped the fashion of Huang T'ing-chien.[11] 10
Adapting to new tunes,
I'm closer in spirit to Chang Yen.[12]
Wandering among rivers and lakes,
I've given myself to women and songs.
A marquis' title I knew 15
Would never be bestowed on a head as white as mine.

(PSTC, 25:10a–10b) *(Tr. Chang Yin-nan)*

Tune: *P'u-sa man* (Deva-like Barbarian)
Title: Climbing Ch'ing-shuo Tower at Yün-chung[13]

Before my goblet of wine, I watch half the sun go down
And then the moon climb over the balustrade.

A horn's note tugs at the hearts of horses going home;
How deep, if at all, is their thought of home?

In an upper-storey room in my home far away
Someone grieving leans at the window,
Gazing fixedly beyond the horizon, waiting for news,
And wild geese flying fill the autumn sky.

(PSTC, 24:8a) *(Tr. Irving Lo)*

Tune: *Shui-lung yin* (Water Dragon's Chant)
Title: Visiting the Temple of Chang Tzu-fang[14]

The iron bludgeon at Po-lang on that day of yore,
What a great pity it didn't hit the Emperor of Ch'in!
Escaping the manhunt at Hsien-yang,
Fleeing for dear life into Hsia-p'ei—
To live unharmed was no easy task. 5
Though Han had the mandate,
If the King of Han[15] had lived,
Would he have submitted to Liu Chi?
True, the three heroes[16] were worthy of rewards,
And Chang, a marquisate of ten thousand families. 10
None of these things
Was ever his life's ambition.

Where his temple stood in his native village of P'eng,
Only moss-strewn fragments
Of a stele scattered on the ground! 15
The post road takes a thousand turns,
And maple leaves cover the mountainside.
A bay in the river's course,
And all life returns to the sea.
The stone marker at Yi Bridge fades into legend;[17] 20
The ancient city gate is shut tight in vain.
Pity the white-haired one, his hair windblown,
Weeping as he passes by,
His gaze turned toward the sunset.

(PSTC, 26:1a–1b) *(Tr. Irving Lo)*

NOTES

1. Present-day Wenchow, in Chekiang, a scenic area immortalized in the poetry of Hsieh Ling-yün (385–433).

2. *Jen-ts'ao*: a kind of grass, according to the *Nirvana Sutra*, which grows on Snow Mountain, and, if eaten by cows, will produce milk with the thickest cream. See Morohashi, 4.10312:44 and 45 under *jen-ju ts'ao*. Also compare the line from the T'ang poet Liu Ch'ang-ch'ing (709–780?): *jen-ts'ao ch'an-chih jao ching-she* ("Arhat grass and Zen branches all around the monastery.")

3. P'eng-lai (the Magic Isles) Pavilion is located near P'eng-lai county, high upon Crimson Cliff Mountain, which overlooks the Yellow Sea in Shantung province, where a Taoist temple was erected in the Sung dynasty. This poem employs a rather uncommon meter—the hexasyllabic form.

4. Located on the border between Kiangsi and Kwangtung, proverbially the demarcation line between the Central Plain and the South, said to be unreachable by the migrating wild geese. Ta-yü ridge was named after the Han general Yü Sheng who conquered Nan Yüeh, and the mountain was best known for its many flowering plum trees.

5. Built in memory of the T'ang poet Chang Chiu-ling (673–740), the leading poet of the K'ai-yüan era, who served as prime minister.

6. The bird's cry sounds like *pu-ju-kuei-ch'ü*, which translates "Why not go home."

7. In the preface to this collection of one hundred Boating Songs on Yüan-yang Lake, Chu wrote as follows: "In the year *chia-yin* [1674], I had to make a living in Lu-ho [in present-day Shansi] and therefore was unable to go home. Recalling old customs of the place, I wrote this series of a hundred quatrains, describing the boat people's affairs; hence, I give them the title of 'Mallard Lake Boating Songs'—roughly in the style of 'Bamboo Branches' and *Lang t'ao sha* tunes; and I would hope that some of my gentlemen friends will compose responses to my compositions."

8. Mou-hsien in Chekiang province.

9. The text reads: *Wu-ling* or the "Five Imperial Mounds"; i.e., Ch'ang-ling, An-ling, Yang-ling, Mou-ling, and P'ing-ling, all around Ch'ang-an, indicating the kinds of places frequented by gallants and men of fashion in T'ang times.

10. The text reads: *Ch'in-ch'i*, or "Ch'in the Seventh," referring to Ch'in Kuan (1049–1100), a Northern Sung lyricist known especially for his love poetry.

11. The text reads: *Huang-chiu*, or "Huang the Ninth," referring to another Sung poet, Huang T'ing-chien (1045–1105), known as the founder of the Kiangsi School.

12. The text reads: *Yü-t'ien* (Jade Field), the style name of Chang Yen (1248–ca.1320), who wrote near the end of the Southern Sung lyric tradition, and who often advocated the twin ideals of *ch'ing* (clarity) and *k'ung* (emptiness) for lyric poetry.

13. Atop Yün-chung Mountain on the Shansi-Shensi border, with a view of the Dragon Gate Pass (Lung-men Kuan), the town of Yün-chung is located northwest of Ho-tse, Shansi province.

14. Chang Liang (d. 189 B.C.), courtesy name Tzu-fang, a native of the state of Han (read in the second tone, not to be confused with the name of the dynasty which is read in the fourth tone). Also see note 17 below.

15. The text reads: *Han Ch'eng*; i.e., King Ch'eng of the state of Han. Liu Chi (line 8) is another name of Liu Pang (256–195 B.C.), the founder of the Han dynasty established upon the ruin of Ch'in in 206 B.C.

16. The three most powerful supporters of Liu Pang: Chang Liang, Hsiao Ho (d. 193 B.C.), and Han Hsin (d. 196 B.C.), all of whom later became high officials.

17. Chang Liang was known as a strategist who helped Liu Pang to the throne. Chang's family had served the *state* of Han for five generations. When Ch'in destroyed Han, Chang swore revenge and hired an assassin to attack the king of Ch'in with a heavy bludgeon at Po-lang Sands but the assassin mistakenly struck the carriage of an attendant instead. Chang was forced to go into hiding. Once when he was strolling along an embankment at Hsia-p'ei, he met an old man who put him through a series of trials to test his patience. In one such encounter, the old man dropped his shoe from a bridge where they agreed to meet and ordered Chang to put it on him. Chang obliged and obtained as a reward from the Old Man of the Yellow Stone the gift of a book on the art of war, with the help of which he became "the teacher of kings," eventually enabling Liu Pang to defeat Ch'in and establish the Han (read in the fourth tone) *dynasty*. It should be pointed out that in the biography of Chang Liang (*Shih-chi, chüan* 55), no geographical name was used to identify the place where the Old Man of the Yellow Stone dropped his shoe, with the word *yi* occurring in the text where the word means "a bridge." However, a place called Yi-ch'iao, located south of P'i-hsien, Kiangsu province, is said to be associated with this legend and identified as the spot where the old man dropped his shoe.

CH'Ü TA-CHÜN

(10 OCTOBER 1630–1696)[1]

Ch'ü Ta-chün's (*Weng-shan;* HUA-FU, LO-FU SHAN-JEN) several personae reflect the turbulence and ambivalence of his time. A native of P'an-yü district (Canton), Kwangtung province, Ch'ü was a student of the famous Ming martyr-to-be Ch'en Pang-yen (1603–1647) when the North succumbed to rebel hordes in 1643–1644; and Ch'ü had just become a licentiate (at age sixteen) when Nanking and Central China were conquered by the Manchus in 1645. When the center of Ming resistance activity shifted to Kwangtung and Kwangsi, Ch'ü was very sanguine to serve the Yung-li Emperor in Kao-yao, but his father's death interrupted these plans; and in 1650 when Manchu forces reasserted control over Kwangtung, Ch'ü took the tonsure and studied for the priesthood under the Buddhist master Han-shih (1608–1685).

Ch'ü continued to be active in literary circles, however, and in 1656 he formed very close ties with Chu Yi-tsun (q.v.), who was to become the most prominent bibliophile and most imperially favored scholar and literary critic of his day. With Chu's assistance, Ch'ü undertook the first of his many travels, sojourning in Kiangsu-Chekiang and in Peking for several years, during which time his fame as a litterateur and as an ardent Ming loyalist grew and spread. Several years later Ch'ü repudiated Buddhism and wrote an apologia for his "return to Confucian life."

Besides associating with many loyalist scholars, would-be heroes, and swashbuckling figures, Ch'ü also had frequent intercourse with men who actively promoted a Ming restoration. His desire to maintain contact with such men, to visit Ming historical sites, and to avoid prosecution by Ch'ing authorities, accounts for the peripatetic nature

1. L. C. Goodrich and Chao-ying Fang, ECCP, 1:201–203.

of most of Ch'ü's life. In 1659, for instance, he was forced to seek refuge in the mountains of western Chekiang. And in 1665–1666 he sojourned in Shansi-Shensi and took trips along and outside the Great Wall with such well-known scholars as Li Yin-tu (1631–1692), who remembered painfully events of the conquest in that area. During this time, Ch'ü was married to Wang Hua-chiang, the daughter of a Ming general who had died fighting the Manchus. Ten years later, after his circuitous return to the Canton area, Ch'ü joined briefly in the revolt of Wu San-kuei (erstwhile collaborationist and Southwest satrap) against Ch'ing rule. When the Manchus recovered control in 1679, Ch'ü's lifelong friend Ch'en Kung-yin (1631–1700) was imprisoned, and Ch'ü fled to Nanking. Nevertheless, he was able to return to Kwangtung in 1681 and thereafter associated freely with Ch'ing officials, apparently considering the Ming cause to be lost.

With Ch'en Kung-yin and Liang P'ei-lan (1632–1708), Ch'ü was known as one of the "Three Masters of Ling-nan." His writing was highly praised not only by Chu Yi-tsun, but also by the most influential poet of his day, Wang Shih-chen (q.v.). These men and others were most impressed by Ch'ü's fresh and unlabored use of ordinary language to achieve vivid poetic effects, and by his untrammeled, inspired style, similar to that of Li Po. As an essayist, he wrote most engagingly about Kwangtung local history and customs in his *Kuang-tung hsin-yü*, 28 *chüan*. As a poet, Ch'ü identified most clearly with his supposed ancestor, Ch'ü Yüan; and many of his poems are anguished flights of imagination in the *Sao* form. Among contemporaries, Ch'ü most explicitly admired Fei Hsi-huang (b. 1664), grandson of Fei Mi (1625–1701) and exponent of the "ancient style" movement of the late seventeenth century.

The seditious (i.e., pro-Ming, antibarbarian) character of much of Ch'ü's writing first came to official notice during the Yung-cheng reign (1723–1735); but it was not until 1774–1775, in connection with the so-called Literary Inquisition of Ch'ien-lung, that Ch'ü's works were officially proscribed, along with those of Ch'en Kung-yin. This accounts for the scarcity of manuscript copies of Ch'ü's collected works, the *Weng-shan shih-wai*, in 20 *chüan*, and the *Weng-shan wen-wai*, in 14 *chüan*. These were printed in the early twentieth century, however, when Ch'ü became a symbol of anti-Manchu Chinese nationalism.

(Lynn Struve)

Snow

All at once nature's sundry sounding pipes are stilled;
Heaven and earth pass into a vast flurried fog.
Blossoms of chalcedony drop down for a myriad leagues,
And distant prospects are consumed in the chilly light.
Spring should come round at the budding of the plum,
But this night turns into the void under moonglow.
A stranger, I sit in a high building facing out—
As coldness and clarity penetrate into the ravine.

(WSSC, 4:18b) *(Tr. Paul W. Kroll)*

Written upon Coming Again to the Tu-hsü Taoist Temple

Stony contours coil round, descending from halcyon heights;
Peak after peak has its cascade, resembling hazy snowfalls.
The ancient trees, ragged and jagged, push forth a protruding pine;
Cold flowers screened from glare send their interspaced leaves soaring.
My white hair will not make the Furred Woman[1] laugh;
Yellow-capped,[2] I am happy to follow the Plumed Persons home.
The transcendents' altar for long years has been without its incense fire;
I would sweep it clear of lichens and liverwort, lest I dampen my cloak.

(WSSC, 5:17a–b) *(Tr. Paul W. Kroll)*

Written at the Year's End, While Visiting Chien-ling

Like a single wall stretching on athwart the sky,
A thousand slanting scarps press down upon the river.
Soaring towers are here placed among the lofty trees,
Their upended shadows covering the flat sandbanks.
Falling leaves tend to startle a stranger,
And when the oriole sings out, one's thoughts turn homeward.
Wildly reeling beyond the curtained awnings,
Wind-driven snow takes the form of flowers!

(WSSC, 3:12a) *(Tr. Paul W. Kroll)*

An Ancient Plum Tree at the K'ai-hsien Buddhist Monastery

Withered and worn, near a cloud-misted cloister,
I take it for a monk of the time of the Six Dynasties!
Its lanky hair hanging down a thousand feet—
Moss-grown majesty covered for several layers.
The dried limbs now wholly transmuted into stone,
Its quenched fire suddenly fused into ice.
There's only shame and chagrin as spring's blossoms burst forth,
When one is made to gaze on its ancient wisteria.

(WSSC, 3:14a) *(Tr. Paul W. Kroll)*

Inscribed on T'ai-po Shrine, at Colored Stone Jetty[3]

From of old men of genius have been prey to kraken dragons;[4]
T'ai-po, along with Ch'ü Yüan, is now become a sylph of the water.[5]
In rhapsodic verse he had matched him like paired sun and moon;
His essential numen still is active in this single mountain stream.
From the broken wall in mid-current his portrait in blue and vermilion shows forth;
By the soaring tower at the edge of the trees are hung the sacrificial trays and platters.
For a thousand years men have acclaimed the excellence of the "poet-sage,"[6]
But *your* flowing charm reaches far beyond that of Tu Shao-ling!

(WSSC, 5:26a) *(Tr. Paul W. Kroll)*

Fishing Jetty

Fu-ch'un Mountains[7] in myriad folds;
Fishing jetty black-green against the snow's glare.
I am like the T'ung River moon,
Long following the Han Guest Star.[8]
Cold gibbons chant against the precipice;
White egrets alight on sandy shores.
An old fisherman waves and waves his hand,
Homeward boat disappearing in the deep haze.

(WSSW, 6:18b) *(Tr. Lynn Struve)*

Tune: *Meng Chiang-nan* (Dreaming of the South)

I

Lament the falling leaves:
The falling leaves, let them fall in spring.
Year after year leaves fly away but more will be found;
Year after year people take their leave, and fewer remain.
On a red sash, the tear stains are new.

II

Lament the falling leaves:
The falling leaves sever the date of return.
Though the blossoms may cover the tree when he returns,
The new branch is not the same as last year's branch;
So why not drift with the river's gentle flow?

(Yeh, p. 30) *(Tr. Irving Lo)*

NOTES

1. The Furred Woman (*Mao nü*) was a trancendent of ancient times. According to the *Lieh-hsien chuan,* she was originally a palace lady of Ch'in Shih Huang-ti, but later fled to Mt. Hua-yin, there subsisting on the bark of pine and cypress trees (symbols of longevity). Fur grew over her body, hence her name.

2. "Yellow-capped": in formal Taoist religious attire. "Plumed (or feathered) persons" (*yü jen*) were early Taoist divine beings who were capable of flight beyond this temporal world. The poet hopes to invoke the Furred Woman and the Plumed Persons through sacred rites at the long-unused altar.

3. According to popular tradition, the inspired T'ang poet Li Po (whose style name was T'ai-po) was supposed to have drowned in a river when, in a drunken state, he leapt from his boat at night in a vain attempt to embrace the moon's reflection in the water. Later, a shrine in his honor was erected at Ts'ai-shih (Colored Stone) Jetty, located near Tan-tu, Anhwei.

4. Krakens are a particularly malevolent breed of dragons who delight in capturing and consuming humankind. See Edward H. Schafer, *The Divine Woman: Dragon Ladies and Rain Maidens in T'ang Literature* (Berkeley: University of California Press, 1973), pp. 20–21.

5. Ch'ü Yüan, the tragic composer of the famous poem "Li Sao" (Encountering Sorrow; for a translation see David Hawkes, *Ch'u Tz'u: The Songs of the South* [Boston: Beacon Press, 1962], pp. 21–34), was also reputed to have met his end by drowning.

6. "Poet-sage" is an epithet applied to Tu Fu, also commonly referred to, as in the next line, as Tu Shao-ling. He and Li Po were traditionally considered the two greatest T'ang poets, with Tu Fu usually being ranked slightly higher. Our poet reverses that judgment.

7. Rising to the west of T'ung-lu district in northwestern Chekiang.

8. A reference to Yen Kuang (fl. A.D. 42), a close companion of Liu Hsiu (6 B.C.—A.D. 57), founder of the Later Han dynasty. After Liu became emperor (posthumously styled Kwang-wu ti), Yen purposely remained incognito as a fisherman on the T'ung River section of the Ch'ien-t'ang River in Chekiang, until he was constrained to join the Han court. After his familiarity with the emperor raised a warning from the court astrologer that a "guest star" had violated the emperor's celestial position, Yen refused to accept a less intimate official post and returned to a simple life in the Fu-ch'un Mountains.

P'ENG SUN-YÜ

(1631–1700)[1]

P'eng Sun-yü (*Chün-sun;* HSIEN-MEN), official, poet, and calligrapher, was a native of Hai-yen, Chekiang province. He passed the *chin-shih* examination in 1659 before he was twenty years old, and began what was to be a successful life in government service. He was appointed to a number of different posts of significance, including that of director of the State Historiographer's Office. His greatest distinction was placing first among the 152 scholars who participated in the *po-hsüeh hung-tz'u* examination held on 11 April 1679. (A total of 188 candidates were summoned to take on the examination, but thirty-six declined. Of the remaining 152 who took the examination, 102 failed.)

Although P'eng Sun-yü's *shih* poetry is overshadowed by that of Wang Shih-chen (q.v.), with whose name his is often linked, it is admired nonetheless and sometimes compared to that of the so-called Ten Talents of the Ta-li era of T'ang times. Wang Shih-chen regarded P'eng as the best lyric poet of the age, and he is certainly one who contributed importantly to the revival of that form in the seventeenth century. He left five collections of verse, all of which are to be found in the *Sung-kuei t'ang ch'üan-chi* (Complete Works from the Hall of Pine and Cassia), which was printed by his son in 1743.

(Daniel Bryant and William H. Nienhauser, Jr.)

---

1. Lien-che Tu, ECCP, 2:616.

Musing beneath a Pine

A sense of autumn grows daily more sparse and open;
The look of nightfall scatters a gentle rain.
A lofty breeze comes from beyond the heavens,
To blow in the boughs of my solitary pine.
Fluttering, murmuring, verdure falls from above
To mingle wanly with the clouds' gray gloom.
Dark and distant, wintry waves are born;
Faintly I hear the dripping of fragrant dew.
A man in seclusion among the stony crags,
Embraces this, honoring what lies beyond the world.
Would that with a mind for the year turning cold[1]
I might preserve and prolong this fading evening.

(SKTCC, 4:2a) *(Tr. Daniel Bryant)*

North-of-the-River Rhymes

I

From withered trees we gather the silkworm floss;
A single day's weaving adds up to a yard or more.
We sell it off to people from south of the River;
How reckless and spendthrift those south-of-the-River girls!

II

Mounted on a mule, to ford the shallow stream,
Don't choose a place where there's no one about.
A tender bride without her husband along,
May spur on her mule, but she'll never get away!

(Nos. 2 and 3 from a series of 3; SKTCC, 6:19a–19b) *(Tr. Daniel Bryant)*

Mooring in the Evening at Plum Village

As the tenth month comes to a river district,
The look of things has turned autumnal and bare.
The harvest now in, a mood of joy is called for;
With no officials, public manners are improved.
There is smoke over the village from a temple as winter approaches;

Torchlight in the grove as people come home in the evening.
Lately, I have been making plans to move;
This neighborhood would be a perfect choice!

(No. 2 from a series of 2; SKTCC, 14:10a) *(Tr. Daniel Bryant)*

On the Road to Tang Lake[2]

In the evening I gaze out from atop a high tower;
The sun's radiance in the forest has been clear all day.
On Lonely Mountain the autumn garrison is cold,
Up the three branches of the Mao River the night tides are born.
Fishermen's fires appear out in the main current,
Gull-topped waves stay bright all night long.
It's time for our boat to stop for a moment:
The misty moon is just too filled with feeling.

(No. 2 from a series of 25; SKTCC, 14:8a–8b) *(Tr. William H. Nienhauser, Jr.)*

Tune: *Sheng-ch'a tzu*
Title: A Traveler's Night

Only a little drunk, I couldn't quite reach the Happy Land;[3]
But only felt the heavy spring chill.
With whom do I share my pillow and mat?
Night after night I share it with sorrow.

Dreams so good they just seem to be real;
An affair over, it only seems like a dream.
I get up and stand without a word
As the waning moon appears above the western lane.

(SKTCC, 38:4b; YLT, p. 4) *(Tr. William H. Nienhauser, Jr.)*

Tune: *Pu-suan tzu* (Song of Divination)
Title: Summer Solstice

Just past those distressing days of languor,
And the rainy season of the Yellow Plum,
I try to roll up the door curtain, lean for a while on the railing,
As a light rain blows red tartness about.[4]

Too hurriedly the span of a hundred years,

How sorely we regret our past mistakes.
Days to come will be as long as those gone by,[5]
And I've no idea what to do.

(SKTCC, 38:9a; YLT, p. 8) *(Tr. William H. Nienhauser, Jr.)*

NOTES

1. Confucius noted that it is only after winter comes that we discover pine and cypress keep their foliage.

2. Located north of Hangchow Bay about fifty miles southwest of Shanghai in modern Chekiang province. Although there are several "Lonely Mountains," none are identifiable in the immediate vicinity of Tang Lake. The Mao River (line 4) emerges from T'ai-hu (Great Lake) and breaks into three channels which eventually join the Wu-sung River.

3. The early T'ang poet Wang Chi (590?–644) wrote an essay entitled "An Account of Drunken Land" ("Tsui-hsiang chi") in praise of the pleasant oblivion brought on by wine.

4. The "red tartness" seems to be a poetic concoction produced by combining the aroma of ripe plums (tartness) with the blossoms (red) of the plum tree which are blow about in the wind and rain.

5. This is both a figurative statement about the poet's future and a literal description of those days before and after the summer solstice. Compare the term *k'un-jen t'ien,* used in line 1, which refers to the first hot days of summer and probably also the the inauspicious fifth day of the fifth lunar month.

YÜN SHOU-P'ING (1633–1690)[1]

Yün Shou-p'ing (Cheng-shu; NAN-T'IEN, TUNG-YÜAN TS'AO-YI-SHENG, PAI-YÜN WAI-SHIH, YÜAN-K'O, SHOU-P'ING-TZU), poet, calligrapher, and painter, was a native of Yang-hu, Kiangsu province. (His native place is sometimes given as Wu-chin, which together with Yang-hu constituted Ch'ang-chou prefecture in Ch'ing times.) And his original name was Yün Ko. Together with Wu Li (1632–1718) and "The Four Wangs"—Wang Chien (1598–1677), Wang Shih-min (1592–1680), Wang Hui (1632–1717), and Wang Yüan-ch'i (1642–1718)—Yün is known today as one of the Six Master Painters of the Ch'ing dynasty, and his reputation as a poet is often forgotten for this reason.

Yün Shou-p'ing was a typical product of the artistic milieu of his time. At fourteen, he and an elder brother followed their father, Yün Jih-ch'u (1601–1678), an ardent Ming loyalist and member of the Fu-she, into Fukien. The father had disguised himself as a Buddhist monk in order to join the forces loyal to Prince Chu Yi-hai. The following year, 1648, when Chien-ning fell to the Ch'ing army, under the command of General Ch'en Chin (d. 1652), the father was separated from his two sons and presumed both of them dead. Actually, only his older son had been killed, and Yün Shou-p'ing was adopted by the wife of General Ch'en. One day in the famous Ling-yin Monastery in Hangchow, the father chanced to see his son visiting the monastery with his adopted mother. But because General Ch'en was then the governor-general of Fukien and Chekiang, the father dared not claim his son; instead, he resorted, with the help of the abbot, to a ruse whereby the governor's wife was told that the boy would die an early death unless

1. Chao-ying Fang, ECCP, 2:960.

he was tonsured as a monk. Thus, left in the monastery, the son was later reclaimed by his father, whom he supported all his life with earnings from his paintings.

As a filial son of a Ming loyalist, Yün refused to enter the service of the Ch'ing government but spent his time learning to paint and to write poetry. He became the friend of many poets and artists, and developed a special relationship with the painter Wang Hui, under whom he studied the art of landscape painting. Soon he came to acknowledge his friend as a supreme master, one he could never excel. So he abandoned the painting of landscapes for flowers and developed the method known as *mo-ku fa*, or "the boneless method," in which genre he won high acclaim. As an exponent of the orthodox school, his friend Wang Hui was known to have painted some rather pedestrian works, and only those landscape paintings of his with the colophon written by Yün Shou-p'ing were treasured as "The Three Perfections" (*san-chüeh*). Meanwhile, the flower paintings of Yün Shou-p'ing were assiduously collected, even by the Ch'ing emperors, and they are still forged to this day.[2]

Yün Shou-p'ing's poems were first printed in 1716, under the title *Nan-t'ien shih-ch'ao,* as part of this collected works, *P'i-ling liu-yi chi.* An expanded collection of his poetic works, entitled the *Ou-hsiang kuan chi* (Collection from the Studio of Teacup Fragrance), was printed in 1844. Most of his poems belong to the variety known as *t'i-hua shih* (poems inscribed on paintings), and quite a number of them involve metrical variations written in a mixture of three-, five-, and seven-word lines in a single poem. His works are generally characterized by a certain amount of freedom and spontaneity, coupled with the frequent use of synesthetic imagery.

(Irving Lo)

Humming My Verse, in My Leisure, beneath Blossoming Cassia Trees

Above the branches, the frosty air pure;
At the foot of the tree, thin blue moss.
Autumn wind is filtered through dense leaves;
On empty steps tiny blossoms fall.

(OHKC, p. 6) *(Tr. Irving Lo)*

2. Ibid.

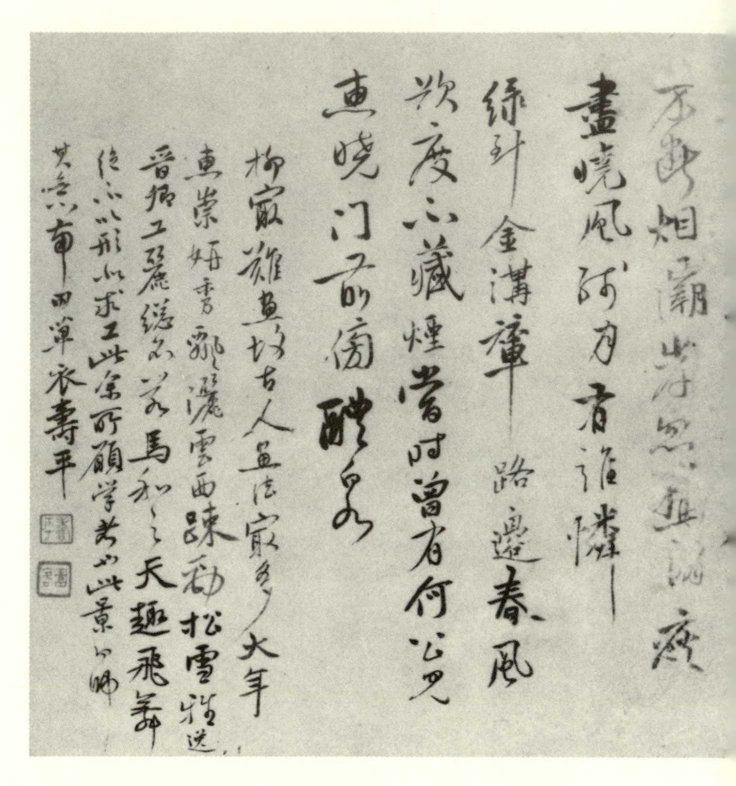

1. "Willows and Boatman in the Style of Ma Ho-chih," leaf from the album *Flowers, Landscapes, and Vegetables* by Yün Shou-p'ing (1674). The Art Museum, Princeton University. Gift of David L. Elliott.

An Inscription for a Painting: "A Forest in the Frost"

A wall of stone against a cloudless sky,
  a mountain stream by a gate[1] gleams bright;
From a stiff wind blowing through a dense grove
  is born the morning chill.
Try to listen to the zither's music
  in a hall in autumn in the mountain's shadow:
There's nothing but the sound
  of falling leaves and misty waters.

(OHKC, p. 9) *(Tr. Irving Lo)*

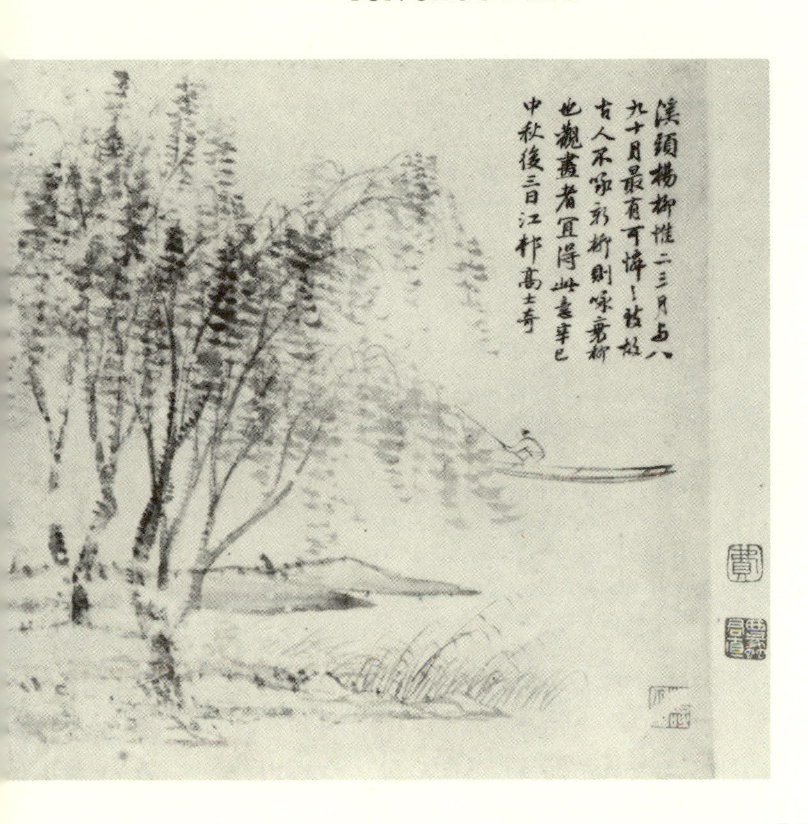

Early Summer, *Jen-tzu* Year [1672], in Playful Imitation of Ts'ao Yün-hsi[2]

A wall of stone against a cloudless sky,
  a mountain stream by a trail hangs in the void.
Through the desolate bamboo leaves the wind blows in the night.
My mind travels to ancient tress and withered vines;
My verses are everywhere in the wintry mist and wild grasses.

(OHKC, p. 41) *(Tr. Irving Lo)*

Tree and Boulder

A gray boulder stands there like a drunken sentry,
An old tree on the verge of bursting into song in the wind,
A pavilion beyond the clouds under an autumn sky—
And the pure sounds of nature permeate the frosty air.

(OHKC, p. 48) *(Tr. Irving Lo)*

Inscription for a Painting

In the wind and rain rising from my inkpot,
there's neither daylight nor dusk;
No one can even tell
where the village lies in the misty distance.
The white clouds serve my purpose
to seal up the mouth of the valley,
For I will never allow horses and carriages
to appear before a recluse's door.

(OKHC, p. 117) *(Tr. Irving Lo)*

A Picture of Village Happiness

The fragrance of rice stalks for a hundred *li* on the west wind,
In the cold ditches, water drops as new grain comes to market.
An old cow, having discharged its debt to the farmer,
Stretches out in the setting sun to chew its cud on the grassy slope.

(OKHC, p. 165) *(Tr. Irving Lo)*

NOTES

1. *Chien-hu* first occurs as a compound used by K'ung Chih-kuei (447–501) in his rhyme-prose composition "Pei-shan yi wen" ("Proclamation on North Mountain"), *Wen-hsüan,* 43:35b–40b. Evidently, the poet was fond of this image, for in another poem below, the first line is identical, and the first four words of the second line are also the same except for the substitution of one word, *lu* (road, trail) for *hu* (door, gate).

2. The courtesy name of Ts'ao Chih-po (1272–1355), a poet-painter of the Yüan dynasty, of Hua-t'ing, Kiangsu province. Ts'ao's courtesy name was Yu-yüan, also Chen-su; his style name was Yün-hsi lao-jen.

WANG SHIH-CHEN

(19 OCTOBER 1634–26 JUNE 1711)[1]

Wang Shih-chen (*Yi-shang;* JUAN-T'ING, YÜ-YANG SHAN-JEN), a native of Hsin-ch'eng, Shantung, was born before the collapse of the Ming dynasty. He was distinguished at an early age by his precocious literary talent and published his first collection of verse at the age of fourteen. After passing the *chin-shih* examination in 1758, Wang entered on a long and generally successful official career, which culminated in his appointment as president of the censorate and subsequently of the Board of Punishments. In 1704, however, he was cashiered for a minor administrative error, and after this he chose to live in retirement.

Widely regarded as one of the greatest of all Ch'ing poets, Wang first achieved celebrity with his set of four poems, "Autumn Willows," written shortly before he passed the *chin-shih* examination. During his official posting, in the city of Yangchow, he traveled to Nanking, where he associated with Ch'ien Ch'ien-yi (q.v.), a senior poet and scholar who had survived the Ming collapse. Ch'ien was so impressed with Wang's poetry and personality that he wrote a laudatory preface to a collection of his verse, in spite of the difference in their critical outlooks. While Ch'ien was an outspoken opponent of the "archaist" (*fu-ku*) movement that had dominated the poetic world for much of the Ming dynasty, it was this movement's ideals that had most significantly influenced Wang Shih-chen's approach to poetry, especially in his earlier years.

Although he wrote many poems in a relatively straightforward manner—favored in our selection here—Wang is best known for his densely allusive style of poetry, in which a single verse may involve

1. Chao-ying Fang, ECCP, 2:831–833.

references that require several paragraphs of annotation to explain. Unlike certain other poets of the Ch'ing, however, Wang does not parade his prodigious erudition for its own sake. Instead, his intellectual command of poetic technique and his sensitive emotional awareness succeed in bringing his learning fully into the service of his poetic intent, with the result that the reader capable of recognizing the allusions discovers in his poetry a richness of meaning attained by few poets. Many of Wang's poems were inspired by historic sites. In these works, he combines a sure grasp of the written (and sometimes legendary) historical sources about the place with a subtle and complex awareness of the interplay between history and individual human experience. In other poems his inspiration is highly visual. In a style reminiscent of Wang Wei (701–761), he succeeds in making a very characteristic statement or suggestion without his personality being explicitly evident.

In addition to being a prolific poet, Wang was also one of the Ch'ing dynasty's most influential literary critics. His earliest training had been in the archaist tradition, as we have seen, a tradition that stressed formal excellence and attention to certain model styles of the past, especially from the most flourishing period of the T'ang. Although these principles tended to degenerate into a dry and imitative formalism in the hands of the lesser archaists, the essential goal of the movement was the cultivation of the highest degree of perception and expression. In the course of his long career as a man of letters, Wang Shih-chen evolved his own distinctive poetics within this tradition, a poetics generally associated with the term *shen-yün,* which he used to suggest the combination of intuitive perception and evocation with personal tone that he found characteristic of great poetry. A striking feature of his criticism is his relatively tolerant attitude toward other critical ideals—unusual in the Ch'ing period, which saw a good deal of friction between competing literary schools. While he continued to favor T'ang poets over those of Sung, and self-cultivation through formal excellence over mere self-expression, Wang did significantly develop the archaist tradition by his stress on the dual nature of poetry as knowledge and expression.

Want wrote widely and extensively in many fields, and his purely belletristic writings alone are voluminous. Both because of the size of his oeuvre and the difficulty of his style, the usually encountered collection of his poetry is not his complete works, but rather his ten-*chüan* selection of the best of his poems, the *Ching-hua lu,* which has been supplied with several commentaries. The generally chronological arrangement of this collection makes it relatively convenient to follow Wang's development as a poet. There is a similarly convenient and accessible selection of some of his critical comments on poetry, the *Yü-yang shih-hua.*

(Daniel Bryant)

Viewing the Sea from the Li-shuo Pavilion[1]

"I climb a lofty hill and gaze toward the distant sea,"[2]
And thus behold ten thousand leagues of waves and surf.
The breadth of the heavens is vast and boundless, its cloudy forms
  are strange;
The shade of spring is lofty and bold, the fish and dragons exalted.
An angry tide is driven by the wind to rise a thousand yards high; 5
Tiger kraken and water oxen flee in tumbling confusion.
A horde of spirits form in secret a million misty mirages;
A single trace, still unsubmerged, of the Three Mountains' crest[3]

And then in a moment their force is spent and the tide too comes to
  rest;
The waves are calm, the heavens clear, as still as a length of
  brocade. 10
Caltrops and moss, an emerald green, grow lush in hollows by the
  shore;
Snails and clams in a shimmering glow are scattered on sandy
  banks.
Isles and islets rough and broken, a realm of open gossamer;
As thick and tangled as starry hosts above in an autumn sky.

I drum on a sword, I listen to your song, 15
If we have wine and do not drink, then what are we to do?
The river in front of the Sun God's shrine is chill and forlorn;
The clouds above the Transcendent's Terrace jagged and lofty.
Hsien-men and Kao-shih are nowhere to be seen;
The First Emperor and Han Wu-ti visited here for nothing![4] 20

Even now as I follow my gaze I feel a pang in my breast;
The regions of Huang, Ch'ui, Chien, and P'ing are all overgrown
  with weeds[5]
The happy moments in human life amount to so few hours;
Ruddy cheeks in a bright mirror can hardly retain their beauty.
I am going to escape from the world on Cricket Hill; 25
Or else drop in my hook from the Ephemera Isles.[6]

(YYSJCHL, 1A:11a) *(Tr. Daniel Bryant)*

Mooring in the Rain at Kao-yu[7]

Wintry rain at Ch'in-yu brings my boat to an evening mooring;
The lake to the south is swollen; the river reaches the sky.
The romantic elegance of Ch'in Huai-hai[8] is nowhere to be found;
Forlorn and lonely, the world of men, these five hundred years past.

(YYSJCHL, 5A:15a) *(Tr. Daniel Bryant)*

On the River

And what of the journey where the head of Wu meets the tail of Ch'u?
Misty rain, as autumn deepens, dims the white-flecked waves.
In evening, I sail the winter tide, on across the river;
Filling the groves are yellow leaves and ever more calls of geese.

(No. 2 from a series of 2; YYSJCHL, 5A:18a) *(Tr. Daniel Bryant)*

Crossing the River at Kuan-yin Gate[9] after Rain

Light sails set and swelling breach the clearing evening sky;
The cold river is dim and still; the ebbing tide is calm.
Shrouded in rain, the hills of Wu vanish here and there;
Along the stream, the fires of Ch'u are lit up one by one.
Famous men are still remembered by Feather Fan Crossing;[10]
In stepping songs is ever lamented the fall of Stone Wall Fort.[11]
Of Southern courts there are heartbreaking histories beyond all count;
Sad and mournful, the sound of jade flutes over the Ch'in-huai.[12]

(YYSJCHL, 5A:18a) *(Tr. Daniel Bryant)*

Climbing to the Very Top of Swallow Rock[13] Once Again, in an Early Morning Rain

For ten thousand leagues the waves of the Min[14] are encompassed in this view;
I brandish my staff on the highest peak of this precipitous rock.
In the hoary green of Wu and Ch'u, I distinguish the farthest coves;
River and hills in the level distance come into the first of autumn.
Those who crossed to the south in Yung-chia[15] times have vanished to a man;

In a westerly wind beside Chien-yeh[16] the river goes flowing on.
Sprinkling wine I lament once more the hazards of Heaven's Moat;
Dabbling ducks and flying swallows cover the banks and islets.

(YYSJCHL, 5A:18b) *(Tr. Daniel Bryant)*

Two Poems on the Ch'in-huai

I

Over the years hearts have been broken on Mo-ling[17] boats,
Dreams entwine the houses beside the Ch'in-huai stream.
For ten days now, in strands of rain and sheets of wind,
This misty scene at the height of spring has seemed like the end of autumn.

(No. 1 from a series of 14; YYSJCHL, 5A:29a) *(Tr. Daniel Bryant)*

II

When the tide ebbed in the Ch'in-huai, autumn after spring;
"Never Sorrow" was fond of outings for pleasure in Stone Wall Town.
For all the years that sorrow has filled it along with the tides of spring,
You wouldn't think the name of the lake would still be "Never Sorrow."[18]

(No. 5 from a series of 14; YYSJCHL, 5A:29b) *(Tr. Daniel Bryant)*

Crossing the River in Heavy Wind

I

Amidst chiseled jasper and drifting cinnabar, all in a haze,
Surf of silver, billows of snow, and thundering torrents.
A ten-foot sail of cloth is like a bird on its wing,
As I lie watching the hills of Chin-ling on both banks of the river.

II

A pair of red-collared swallows gently brush the waves:
From both banks, flowing foam and tiny ripples are born.
Heading south or north, two boats pass each other without a word,
As a sail in the wind cuts a swath on the river just for one instant.

(YYSJCHL, 5A:32b–33a) *(Tr. Irving Lo)*

Chen-chou Quatrains

I

At dawn I climb a river tower to its very highest storey,
The gentle and delicate look of departing sail is hard to bear.
The tide stretches a thousand yards below White Sands Pavilion;
Sending a homesick heart all the way back to Mo-ling.

II

Most of the houses along the river are those of fisherfolk;
Spaced well apart in a band of willow paths and caltrop ponds.
Perfect now that the sun is low and the wind has died away,
And they sell their perch beneath the scarlet trees along the river.

(Nos. 3 and 4 from a series of 5; YYSJCHL, 5B:11a-b) *(Tr. Daniel Bryant)*

NOTES

1. Located in Lai-chou, on the coast of Shantung.
2. An ancient *yüeh-fu* tune title, and also the first line of a ballad by Li Po.
3. A mountain fifty *li* north of Lai-chen, Shantung province, where numerous shrines were built by visiting emperors of ancient times.
4. The First Emperor of Ch'in and Emperor Wu-ti of the Han both made progresses to Shantung, where they carried out sacrifices to various spirits, including the "Sun God," and sought the arts of immortality of such legendary transcendents as Hsien-men and Kao-shih.
5. Huang, Ch'ui, Chien, and P'ing are all districts in which sacrifices were carried out.
6. Cricket Hill and the Ephemera Isles were likewise places associated with spiritual escape from the world.
7. Kao-yu, also called Ch'in-yu, is located north of Yangchow, Kiangsu province.

8. Kao-yu is the birthplace of the Sung lyric poet Ch'in Kuan, whose style-name was Huai-hai.

9. North of Chiang-ning, Kiangsu province, an important garrison town.

10. Referring to the victory of the Tsin dynasty general Ku Jung who used a fan made of feathers to direct his troops.

11. I.e., Nanking.

12. See Ch'ien Ch'ien-yi, note 3.

13. A promontory that juts into the Yangtze at Nanking, a city known as "Heavenly Moat" since the Yung-chia period (307–313).

14. The Yangtze is sometimes called the Min, since its headwaters are located in the Min Mountains of Szechwan province.

15. See note 13 above. This was a time of foreign invasion and political turmoil.

16. I.e., Nanking, a city sometimes said to be protected by Heaven's Moat because of its location on the south shore of the Yangtze.

17. Ancient name for Nanking.

18. A famous lake in Nanking named after Mo-ch'ou (Never Worry), a beautiful girl from an ancient ballad said to have been married into a rich family and later expressing regret or worry for not marrying a young man next door.

TS'AO CHEN-CHI

(1634–?)

Ts'ao Chen-chi (*Sheng-chieh* and *Sheng-liu*; SHIH-AN), a native of An-ch'iu, Shantung province, received the *chin-shih* degree in 1664 and subsequently entered government service, where he ultimately attained the position of Senior Secretary of the Board of Ceremonies. Little else is known about his personal life, save that he was a friend of the poet-official Shih Jun-chang (q.v.). He was a serious student of the art of poetry, and several of his collections of *shih* and *tz'u* poetry have survived to the present. Although his accomplishments in both genres were recognized in his own time, today his reputation as a poet rests almost exclusively on his lyrics. These are to be found in his *K'o-hsüeh chi* (Jade and Snow Collection) in two *chüan* (SPPY edition).

His best works in the lyric mode possess a purity of spirit, a vigorous manner, and a considerable breadth of topical interest. As such, he is somewhat reminiscent of the Southern Sung masters and certain of his contemporaries, such as Ch'en Wei-sung (q.v.).

(William Schultz)

Tune: *Mu-lan hua* (Magnolia Blossoms)
Title: Late Spring

One slash through the dense growth—the road south of the city,
Where frail catkins follow the wind as reckless as rain.
Dangling my whip, I often ride till the hour of sunset;
Seeing off guests, each time I come upon a heartbreaking place.

So quiet is the lane to my gate when spring's about to end;
Beneath the trees the captivating crimson blooms, sad
beyond words.
On painted rafters the swallows just sound asleep—
Once the ground's been perfumed with fragrant petals, they fly off.

(KHT, 1:5b) *(Tr. William H. Nienhauser, Jr.)*

Tune: *Huan hsi sha* (Sands of Silk-washing Stream)
Title: Inscribed on a Painting

Crab shops and fishing village—in an out of the way place;
Tall trees dense and dark, and flooded fields level with land.
Rivers and lakes all peaceful, and a white-gull sky.

Watercress leaves and rush blossoms blur the distant crossing;
Slanting winds and a fine mist hug the boat heading home;
But where will the old fisherman, pillowed on his straw cloak, find
a place to sleep?

(KHT, 1:1b) *(Tr. William H. Nienhauser, Jr.)*

Tune: *Shui-lung yin*
Title: White Lotus Flowers

A level lake, mist on the waters, obscure and indistinct—
Vaguely recalls the girl living at Heng Dike:[1]
At the sudden rise of dark clouds,
Donning a feather cloak for the first time,[2]
Tenderly peering at her makeup. 5
As dew descends in the third watch of the night,
And the moon stretches bright over a thousand miles,
Stealthily she disappears without trace.
Imagine, reed flowers and duckweed leaves,
A misty void all of one color. 10

I feel lost by a jade well,
On a road to the mountain's peak.

Could it be that unmarried daughter of Chu-lo Mountain,[3]
With her pendants dangling
Returning to Jo-yeh Brook? 15
My dream of the playful transcendent is distant—
As if an immortal crane rode off into the empyrean,
Or a woman's tiny steps walked the waves.[4]
When egrets fly back to their perch,
I can still faintly recognize the scene; 20
A gentle breeze comes up,
A light magnolia boat sails away;
Half-hidden by thin damask,
What family can she be from?

(KHT, 2:4b–5a) *(Tr. William H. Nienhauser, Jr.)*

Tune: *Pai-tzu ling* (Hundred-word Song)
Title: On a Historical Topic [Ching K'o][5]

T'ien Kuang has grown old.[6]
Once he laughed at Prince Tan's retainers, among them not one real man.[7]
"Horns on a horse and a white-headed crow?"[8]—the remorse of a thousand years!
The dagger in the casket gleaming like snow,[9]
The setting sun desolate, 5
The song in the key of *yü* so stirring,
A brave man's hair bristled against his cap.
Ah, that young boy!
Why should an angry Wu-yang turn ashen-faced?[10]

Let me ask: the lute-player Chien-li,[11] 10
Where was he then?
Why couldn't he have shared the same carriage for the journey?
The sword-carrying First Emperor, startled at his sleeves being pulled,
Succeeded barely in leaping across a six-foot screen!
When the sun might have been strung on that long rainbow,[12] 15
That the king should run around a copper pillar—
Thus the calamity of Ch'in was perpetuated by Heaven's will.

The mournful wind over the River Yi[13]
Still sobbing and choking to this day? 20

(KHT, 1:25a) *(Tr. William H. Nienhauser, Jr.)*

NOTES

1. "Living at Heng Dike" (Heng-t'ang) recalls Li Ho's (791–817) "Song of the Great Dike" ("Ta-t'i ch'ü"). The word *t'ang* can also be translated as "pond." See Wu Wei-yeh, note 10.

2. Line three may refer either to a woman's hair (see Li Ho's "Song of the Great Dike") or to the leaves of the lotus. The fourth line ostensibly describes the flower, but may also suggest the shamanistic references of the second stanza, since shamans often wore clothing made of feathers.

3. The unmarried miss of Chu-lo Mountain is Hsi Shih, the famous beauty of the state of Yüeh. The "bright pendants" again recall Li Ho's poem cited in note 1 above. The area near Jo-yeh Brook had long been associated with beautiful women who picked lotus flowers.

4. Line 17 is taken verbatim from Ts'ao Chih's (192–232) "Prose-poem on the Lo River Goddess" ("Lo-shen fu"). In Ts'ao Chih's work, too, the poet watches a beautiful water goddess who then leaves him. *Wen-hsüan*, 19:8a–11a.

5. Ching K'o, also known as Master Ching, attempted to assassinate Yung Cheng, the King of Ch'in and the future Ch'in Shih Huang-ti, at the request of his master, Prince Tan of Yen, in 227 B.C. Knowing that Ching K'o would never return alive from this mission, the prince bade farewell to him with funeral obsequies at Yi River.

6. In the *Yen-tan tzu* version of the Ching K'o story apparently used by the poet, T'ien Kuang was first asked by Prince Tan of Yen to find some means of stopping Ch'in's conquests. T'ien, however, said he was too old for the job and recommended Ching K'o. After the prince inadvertently offended T'ien by asking him to keep their discussion secret, he arranged for Ching K'o to see the monarch and then slit his own throat to prove his honor.

7. T'ien Kuang dismissed all of the prince's men, because none of them could disguise their emotions well enough.

8. The prince had formerly been held a captive by Ch'in. The king of Ch'in said he'd never release him until crows had white heads and horses grew horns. When miraculously such events in fact transpired, the king kept his promise and released the prince. This was the beginning of the latter's desire for revenge.

9. The prince obtained an especially sharp dagger and had it coated with a particularly deadly poison, with which to stab the king of Ch'in.

10. Wu-yang, or Ch'in Wu-yang, was the young man appointed by the prince to accompany Ching K'o. T'ien Kuang had rejected him in his analysis of the prince's retainers, because his face turned white when he was angered. Later, when approaching the king of Ch'in with Ching K'o, Wu-yang does go pale and possibly (so Ts'ao Chen-chi implies) forewarns the king, despite Ching K'o's assurance that Wu-yang was merely overcome by the splendor of the king's court.

11. Kao Chien-li was considered to be a man of Ching K'o's stature. After Ching's failure he was finally brought to Ch'in to be executed. But the king was moved by his character and only had him blinded. Kao then filled his lute with lead and attempted to bludgeon the king to death with it. Ts'ao seems to imply that if Kao had gone with Ching K'o instead of Wu-yang, the mission may have been successful.

12. When Ching K'o approached the king, he grasped him by the sleeve. The king, unable to draw his sword, jumped a screen and evaded Ching K'o by running around a pillar. The rainbow metaphor was used to describe Nieh Cheng's successful assassination of Han Wei, a story also recorded in the chapter on assassins in the *Shih-chi*.

13. Alluding to a line of a song Ching K'o sang as he departed Yen.

WU WEN

(1644–28 JUNE 1704)[1]

Wu Wen (*T'ien-chang;* LIEN-YANG, YÜ-CHIEN-TZU) was a native of P'u-chou, Shansi province, even though his ancestral home had been in Liao-yang, Feng-t'ien. His father, Wu Yün-sheng (?–1656), was a *chin-shih* and a director of studies in P'u-chou until his death. It was his father who aroused his interest in books. He read widely and his hunger for knowledge was never satiated. He became a pupil of the celebrated Shantung poet, Wang Shih-chen (q.v.), who praised his genius and, after his death, edited a collection of his poems with commentary.

Unlike his father, Wu Wen did not want to confine himself to one place, and he traveled extensively. In 1679, he was summoned to take the special *po-hsüeh hung-tz'u* examination, but he failed to pass. Afterwards, he had no interest in becoming an official. He settled down in the Yung-lo district, Shensi province, where the famous *Yü-hsi* or Jade Stream was located, where the T'ang poet Li Shang-yin had lived. He may have thought of himself as a latter-day Li Shang-yin; however, neither his style of poetry nor his point of view was like those of Li. Instead, he was a true exponent of the Wang Wei manner. Wang Wei's "natural" style and "Buddhist" viewpoint inspired him so deeply that he wrote poetry in the same vein, and there is a strong visual quality to his verse. Even though he was not known as a painter, he was, nevertheless, an excellent calligrapher. His contemporaries admired him greatly, and Chao Chih-hsin (q.v.), a nephew of Wang Shih-chen and a fine poet himself, considered Wu Wen's poetry to be superior even to that of Wang Shih-chen.

---

1. Chao-ying Fang, ECCP, 2:883.

In recent years, because of the impress of Buddhist philosophy and allusions on his poetry, Wu Wen has been criticized for his "incomprehensibility." Thus, his poetry has been little anthologized and he is seldom read.

Three editions of his collected works appeared during his lifetime. The most complete one, entitled *Lien-yang chi* or *Lien-yang shih-ch'ao,* in 20 *chüan,* was printed in 1774.

(Chang Yin-nan)

The Jasper Cloud Monastery

At this old monastery, long corridors are lost in the shade;
Above green mossy steps, birds sing noisily.
In the empty woods echo a pair of wooden clogs,
Frightening the cranes into the pines.
At the opening of a cave, flowers grow dense and dark; 5
Before a precipice, clouds stretch on and on.
Beneath dangerous rocks, a mountain stream—
What ancient hand could have sculpted this!
To quench these burning desires in my heart,
I will pour a libation from this brass ewer. 10

(LYC, 1:1b) *(Tr. Chang Yin-nan)*

Poems on Yi Garden: Written for Mr. Juan-t'ing[1]

I
Crane Lodge

A pure cry sounds the alarum at midnight,
Bamboo dew dampens the flower-strewn well.
This mountain man opens his gate at dawn:
How majestic is this bird, how cold its feathers!
Suddenly, upward it flies to the tiered empyrean,
Leaving in the courtyard tangled shadows of pine trees.

II
The Bridge of Drifted Fragrance

A forest wind blows from a flower-hidden spring,
A dense mist passes over the brook.

A traveler sits by the stone bridge,
His heart suffused with a strange fragrance
From somewhere betwixt wind and water,
But none can tell where it comes from!

(Nos. 2 and 3 from a series of 12, LYC, 2:1b–2a) *(Tr. Chang Yin-nan)*

In the Mountains

From endless rains comes autumn's dusk;
A flying cataract emerges halfway down the peak.
Returning wild geese cross the mountain ridge in haste;
Falling leaves keep me company in my idle hours.
Small isles o'ergrown with bamboo, high and low;
A monk's quarters provide me with lodging, coming and
going.
What's there to anchor my feelings of loneliness?
All day long the sound of rushing waters.

(No. 1 from a series of 2, LYC, 3:10b) *(Tr. Irving Lo)*

Starting Out on a Journey in a Windstorm

I

All day I fret over wind and sand,
While the water of the river ripples green.
Willows are the most heartless of trees,
Blowing across ferry passengers at dawn.

II

A heart that yearns for fame never dies,
This drifting life, what is it all about?
It's like ladling out water for sale in the wind—
Blown thither and yon into ripplets and waves.

(Nos. 1 and 2 from a series of 3, LYC, 16:4a) *(Tr. Irving Lo)*

NOTE

1. The courtesy name of the poet Wang Shih-chen (q.v.).

HUNG SHENG

(1645–1704)[1]

Hung Sheng (*Fang-ssu;* PAI-CH'I), a native of Ch'ien-t'ang, Chekiang province, is best known today, as he was during his lifetime, for his long dramatic work *Ch'ang-sheng tien* (The Palace of Everlasting Life). Written in the *ch'uan-ch'i* form and so containing a wealth of musical verse, the play recounts the famous ill-fated love affair of the T'ang emperor Hsüan-tsung and his paramour, the Precious Consort Yang. In many ways the culmination of a number of earlier treatments of the tale in poetry and music drama, Hung's play (completed around 1684) attained an immediate and widespread popularity.

Hung had first come to Peking as a student in the Imperial Academy and soon gained the friendship of some of the most important poets of the day. He accepted the patronage of Wang Shih-chen (q.v.), becoming a disciple of that influential critic, although his own ideas about poetry were to develop rather differently from the theories advocated by Wang. He was also on familiar terms with Chu Yi-tsun, Chao Chih-hsin, and Shih Jun-chang (qq.v.). But in 1689 he was dismissed from the academy, after a special performance of *Ch'ang-sheng tien* was staged in his honor during a period of imperial mourning. He returned home and lived thereafter the life of a retired scholar, taking special pleasure in the solace of nature.

Hung's dramatic works (he wrote several other plays besides his most famous one) attest to his skill as a writer of lyric verse. Contemporaries felt that his *shih* poetry (all the poems translated here are of this kind) had a lofty and untrammeled air that set it apart from the conventional verse being written at the time. But, as is true of many Ch'ing poets, there is also a heavy undercurrent of melancholy in his

---

1. Tai Jen, ECCP, 1:375.

works. Hung's death by drowning (it is reported that he fell overboard while drunk) recalls the apocryphal story of the similar end of the great T'ang poet Li Po.

(Paul W. Kroll)

The Thatched Cottage

In the thatched cottage I have settled, lingering long;
With springtime's coming, the air turns gradually milder.
Scattered flowers open frozen buds,
As the hidden stream grows a new scar.
Wild birds content to bid the valley farewell,
And mountain clouds lazily enter at the gate.
Except for two or three shepherds and woodsmen,
No one comes anymore to the deserted village.

(PCHC, p. 163) *(Tr. Paul W. Kroll)*

An Old Sophora Tree

An old sophora tree, utterly withered and bare,
Its sparse shadows carelessly shudder now and sway.
Leaves stripped, it lets down the scantiest shade;
In the emptiness of the courtyard it receives most of the moonlight.
Autumn crickets raise their clamor in vain;
The sunset birds come past here no longer.
——If a planted tree has now come to this,
What recourse can there be for our floating life?

(PCHC, p. 44) *(Tr. Paul W. Kroll)*

Passing the Night at the Monastery of Eternal Peace

In darkness I sought lodging at a mountain monastery,
Where the vapors of the rocks brushed my garments cold.
In the faintness of a breeze, crickets intone autumn;
With the chill of dew, cranes take warning.
As the bell's tolling fades, monks chat together;
As the night grows long, my heart is more at peace.

And just when one would glimpse the glow of the luminous moon,
The deep-set pines spill out their scattered shadows.

(PCHC, p. 20) *(Tr. Paul W. Kroll)*

On Rising at Dawn and Seeing the Mountains

Lying abed I heard the din of magpies in the grove,
And by the feel of the air knew the day would be fair.
I flung on a cloak, went out the courtyard door,
As the fading moon lay athwart the southwest.
The wind-gap mist already breaking up gradually, 5
The halcyon blue of the void seemed to welcome me.
Stickle-backed as fish scales, auroral clouds of pink rose up;
Sharp-honed as sword blade, a cooling breeze was born.
In the solitary stillness, my ears and eyes were opened;
By the broad expanse, heart and spirit were purified. 10
What is one now to make of men of court and marketplace,
Who, roiling and riling, contend for fame and profit?
As the cocks of morn are heard they bridle their steeds,
And take uneven bumpy paths to call on dukes and lords.
——But for just a moment's glimpse of happiness such as *this,* 15
I decide to live out my years farming beneath the cliffs.

(PCHC, p. 21) *(Tr. Paul W. Kroll)*

The Fire of the Fireflies

Leaning on the oars, I watch the fire of the fireflies,
Flitting and fluttering, airily at their will.
Along with the breeze, carrying a remote light;
Crossing the water, sporting their faint gleam.
Over shoreside trees the clouds are wholly black;
In the river sky the moon is not yet born.
—How long can your glimmering last,
In the darkling night, to assert your wish?

(PCHC, p. 185) *(Tr. Paul W. Kroll)*

CHA SHEN-HSING

(5 JUNE 1650–14 OCTOBER 1727)[1]

Cha Shen-hsing (*Hui-yu;* CH'U-PAI, T'A SHAN, etc.) was a native of Hai-ning, Chekiang province. Although he belonged to a wealthy and influential clan, his immediate family was apparently less financially secure. Thus, when his father died in 1678, Cha was compelled to seek gainful employment rather than continuing his preparations for the civil service examinations. He served on the staff of a provincial governor for three years, after which he returned to his native place to study with the famous scholar Huang Tsung-hsi (q.v.). Still later he accepted a position as the tutor of K'uei-hsü (1674?–1717), the second son of the grand secretary Mingju (1635–1708) and younger brother of the poet Singde (q.v.). Thereafter, he was employed by Hsü Ch'ien-hsüeh (1631–1694), an influential scholar and powerful civil official, to assist in the compilation of the *Ta-Ch'ing yi-t'ung chih* (Comprehensive Geography of the Empire). This work took him to the city of Soochow and was in part responsible for his being employed in other similar scholarly endeavors in later years, including the compilation of the phrase dictionary *P'ei-wen yün-fu,* a companion anthology of poetry, and several local gazeteers.

In 1693, Cha was successful in the examination for the *chü-jen* degree, and ten years later he was awarded the *chin-shih* degree. This led to appointments in the Imperial Study and the Hanlin Academy. He retired from public service in 1713, returned to his native place, and lived there quietly until he and other male members of the family were imprisoned. Ostensibly his brother had impugned the imperial name, but it is more likely that his family's long association with K'uei-hsü, who had become embroiled in the Yung-cheng succession affair,

1. Chao-ying Fang, ECCP, 1:21–22.

was the real cause. In any event, one brother died in prison, another was sent into exile, and Cha himself died shortly after he was released and allowed to return home.[2]

Very much a man of his times, Cha led a rich and full official life, one not of course without its dangers and uncertainties, and he played an active and important role in the various group research and compilation projects which were sponsored by government and wealthy individuals alike. The results of his own scholarly interests include a commentary on the *Yi-ching* and an annotation of the works of the great Sung dynasty poet Su Shih.

Except for one play and a large collection of casual essays, poetry was Cha's main creative outlet. Like the two poets Su Shih and Lu Yu (1125–1210) of Sung times, whose accomplishments in poetry influenced him and with whom he has sometimes been compared, poetry was for Cha Shen-hsing a congenial and flexible medium for the recording of his daily thoughts, emotions, experiences, and personal observations. That he consciously regarded poetry in this way is revealed in the scope of his poetic corpus, approximately six thousand poems, the vast thematic range of his verse, and the personal attention he gave to the organization of his collected poems. Shortly before his death, he put his poems in chronological order, divided the whole into a number of sections and subsections, assigned each of these divisions separate titles, and wrote brief introductions to each, including useful biographical detail. Apparently, he wanted later generations to understand his poetry correctly and to judge him well.

Cha Shen-hsing has been credited with the creation of a distinct poetic style for his times, one of clarity and precision of manner. His nephew once said he learned from his uncle that "the profundity of poetry lies in its meaning, not in its language; the power of poetry lies in its vital force, not in its upright manner; the sensibility of poetry lies in its emptiness (intangibles), not in its craft; the simplicity of poetry lies in what it casts off, not in what is easy. . . ." These principles of profundity, power, sensibility, and simplicity were the qualities Cha sought to capture in his poetry. Chao Yi (q.v.) was later to say that the dominant feature of his poetry was the clarity of language and manner which precluded heavy ornamentation and bodied forth his ingenuity and excellence as a poet.

(William Schultz)

---

2. Ibid., p. 22.

A Song of Crows Gleaning the Grain

In front of the ox, he raises his head to hoe;
Behind the crows, he bends down to gather the grain.
Why should the ox till for the crows?
Crows, because of the ox, get their fill.
The farmer tends the ox, but always he suffers hunger;
Better to be a crow—to flock together, fill one's belly, and fly off, east or west!

(CYTSC, 35:6b) *(Tr. William Schultz)*

After a Rain

From one shower comes hopes for a bumper harvest;
Perhaps it is human nature thus to take comfort in the present.
But, compared to the old farmer, mine is an even shorter view:
Merely to covet this one night, one night of cool slumber.

(CYTSC, 13:3a) *(Tr. William Schultz)*

Autumn Impressions

I

A cricket chirrups near my bed;
A cicada is silent, voiceless.
These two insects exchange their roles,
And, in the process, summer becomes winter.
Great, indeed, is the Maker's principle,
Made manifest through such small things.
The aging of man proceeds from this:
Hurrying and scurrying; so much scheming!
The Celestial Order is obscured by the myriad activities,
With tranquility I will view my life!

II

Chrysanthemum pistils daily yellow;
Maple leaves daily redden.
The natures of things determine young and old,
Their transformations following the frost and wind.

The frost and wind certainly show no partiality,
Yet blooming, fading, how different these two things!
Most everyone admiring its coloration:
A blind ancient follows a sightless youth.

(Nos. 1 and 3 from a series of 6, CYTSC, 23:7b–8a) *(Tr. William Schultz)*

A Song of Bitter Drought

Uncaring, the God of Fire causes the farmers grief:
Thirty days and more of cloudless skies, not a drop of rain.
Well sweeps lift the water into trenches for distant fields;
The sun rages, winds blow, the fields turn hard as salt.
Several families together continue to plant their rice, 5
But the young shoots, green and tender, quickly turn a yellow hue.
Up in every field, by every dike, they irrigate,
But soon, faint clouds of dust rise from river beds.
"Sir, haven't you heard;
With a tidal roar, the cistern broke, a monstrous calamity, 10
And the water drained away, the fields went dry, doubling our troubles.
For the present, do not worry about the distant Milky Way;
Instead, worry that the 'mulberry fields may become a sea.' "[1]

(CYTSHC, 1:5b) *(Tr. William Schultz)*

The Customs Station at Weed Lake[2]

Yesterday, we left Dragon River,[3]
Arrived this morning at Weed Lake.
A following wind filling the sails,
We passed the customs station in a flash.
An officer, duty bound to impose the levy, 5
Blocked our way, loudly shouted at us.
The boatmen, not daring to proceed,
Shifted the rudder, hauled on the windlass.
I smiled and spoke to the customs officer:
"Of rare goods, I have none at all! 10
For linking verses, only one short brush,
And, as ballast, one hundred scrolls.
In the prow, there are two chests;
In the stern, a jug of wine.
Beyond this, what more can there be 15

But my companion, this long-bearded servant?"
Distrusting me, the officer advanced
To overturn chests, topple wicker baskets,
Ignoring not a single article.
Regarding one another, he fixed me with his gaze: 20
"To buy us drinks, the law requires payment."
He turned away as if I was a tax dodger.
If one has goods, officials press for the levy;
If one has none, officers are perversely harsh.
Goods or no, neither can be avoided, 25
So how can one console one's self on a long journey?

(CYTSC, 1:3b) *(Tr. William Schultz)*

NOTES

1. I.e., a common proverb indicating the vicissitudes of life.
2. Wu-hu (Weed Lake), the name of a lake and a district in Anhwei province, the latter being a prosperous communications and trading center.
3. Located in Kiangsi province.

HSÜAN-YEH (Emperor K'ang-hsi)

(4 MAY 1654–20 DECEMBER 1722)[1]

Hsüan-yeh (T'I-YÜAN CHU-JEN), the second emperor of the Ch'ing dynasty, occupied the throne from 1661 to 1722 under the reign title K'ang-hsi. He was only seven years old when his father, Fu-lin (1638–1661), died, and for the next six years political authority rested in the hands of four regents, all senior members of the Manchu conquest elite. In 1667, while still only thirteen years of age, K'ang-hsi wrested power from the regents with the aid of Songgotu (d. 1703?) and other members of the court. Thereafter, he ruled both in name and in fact. Several years later he displayed a similar boldness in challenging and destroying the independent power of the Three Feudatories in south and southwest China after a protracted war. The consolidation of Ch'ing rule was carried another step forward with the subjugation of Taiwan and the stabilization of the northwest frontier. K'ang-hsi personally took the field in one campaign into the northwest territories. With the successful conclusion of these enterprises, Manchu supremacy was essentially established and an era of relative peace and stability was ushered in.

K'ang-hsi was a diligent, conscientious, and frugal administrator; however, his sense of duty did not prevent his enjoying the pleasures of the hunt, or his making numerous grand tours of the south. By nature an intelligent and inquisitive man, he took a lively interest in the arts and sciences. His sponsorship of scholarly projects had important results: the involvement of dissident literati elements in imperial undertakings and the publication of such major works as the *K'ang-hsi tzu-tien* (the K'ang-hsi Dictionary), the *Ming-shih* (The Ming History), the *Ch'üan T'ang shih* (Complete T'ang Poems), and the phrase

1. Chao-ying, Fang, ECCP, 1:327–331.

dictionary *P'ei-wen yün-fu*. He also took a personal interest in calligraphy and the literary arts. Extant specimens of his calligraphy do not possess any high distinction. Nor do his prose essays and poems attain the high standards of the masters of the time, although they are of considerable historical interest and are at times much superior to the poems of most rulers of the past. Nonetheless, as Professor Spence has noted in his masterful *Emperor of China: Self-Portrait of K'ang-hsi*, he wrote with a "simplicity and directness" that has its own charm. Three collections of his verse in twenty-eight *chüan* were compiled by the scholar-poets Kao Shih-ch'i (1645–1703) and Sung Lao (1634–1713). All three collections are included in his collected works, *K'ang-hsi ti yü-chih wen-chi*.

(William Schultz)

Hunting in the Ordos, the Pheasants and Hares Were Many[1]

Open country, flat sand,
Sky beyond the river.
Over a thousand pheasants and hares daily
Trapped in the hunters' ring.
Checking the borders,
I'm going to stretch my limbs;
And keep on shooting the carved bow.
Now with my left hand, now my right.

(KHTYCWC, 47:11b [p. 1308]) *(Tr. Jonathan D. Spence)*

Lines in Praise of a Self-Chiming Clock

The skill originated in the West,
But, by learning, we can achieve the artifice:
Wheels move and time turns round,
Hands show the minutes as they change.
Red-capped watchmen, there's no need to announce dawn's coming.
My golden clock has warned me of the time.
By first light I am hard at work,
And keep on asking, "Why are the memorials late?"

(KHTYCWC, 32:3a–3b [p. 2428]) *(Tr. Jonathan D. Spence)*

Gift for an Old Official

How many now are left
Of my old court lecturers?
I can only grieve as the decays of age
Reach ruler and minister.
Once I had great ambitions—
But they've grown so weak;
Being disillusioned by everything,
I don't bother to seek the truth.
Shrinking back I look for simple answers,
But everything seems blurred.
Complexities bring me to a halt,
Exhausting my energies.
For years past, now,
I've neglected my poetry
And, shamed as I grope for apt phrases,
Find dust on my writing brush.

(KHTYCWC, 35:11a–11b [p. 2468]) *(Tr. Jonathan D. Spence)*

NOTE

1. Jonathan D. Spence, *Emperor of China: Self-Portrait of K'ang-hsi* (New York: Knopf, 1974). Jonathan Spence gratefully acknowledges the help of Andrew Hsieh (Cheng-kuang) in making the original draft of this and other translations of the poems by Emperor K'ang-hsi.

SINGDE (Na-lan Jung-jo)

(19 JANUARY 1655–1 JULY 1685)[1]

Singde (*Ch'eng-te, Jung-jo;* LENG-CHIA SHAN-JEN), sometimes also given as Nara Singde, was a noble descendant of the highly placed and influential Yehe Nara clan which traced its origins to Turmed Mongol stock, and the firstborn son of Mingju and his wife, a daughter of the Prince Ying, Ajige (1605–1651), the twelfth son of Nurhaci. Mingju enjoyed a spectacular official career, culminating in his being named a grand secretary in 1677. For the next decade, he was one of the most powerful men in the empire. He was a patron of the arts, an avid collector of *objets d'art,* and a host to many of the leading poets of his day. Ch'en Wei-sung, Chu Yi-tsun (qq.v.), Yen Sheng-sun (1623–1702), and Ch'in Sung-ling (1637–1714), among others, were guests at one time or another at his palatial residence in the Forbidden City.

Singde was tutored in traditional letters by Chinese scholars, and in 1676 he placed well in the palace examinations. As a member of the Plain Yellow Banner, he was appointed to the Imperial Bodyguard as an officer of the third rank, thus becoming a member of the imperial retinue. In that capacity, he regularly accompanied the K'ang-hsi emperor on state visits to sacrificial shrines, the ancestral tombs, hunting parks and watering spas, and the Manchu ancestral homeland. In 1684, he visited the Yangtze valley region as a member of the imperial entourage. Two years earlier he had been sent north to the Amur River valley as a member of an imperial mission investigating Russian encroachments in that area. At the age of thirty, he took ill and died quite suddenly, thus ending a short but brilliant political and literary career.

Singde is widely regarded as one of the finest *tz'u* poets of the seventeenth century, and by some as the leading master of that form

---

Chao-ying Fang, ECCP, 2:662–663.

during the last three centuries of imperial rule. The modern critic Wang Kuo-wei (q.v.) is unstinting in his praise: "Singde observed things with an unclouded vision and described emotions in the patterns of natural speech. . . , and thus is his poetry genuine and incisive. Since Northern Sung times there has been only one such person as this." A close student of the *tz'u* form, Singde admired especially the early masters, such as Li Yü (937–978), and it is therefore not surprising that he favored the shorter, or *hsiao-ling*, modes, although he did not fail to utilize the longer modes as well. As Wang Kuo-wei and others have noted, his *tz'u* poems are graced by a simple, direct language, one that is relatively unencumbered by heavy ornament and allusion. Like the earlier poet Li Yü, to whom he has often been compared, his verse is imbued with emotion, often of a personal nature, and almost always melancholy in tone. The sorrows of separation and longing, of the partings of friends, of the death of his wife, or the transience of human life, of a nostalgic yearning for an untrammeled, simple life—all conventional enough as traditional themes—are movingly and beautifully expressed in his verse. Where one might have expected this poet of alien ancestry to have sounded a different note, that is not the case, for even his *pien-sai* ("border") verse assumes a conventional Chinese view of the northern desert regions as an unfriendly, inhospitable land. And it is these Chinese rather than alien visions that characterize the content of his poems, and which account in part for his popularity.

Although seldom remarked on, Singde was also an accomplished master of other poetic and literary forms. The same qualities of language, diction, and emotional texture are to be found in his *shih* poetry, which accounts for approximately 40 percent of his total corpus. His collected works also include casual essays, as well as prefaces written for scholarly works, such as the well-known collectanea *T'ung-chih-t'ang ching-chieh*, of which he was one of the sponsors and possibly also a compiler.

Although he was the scion of a great and powerful family and courtier to the illustrious K'ang-hsi emperor (q.v.), the poetry of Singde reflects less the wealth and grandeur of his place and time than it does the inner turmoil and frustrated longings of a remarkably gifted and sensitive man caught up in one kind of existence but longing for another.

(William Schultz)

A Song of the Wild Crane: Presented to a Friend

Once a crane lived in the wilds,
Year around never seeing the sight of man;
At dawn it drank blue ravine waters,
At dusk nested along azure streams.
Then, without warning, struck by a crossbow bolt, 5
It raised its head to gaze at the blue clouds.
I, too, was once a mad scholar,
Viewing wealth and honor as mere swansdown;
I sought to break free, but the way was closed,
So I turned about and sought an official's tassels. 10
In action, I appear to follow the wall;
Secretly, I hide myself, flee from fame.
Fortunately, you are a true friend,
Unchanged by the ways of the world.
How I wish to go away with you, 15
Our hearts in tune, pure as the flowing water!

(YSSC, 11b–12a) *(Tr. William Schultz)*

In Imitation of Ancient-Style Poetry

The north wind blowing through the barren willows,
The temporal sequence suddenly resumes its pace.
Pavilion grasses have withered all away;
Looking back, I see the white sun quicken its race.
Originally, I was an easygoing man, 5
Doing nothing to restrain or bind myself.
Free and easy, I put my trust in Heaven,
For a cage was not what I desired.
Alas, the cries of the Hua-t'ing cranes![1]
Honor, fame—nothing but disgrace. 10
A traveler in this world, I sigh over middle age,
Take up the goblet and write a Golden Valley preface.[2]
The wine jar empty, everyone departs;
In these comings and goings, why be hasty?
Clutching my clothes about me, I take up a song; 15
The bright moon is as lustrous as a jewel.

(No. 40 from a series of 40; YSSC, 7b) *(Tr. William Schultz)*

Tune: *P'u-sa man*

I

Yellow clouds, purple ramparts—three thousand *li;*
West of crenelated walls, tower ravens take wing.
  In the setting sun, the myriad hills are cold;
  Whinnying, the hunting horse returns.

  Unbearable is the sound of reed pipes;
  Night approaches, the empty tower grows dark.
  Autumn dreams fail to carry me home;
  From a fading lamp fall fragments of flowers.

(NLT, 1:10a) *(Tr. William Schultz)*

II

The north wind blows, scattering the third-watch snow;
Lady Ch'ien's soul still loves the peach blossom moon.
  The dream is good, so don't awaken her;
  Leave it to wander in pleasant realms.

  Why now do I hear the sound of the painted horn?
  Beside the pillow, a few frozen rogue tears.
  The border horse nickers but once;
  Scattered stars brush the great banner.

(NLT, 1:9a–b) *(Tr. William Schultz)*

Tune: *Huan hsi sha*[3]

I

Who knows how cold, how lonely the west wind?
Yellow leaves dryly rustle, choking the latticed window.
Lost in thoughts of bygone days, I stand in the fading light.
Intoxication with wine did not disturb our deep springtime slumbers;
The quoting game dispersed the fragrance spreading from the brewing tea—
Those were pleasures we regarded then as everyday affairs!

(NLT, 1:4b) *(Tr. William Schultz)*

II

Heading for cloud-mantled mountains, I press on to the other side;
The north wind rages, cutting off the sound of the horse's neighing.
Late autumn and a distant border conspire to stir my emotions!

One slash of evening mist above a deserted rampart;
Half a staff high, the sun slants across an old frontier town.
Dark regrets of past and present, when will they be put to rest?

(NLT, 1:6b) *(Tr. William Schultz)*

Tune: *Ch'ing-yü an* (Green Jade Cup)
Stopping Overnight at Black Dragon River

The east wind churns the ground, whirling upwards elm tree
 pods;
 Now that it has passed by—
 This vast pall of snow—
I envision fragrant chambers, incense permeating everything.
 Who could know that tonight, 5
 By Black Dragon River,
 Alone, I would face the new moon?

The passionate are not inclined to frequent partings;
Partings are devised only for the passionate.
Butterflies dream of the myriad flowers; flowers dream of
 butterflies. 10
 When will we meet again
 By the west window to trim the candle
 And talk at length of today's affairs?

(NLT, 3:10b–11a) *(Tr. William Schultz)*

Tune: *Yi Chiang-nan* (Remembering the South)

I

Beautiful is the South,
 But who will transmit, who cherish its ancient lore?
By Swallow Promontory, the moon over red smartweed
 flowers;

Along Blue Coat Lane, mists clinging to blue willows—
A scene to recall those years.

(NLT, 5:1b) *(Tr. William Schultz)*

II

Title: Impressions of a Night's Stay at Shuang-lin Temple

Heart turned to ashes,
Hair long, not yet a true monk am I.
Eroded by wind and rain: life and death partings;
How like an old companion: a solitary lamp.
Feelings persisting, I cannot awaken.

(NLT, 2:9b–10a) *(Tr. William Schultz)*

III

After the leaves have quivered and fallen,
How can one bear to hear the clear wind blowing?
In the dark, whirling leaves at Golden Well rustle, rustle,
And suddenly the sounds of still air and bell are heard;
This luckless one salutes a famous beauty.[4]

(NLT, 2:9b–10a) *(Tr. William Schultz)*

IV

Even the crows have gone.
I linger, alas, for whom?
Impatient snow flutters like catkins into the fragrant room,
A breeze stirs the plum branch in the vase,
That "heart" has already turned to ashes![5]

(NLT, 1:1a) *(Tr. Julie Landau)*

Tune: *Che-ku t'ien* (Cuckoo Sky)

Cold and silent, the dew deep in the night;
The crows unsteady, perching in the winter wind
How I hate the insistent battle drum from the tower
That keeps a soldier from returning—even in dreams!

Drab autumn,
A crescent moon,

No one gets up to gaze into its depths
At dawn a horse will take me on, another place—the same longing
If you knew how many mountains are rising between us!

(NLT, 3:1b) (Tr. Julie Landau)

Tune: *Chin-lou ch'ü* (Song of Gold-Thread Jacket)
Title: Sent to Liang-fen[6]

I fear the fragrance of a full cup
When, deep in the night, vague drunken shadows
Dance with the fading lamplight
The new moon hangs in the curved passage as it did, still
Unstable; the sound of the bamboo, discordant 5
I ask: is sorrow deep as a spring night is long?
Is Swallow Tower[7] empty? Are the strings of the lute cold?
Let the pear blossoms fall—no one can stop them
In dreams I hear their whispered call

I wish the east wind would wash away this feeling 10
Instead it brings a trace of perfume when I'm already sick with wine—
And doubles it!
Pity Chiang Yen,[8] worn by separation—
How can I bear light cold light warmth
When I remember talking endlessly over tea
As drop by drop the candles shed red tears in the west window?
My anguish then, compounded day by day,
I confide to angular pillows
In lonely inns

(NLT, 4:8a–8b) (Tr. Julie Landau)

NOTES

1. The poet Lu Chi is reported to have lamented, on being led off to the execution ground, that he would never again hear the crying of the cranes at Hua-t'ing, the family estate located in the lower Yangtze valley.

2. Shih Ch'ung (249–300), a man of great wealth, made his famous estate called Golden Valley a meeting place for poets and a place for extravagantly lavish parties. These events were recorded in a famous preface by Shih Ch'ung himself.

3. Given here in its more popular form. *Na-lan tz'u,* followed by some other editions, gives the title as *Huan sha ch'i* (Silk-washing Sand Stream), referring to the same tune title.

4. Some editions of Singde's poetry make this poem the second stanza of the poem immediately above, but distinctive differences between the two in topic and tone recommend their being taken as separate verses, as the modern critic Li Hsü has done.

5. Alluding to a poem by the poet Yang Wan-li (1124–1206), where the word "heart" has a double meaning: the incense and the poet's heart, both of which have turned to ashes.

6. The courtesy name of the lyric poet Ku Chen-kuan (1637–1714?), one of Singde's closest friends.

7. Swallow Tower (Yen-tzu lou), located in Hsü-chou, Kiangsu province, is said to have been built by a T'ang official, Chang Chien-feng (735–800), for his favorite concubine Kuan P'an-p'an. Upon Chang's death, Kuan refused to remarry and lived in this tower for fifteen years until she eventually died of self-induced hunger.

8. Chiang Yen (444–505), a poet of the Six Dynasties period, was admired for his literary talents as a young man and as the author of two rhyme-prose compositions entitled respectively, "On Parting" and "On Remorse."

CHAO CHIH-HSIN

(1 DECEMBER 1662–27 DECEMBER 1744)[1]

Chao Chih-hsin (*Shen-fu;* CH'IU-KU, YI-SHAN), poet and calligrapher, was born in Yi-tu, Shantung province. He was a precocious young scholar, receiving his *hsiu-ts'ai* degree at the age of fourteen and his *chin-shih* at eighteen. He became a compiler in the Hanlin Academy, an editor of the *Ming-shih,* and a friend of such luminaries as Chu Yi-tsun (q.v.) and Mao Ch'i-ling (1623–1716). He later became a secretary in the Supervisorate of Imperial Instruction, at which time his potentially illustrious career came to a halt due to his friendship with another great poet, Hung Sheng (q.v.).

In the autumn of 1689, Chao attended a special showing of Hung Sheng's drama *Ch'ang-sheng tien* (The Palace of Everlasting Life)—unfortunately at a time when a member of the imperial family had just died and there was a proscription on such frivolous entertainments. An imperial censor whom Chao had earlier rebuffed in an arrogant manner took this opportunity to attack him and the other scholars who attended the performance. Hung Sheng and Chao were both dismissed from office at the time. At the age of twenty-eight, Chao's official career came to an end, and he never held another office.

In his retirement, he traveled widely in southern China, made many friends, and devoted himself to the writing of poetry and literary criticism. Although he was related by marriage to Wang Shih-chen (q.v.), he was a strong opponent of Wang's "spirit and tone," or *shen-yün* theory of poetry, attacking Wang in his *T'an-lung-lu* (1709). His *Yi-shan shih-chi,* in twenty *chüan,* was published in its first complete

---

1. Chao-ying Fang, ECCP, 1:71.

edition in 1752, eight years after his death. Most of his poetry is occasional, and a very great deal of it is concerned with the depiction of nature during Chao's travels. For the most part he writes very calm, almost wistful descriptions of nature in the style of the T'ang and Sung masters. He also left a manual on prosody, under the title of *Sheng-tiao p'u*, which contains his views on the rules for the "even" (*p'ing*) and "deflected" (*tse*) tones in T'ang poetry.

(Michael S. Duke)

A Mid-Autumn Night

The autumn air banishes lingering rains,
An empty courtyard invites distant breezes—–
One glass of mulberry dew wine,
At midnight in the moon-bright season.
A longtime traveler feels the night is endless,
In early coldness grows drunk too slowly.
Still resigns his bleak and lonely feelings
To a rendezvous with far-off chrysanthemums.

(YSSC, 1:3a–3b) *(Tr. Michael S. Duke)*

Fireflies

Once more coming through the door with rain,
Suddenly flying over the wall on the wind,
Although they need the grass to achieve their nature,
They do not depend on the moon for light.
Understanding the secluded one's feelings,
I briefly invite them to dwell in my gauze bag.
Just look: falling through vast empty space,
How do they differ from the great stars' rays?

(YSSC, 2:5a) *(Tr. Michael S. Duke)*

Presented to a Mountain Dweller

Looking like a wild deer sleeping against the cliffs,
Casually wandering out of the valleys with the flowing streams.

Since the travelers asked him about the frosty trees,
They all came to know his face, but do not know his name.

(YSSC, 3:2b) *(Tr. Michael S. Duke)*

On Poetry

An expert painter who scrutinizes a marvelous scene is equal to a god:
High and low, he dabs on the crimson and the blue to draw trees in October.
He ought to know that autumn's colors are the brightest
Only where the quiet hills are caught in the sun's dying glow.

(No. 1 in a series of 2; YSSC, 7:6a) *(Tr. Irving Lo)*

Miscellaneous Poems on Mountain Travel: Two Selections

I

Where the summit road twists and turns, I'm soon to lose my way,
With close of day comes frost and sleet, and sudden chills arising;
Winds slip through the forest trees and then the leaves,
Coldness wanes in the valley depths, which now turn into mud;
As my horse's hoofs rear back in fright, I suspect the earth has vanished,
Where valley clouds gather in drifts, I sense the sky has lowered;
A weary traveler should not be surprised when frightened time and again:
It's late in the year, the mountains are empty, and birds are jabbering crazily.

II

Evening clouds suddenly scatter and peaks come into view,
A distant temple's tolling bells bring sadness to my thoughts;
Heaps of snow are fitting indeed to reflect the new moonlight,
Gentle mists cannot conceal cascades streaming in darkness.
I make my way like a nesting bird, hurrying home to the forest,

I envy the comfort of a mountain monk, dozing off, clutching at his quilt;
A welcome wind from the valley stirs, sending me on my way,
A single lamp flickers and dims within the lookout tower.

(Nos. 1 and 2 from a series of 4; YSSC, 1:5b–6a) *(Tr. James M. Hargett)*

PART II

Poets of the Eighteenth Century

SHEN TE-CH'IEN

(24 DECEMBER 1673–6 OCTOBER 1769)[1]

Shen Te-ch'ien (*Ch'üeh-shih;* KUEI-YÜ), a native of Ch'ang-chou, Kiangsu province, came from a poor but scholarly background. He led an undistinguished official life until his late sixties, when he passed the *chin-shih* examination and won the admiration of the Ch'ien-lung emperor. Thereafter, until his death in 1769 at the age of ninety-seven, he served in a variety of educational posts and received numerous honors. In 1742, as a compiler in the Hanlin Academy, he edited the *Chiu T'ang Shih* and the *Hsin T'ang Shih* [Old and New Histories of the T'ang dynasty], and he participated in the compilation of the *Mirror of History* for the Ming dynasty. Among the posts that he held were those of expositor in the Hanlin Academy (1743), imperial diarist, examiner of the Hupeh provincial examination (1745), vice-chancellor of the Grand Secretariat (1746), tutor to the imperial princes and second vice-president of the Board of Ceremonies (1747), and assistant director of the metropolitan examination (1748). He was honored with two imperial prefaces to his own works, and was made honorary president of the Board of Ceremonies (1747) and Grand Tutor of the Heir Apparent (1765). All these titles, however, were stripped from him posthumously in 1778 when he was denounced for having written a biographical sketch of Hsü Shu-k'uei (*chü-jen,* 1738), in whose works were discovered seditious sentiments.

Shen Te-ch'ien is now chiefly remembered as an anthologist and editor. Many of his works are still used as standard texts. These include the following titles: *Ku-shih yüan* (1725), *T'ang-shih pieh-ts'ai chi* (compiled in collaboration with Ch'en Shu-tzu in 1717 and revised in 1763), *Ming-shih pieh-ts'ai chi* (compiled with the aid of Chou Chun in 1739),

1. Man-kuei Li, ECCP, 2:645–646.

Kou-ch'ao shih pieh-ts'ai chi (1759), *T'ang Sung pa-chia wen-hsüan* (1752), and *Tu-shih ou-p'ing* (1753). In these works, Shen Te-ch'ien attempted to promote a revival of classicism in both form and content. Poetry, he claimed, should serve a didactic and moral function. On this point he opposed his contemporary, Yüan Mei (q.v.), who emphasized individual genius (*hsing-ling shuo*) by stressing, in its stead, the primacy of the poetic form (*ke-tiao shuo*).

His poetic works, collected into the *Kuei-yü shih-wen ch'ao* (1752 and 1766) and *Shih-yin* (1753), are marked by a similar concern with recapturing the restraint and economy of the poetry of the Han, Wei, and T'ang dynasties.

(Marie Chan)

Ditty: Below the Frontier

I

Urgent the cry of the wild geese, wailing amidst the void;
The wind whirls the Dragon Sand[1] as it forms a dune.
The kumiss all drunk, the sky turns to dusk.
Under a bright moon alone I climb Li Ling's tower.[2]

II

The troops are moved to a distant region, they leave Yi and Kan;[3]
White geese, gold-edged pipes, they cannot bear to hear.
Twenty thousand men turn back to gaze afar.
The source of the Yellow River lies south of the great wasteland.

(Wu, p. 51) *(Tr. Marie Chan)*

Mooring My Boat at Pan-ch'a[4]

Clear are the Huai currents, I see the river's depth;
Loving this, I rest my oars at evening.
The marketplace abustle, I know winter is over;
A monk at leisure, I sigh at a traveler's toils.
On the embankment, a lad makes offerings to the kitchen god;[5]
In the village shop a dame presides over her stove.

Tomorrow I'll ride upon my mule and leave,
As the spring wind brushes my hemp robe.

(Wu, p. 105) *(Tr. Marie Chan)*

Song on a Pine on Yellow Mountain[6]

All at once I see a coiled dragon forming the base of an ancient bronze plate:
Its scales severely scuffed, blotched with dark green moss,
Its body half submerged in barely three feet of dirt.
Might it not be the same lone-standing pine atop Mount Omei[7]
Whose visage has suffered no change for ten thousand years? 5
I ask the pine: from where do your roots receive their nurture?
It comes from Yellow Mountain's thirty-six majestic peaks.

So high is Yellow Mountain that its summit abuts on heaven:
This ancient pine, writhing and curling, hangs from a cliffside.
Boulders angrily split asunder, robbing it of earth's moisture: 10
Its trunk and branches are steeped in the light of sun and moon.

What craftsmen skilled with pike and chisel—
Their bodies dangling by long lines—
Lowered themselves down, peering into the abyss,
Suspended ten thousand fathoms in the void, 15
And from the mountain's miraculous anatomy,
Cut and fashioned this curious boulder for a linked-root tree?

As if transported from a distant magic kingdom's deepest recesses,
It provides, a thousand leagues away, lodging for a recluse,
Where, in its empty hall, mist and fair clouds constantly arise, 20
And the watery vapor of Heavenly Peak[8] seems to gather in a corner of its courtyard!

As I face the pine on Yellow Mountain,
My spirit roams Yellow Mountain's peaks,
Where the immortals Fu-ch'iu and Jung-ch'eng[9]
Keep me company on the edge of the clouds. 25

Of, if only I could ride a white deer, lose myself in these dark green cliffs,
Then, after feasting on pine nuts, lightly rise
To join hands with the crowded pinnacles in greeting the immortal company!

(HHSC, p. 166) *(Tr. Irving Lo)*

2. The pine of Huang-shan: a photograph. Courtesy of the Embassy of the People's Republic of China.

NOTES

1. I.e., the border desert areas of northwestern China.

2. Li Ling (d. 74 B.C.), a Han general who led a major expedition against the Hsiung-nu tribe, was compelled to surrender when his forces were greatly outnumbered, and died in captivity twenty-five years after his defeat.

3. I.e., Ili in Sinkiang province and Kansu province.

4. The sluice gate at Huai-an, modern-day Huai-yin, Kiangsu province, on the historic Huai river.

5. Offerings to the kitchen god were traditionally made on the twenty-fourth day of the twelfth lunar month.

6. Yellow Mountain (Huang-shan), located in the southern part of Anhwei province, is probably the most celebrated of all scenic areas in China. It derives its name, since the T'ang dynasty, from the legend that the mythical Yellow Emperor once prepared the elixir of immortality on this mountain, in the company of the Taoist immortals Fu-ch'iu and Jung-ch'eng (line 24). The mountain is famous for its thirty-six peaks, the tallest of which are over 1,800 meters; and the area is also known for the so-called Four (Scenic) Wonders; namely, seas of clouds, warm springs, marvelous pines, and fanciful rocks.

7. A famous mountain in Szechwan province.

8. T'ien-tu (Heavenly Capital) Peak, the highest of the thirty-six peaks of Huang-shan.

9. Both legendary immortals, companions of the Yellow Emperor. Duke Jung-ch'eng was said to have been the latter's teacher and to have also written a book on sexual practices which enabled a follower of his to live past the age of 160 years.

LI E

(16 JUNE 1692–17 OCTOBER 1752)[1]

Li E (*T'ai-hung*; FAN-HSIEH), a native of Ch'ien-t'ang (Hangchow), Chekiang province, was by contemporary acclaim the foremost landscape poet of his time, and particularly renowned for his pentasyllabic verse and his memorable sketches of the Chiang-Che region. A prolific author, he left behind eight titles, totaling close to 200 *chüan*, including twenty *chüan* of *shih* and *tz'u* poems. He was also known for his compilation *Sung-shih chi-shih* (anecdotes about Sung *shih* and their authors, in 100 *chüan*), and for the annotated edition of a collection of *tz'u* compiled by the Sung poet Chou Mi (1232–1298), known as the *Chüeh-miao hao-tz'u* (*An Anthology of the Best Loved Lyrics*), which Li edited with Cha Wei-jen (1694–1749).

Li E's success as a poet and scholar is a classic case of personal industry and literary patronage. Coming from a very poor family and orphaned early in life, he was self-educated and had to pursue a vigorous course of study under the most difficult circumstances. His erudition and poetic talents eventually won him a large circle of literary friends and admirers, including the celebrated Ma brothers of Yangchow—two opulent salt merchants who were also bibliophiles and the most generous literary patrons. Li E enjoyed the hospitality of the Ma brothers on many occasions; and it was at the latters' private library—the famous Ts'ung-shu lou at Yangchow—that he did the research and writing for his voluminous *Sung-shih chi-shih* (Records of Sung Poetry). There are indications that Li E sorely needed this patronage for, despite his growing fame as a man of letters and his receiving a *chü-jen* degree in 1720, he never seriously sought or ever received an official appointment.

1. Lien-che Tu, ECCP, 1:454–455.

Equally outstanding in the *shih* and in the *tz'u*, Li E had a creative career that spanned over four decades. His early poems are dominated by pure landscape themes and are at times suffused with an ambience quite reminiscent of Wang Wei and Meng Hao-jan (689–740), exhibiting the qualities known as *p'ing-tan* (tranquil and bland) and *k'ung-ling* (ethereal), which became the mode cherished by the Sung poets. His later poems, however, often blend landscape descriptions with contemplative references to personal experience. As a writer of lyrics, he was first inspired by Southern Sung poets like Chiang K'uei and Chang Yen (hence his reputation for belonging to the Che-hsi school), but eventually he returned to the *hsiao-ling* of earlier times, thereby showing a versatility and an awareness of tradition that characterizes a true master of that subgenre.

(Shirleen S. Wong)

Spending the Night at Monk Ch'ao Yün's Retreat on Mount Lung-men[1]

A cliffside pavilion juts out from the treetops,
Where I lodge for one night amid ten thousand hills.
A tiger's roar won't startle a monk in his meditation;
The sound of bells must come from somewhere in the sky.
Facing away from the window, I see the shadows of roosting birds;
Blowing out the candle, I listen to the wind in the pines.
Tomorrow I'll look for fresh water by the stone steps.
Surely it will fill up a dozen bamboo pipes.[2]

(FHSFC, 1:3b–4a) *(Tr. Shirleen S. Wong)*

South Lake[3] in the Rain

Blossoming peach trees among the bamboos: patches of moistened red.
Fish traps adrift in a rising tide, half hidden by the reeds.
Spring scenery at South Lake has nobody in charge,
Except for the slanting wind and fine rain everywhere.

(FHSFHC, 7:4a–b) *(Tr. Shirleen S. Wong)*

Passing through South Lake Again

Approaching South Lake, I already begin to dread the journey,
A place of old memories, each corner reopens a wound.
Watching plum blossoms in a small courtyard could be but a dream fulfilled;
Listening to rain in a quiet room is like entering another life.
Autumn waters are bluer for reflecting my graying temples;
The evening bells sound crisper for breaking a sorrowful heart.
Lord of Emptiness, take pity on this homeless soul—
Out of this incense smoke make me the City of Refuge.[4]

(FHSFHC, 2:9a–b) *(Tr. Shirleen S. Wong)*

A Cowherd's Song: In Imitation of Chang Chi[5]

My master gave me a black cow to tend,
And I said to my master, "You have nothing to worry about.
Mornings I look for water and grass; at dusk I return home.
I won't allow even a gadfly to trouble its eyes."

I led the cow to the southern slope to have a good time;
I hardly knew if the cow was hungry or had a full stomach.
Should the cow get sick, I'll run from my master's whip,
For the master can always consult a vet.

(FHSFC,1:2a) *(Tr. Irving Lo)*

Leaving Southern Screen Hill[6] at Dawn and Crossing the [West] Lake: A View from the Boat

Dawn spreads out its colors before my boat has barely left the shore;
Glancing back, I watch the abbot's lodge recede, become smaller than a bird's nest.
Now the full springtime lake may peep at the hill's reflections
As the sun's early rays, for ten *li* around, mount up the willow tips.
My unconventional, wild fame is known only to the hidden birds;
This old man's toddling gait is the mockery of rural folks.
My wandering steps do not yet pursue the fragrant dust;
Far on the opposite shore, I hear a fisherman tapping on his boat.

(FHSFHC, 6:24a) *(Tr. Irving Lo)*

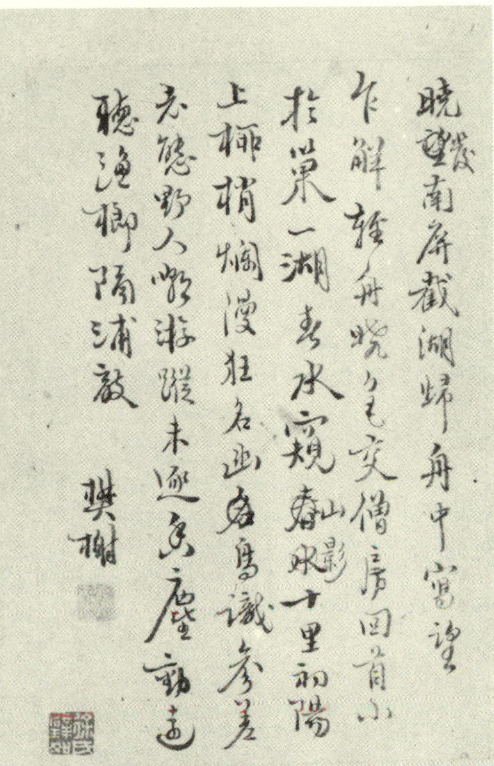

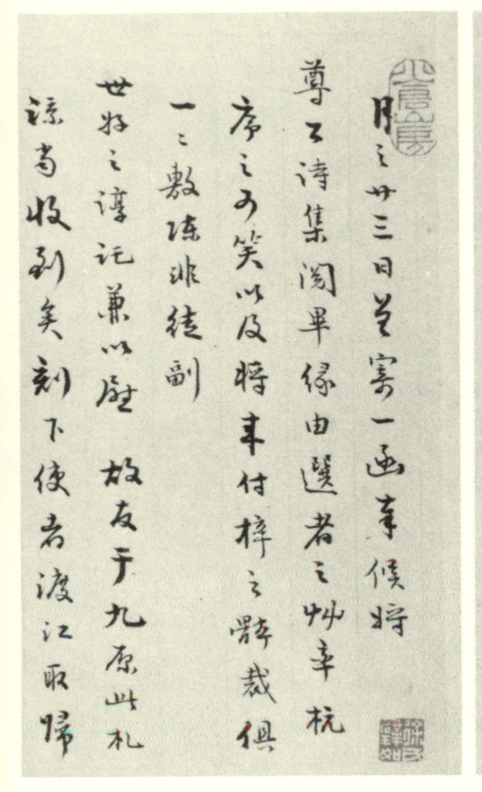

3. Calligraphy by Li E: "Leaving Southern Screen Hill at Dawn." Courtesy of the Shanghai Museum, People's Republic of China.

Tune: *Yeh Chin-men* (Paying Homage at Golden-Gate)
Title: Written on the Lake after a Shower, On the Sixteenth of the Seventh Month

She leans against the painted railing—
Autumn ablaze with colors after rain, but paler she looks.
Across the water the sunset clouds are still bright,
Against small hills, three or four.

When will we sail together on a boat, you and I?
Wait for the day we can break off the flowering lotus and look into our mirror.

Then, day after day, the green round plate and the lightly touched-up beauty—
No place for the west wind to dim its glory.

(FHSFHC, 10:11a) *(Tr. Shirleen S. Wong)*

Tune: *Pai-tzu ling*

Title: Passing Seven-Mile Rapids[7] on a Moonlit Night, I Encountered This Marvelous Scenery and Composed This Tune Which Almost Made the Many Hills Echo to My Song.

Fine autumn scenery tonight
Has led me to the T'ung River, to discourse on high exploits of long ago,
Where the wind and dew no longer belong to the human world.
I sit on the stern of my boat, blowing on my flute.
Myriad sounds of nature rise from the hills; 5
One star shines in the water.
I again imagine myself in a dream seeking immortality,
Until the oars' sound drifts far away[8]
To where the fisherman from the Western Cliff lodged for the night.[9]

Recalling the somber days of the Evening Tide Society,[10] 10
Such high-minded spirit no longer to be seen
Has made me appear the more forlorn.
Silently, the cold light of three or four glowworms
Winding their way past a thatched hut near the bay in front.
Spotless, the forest garners the mist; 15
Straight up stands the cliff obstructing the moon's path.
My sail's shadow, unsteady in the limpid green,
Bobs and drifts with the flowing current—
White clouds returning to their rest in the deep valley.

(FHSFC, 9:11b–12a) *(Tr. Irving Lo)*

NOTES

1. Lung-men Shan is located to the southwest of Hangchow, nicknamed Hsiao-ho Shan. The monk's name Ch'ao-yün means "Nestling-in-the-clouds."
2. Constructed as a conduit for water.

3. Nan-hu, located south of Hangchow, consisting of an upper and a lower lake. These lakes, originally dug during the Han dynasty, were significantly improved and enlarged during the governorship of Fan Ch'eng-mo (1624–1676) during the K'ang-hsi reign.

4. Hua-ch'eng (City of Refuge) is the name of the illusory city depicted in the *Lotus Sutra*. It is a temporary resting place created for the comfort of seekers of nirvana.

5. Chang Chi (765?–830), a T'ang poet who won the praise of Po Chü-yi as the best writer of *yüeh-fu* poetry.

6. Southern Screen (Nan-p'ing) Hill, so named for its resemblance to a decorative screen, located southwest of Hangchow, is a famous scenic spot in the West Lake region.

7. Located near T'ung-lu prefecture in Chekiang, west of Yen-lin Mountain; also known as the Fu-ch'un Islet. Between two precipitous cliffs, the water of this shallow is so swift that boatmen speak of the distance as "consisting of seven *li* when there is wind and seventy *li* when there is no wind."

8. Alluding to an apocryphal story in the *Chuang-tzu* which relates that once Confucius played on a lute and sang and a fisherman came to listen. When Confucius tried to seek him out and engage him in conversation, the fisherman took off in his boat, to the great disappointment of the sage, who waited on the bank until he could no longer hear the oars' sound.

9. Echoing the poem "The Old Fisherman" by the T'ang poet Liu Tsung-yüan (773–819), written while Liu was an exile in Yangchow:

The old fisherman lodges for the night by the Western Cliff,
Mornings he drinks from the clear Hsiang River and burns the bamboo of Ch'u for fuel.
Mist dissolves, the sun rises, but there is nobody near;
At one sound of *yiya*, the hills and the water suddenly turn green.
Looking back at the horizon, he floats out into midstream;
On the cliff the carefree clouds chase each other.

[*Liu Ho-tung chi*, 43:25b–26a]

10. The Evening Tide Society, or Hsi She, refers to the meetings of a group of friends of the Sung lyric poet Hsieh Ao (1249–1295), a man especially admired for his integrity and high-mindedness. It was said that he was so driven by grief over the death of Wen T'ien-hsiang (1236–1283) that he took up the life of a recluse in the Chekiang region, and he once performed sacrifices to the spirit of Wen at the famous Yen Jetty (Yen Lin) on the banks of the Fu-ch'un River. Wen was known as the author of the "Song of Righteousness" ("Cheng-ch'i ko"), composed just before his death, after he had fought against the Mongols in a series of losing battles on the coast of Chekiang and Fukien provinces until his ultimate capture and execution by Kublai Khan (1215–1294).

CHENG HSIEH

(1693–1765)[1]

Cheng Hsieh (*K'o-jou;* PAN-CH'IAO), a native of Hsing-hua, Kiangsu province, was known in his own time, and to this day, for his painting, poetry, and calligraphy. Also counted among the celebrated "Eight Eccentrics of Yangchow," Cheng's reputation as an eccentric may be based partly on his calligraphic style, which in later years was a unique combination of clerical and seal scripts, and partly on his sense of humor, which is well illustrated in his famous "Pan-ch'iao Price List":

> Large scrolls, six taels; medium scrolls, four taels; small scrolls, two taels; parallel couplets, one tael; inscriptions on fans, half a tael. Hard cash is infinitely preferable to gifts or presents of food, for your idea of what constitutes a good gift might not be mine at all. An offer of cash will warm the cockles of my heart, and my brushwork will be all the better. Gifts are an entanglement for me, and for you, credit buying is worse then repudiating a debt. I am an old man who tires easily, so I am unable to join you gentlemen in profitless talk. It's more expensive to paint bamboo than to buy one: six feet of paper will cost you three thousand. All talk of olden days and friendship is just so much autumn wind blowing by my ears.

But merely to brand Cheng Hsieh an eccentric is to do him a gross injustice, for he was a well-rounded human being: he was a serious student, a veteran traveler, an accomplished scholar (a K'ang-hsi *hsiu-ts'ai,* a Yung-cheng *chü-jen,* and a Ch'ien-lung *chin-shih*), a concerned and active public servant, a devoted family man, and a bit of a philosopher as well.

---

1. Chao-ying Fang, ECCP, 1:112.

Most of this first thirty years were spent at home or in school in nearby Chen-chou. In 1724 he traveled south to Kiangsi province where he became acquainted with Buddhist monks on the famed Mount Lu. In later travels, as far north as Peking, he would spend much time in Buddhist temples, where he studied the Confucian classics, history, and literature, and made friends with many Zen monks. He visited Yangchow (the city with which his name is so often associated) in 1731, but does not seem to have actually taken up residence there until 1737, the year after he had become a *chin-shih* in Peking. He lived in Yangchow until 1741, when he traveled to Peking for the third time, probably in search of an appointment. Indeed, the next year, at the age of forty-nine, he received his first official post as magistrate of Fan-hsien in Shantung province. In 1746 he was transferred to Wei-hsien in the same province, where he served with distinction, opening the granaries during an extended famine and creating large-scale public works projects so that the poor might have a source of income to pay off their debts. During his tenure as magistrate of Wei-hsien, he offended his superiors by requesting relief aid for the people of his district, and in 1753, he resigned his post, much to the disappointment of the common folk, who had benefited from his presence for seven years. The remaining twelve years of his life were spent around his home town of Hsing-hua, or in Yangchow.

As a poet, his style has been compared to that of Po Chü-yi and Lu Yu, T'ao Ch'ien (365–427) and Liu Tsung-yüan, Fan Chung-yen (989–1052) and Yüan Mei (q.v.). In fact, none of these comparisons is quite accurate, while each holds a kernel of truth. Cheng shared with T'ao Ch'ien a love of family and the simple life together with a distaste for the company of officials. Like Liu Tsung-yüan, he kept company with Buddhist monks, exchanged poems with them, and was at the same time a concerned and active official to whose memory the people of his district erected altars after he resigned from office. Like Po Chü-yi, he wrote simple ballads in which he depicted with great power the misery of the common folk, who suffered not only from famine, but from excessively harsh officials as well. Like Lu Yu, he was unrestrained in his writing, and he had much in common with the "inspirational" school of poetry most often associated with Yüan Mei. Yet it would be unfair to limit him by any one of the above comparisons. He describes himself rather well:

> My poems and prose writings are all forms of self-expression, my own ideas, although their truths are always traceable to the sages, and their style is always drawn from ordinary usage. There are those who claim to write in a style loftily and anciently rooted in the T'ang and Sung; I

> can't stand these people. I say: "If my writings are to be preserved, it will be as Ch'ing poetry and Ch'ing prose. If they are not preserved, it will be because they are unworthy of being Ch'ing poetry and Ch'ing prose." Why rave about ages that are long gone?

Cheng's poetic depictions of the people, cities, historical sites, landscapes, temples, plants and flowers, and natural phenomena he experienced during his seventy-two-year life are both sincere and romantic at once. Again, this aspect of the man is best expressed in his own words:

> I haven't done too much traveling through the countryside, but then again I've done a bit; I haven't done too much studying either, but I have done some; as for hobnobbing with brilliant and famous persons, I haven't done too much, but again I've done a bit of that too. I started out in dire poverty, then later came to be rather well-off; even later, once again I became rather poor. Therefore you'll find a taste of almost everything in my writings.

Cheng was not an innovator in verse technique, thematic treatment, or poetic style, but he was a master of the inspired description of genuine emotions based on his personal appreciation of the entire gamut of human experience. He knew, for example, that man is a social animal with responsibilities to his fellows. He was equally aware of the ultimate vanity of all human social endeavor, as illustrated by all the tattered remnants of once glorious enterprise he saw dotting the Chinese landscape. At the same time he was very much an individual, conscious of his individuality and demonstrating it in his own style of painting and calligraphy. The poems, like the man, are unaffected, fresh, and free-flowing. Even the seriousness with which he viewed his poems is expressed with characteristic humor in the last line of his last preface to his collected verse:

> This will be the final edition of my poems. If, after my death, anyone should misappropriate my name to produce an unauthorized edition and stealthily insert his ordinary run-of-the-mill verse therein, he will surely suffer a thump on the noggin from my aggrieved ghost!

(Jan W. Walls)

Martyred Widow Liu of Hai-ling:[1]
A Ballad

The martyred widow's husband, a successful military candidate, died in Tso Liang-yü's (1598–1645) ranks. He left no sons. His widow vowed

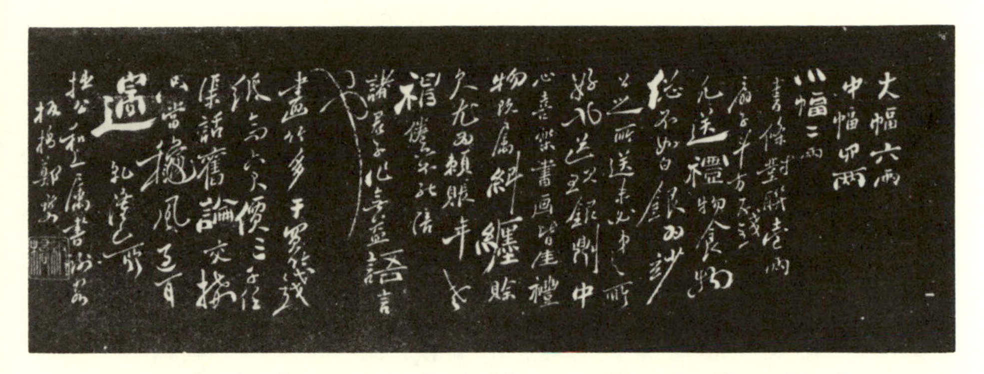

大幅六兩
中幅四兩
小幅二兩
書條對聯壹兩
扇子斗方五錢
凡送禮物食物
總不如白銀為妙
公之所送未必弟之所
好也送現銀則中
心喜樂書畫皆佳禮
物既屬糾纏賒
欠尤恐賴賬年老
神倦不能陪
諸君子作無益語言
也
畫竹多于買竹錢
紙高六尺價三千任
渠話舊論交接
只當秋風過耳
邊 乾隆己卯
拙公和上屬書謝客
板橋鄭燮

4. Cheng Hsieh's famous price list in his own calligraphy. Reproduced in *Pan-ch'iao shu-hua t'o-p'ien-chi* by the Wei-fang (Shantung) Municipal Art Institute, n.d.

5. "Bamboos in Mist," four hanging scrolls by Cheng Hsieh. The Art Museum, Princeton University. Anonymous loan.

to serve her parents-in-law, and when they passed away she immediately hanged herself. The people of the prefecture mourned her, and called her the Martyred Widow Liu.

Damp clouds press on the window, the lamp about to die,
The young woman stops her shuttle, brushes her skirt and stands.
Her heart lonely through the night's gloom, she lies down tired,
And deep into her bedroom comes a dream of the battlefield.
Broken armor and tattered flags enfold stains of blood. 5
Dangling a defeated drum, an aggrieved soul howls,
Saying, "I've lost my life in one of many battles;
My body broken, my bones drift in the Yellow River torrents."

Terrified and trembling she awakens with a start,
To the wild baying of dogs beneath an autumn fence. 10
In the depth of night she wails, but even wailing fails.
Teardrops stream down, her silken quilt is soaked.
She wipes her rouge away and abandons all makeup,
Kingfisher coiffure, cloudlike tresses, lose their sheen.
Then comes the ominous news: our troops have fallen in defeat, 15
No different, after all, from the dream.

With warm words, small talk, she soothes the old couple.
But in her darkened room, she rips apart skirts of silk brocade.
In her greatest grief, streams of tears become bowls of blood;
Sacrificial offerings drift away to distant autumn clouds. 20
In the lonely stillness of a hut, weasels squabble with squirrels,
A sickly widow keeps the home for a family grown destitute.
Night after night her cold loom spins until the break of day.
Morning after morning from the broken well she picks up lovebird
 tiles.
Ten acres of wasted land, no harvest for the year, 25
A garden full of flowers and willows booms in vain.

When Father- and Mother-in-law die, the widow will soon follow:
"No one left to serve ancestral souls, what place is there for me?"
She presses her pale neck against a red silk rope,
Hoping to send her fair soul in search of that battlefield. 30
The husband died for the state, the widow dies for him;
But loyalty and righteousness cannot bring back their breath.
Once the mind gives way to doubt, the deed is lost,
And filled with shame in the nether world, it is too late for regret.
Even now the graveyard trees at night cry in sorrow: 35
Desolate river, withered grass, high autumn plains.

A cold crow perches alone, unsettled through the night:
Sadly moaning to the moon, begging for its mate.

(CPCC, p. 35) *(Tr. Jan and Yvonne Walls)*

Poor Scholar

A poor scholar, hit by hard times,
Rises at night, opens his gauze curtains.
Pacing back and forth, he stands by the courtyard tree,
A bright moon sinking in the light of dawn.
He thinks his old friends would do him well; 5
If asked, they surely would not decline.
Leaving home, his air is fairly bold;
Halfway there, his spirit already has failed.
When they meet, they exchange cool words,
So, he swallows his request and goes back home. 10
Returning home, he must face his wife,
Embarrassed, bereft of dignity.
But to his surprise, she comforts him,
Takes off her jade hairpin, pawns her old clothes;
Going to the kitchen, she heats the broken cauldron, 15
Bright smoke congealing in the morning light.
In the platter, leftover buns and nuts
Are divided among the hungry children.
I said, "By the time wealth and honor come to me
My hair will be short and thin." 20
She replied, "Never seize some new flowering bough
To mock this coarser fare."[2]

(CPCC, p. 67) *(Tr. Jan and Yvonne Walls)*

Flight from Famine: A Ballad

Ten days ago, he sold a son,
Five days ago, he sold his wife,
One more day, and he will be alone.
On and on the long road stretches:
The long road stretches into the distance, 5
To mountain passes thick with wolves and tigers.
In a famine, tigers never starve,
And cunning men lurk by mountain crags;
Wolves come out in broad daylight,
And villagers wildly beat their drums. 10

Ah, his very skin and hairs are scorched.
His bones broken, his back twisted.
Meeting people, at first he only stares,
Getting food, he vomits all he swallows.
Not enough of him to fill a tiger, 15
So even the tigers leave him alone.
He sees an abandoned child by the road,
Picks him up, carries him in his cooking pot.
All of his own children sold,
Now he cares for another child. 20
There is a woman on the road
Who pities the child, gives him suck.
A gulping sound at her breast,
A babbling noise from his little lips,
He seems to be calling for mom and dad, 25
The more pitiful as he coos and smiles.

A thousand miles to the Mountain-and-Sea Pass,[3]
Ten thousand to the Liao-yang[4] garrison.
Rugged walls glower at evening stars,
Village lamps shine on autumn swamps. 30
A long bridge floats on the water,
Winds howl and waves are enraged.
He starts to cross, but loses his nerve,
For the bridge is slick and he has no shoes.
Someone pulls in front and someone pushes from behind, 35
A single slip, and you will never get up again.

Across the bridge, he rests in an ancient temple,
All attentive, he hears his village tongue:
Women talking about kinsmen and relatives,
Men speaking of families and marriages. 40
So happy to talk, he cannot sleep that night,
And for a while, he nearly forgets his sad and bitter lot.
Before dawn, he is up and on the road again,
In the morning light, his shadow traveling alone.
A little south toward the border walls, 45
Yellow sands are vast without end.
Some say the white-robed Hsüeh[5]
Set out from here to fight in Liao-tung.
Some say the Emperor Yang of Sui
Visited here with bold warriors from Korea. 50
On first arrival, things are as bad as before,
Nothing but hardship and talk of long ago.

Fortunately, he meets a new master,
Who at least gives him a place to sleep.
With a long plow he tills the ancient gravel, 55
Ploughs spring fields in the drizzling rain.
He learns to tend horses, cattle, and sheep,
In the slanting sun, to measure out the grain.
His body now safe, his heart begins to mourn;
The southern horizon is vague and far away. 60
So many things that cannot be put in words,
Face to the wind, his tears seem to pour.

(CPCC, p. 103) *(Tr. Jan and Yvonne Walls)*

Tune: *Jui-ho hsien*
(An Immortal on an Auspicious Crane)
Title: The Fisherman

When wind and waves rise upon the river,
They tie the little boat to a green willow tree,
In the village of red apricot blossoms.
How I envy the fisherwoman's air:
She uses no rouge or powder, 5
Only occasionally works her hair.
A wild flower on her bun
Surpasses any jeweled earring or hairpin.
Suddenly she calls her man to toss the net, sound the rattle,
And they row the boundless river-sky. 10

The profit's good.
Rush bags encase their crabs,
Bamboo baskets hold their shrimp,
And willow strands string their carp.
The city's not far away: 15
Go there in the morning,
Be back at noon.
They bring along a vat of someone's fine brew:
Men and gulls get drunk together,
Lying among blossoming reeds, a vast stretch of white, 20
And miles and miles of setting sun.

(CPCC, p. 149) *(Tr. Jan and Yvonne Walls)*

Tune: *Jui-ho hsien*
Title: The Tavernkeeper

A green flag—wineshop by the river
Amid fine rain and blossoming pear trees.
At this time of the spring festival.
Shrimp and snails, mixed fish and lotus roots,
And of course the old jug under seal, 5
Opened only now,
Pure, mellow, sweet,
Enough to souse a fisherman or a woodsman.
The road back to village and town grown blurred,
Man and setting sun are flushed through and through. 10

Did you know
There are rich and poor in the human world,
Growth and decay among the leaves,
Ins and outs on fortune's wheel?
So why worry? 15
Raise the winecup,
Long life to you,
May you sweep away your old dreams of the capital
And come to find your thirsty friends here in the hills.
Take off that golden sable and give it to the tavern hand! 20
From now on, let go!

(CPCC, p. 149) *(Tr. Jan W. Walls)*

Tune: *Jui-ho hsien*
Title: The Monk

The thatched temple, leaning toward collapse,
Is supported by an ancient tree,
Encircled by white clouds.
The forest deep, no visitors arrive,
But a spring babbles at the bottom of the brook 5
In the valley of hidden birds.
Gentle winds come to sweep
And sweep the fallen leaves into the stove,
So he may close the door, bake potatoes, trim the lamp.
The lamp expires, potatoes smell sweet, day dawns. 10

No fakery—
Though he hobnobs with nobility,
Though he treads the red dust,
Still he always returns to the rosy clouds;
Tattered shirt, frazzled patches, 15
Unmendable,
Unsewable.
He has less hair than a man of the world,
But fewer troubles, too.
He lights incense before the Buddha, 20
Takes a nap at ease.

(CPCC, p. 150–151) *(Tr. Jan W. Walls)*

Tune: *Jui-ho hsien*
Title: Powerful Officials

Music and song wandering beyond the clouds,
Candles burning, stars bright,
Flowers thick, the night goes on and on.
Glowing sunrise in a cold upper room,
Peonies greedy for a little more sleep, 5
The parrots have not wakened.
Amid the halberdlike shadows of the locust tree,
Stand so many dignitaries with their insignia of office,
In no time, the fog disperses and clouds disappear,
So desolate, a sparrow net could be spread outside the gate. 10

Suddenly he knows:
Swallows have taken the spring away,
Wild geese have brought the fall.
And frost and snow press in,
Some households feel the cold 15
That forces out
The sign of the blossoming plum.
Ah, how closely Heaven divides and multiplies human fortune—
waxing and waning!
Not circumscribed by the greed of a single house,
Even though cast with iron, molded of bronze, 20
All are like cakes drawn on paper!

(CPCC, p. 151) *(Tr. Jan W. Walls)*

Tune: *Jui-ho hsien*
Title: Kings and Emperors

Mountains and rivers are like discarded shoes:
How I envy the sage ideal of Emperor Yao
Who passed over his son, ceded his throne to the worthiest man.
And Emperors Yü and T'ang who hatched no schemes,
But let their sons and grandsons 5
Bear the burden of the universe.
In a thousand generations, a myriad ages,
How many heroes have been wasted—
Now only reams of old paper!
Why regret the founding of Ch'in upon the heels of Ch'u! 10

Rely on no one!
Neither on eunuchs,
Nor on princes,
Nor on royal kin!
Prop up the east, and the west will fall; 15
Lean heavily to one side,
And there is friction and quarrel.
In other years, palace walls will be broken bits of tile,
Lotus leaves will flap about on autumn waters;
There remains a rustic on a tattered boat in the slanting sun, 20
Leisurely picking the wild rice.

(CPCC, p. 151) *(Tr. Jan and Yvonne Walls)*

NOTES

1. A salt-producing area on the sea coast, near present-day T'ai-hsien, Kiangsu province.

2. Literally, "To mock this deer-parsley," meaning the wife herself. This expression alludes to two lines of an ancient-style poem: "I go up the mountain to gather deer-parsley,/I come down the mountain to meet my husband." See Wang Shih-chen, ed., *Ku-shih hsüan,* 1:4*a*. Also cf. David Hawkes, *The Songs of the South,* p. 40, Line 1 of "Shao Ssu Ming," for his translation of *mi-wu* as "deer-parsley."

3. Shan-hai kuan: see Wu Wei-yeh, note 3.

4. Liao-yang: located in Liao-ning province in China's northeast, an ancient town established during the Ch'in dynasty. Once conquered by Korea, it has been an important Chinese administrative center since T'ang times.

5. Hsüeh Jen-kuei (612–681) is a popular hero of Chinese military romance; he followed the T'ang emperor T'ai-tsung (*reg.* 627–650) on his campaign to Liao-tung, achieved great success in battle, and rose to the rank of general.

YÜAN MEI

(25 MARCH 1716–3 JANUARY 1798)[1]

Yüan Mei (*Tzu-ts'ai;* CHIEN-CHAI, TS'UN-CHAI, SUI-YÜAN) is unquestionably the Ch'ing dynasty poet best known in the West. The early presentation of extracts from his cookery book, the *Sui-yüan Shih Tan* in Giles's *History of Chinese Literature* established Yüan Mei as an object of exoticist interest, and Arthur Waley's fine short biography very clearly presented the multifaceted, and not uncontroversial, nature of the man himself. Waley's translations provide a fair insight into the warmth and wit which mark both the man and his poetry. His works show not only a truly creative use of the poetic tradition, but also more than a few flashes of real originality—all of this in a period when poetry was often marked by bookishness and slavish imitation of the past.

Born in Hangchow into genteel poverty, Yüan was early recognized as a prodigy. He achieved his first degree at the age of twelve, and took the *chin-shih* degree at the age of twenty-three in 1739. Assigned to study the Manchu language, he failed an examination on the subject in 1742, and was appointed to a succession of minor district magistrateships. When a recommendation for promotion was rejected by the court in 1749, Yüan chose to enter a life of retirement which was to last almost fifty years. It would be tempting to view Yüan's failure of the Manchu examination as a deliberate defiance of the Manchu rulers, were it not for the fact that he seems to have been little suited by temperament to high political position. He was devoted, even while studying assiduously for the examinations, to the study and writing of poetry. It ought to be noted in his favor, however, that he was beloved by the common people in each of the districts in which

1. Man-kuei Li, ECCP, 2:955–957.

he served; his tenure in Nanking, 1745–1748, was, indeed, the subject of many popular ballads.

From 1749 until his death in 1798 Yüan Mei dwelt mainly, though with many lengthy excursions, within the confines of his famous garden villa, the Sui-yüan, or Garden of Contentment. Yüan Mei's poetry and prose were immensely popular during his lifetime. His works, which included in addition to poetry, and the previously mentioned cookery book, ghost stories, literary essays, an important work of poetry criticism (*shih-hua*), letters, and example examination essays (*pa-ku-wen*), were in great demand. His poems were constantly pirated, and they are known to have been searched out even by foreign visitors as examples of the best of contemporary culture. Yüan proudly asserts in his will that he was once paid a thousand taels of silver for a funerary inscription.

Partially accounting for this popularity may be Yüan Mei's critical stance. Countering the prevailing demand that poetry must be didactic, a position best represented in the works of Yüan's older contemporary, Shen Te-ch'ien (q.v.), Yüan held that the function of poetry is to delight. As a result, Yüan published many humorous and even erotic poems of the type which had previously been written and circulated only within closed circles of intimate friends. Always devoted to the honest representation of life and things as they are, Yüan's poems appealed to the same audience that was buying and reading novels and short stories written in the colloquial language. These works of fiction, though they are now generally considered the true florescence of Ming and Ch'ing culture, were in their own times reputed to be low and vulgar. Yüan's independence of thought and feeling is the independence of the urban man and the commonsense rationalist. His outlook was for its time an extraordinarily egalitarian one. He scandalized Confucian purists by writing an epitaph for Miss Fang, his concubine, and by personally tending the grave of his respected gardener, whom he had interred within the confines of the Sui-yüan itself. All those things which combined to make him anathema to the strictest of the Confucianists (of whom there seem, really, to have been very few, outside the Court itself) at the same time recommended him, and his work, both to the rising class of literate townsmen, and to the traditionally educated scholars and scholar-officials who were both writing (anonymously) and reading the new colloquial literature.

Yüan's works would hardly seem wildly experimental to the modern Western reader. Though he does toy with colloquial usages, and occasionally takes great liberties with the traditional forms themselves, his work is down-to-earth, but never "earthy"; witty, but hardly ever indecorously so. He is a master of traditional poetic technique and vocabulary, a true renovator of the grand tradition of poetry rather than a rebel against it: a poet whose life and works fully deserve further study and translation.

I can think of no better encapsulation of the man than the following, from Waley's preface to *Yüan Mei, Eighteenth Century Chinese Poet*: "Personally, I find him a lovable, witty, generous, affectionate, hot-tempered, wildly prejudiced man; a writer of poetry that even at its lightest always has an undertone of deep feeling and at its saddest may at any moment light a sudden spark of fun:[2]

(J. P. Seaton)

Written at the Graveside

I recall a small, young boy
By his grandmother most dearly loved.
A toddler first to be cuddled
Still shared her bed in his teens.
His braids silhouetted by her red lamp, 5
He read aloud before her white hair.
A pampered boy who nagged her for fruits
Played hooky, she spared him the whip.
His tutor's meals she served with reverence
And herself made the boy's gown of silk. 10
Truly she prized this pearl of her palm,
Expected him to soar like a crane.
She leaned on his back oft when they played
And hugged his shoulder when viewing flowers.
Neighbors and kin marveled at such great love; 15
His sisters were jealous of such dotage.
When envoys left the royal jade steps,[1]
When autumn wind brought forth the name list,
Her hopes for his day of success would rise,
Though she said, "I might not live to see it!" 20
In silence her words still seemed to linger,
But quietly a few years have passed.
Indeed, one comes in palace-silk robe
To bow before the grave, smoke-shrouded.
Though he's keen to do his filial duties, 25

2. Arthur Waley, *Yüan Mei, Eighteenth Century Chinese Poet* (London: George Allen and Unwin Ltd., 1956), preface.

Her dream of fun with grandson is lost.
Kindness cannot requite those white bones,
Though tears might reach the Yellow Spring.
As old grass shimmers in the twilight,
The nightjar weeps in the hills of autumn. 30
Let not the bright, clear moon tonight
Attain above her grave its fullness!

(HTSFSC, 2:2a–b) *(Tr. Anthony C. Yu)*

Climbing T'ai Mountain

If one did not climb the T'ai Mountain tall,
How could one know that the world was small?[2]
But once having reached this very place,
Dare one not hasten to climb at all?
The natives braided ropes to make a wooden basket, 5
In which I was made to lie like a spring silkworm.
Two men carried it and like crabs they walked
Sideways and straight up, mumbling all the while.

First we entered the Immortals' Tower,
Then ascended the Water-Curtain Cave;[3] 10
Many peaks, like sons and grandsons,
Stood in rows vying to send us off.
The path meandered like a long, coiling snake;
The withered boughs hung like iron chains suspended.
A layer of white clouds, then a layer of water— 15
They trembled like a thousand, ten thousand hibiscus flowers.
Maple red stairs and jade green steps turned round and round.
Suddenly a sheer cliff reared up, brushing the sky;
Below it, deep canyons gaped;
Above it, Heaven's gate yawned. 20
As clouds already sealed the path on which we came,
We had to risk death to rise straight into the void.
The head of one behind followed the heels of one in front;
An inch of grass seemed taller than a thousand-foot pine!
We had no fear of not reaching the P'eng-lai Palace,[4] 25
Only the fear that light frames and small bones could not withstand
 the winds of Heaven.[5]

Would you like to know the shapes of Ch'i and Lu?[6]
A few packs of snails, a bustling beehive!
A band of yellow water which seemed a sash

Did pierce this world to reach the Milky Way. 30
We regretted only that wine cups were so few in Heaven;
We could not believe there were many people on Earth.
We stooped to listen: the whole empire below
Was silent, opaque, and endless like a single breath.
Leaves beneath our feet soared higher than the backs of birds; 35
The sea before our eyes would surge around our chests.
Then I knew that Heaven did not show its solemn hue;
Otherwise, how could I stare at the yellow earth as if it were the
azure sky!

A Taoist bade me worship the mountain god.
Jade towers and scarlet halls, how brilliant they were! 40
Our Sage Court, full of virtue, does not perform these rites.[7]
Boredom would kill Hsiang-ju if he did not write![8]
Ornate monuments of seventy-two generations,[9] now half sand and
dirt.
Caused me to think of the past with grievous hurt.
Quickly I descended for I feared the sun would set. 45
What could I do but face again the Red Dust?
I did not see the golden wheel bring forth the divine tree,[10]
Only above the peak the bright moon big as a silver tray.

(HTSFSC, 3:3a–b) *(Tr. Anthony C. Yu)*

Leaving My Post to Retire at the Sui Garden

I

A stabled horse[11] bearing a thousand weights
Which was made by the long whip to run,
But suddenly set free in the hills,
So this body is now all mine!
The royal minister of yesteryear 5
Now retires to go back to the fields.
No word's exchanged in the farewell party;
I only drink with abandonment.
I gaze at the jade green brook:
Are there changes in my looks? 10

II

The whole garden's full of hills;
The hills are full of books.[12]

Each thing is in its place,
Is Master set to go home?
Children send me on my way 5
With incense along the road.
I smile when I look at them,
For fame, too, seems empty and vain.
I've no shame and that's my comfort;
To come or go is my privilege. 10
I look to the wide distant space:
Even birds fly at a leisure pace.

(HTSFSC, 5:13b) *(Tr. Anthony C. Yu)*

Life at the Sui Garden

I

Officialdom does not come by birth;
Full grown, we walk the royal path.
If such flavor I've tasted once,
To plain nature I can thus return.
The flower watcher wants to go home—
Why wait, then, for the end of spring?
When white clouds roam in the sky,
They come and go too without cause.

II

Joy and rage are not caused by things;
They spring by chance from our hearts.
Fate has no say o'er win or loss;
It is by sheer accident wrought.
If you gain nothing from your books,
Leave them, rise, and take a walk.
If you can reach the bamboo grove,
You'll hear there spring water flow.

III

In building houses, I'm content with few;
In building ponds, I'm content with many.
Few houses will not block the mountains;

Many ponds will not stunt the lotus flowers.
Fishes, swimming, fully a foot long
Leap o'er the clear waves in daylight.
They know I love the lotus flowers
And would not dare spread the nets.

IV

Flowers will arrive with spring,
But spring may not leave with flowers;
Clouds will flow away with water,
But water can't detain the clouds.
I would ask for an explanation,
But none has a tree tall enough.
Idly I think beneath the trees:
Whither have the clouds and spring returned?

V

Eyes, nose, ears, mouth, and mind—
By chance they're my possessions.
If I cling to what I possess,
For whom do I guard these things?
The mind is the body's host;
The body's the friend of the mind.
Let our host serve our good friend:
Gladly let's drink a barrel!

VI

You musn't laugh at my tall tower;
The tall tower, after all, is nice.
When you're still ten miles away,
I can already spot you coming.
When you come, don't take a cart;
The cart's noise alarms my birds.
When you come, don't ride a horse;
The horse will feed on my grass.
When you come, don't come at dawn;
The hermit hates to rise early.

When you come, don't come at dusk;
At dusk all flowers will age.

(Nos. 1–2, 4–6, and 10 from a series of 10; HTSFSC, 6:3b–4b) (Tr. Anthony C. Yu)

Self-Ridicule

I suffer, being ruled by poetry and books,
And day's passing alarms me frequently.
I crave a seal carved on all three sides[13]
I'm used to grinding an ink stick on both ends.[14]
To copy the aged, I take up early a cane;
To flee officialdom, I'm long averse to boots.
The names of friends I often forget;
The ancient sages I promptly recall.

(HTSFSC, 12:7a) *(Tr. Anthony C. Yu)*

For My Wife: A Poem Written in Sickness

Tossing, turning—this poor man can't fall asleep:
As we grow old, my care is your travail.
A thousand goldpieces may buy every flower's smile;
In sickness comes the proof of wedded love.
Jade trees without wind: the silvery candle's safe;
Rainfall on autumn river: the bamboo tower's cleansed.
I love, my dear, your kind inquiring words
Which never wait until the cock crows twice.

(HTSFSC, 18:7b) *(Tr. Anthony C. Yu)*

In Early Years

In early years I governed, early I retired—
This, my nature, is peculiar among mankind.
Though old, I claim more attentive might than Ch'an;[15]
Though poor, I have my fun through cleverness.
I know I'm rather blessed in this life;
I might not be nameless e'en after death.
I sort out my books and console myself:
Renowned of old were not all dukes and earls.

(HTSFSC, 19:4a–b) *(Tr. Anthony C. Yu)*

Mocking Spectacles

Our vision is by nature free.
Why depend on the lenses' power?
Though far out eyesight may reach,
There's still an awkward barrier.
The strings first entangle your nose,
And ice forms even without tears.
E'en if Hsü Yen's state did not fall,[16]
His stare would still be a horror.

(HTSFSC, 19:4b) *(Tr. Anthony C. Yu)*

Praising Spectacles: Within three years I have both mocked and praised spectacles.

How swift is the coming of old age!
These old eyes are young once more;
My pupils are born from a box!
Spring ice reveals my reflection;
The sky glows with an autumn moon.
Small print I can find in twilight;
A lone flower in thin mist seems clear.
Henceforth where'er my gaze I turn,
Dare I your companionship spurn?

(HTSFSC, 20:11b) *(Tr. Anthony C. Yu)*

Willow Flowers

Willow flowers, snowflakes
The same; they're feckless—
No matter whose garden they fall in,
They'll always follow the wind away.

(HTSFSC, 21:7a) *(Tr. J. P. Seaton)*

Money

There's something to love in each thing in the world
Except money: that most insipid of all things:

In life, you can't get it;
In death, you can't take it.

(HTSFSC, 35:3b) *(Tr. J. P. Seaton)*

Rain Passes

Rain passes, washing the face of the mountain;
Clouds come, the mountain's in a dream.
Clouds, rain, come and go as they please.
The green mountain, as always, is unmoved.

(HTSFSC, 31:14a) *(Tr. J. P. Seaton)*

Sleeplessness

One rain, and all the flowers done!
Third watch, and all the music still.
Except what strikes my ear and stays my sleep:
From windy branches the last drops fall.

(HTSFSC, 18:7a) *(Tr. J. P. Seaton)*

Delirium: Jesting at Illness

I don't want to come, yet suddenly I'm here;
I don't want to go, and suddenly I'm gone.
Don't know where I've come from or where I'm going.
In this, of course, there is true waxing and waning.[17]
Since Heaven can't speak, I'll tell on its behalf:
Just wait for Old Master Chaos[18] to give back my life—
If he looks for me, he'll naturally find me.

(HTSFSC, 27:3a) *(Tr. J. P. Seaton)*

Mad Words

To learn to be without desire, you must desire that;
Better to do as you please: sing idleness:
Floating clouds, and water running—where's their source?
In all the vastness of the sea and sky, you'll never find it.

(No. 3 from a series of 3, HTSFSC, 34:11b) *(Tr. J. P. Seaton)*

NOTES

1. Messengers announcing the winners' names from the list of candidates who had successfully passed the palace examination.

2. An allusion to an oft-quoted statement in *Meng-tzu* (*The Book of Mencius*, 7a:24): "Mencius said, 'Confucius ascended the eastern hill, and Lu appeared to him small. He ascended the T'ai mountain, and all beneath the heavens appeared to him small. So he who has contemplated the sea, finds it difficult to think anything of other waters, and he who has wandered in the gate of the sage, finds it difficult to think anything of the words of others' " (Legge's translation). One of the five sacred mountains of China, T'ai-shan is located north of T'ai-an, Shantung province. It is the site visited by emperors of China, beginning with Ch'in Shih Huang-ti, to perform their *feng-shan* rites, to signify their possession of the mandate to rule.

3. An allusion to the birthplace of Sun Wu-k'ung, the Monkey of the Ming novel, *Hsi-yu chi* (The Journey to the West).

4. One of the three legendary islands famed for being the abodes of immortals.

5. Possibly a parody on Su Shih who wrote a *tz'u* poem to the tune, *Shui-tiao ko-t'ou*: "I was just about to ride there on the wind,/ But feared that heaven's crystalline palaces and towers so high, would be for me too cold." See Wu-chi Liu and Irving Yucheng Lo, eds., *Sunflower Splendor: Three Thousand Years of Chinese Poetry* (New York: 1975), p. 350.

6. Two ancient feudal states whose territories comprised the province of Shantung and whose boundaries were visible from the top of T'ai-shan.

7. A reference to *feng-shan*, sacrifices to Heaven and Earth performed on this famous mountain by Chinese emperors.

8. Referring to Ssu-ma Hsiang-ju (179–117 B.C.), who was said to have composed an essay (now lost) on *feng-shan* for Emperor Wu of the Han Dynasty.

9. According to the *Shih-chi, chüan* 28, there were seventy-two rulers in antiquity who had performed these sacrificial rites on T'ai-shan.

10. *Fu-sang*, a mythical tree with a double trunk, supposedly located in the Eastern Sea. Ten suns were reported to shine on this tree. See the *Shan-hai ching* (Classic of the Mountains and Seas), *chüan* 9, pp. 3a–b (SPPY edition).

11. Alluding to two famous lines from Ts'ao Ts'ao: "Yet ancient steeds in stall that lie/ Dream of the leagues they ran." Translation by John A. Turner, *A Golden Treasury of Chinese Poetry* (Hong Kong: The Chinese University Press 1976), p. 63.

12. Artificial hills in the Sui Garden. A study was probably located on top of one of these hills.

13. A seal carved on all three sides accommodated the many sobriquets and official titles of the owner.

14. A reference to rubbing an ink slab with a stick of ink.

15. I.e., the power of meditation (*samadhibala*), the ability sought by Zen priests to overcome and to dispell all distractions. A life-long critic of Buddhism, Yüan is always poking fun at this religion in his writings.

16. Hsü Yen was reputed to have lived in the eleventh century B.C. He was said to be so benevolent a ruler that he refused to go to war when his territory was invaded by the forces of the state of Ch'u and he thereby lost his country. In a footnote to his own poem here, Yüan Mei cited a passage in the *Hsün-tzu* (*chüan* 5), which declared that "the eyes of King Hsü Yen could

only see with a stare." Yüan interpreted the phrase "with a stare" to mean nearsightedness.

17. "Waxing and waning." Possibly intended as a pun is the compound *hsiao-hsi*, which, on a colloquial level, means "news" or "message." Structurally, in our interpretation, this line mimics the penultimate line of T'ao Ch'ien's famous poem "Drinking Wine, Number Five": "In this there is true meaning." The final line of T'ao's poem also expresses, in much more serious vein, an inability to communicate experience clearly: "But when I try to speak I cannot find the words." The translator is indebted to Professor Anthony C. Yu for calling his attention to this allusion, which also occurs in Chia Yi's (200–168 B.C.) "Peng-niao fu" (*Wen-hsüan*, 13:12a).

18. P'an-ku, the legendary creator and first ruler of the universe in Chinese mythology.

CHIANG SHIH-CH'ÜAN

(2 DECEMBER 1725–1 OR 3 APRIL 1785)[1]

Chiang Shih-ch'üan (*Hsin-yü;* CH'ING-JUNG), a native of Nanchang in the Yüan-shan district of northern Kiangsi province, was one of the foremost literary men of his time, but his lasting fame as the leading dramatist of the Ch'ien-lung period has overshadowed his contributions in the field of poetry. Chiang, Yüan Mei, and Chao Yi (qq.v.) were known to their contemporaries as the "Three Masters of Chiang-tso" and were the recognized masters of poetry in South China during the reign of Ch'ien-lung (q.v.).

In spite of his early success as a dramatist, Chiang was not as successful in the capital examinations. After several failures he finally won the *chin-shih* degree in 1757. It has been suggested by Li T'iao-yüan (1734–1803) that the element of criticism in Chiang's earlier plays hindered his progress in the examination system and clouded his career. Advancement within the bureaucracy may not have been foremost in his ambitions, however. After serving in successive minor positions in the capital, Chiang retired in 1763 to care for his mother. Memories of a bitter existence caused by his father's lack of achievement as an official, and the success of his friend Yüan Mei, who had already retired from government service to devote his time to poetry, weighed heavily in Chiang's decision to pursue a career as an educator. In 1781, however, Chiang returned to government service in the capital. He was soon stricken with partial paralysis and was forced into permanent retirement at his home in Nanchang near Lake P'o-yang.

As a poet and a critic, Chiang was a proponent of the *hsing-ling* school of literary theory, which emphasized one's inner nature and true emotion or spirit as the two most essential elements in literary

1. Lien-che Tu, ECCP, 1:141–142.

creation. Chiang wrote a cycle of poems criticizing the works of other poets and was especially critical of Wang Shih-chen's (q.v.) poems, which he characterized as "empty and floating." He also expressed little regard for those of Li Po's poems which seemed to him to dwell on the pleasure-seeking nature of man. The subject matter of Chiang's own poems falls largely within the realm of tradition. The central themes of conscientiousness, filiality, righteousness, and honor are frequently expressed through historical events or personalities. Chiang Shih-chüan's collected poems, under the title *Chung-ya t'ang shih chi,* were published shortly after his death and reprinted in Canton in 1816.

(Coy Harmon)

An Evening Prospect: City Lights

Market torches, boat lanterns: a jumble of fireflies.
Grasses and clouds—a trail of black ink—the night long and dark.
I imagine myself among the layered clouds,
Looking down upon the human world with its galaxy of stars.

(CYTSC, 16:10b) *(Tr. Irving Lo)*

Toasting the Moon at Ten-Thousand-Year Bridge[1]

A thousand paces long, the flying arch leaps the river,
Appearing at the edge of the void, people come and go.
Like a rainbow it links jumbled peaks halfway broken off.
Below lies the flood dragon, awed into submission.
From the blue sky the light of the crescent moon touches the water
below; 5
On its glassy surface lies the brilliance of a myriad things.
Off the wind fall drops of dew; vast are the waves—
Now all between heaven and earth is cleansed of dust.
In midstream, twenty-three mirrored arches;
Up and down, reflections of the vaulted heaven in the autumn
river. 10

Crossing the bridge the traveler feels the river winds,
Treading on cold light yet unaware of the chill.
For a thousand feet the water flows in the glimmering moonlight,
Broken now and then by the splash of a fish.

With eyes glancing all about, I hardly knew I was in this world, 15
And with goblets flying, I lost track of time.
Like ice and snow, the moon and water rival one another in clarity.
I only regret that in the presence of guests there is not the sound of
a flute.

Lights of the fishermen are motionless, wild gulls asleep;
Temple bells ring out, startling the nesting crows. 20
Gala outings amidst scenic splendor are few indeed;
In his heart the Master[2] knows he can achieve immortality.

Among prominent officials, who can take pleasure in the mountains
and water?
Perhaps, as a poet, I am inferior to the Dragon and the Tiger.[3]
With full cup in hand, I should enjoy myself to the full, 25
For the cool night brims with song, laughter and verses,
And our eyes and ears are restored to the calm of the shimmering
waters.
In moments of clarity, the breeze and moonlight must be treasured.
Bending down, I gaze at stars falling on the rapids below;
Alas, even the sun and moon in their races are but straw dogs.[4] 30
We have come this evening to the bridge of ten thousand years;
Perhaps only True Perceivers can partake of immortality.

(CYTSC, 1:12a–12b) *(Tr. Coy Harmon)*

Expelling Witches

Shamans scurrying everywhere propagate ghostly teachings.
Alas, they've not yet met a Hsi-men Pao![5]
Cursing at spirits, howling at ghosts, they weep and sigh.
The sick are fearful and suspicious when medicine effects no cure.

At my eastern neighbor's house, at midnight they strike the
shaman's drum, 5
Stirring me from deep sleep, disturbing my dreams.
Dressing and going into the moonlight, I ascend my neighbor's hall;
Wife and children hold back their tears as the old man lies abed.

An old shamaness shakes her head and mumbles incantations;
Holding a dragon's horn, she invokes the White Tiger. 10
Hideous and repulsive, ugly and strange, images are set in rows,
Intermixed with pictures of lascivious women, truly detestable.
Wooden phoenixes, golden placards are hidden by flags and
pennants;

On high a lamp burns in front of a life-giving tally.
I rip up the demon images, put them to the torch, 15
Then trample on the ashes, smash their bows.
I blow out the lamps, curse the shamans, and all take flight.
Guests and friends, their tongues hanging out, all depart;
Spirits and ghosts scatter and flee the place.

At break of day the sick man rises to eat rice gruel. 20
Master Hu wrote a poem on expelling witches,
And in three days it was chanted in villages and towns.
Formerly I heard of a magistrate summoning a shamaness to
summon his own spirit.
With drums and music, she was escorted to the temple gate.
Alas, who has not heard that demons come from among men? 25

(CYTSC, 14:5b–6a) *(Tr. Coy Harmon)*

Sixteen Songs of the Capital: Chicken Feather Shop[6]

Icy sky, snow-blanketed earth, the wind like a tiger,
The naked and weeping have no place to perch.
At dusk, they chatter ceaselessly begging three coins
To buy one night's rest in the chicken feather shop.
Cow sheds and pig pens are all much the same; 5
Who will provide wheat stalks and hemp straw?
Chicken feathers, spread thick on the ground, make a carpet;
Chicken feathers they gather to fashion a quilt.
People lie criss-cross, all ajumble; snoring sounds fill the air;
The foul air, rising like steam, keeps their bodies warm; 10
Calm and peaceful, the shop nearly matches a bridal chamber,
Surpassing even a guest house with quilts, curtains, and blankets.
Though their backs and bellies grow feathers, they cannot fly,
But, facing the wind as they pluck themselves, goose pimples rise
up.
On the street at daybreak, they screech like winter crickets, 15
And they regret not having feathers like a real chicken.
Alas! Alas!
"If I can't beg three coins for tonight's stay,
Tomorrow the magistrate will proclaim a deed of charity,
Lay me in a poplar coffin to take my eternal sleep."

(CYTSC, 8:10b–11a) *(Tr. Irving Lo)*

NOTES

1. Built near Hsü-men in the district of Wu, Kiangsu province, during the reign of the Ch'ien-lung emperor.

2. I.e., the poet himself.

3. The poets Ts'ui Yin (d. 92) and Ts'ao Chih, respectively.

4. Alluding to the famous metaphor found in the fifth chapter of the *Tao-te ching*: "Heaven and Earth are not humane./They regard all things as straw dogs."

5. In the fifth century B.C., as a newly appointed magistrate in modern Honan, Hsi-men Pao quickly rid the area of sorcerers and prominent citizens who worked in collusion to extort sums of money from the populace by providing young girls as sacrificial wives to the River God.

6. A chicken feather shop was a place where the homeless poor could spend the night after the payment of a small fee.

CHAO YI

(4 DECEMBER 1727–5 JUNE 1814)[1]

Chao Yi (*Yün-sung*; OU-PEI), a native of Yang-hu, Kiangsu, was a noted historian and—along with Yüan Mei and Chiang Shih-ch'üan (qq.v.)—one of the most acclaimed poets of the Ch'ien-lung era. Son of an impoverished scholar who made his living as a tutor in private families, he was known to be a precocious child. When he was fourteen, his father died and Chao Yi was invited to succeed to his father's tutoring post, thus becoming tutor to all his former schoolmates. He continued tutoring and secretarial work until he passed the *chin-shih* examination with highest honors, as *chuang-yüan* or optimus; but because the emperor noticed that the candidate in third place was from the province of Shensi (which had not produced a *chuang-yüan* during the entire Ch'ing era), he ordered that the two names be interchanged and that Chao be given third-place honors, as *t'an-hua*. After Chao achieved fame as a poet and his name was frequently mentioned along with Yüan Mei and Chiang Shih-ch'uan, he constantly chafed at his failure to emerge as *the* leading member in a trio of preeminences.

Chao Yi's reputation as a scholar and historian rests largely on a well-known and highly respected critical study of the twenty-two dynastic histories (*Nien-erh shih cha-chi*), a large work in 36 *chüan* which he completed in 1796 and which was printed three years later. His poetic output consists of fifty-three *chüan* of poems published under the title *Ou-pei chi*; he also left a volume of discourses on poetry entitled *Ou-pei shih-hua*, in which he made a critical study of ten earlier poets. His choice of subjects for examination was exemplary in that the list included two of his near-contemporaries (Wu Wei-yeh and Cha Shen-hsing—qq.v.) along with four T'ang poets (Li Po, Tu Fu, Han Yü, and

---

1. Lien-che Tu, ECCP, 1:75–76.

Po Chü-yi), two Sung poets (Su Shih and Lu Yu), and two poets of the Yüan and Ming periods (Yüan Hao-wen and Kao Ch'i, 1336–1374). He took the position of never recognizing the superiority of the ancients over the moderns, and he maintained that great poetry should have a bearing on all areas and levels of human experience and not be confined to any particular mode of expression. Strong in his condemnation of the Archaic School of Ming poets, Chao Yi insisted on originality of expression, but not at the sacrifice of relevance. This view is most evident in his appraisal of some T'ang and Sung poets—for instance, he considered the poetry of Yüan Chen and Po Chü-yi superior to that of Han Yü and Meng Chiao among the T'ang poets because Yüan and Po showed a naturalness and a sense of fact which were lacking in Han and Meng; similarly, among the Sung poets, he ranked Su Shih much higher than Huang T'ing-chien despite the latter's reputation as a technical virtuoso. He suggested four criteria for poetry: power of imagination (*ssu-li*), human nature and feeling (*hsing-ch'ing*), learning (*hsüeh*), and experience or perspicacity (*shih*). His own poetry touches on a wide range of subjects, with serious thoughts often couched in witty language and a mocking tone. He is particularly admired for his poems on the subject of "Remembering the Past" (*huai-ku shih*), where he combined adept use of allusions with contemporary idiom and powerful imagery.

(Shirleen S. Wong)

On Poetry

I

The world is alive with inspiration to a potter who turns the wheel.
By nature's doing and human skill, too, one strives daily for
 something new.
I predict, though, a new thought that holds for five hundred years
Will become, in another five hundred, hackneyed and stale.

(No. 1 from a series of 5; OPSC, pp. 483–484) *(Tr. Irving Lo)*

II

The poems of Li Po and Tu Fu, passed along by myriad voices,
No longer seem in this modern era so fresh and new.

Every age these rivers and hills produce a genius,
Each capturing in spirit the *Odes* and *Songs*[1] for scores of decades.

(No. 2 from a series of 5; OPSC, p. 484) *(Tr. William Schultz)*

III

The best of poetry comes from the destitute, but my pocket is not
yet empty;
I gather, it's all because I haven't perfected my skill as a poet.
Having fish to eat or bear's paw?[2] I admit, I'm greedy for both:
I yearn for skill in poetry, yet how I dread being poor!

(No. 5 from a series of 5; OPSC, p. 484) *(Tr. Irving Lo)*

Mocking Myself

A bowl of gruel and greens, beard wet from steam and snivel,
Hands clutching a brazier, my back is arched toward the sun;
Of all the portraits in the Unicorn Pavilion,[3] surely,
Does a single one depict a shape and form like mine?

(OPSC, p. 502) *(Tr. Shirleen S. Wong)*

Sleepless at the Fifth Watch

Stars beyond the railing, a thin thread of moon—
Boom, boom, the watchman's drum, the night as long as a year.
An old man wakes from his dream to a wild rooster's crowing:
One on each side of the window, sleepless night for both!

(No. 2 from a series of 3; OPSC, pp. 535–536) *(Tr. Shirleen S. Wong)*

Watching An Opera: Impressions

I

With sticks and staves on a makeshift stage—all are engrossed in a
child's game.
Looking around me, I am pained by a thought that only I know:
I have gold coins now to purchase song and dance;
But, alas! the prime of my youth is already spent.

II

Knowing full well the tragic and comic are bits of stagecraft,
Still I can't bear the singing when the arias are sad.
Make-believe weeping has caused real tears to flow,
So people laugh and call me a silly, credulous old man.

(OPSC, p. 478) *(Tr. Shirleen S. Wong)*

The Red Cliff[4]

Even today this natural barrier commands the Ching-hsiang region;[5]
Before Red Cliff Mountain, ancient ramparts stretch on and on.
But where "the magpie flies south" is no longer the land of Wei;
And where "the Great River flows east" we think of the young Lord Chou—
A man for a thousand ages, from a tripartite kingdom;
An expanse of hills and rivers, the field of a hundred battles.
Now, passing by, we see only the vestiges of the past;
Under a bright moon, a fisherman sings the song "Blue Waves."[6]

(OPSC, p. 306) *(Tr. Shirleen S. Wong)*

Responding to a Poem on T'ai-po Pavilion at Colored Stone [Jetty][7]

By Aloeswood Pavilion, you once walked in your stocking feet;[8]
This place now bears witness to your sailing away under a bright moon.
Into the chalky waves of the river have dissolved an inspired immortal's bones,
But as high as the green mountain, for ten thousand ages, rears a poet's name.
Your brocaded gown was the envy of thousands those days;
But when can the Golden Grain Tathāgata[9] be brought back to this world again?
From a hundred-foot tower, looking down into an abyss,
Let me sing a song to your proud spirit's everlasting praise!

(OPSC, p. 307) *(Tr. Irving Lo)*

NOTES

1. The *Shih-ching* and the *Ch'u Tz'u,* the two oldest anthologies of Chinese poetry.

2. Alluding to a famous parable in the *Meng-tzu,* in which Mencius points out that when two delicacies, fish and bears' paw, are placed before a person and he can only have one of the two to eat he has to make a difficult choice.

3. The Unicorn Pavilion (Lin-ko) was first built on the order of Emperor Wu of the Han dynasty to celebrate the capture of the mythical, auspicious *ch'i-lin,* the unicorn. Later, portraits of meritorious ministers and military heroes were painted on its walls.

4. Ch'ih-pi, the Red Cliff, situated along the middle reaches of the Yangtze in modern Hupeh province, was commonly believed to be the scene of a decisive battle fought in the winter of A.D. 208. At this battle, the power of Ts'ao Ts'ao in the north (later known as the Wei Kingdom) was crushed by the naval forces of Wu under the command of Chou Yü, a young aristocrat related by marriage to the ruling house of Wu. The first half of line 3 is a direct quote from a poem by Ts'ao Ts'ao, "A Short Song" ("Tuan ko hsing"), and line 4 contains a quotation from a famous lyric by the Sung poet Su Shih on the subject.

5. The modern provinces of Hupeh and Hunan, where Ching-chou and Hsiang-yang are the principal cities.

6. The song of the "Blue Waves" ("Ts'ang-lang") identifies an ancient folk song quoted both in the *Meng-tzu* and in the "Fisherman" poem in the *Ch'u Tz'u.* The text reads, "When the waters of the Ts'ang-lang are clear, I wash my tassels in them;/When the waters of the Ts'ang-lang are muddy, I wash my feet in them." This song is generally taken to mean that one must choose between public office (tasseled hat strings symbolizing official ranks) when there is good government, and a life of reclusion when times are corrupt.

7. Ts'ai-shih chi (Colored Stone Jetty), located northwest of Tang-t'u, Anhwei, is where, according to legend, the T'ang poet Li Po died and was last seen riding away on a whale. Li Po, whose courtesy name was T'ai-po, often referred to himself as a "banished immortal," from a sobriquet given him by his contemporary poets.

8. This alludes to the legend that, when summoned to the Aloeswood Pavilion in the palace of the emperor (Hsüan-tsung) to compose poems, he would have his boots pulled off by Consort Yang's favorite attendant Kao Li-shih.

9. *Chin-su ju-lai,* or Golden Grain Tathāgata, in Buddhist terminology, refers to the Buddha of the Future. It was also said that the Indian monk Vimalakīrti (who came to China in the Han dynasty) was his reincarnation. In a poem by Li Po, entitled "Replying to the Question, 'Who Is [Li] Po?' Asked by Magistrate Chia-yeh [Chi] of Hu-chou," the poet himself wrote: "Why must the Magistrate of Hu-chou ask [such a question]?/Golden Grain Tathāgata is my previous reincarnation." Chin-su is also the name of a hill, northwest of P'u-ch'eng, Shensi, where the tomb of Hsüan-tsung was situated. Kao Li-shih was said to have been buried there also (as a companion to the dead emperor).

YAO NAI

(17 JANUARY 1732–15 OCTOBER 1815)[1]

Yao Nai (*Chi-ch'uan, Hsi-pao,* and *Meng-ku*), scholar-official, calligrapher, anthologist, literary theorist, and poet, was born in T'ung-ch'eng, Anhwei province, where he was tutored in the traditional curriculum, first by his uncle Yao Fan (1702–1771), and later by a fellow townsman, Liu Ta-k'uei (1697?–1779). The literary values these two men instilled in their young charge were those of *ku-wen,* or the ancient-style prose movement. After receiving the *chin-shih* degree in 1763, Yao Nai was appointed to the Hanlin Academy, and thereafter to terms of service with the Boards of War, Ceremonies, and Punishments. Later, he served on the imperial commission engaged in the compilation of the *Ssu-k'u ch'üan-shu tsung-mu t'i-yao* (Annotated Catalogue of the Four Libraries Collection). In 1774, he resigned from public office to devote himself to teaching in private academies in the lower Yangtze River valley.

An advocate of ancient-style prose standards, he was so successful in that enterprise that the movement came to be known as the T'ung-ch'eng School, after his hometown and that of his predecessors. A key factor in that development was the publication of an anthology of model prose essays and poems Yao Nai compiled to illustrate the school's principles: the *Ku-wen-tz'u lei-tsuan* (A Classified Compendium of Ancient-Style Prose and Verse). Once this work was printed, it quickly became a widely popular reference work and reader, and it has since been supplemented and imitated many times, but without diminishing the popularity of the original compilation.

Yao Nai was however more than an anthologist, for he provided theoretical sanction for the literary values sponsored by the T'ung-

1. Chao-ying Fang, ECCP, 2:900–901.

ch'eng School. In terms of his general philosophical outlook, he belonged to the orthodox Ch'eng-Chu tradition of Neo-Confucianism, and the metaphysical and ethical concepts he derived from those teachings were useful in his formulation of a theory of literary value. In the preface to the *Ku-wen-tz'u lei-tsuan,* specific literary genres are equated to such larger philosophical concepts as *shen* (spirit), *li* (principle) and *ch'i* (vital force). The ancient concepts of the *yin-yang* duality were made to serve a two-part theory of beauty, the masculine and the feminine. His system, although not always sharply defined in its primary components, was nonetheless a flexible and sophisticated one that well served several generations of writers prior to the advent of Western concepts on the Chinese scene.

Yao Nai's interest in literature was more than theoretical and pedagogical, however. In addition to a variety of scholarly writings (he was an indifferent scholar), miscellaneous notes, letters, and essays, which manifest a simple and lucid style, his collected works, the *Hsi-pao-hsüan ch'üan-chi,* contains eleven *chüan* of verse. At his best, often in those poems couched in the ancient-style pentasyllabic form, Yao Nai evokes in an uncomplicated, straightforward manner the human emotions stimulated by a visit to an ancient historical site or a scene of natural beauty. There is little, if anything, that can be described as really new or innovative in his poetry. However, within the confines of the received tradition, he speaks with a voice distinctly his own.

(William Schultz)

A Temple in the Hills

All hills resound with the tones of autumn;
Lofty woods grow dark as dusk draws near.
Breaking through the clouds and crossing the cold hazels,
Twilight shade descends the wall in front.
In the temple gateway the wind soughs and sighs; 5
Flying leaves fill the gathered crags.
A bamboo islet darkens the deep stream
Whose murmuring voice emerges from great boulders.
I call to mind, beyond the valley entrance,
The setting sun on the jade of distant peaks. 10
A single chime within the flowing mist,
Ten thousand glens in a crevice of enclosing eaves.
Surely there must be a man of profound seclusion

Living here and dressed in hemp and vines.
The glow of the new moon is soon extinguished; 15
Sadly gazing, I halt and rest on my staff.

(HPHSC, 1:1b–2a) *(Tr. Daniel Bryant)*

The Government Pond

Dark jade clouds over cliffs and canyons coil in distant shapes;
A setting sun on hazel woods glows in evening calm.
The valley tiger is about to come, a breeze fills the glens,
And on the surrounding hills the autumn leaves in unison resound.

(HPHSC, 7:4b) *(Tr. Daniel Bryant)*

The Pavilion of the Infinite Heavens

Thirty years ago I climbed to the top of this pavilion,
Hand in hand with glossy temples, writing poems on Ts'ang-chou Isle.[1]
Varied trees on the surrounding hills enter through extended eaves;
A clear river, ten thousand leagues long, flows encircling the district.
Through clouds and mist before my eyes I peer beyond the world;
As I lean on the railing, blossoms and birds appear on the twigs once more.
Still there remains the setting sunlight white on storeyed verandas;
And again I face the bright glow of sunset, gazing at departing gulls.

(HPHSC, 8:6a) *(Tr. Daniel Bryant)*

NOTE

1. Ts'ang-chou Isle was a legendary paradise located in the Eastern Sea.

HUNG LIANG-CHI

(17 OCTOBER 1746–24 JUNE 1809)[1]

Hung Liang-chi (*Chün-chih, Chih-ts'un*; PEI-CHIANG, KENG-SHENG), a native of Yang-hu, Kiangsu, is chiefly remembered today for his scholarship; in his own lifetime, however, he was better known as a poet and as a calligrapher. Orphaned at an early age, he began his schooling in his mother's family; after failing twice in the provincial examinations in the early 1770s, he found employment—along with his friend Huang Ching-jen (q.v.)—on the secretarial staff of Chu Yün (1729–1781), who initiated the concept of compiling the vast *Ssu-k'u ch'üan-shu* (The Complete Collection of the Four Treasuries). Toward the end of the decade, he went to Peking as a member of the *ssu-k'u* commission under the editorship of Chi Yün (1724–1805). Later he also served on the staff of Pi Yüan (1730–1797) and contributed to the compilation of the *Hsü Tzu-chih t'ung-chien* (Continuation to the Mirror of Government).

He did not earn his *chin-shih* degree until 1790, when he took the second-highest honor at the metropolitan examination, after four repeated failures.

Over the next twenty years, Hung served in the Hanlin Academy and held both provincial and court positions. He traveled extensively in the empire, including a brief period of banishment to Ili, Sinkiang province, and compiled important scholarly treatises on the classics, lexicography, hydrology, historical geography, as well as local gazeteers. His views on China's population problem have been considered by modern writers to be very close to the Malthusian theory of the West.

---

1. Lien-che Tu, ECCP, 1:373–375.

Hung Liang-chi was a prolific poet, with several thousand of his poems collected in five different collections which he edited himself. He wrote in both *shih* and *tz'u* forms, although he clearly favored the former; and he showed particular fondness for imitating the style of the *yüeh-fu*, or folk songs, of different periods and regions. Highly eclectic, he frequently combined in one poem (of the *shih* variety) lines of unequal length, in addition to experimenting with other metrical variations. The following selections are indicative of his versatility as well as his wit and humor.

(William Schultz)

Chatting about the Past with Huang the Elder [Ching-jen][1]

All ambitions of youth yield place to calamities;
Parted as in a dream—reunited, we can't trust our eyes.
Shall we match our strength in climbing one more mountain?
Winning fame in literature, there's you alone.
In a sea of dust, we still can tarry for a little while;
Or sit in a granary of books, all day, without food.
This morning I took myself to Yen Pavilion[2] for a look,
Trying to find the leanest horse to ride down the capital street.

(HPCSWC, p. 383) *(Tr. Irving Lo)*

A Ballad of a Springtime River: Presented to Wang the Elder

A railing of crimson hue,
Its shadow touches the sky;
In front of the railing, a river in spring flood.
The railing shimmers red, the water shimmers green;
The railing's pattern upon the waves; a hundred twists and turns. 5
We eat the same fish of the springtime river;
We both drink from the surging springtime flood.
The tide pulses in and out of the carp's belly;
And upon the ripping water—me, a gourd-head of Soochow.

At my home in Soochow 10
Flowers overspread the dikes.
When spring breezes come,
They fly north of the river.

Before the gate of your home,
A host of peachtrees. 15
When spring rains fall,
They waft south of the river.

Drinking from the water at dawn or dusk,
I think of you whom I cannot meet.
Vast, vast is the water; 20
Less than two feet is my pole.
Remote, remote my dreams,
Nineteen bridges away.

(HPCSWC, p. 395) *(Tr. William Schultz)*

To Dispel the Cold: Two Poems on Spring[3]

I
Small Pavilion

Where is the first sign of spring?
Spring comes earliest to a small pavilion:
Upon the shadow of a bamboo blind in the
moonlight,
In the tender notes from a flute in the breeze,
In the greening of a branch breaking out at the tip,
In the drippings of a candle of red passion.
In the whispered words overheard past midnight,
In the scented breath wafted beyond the wall.

II
Winding Pond

Where is the first sign of spring?
Spring comes earliest to a winding pond:
When water blossoms forth patterns of delight,
When a darting fish's eyes stir longing thoughts,
When faded dreams are enmeshed among fresh duckweeds,
When new sorrows are adrift in the silken rain.
Daybreak finds me rolling up the blind for a look
And the shadow upon the ripples comes up slowly.

(Nos. 1 & 4 from a series of 4; HPCSWC, p. 449) *(Tr. Irving Lo)*

Written on a Boat on the Ch'ien-t'ang River

Peonies blooming on paired pillows,
Lotus embroidered on a petticoat—
Unable to tell the flowers from needlework,
Butterflies come flying into my bed.

(HPCSWC, p. 508) *(Tr. Irving Lo)*

On the Road to An-hsi[4]

Flying for ten thousand ages, yet never exhausted
Are the snow and sand of T'ien-shan.
Weird winds issue from caves and grottoes,
Not a blade of grass or hemp on the battleground.
Another year is coming to a remote garrison,
Though the sun's warmth does not enter a yurt.
But I would still question closely my attendant
Lest there lie a three-forked road ahead.

(HPCSWC, p. 1112) *(Tr. Irving Lo)*

Upon Arriving at Ili, Recalling What I Saw on the Road

Before Chia-yu Pass[5] gathers the evening fog,
Behind Bulungir River[6] morning stars seem to float.
The horse's mane, capped with snow, glistens for hundreds of miles;
The dragon's breath, forming clouds, darkens the whole continent.
A valley of ice facing my bed, I find myself suddenly dumb;
With Flame Mountain[7] before my door, I break into a sweat.
All my life, I tire of the universe being narrow;
Now outside the empire, I can stretch my head for once.

(No. 1 from a series of 6; HPCSWC, p. 1125) *(Tr. Irving Lo)*

NOTES

1. The poet Huang Ching-jen (q.v.).
2. Yen-t'ai, outside of Peking, near the Yi River, was said to have been constructed by King Chao during the Warring States period as a gathering place of literary talents of the time.
3. The full title of this series of poems is: "To Dispel the Cold: The Seventh Collection—Summoning Friends to Gather at Morning Splendor Pavilion [Chao-

hua ko] to Write Poems As Responses to 'Poems on Spring' [''Sheng-ch'un shih''] in the *Ch'ang-ch'ing chi* [by Po Chü-yi].''

4. An-hsi *hsien* in Kansu province, belonging to the administration of present-day Tun-huang.

5. Chia-yü Kuan, located near An-hsi, Kansu province, at the western terminus of the Great Wall, had been a major fortification since Ming times.

6. Also called Su-lo River, in Kansu province, flowing from the northern foot of the Ch'i-lien Mountain into An-hsi.

7. Huo-shan, or Huo-yen Shan, is located in Sinkiang province, east of Turfan.

WU HSI-CH'I

(1746–1818)[1]

Wu Hsi-ch'i (*Sheng-cheng;* KU-JEN), a native of Ch'ien-t'ang (modern Hangchow), Chekiang province, obtained the *chin-shih* degree in 1775. After serving in a number of positions at the capital, he was appointed tutor to the imperial great-grandson and for several years worked closely with Yung-hsing (Prince Ch'eng; 1752–1823), the eleventh son of Emperor Ch'ien-lung. Several times in his life he left his official duties and returned home to support his parents. He was well known as a man of letters, and, as director of the An-ting Academy, he assisted in collating the *Chüan T'ang wen* (Complete T'ang Prose). In both his official and personal relationships he showed himself to be a man of integrity and humility. His collections of both prose and poetry won him great acclaim during his lifetime. In the area of prose he is best known for his *p'ien-t'i-wen*, or Parallel Prose; and he is one of the eight writers whose works were included in the *Pa-chia ssu-liu*, an anthology of balanced prose. As a poet he is best known for his *tz'u* and *san-ch'ü*. In working with these two genres he stayed very close to accepted traditions, writing mostly on themes such as nature, loneliness, love, and old age. However, in his poems he demonstrates a mastery of both language and technique and an unusual sensitivity to his environment. He combines poetic skill with a keen sense of emotional involvement and this is the basis for his success as a poet.

(Frederick P. Brandauer)

---

1. Rufus O. Suter, ECCP, 2:868–869.

Tune: *P'u-sa man*

Curtain hooks sway gently in the spring breeze,
And a thin overcast sets off the misty landscape.
Tiny blossoms fall from the cherry trees,
And someone crosses the bridge unnoticed.

Under the dew the deep green moss is wet,
And she stands alone in her unlined gown.
She finishes lighting the Daughter Incense,[1]
And she worships her shadow, making a pair.

(YCWCT, p. 1) *(Tr. Frederick P. Brandauer)*

Tune: *Ch'ang hsiang-ssu* (Eternal Longing)
Title: Colophon Written on the Flyleaf of a Book Sent to My Several Friends at Hsi-ling

Speak of our love,
Ask of our love.
The wild goose is late in departing as maple leaves fall in the river Wu.
Cold is the weather at Double Ninth time.

Who knows my complaints,
Who knows my dreams?
I'd send a sprig of plum blossoms if I could.
When the snows come, kingfishers take wing.

(YCWCT, p. 26) *(Tr. Frederick P. Brandauer)*

Tune: *T'iao-hsiao ling* (A Song to Induce Laughter)

Autumn rains,
Autumn rains—
Cold words falling on plaintain leaves.
Only when the waning moon appears at the fifth watch
Can I dream of returning from this distant place.
Dream of return,
Dream of return,
With a chorus of insects to send me off.

(YCWCT, p. 39) *(Tr. Frederick P. Brandauer)*

NOTE

1. Incense made from the plant *aquilaria sinensis,* so named because its cultivation is associated with women.

LI CHIEN

(23 MAY 1747–7 NOVEMBER 1799)

Li Chien (*Chien-ming*; ERH-CH'IAO), a native of Shun-te, Kwangtung, did not achieve fame in life beyond a select circle of friends who genuinely admired his genius. Son of a moderately successful businessman, Li was known as a prodigy at the age of nine; his poetic talent was later discovered by the bibliophile-scholar-official Li T'iao-yüan (1734–1803) who went to Kwangtung in 1777 as an assistant examiner. Yet, despite much encouragement, Li Chien only achieved the rank of a licentiate, as late as 1789. Suffering from asthma and frail health, Li spent his life among books and the hills and streams of his native province which he loved. Known also for his painting and calligraphy, he was often spoken of as one of the "Four Masters of Ling-nan" (the other three being Chang Ching-fang, Huang Tan-shu, and Lü Chien, all three among his closest friends).

Despite the lack of official distinction, however, Li was held in high regard by his contemporaries. The poet Yüan Mei (q.v.) was said to have invited him to come to Hangchow for a visit, which he declined. The poet Hung Liang-chi (q.v.) compared his poetry to the cry of an "enraged lion drinking from a mountain stream," or "the swift lightning illuminating a forest."

Li's oeuvre consists of 1,825 *shih* poems, written between 1771 and 1795, which he himself edited into twenty-five Chinese volumes (arranged one year per volume). This work was published in 1796, on the poet's fiftieth birthday, under the title *Wu-pai-ssu feng ts'ao-t'ang shih-ch'ao* (Poems from the Thatched Hall [Facing] Five Hundred and Four Mountain Peaks). At the time of his death, he also left two separate, smaller collections of his lyrics (*tz'u*) and his *yüeh-fu* poetry, respectively, under the titles of *Yao-yen-ko tz'u-ch'ao* (Lyrics from the

Pavilion of Steaming [Herbal] Medicine) and *Fu-jung-t'ing yüeh-fu* (Ballads from the Hibiscus Pavilion).

Li was fond of describing himself as *k'uang* (unconventional) and *chien* (simple and plain). In his poems on poetry, he compared the writing of poetry to a game of chess ("Be not mindful of ulterior purpose and forget fame"), or to the shooting of an arrow, or being engaged in battle. ("When the mind is quiet, it [the arrow] can hit the target of a myriad things": *ching p'o wan-wu ti.*) And he would quickly add, "No one can write a good poem without sincerity." Li's voice is distinctively his own; his verses evoke the virility of the T'ang poet Han Yü and also the sparseness of another T'ang poet, Meng Chiao. In the words of the poet-anthologist Wang Ch'ang (1725–1806), writing in 1803, Li's originality consists of "exercising his mind singly, with the result that he can say what has not been said by others" (*Hu-hai shih-chuan, chüan* 38).

(Hsing-sheng C. Kao)

Bent Willows

The river's waves reflect a bent willow,
Unbothered by the darkening sky at dusk.
If this tree can be said to hold a grievance,
Who hasn't felt the pangs of lost love?
I'm listless and the road home for a traveler is far;
And autumn winds rise after our leave-taking.
One day sporting a young girl's pearl coiffure,
This morning I dread to look into the mirror bright.

(WPSFTTSC, 11:27) *(Tr. Hsin-sheng C. Kao)*

My Little Garden

Reflections on the water catch the stirrings of dense trees;
The gleam of the mountain peeps over the short wall.
The village in autumn is covered with yellowing leaves,
A full half of them under the slanting sun's rays.
Secluded bamboos are as quiet as the visitor,
Blossoms in the cold air send forth fragrance for me.

It suits me to stand a while in my little garden:
The new moon is exactly like the new frost.

(Ch'ien, pp. 46b–47a) *(Tr. Irving Lo)*

Strolling under the Moon

Moonlight streams down unbroken until it ruffles my cloak;
Motionless is the visitor's shadow as he comes upon a brook.
The dew is still upon clusters of white rushes,
Much rain has turned the barren marshland green.
Among the shimmering waves waterbirds can be heard,
Amid darkened leaves, a steady glow of a firefly in the wind.
I remain sleepless under the paulownia-shaded eaves:
Mysterious is the night air upon the flowering wisteria.

(WPSFTTSC, 12:10b) *(Tr. Irving Lo)*

A Modern Poem in Response to "Wild Geese on the Lake" by Shen Yüeh[1]

They really scheme for millet and grain;
How can one say that they are high-minded and pure?
They only seek the grounds that aren't steep,
Knowing that they are fated to a life of toil.
Winter, summer: the difference between heaven and earth;
Up in the clouds or down in the mud: the selfsame feathers.
The year is late, the water in the field is shallow;
To sustain life is all I care for, as I look around me.
Let me say to the gulls and egrets in parting:
How often do we chance to meet in one's lifetime?
In the long journey ahead, think of your quiet companion,
In frost or moonlight, dreaming of mist and waves.

(WPSFTTSC, 23:12b) *(Tr. Irving Lo)*

The Dying Lamp

At fourth watch a single star peers over a cloud,
Here below, a dying lamp shines on us two.
My heart alone feels concern for heaven and earth,
Wearied and worn, the light pales in the wind and dust.

In the forest, cold and dark, a firefly glows,
The air almost red with a wild phosphorescence.
The sick woman weaves her silk into the dawn,
Making the scholars feel ashamed of their poverty.

(WPSFTSC, 12:15) *(Tr. Hsin-sheng C. Kao)*

NOTE

1. The original poem by Shen Yüeh (441–512) is included in *Sunflower Splendor,* p. 71.

HUANG CHING-JEN

(20 FEBRUARY 1749–25 MAY 1783)[1]

Huang Ching-jen (*Chung-tse, Han-yung*; HUI-TS'UN, LU-FEI-TZU) was a native of Kao-ch'un, Kiangsu province, and his family moved to Wu-chin when he was six years old. Although he came from a distinguished family—he claimed to be a remote descendant of Huang T'ing-chien, a disciple of Su Shih and one of the leading poets of the Sung dynasty—Huang Ching-jen led a short life plagued by continual poverty and repeated failures. In further contrast to his illustrious ancestor, who was particularly known for his close attention to formal excellence in his verse and for his respect for the T'ang poet Tu Fu, Huang Ching-jen was a romantic and expressive poet above all, and a self-conscious follower of Tu Fu's very different contemporary Li Po. Huang did succeed in passing a few low-level civil service examinations, but for most of his life he depended on the good will and patronage of others for his livelihood, a situation that lends a tone of bitterness and desperation to much of his work. The one successful facet of his career was literature, for he was widely recognized among his more discerning contemporaries, most notably by his close friend Hung Liang-chi (q.v.), as a genius in the realm of poetry. His early death and the emotional intensity of his poems inspired great sympathy for him after he was gone, and his work has been repeatedly published. Huang's poetry first appeared in print in Pi Yüan's *Wu-K'uai yin-ts'ai chi* (A Collection of Works of Genius from Kiangsu and Chekiang), 1793. In 1796, the poet Weng Fang-kang printed a collection of his *shih* as *Hui-ts'un shih-ch'ao.* A larger collection of the poet's oeuvre was printed in 1799 under the title *Liang-tang-hsüan shih-ch'ao,* which was reprinted many times in the nineteenth century. In 1858, his grand-

1. Chao-ying Fang, ECCP, 1:337–338.

son printed the complete works consisting of over 1,000 *shih* and more than 200 *tz'u*, as *Liang-tang-hsüan ch'üan chi* (Complete Works from the Studio of Two Proprieties), in 1876. Still unpublished, scattered poems were found, and they were included in a modern edition of *Liang-tang-hsüan chi*, published in 1983. In the same year, to mark the bicentennial anniversary of the poet's death, a memorial volume of the poet, *Chi-nien shih-jen Huang Chung-tse*, was also issued, consisting of poems and paintings by contemporary scholars and artists in the People's Republic of China.

(Daniel Bryant)

A Sail on the Lake after Rain

The wind picks up and the water grows rough and choppy;
My boat is light and the going begins to slow.
After fresh rain over the lake,
The time for mist to gather in a myriad trees.
Here is a stranger leaning on his orchid sweep;
Who is it singing a Bamboo Branch Song?[1]
The lotus girls have now all gone home;
Leaving only longing in the farthest reaches of the cove.

(LTHC, p. 15) *(Tr. Daniel Bryant)*

Dawn Snow

The Master's hut is as tiny as that of Wan-ch'iu[2];
Late in the year, it is dreary to listen to the sorrowful sound of the wind.
For a single night, the wind dies away and I get some peaceful sleep;
Leaden clouds have come to rest now down along the eaves.

As dawn arrives my feet aren't warm, even under several covers; 5
And yet how odd the light should pierce so through my paper window!
Wild with delight, a little boy comes bursting through the door
To announce that out in the vacant courtyard snow has drifted deep.

Scattered salt and drifting catkins are still thick and flurried,[3]
Cut off by only a sheet of paper, yet not a sound to be heard. 10

With a sheepskin robe on inside out, in the empty gateway I stand;
Glowing bright in my mind's eye is the cold without an end.

Now that inspiration strikes, the imps of sleep are gone;
This is my very first chance this year to see it snow.
I empty my purse—there is just enough to buy some village
brew— 15
Warm my inkstone and prepare to turn my verses loose.

Faintly humming, I muse abstracted, remember former companions,
When at the end of the year *ping-hsü*[4] I was on a boat to Wu-ling.
Crouched under a mat in the heavy snow, suffering with nothing to
drink,
For even now the furs of Ssu-ma Hsiang-ju are still in hock.[5] 20

Glancing back toward this scene as though in a flash of lightning,
All those meetings and separations gone in the twinkling of an eye.
The noble lord of Fan-yang[6] was a true hero in poetry;
When did he ever hold an inch of steel in "unarmed combat"?[7]

This snowfall must be less in amount than that on the hills of
Yen; 25
Plucking their lutes, the men of old sang when they were grieved.[8]
Who will come on this cold night to visit Shan Stream?[9]
If I wanted to go, just as it pleased me, what would I do?

What would I do? The snow won't stop.
Along with the wind it floats and soars, down and then back up; 30
Scattered over a thousand groves and into ten thousand hamlets.
A mountain monk holds his broom and looks up into the sky;
Yesterday evening in the empty kitchen there wasn't a grain of rice.

(LTHC, pp. 16–17) *(Tr. Daniel Bryant)*

A Note to My Friends, While Slightly Ill

Stinking drunk from morning to night, a thousand times over now,
I give offence to Ssu-ma Hsiang-ju's old diabetic innards.[10]
Beneath the lamp my worn-out shirt is streaked with wine and
tears;
Facing the wind my weary bones are at war with frost and ice.
I persist in poetry without necessarily growing thin from poetry;[11]
To prolong my illness has truly become my way of treating illness.
Since all that I have got wrong with me is really very minor,

There is nothing to keep you from dropping in for a chat beside my
hammock.

(LTHC, p. 62) *(Tr. Daniel Bryant)*

The Grave of Li Po[12]

When I bound up my hair I was reading your poems;
Now I have come to visit your grave.
A cooling breeze comes fresh and clean across the river;
And I should like by way of it to convey my humble homage.

Alas! That genius as great as yours could not escape from death! 5
I myself am firmly convinced that dying, you did not die.
The planet Venus fell to earth three thousand years ago,[13]
And here it is, apocalyptic ash from K'un-ming Pool.[14]

Your lofty headgear towering high and girdle pendants dangling,[15]
With brave adventures and vigorous swordplay, the genius within
your breast, 10
You smelted and forged Ch'ü Yuan and Sung Yü, combined with
the Greater Odes,
Brandished and scattered the sun and moon to create your flawless
lyrics.
In those days, though you were here, no place to make your mark;
And yet today your remnant relics are still remembered fondly.

When you were sober you toiled and moiled; when drunk—a
thousand poems! 15
It must have been the Creator itself making your hand its own.
Heaven and Earth had no occasion to enter your fond embrace;
Your only concern, the quest for transcendence—that and drinking
wine.

Throughout your life, you bowed your head to none but him of
Hsüan-ch'eng;
The gate of your tomb is directly across from the green of his Green
Hills.[16] 20
Your romantic spirit's radiant glow is today as long ago;
Also here is a donkey-riding sojourner from Pa Bridge.
Here in this place beneath the earth a truly excellent sight;
Small wonder the rivers and hills bring together so much living
beauty.

Rivers and hills to the end of time abide in the light of the moon; 25
Your drunken soul sank lower and lower, when called did not return.[17]
Brocade robe[18] and painted boat, alone with no one near;
Dim and dark the sound of a song encircling the river waters.
Remnant richness, enduring fragrance, were scattered in the six directions;
But active yet in the world of men, the Master of Ten Thousand.[19] 30

Omissioner Tu was a man who lived in the same age as yourself,
And yet his gravestone is set apart, on the banks of the Hsiao and Hsiang.
Once long ago on a southward voyage, I paid a visit there,
The clouds of Heng-shan were dense and unbroken as far as Nine Doubts Peak.[20]
Even when it came to a place to rest your bones when you were gone, 35
You proudly galloped off in another direction, as in the realm of verse.[21]
In the end, I am wary of that old man as too irascible and aroused;
The one I recognize as teacher is no one if not you.

For the hundred years of human life we ought to take our pleasure;
A thousand cups in a single day is nowhere near enough. 40
Laughing, I watch the woodsmen and herdboys talk in the setting sun;
Once dead I ought to be buried here at the foot of this very hill.

(LTHC, pp. 76–77) *(Tr. Daniel Bryant)*

A Caged Tiger: A Ballad

At the city gates in the New Year season, a hundred skills are displayed;
Fish and dragons and outlandish creatures, hardly a one is missing.
What could it be that brings out on the town the idle-handed lads,
To issue commands to a mountain lord become the sport of boys?

First they drag out a tiger cage, brought to the open field; 5
The city is emptied as an audience forms, tiered like a solid wall.
On all four sides they set up bars and lead the tiger out,
With furry paws and ears relaxed, his spirit unaroused.

First they pull on the tiger's whiskers; the tiger still submits;
Then they prop up a club on the ground and the tiger stands like a man. 10
The trainer shouts, the tiger roars, the noise is just like thunder;
With teeth and claws bared in a cluster; he rushes into the ring.

The tiger's mouth is agape in a yawn, as wide as a bushel basket,
Into which, as cool as can be, the trainer extends his hand.
Then he lowers his very own skull in front of the tiger's mouth, 15
As though he were serving it to the tiger, but the tiger will not eat;
A tigerish tongue laps the man as though it were lapping milk.
Suddenly leaning on the tiger's back, he grunts to make him go;
And then the tiger begins to run back and forth around the ring.

Rolling over, he scratches the ground, kicking the frozen dust, 20
His entire body changed with a shake to a blossom embroidered cushion.
Around and about in dancing poses, copied from a nomad whirl;
As though to bend his tiger's might and make it pleasing to men.

Then for a moment he lies on his back pretending to be dead;
But as soon as some meat is thrown before him he leaps to his feet in a flash. 25
The crowd of onlookers laugh out loud as they hurry to pool their coins;
Once the trainer has picked up the money, the tiger wags his tail.

Then he is driven into his cage—pride showing in his speed;
So happy is he to be inside, his mountain home is forgotten.
Obeying his trainer, the tiger allows the man to command him by nods; 30
Befriending the tiger, the man is covered with the last of the tiger's spittle.

As for me, I watch this sight feeling drained and depressed at heart;
Alas for you, my stupid slave, what a wretched sight you are!
You lack the wisdom to break out of your trap;
You lack the valor to smash your bars.
This churl is fed and clothed by you for all the rest of his life; 35
Is his power really the same as that of the Earl of Chung-huang?
How can his approval or anger equal those of Liang Yang?[22]
If you get only leftover food to eat, who is there to help you?
A shamefaced, tiger-chewed ghost[23] has now become your master. 40
If you were to meet with one of your old companions from the hills,

He would laugh at you in your traveling lockup, no better than a rat!

(LTHC, pp. 354–355) *(Tr. Daniel Bryant)*

NOTES

1. The title of a popular folksong.

2. Master Wan-ch'iu is a legendary person said to have been the teacher of P'eng-tsu, China's Methuselah. Su Shih once referred in a poem to Wan-ch'iu's study being as small as a boat.

3. This line alludes to an occasion in the Chin dynasty. Hsieh An (320–385) called upon members of his family to make up metaphors to describe the falling snow. His nephew Lang likened it to scattered salt, but An's preference was for "willow catkins," suggested by his niece Tao-yün.

4. I.e., 1766.

5. Once, when the Han writer Ssu-ma Hsiang-ju, best known for his *fu* (rhyme prose), was in financial straits, he pawned his fur robes and bought wine with which to celebrate with his wife, Cho Wen-chün.

6. The "noble lord of Fan-yang" is identified by a note in the original text as one Min Chen, a friend of Huang's.

7. An allusion to an incident in the Sung dynasty, when Ou-yang Hsiu (1077–1072) and some of his friends held a poetry competition during a snowfall. The rules stipulated that various common similes were disallowed. Su Shih later referred to the incident in a poem, one line of which goes, "In unarmed combat not allowed to hold an inch of steel."

8. See Ts'ao Chen-chi, notes 6–13.

9. Wang Hui-chih awoke after a snowfall and, struck by the beauty of the scene, was inspired to visit his friend Tai K'uei (d. 396), who lived on Shan Stream. When his boat arrived at Tai's house, however, he turned around and returned home. Asked why, he replied, "I went just because it pleased me and came back just because it pleased me; there was no need for me to see K'uei."

10. The Han writer Ssu-ma Hsiang-ju is recorded to have suffered from diabetes.

11. Li Po addressed a well-known poem to Tu Fu in which he remarks that Tu has grown thin because he "suffers from poetry."

12. Li Po's grave is located in Tang-t'u, Anhwei.

13. Because the planet Venus had appeared to his mother in a dream, Li's parents named him Po (white).

14. When a layer of ash was discovered during the excavation of K'unming Pool, in Ch'ang-an, a Buddhist interpreted it as being left over from a previous destruction of the world.

15. This line echoes a couplet from Ch'ü Yüan's *Li Sao*.

16. The Six Dynasties poet Hsieh T'iao (464–499), who had governed Hsüan-ch'eng and whose work Li Po greatly respected, was buried at the site of a residence he had built south of Green Hill near Tang-t'u. Li Po's grave was nearby. So too was Chia Tao, a Middle T'ang poet, who once encountered Han Yü while riding his donkey in the capital near the Pa Bridge.

17. See Ch'ü Ta-chün, note 3.

18. I.e., Li Po.

19. This couplet is derived from an early encomium on Tu Fu, who is explicitly named in the following stanza of Huang's poem.

20. Heng Shan is a mountain range in Hunan, one of China's five sacred mountains. Nine Doubts (*Chiu-yi*) Peaks, also located in Hunan, is the site of the grave of the legendary sage-king Shun.

21. Tu's grave was to the southwest, in Hunan. Although Tu Fu admired Li Po, his slightly older contemporary, their poetic styles are remarkably different.

22. The Chung-huang Earl and Liang Yang are animal trainers mentioned in early Taoist texts.

23. According to an old Chinese superstition, the ghost of a person killed by a tiger would be ashamed to appear in the nether regions, because disfigured by the animal's toothmarks, and so would serve the tiger as a ghostly attendant, aiding its depredations.

WANG TS'AI-WEI
(1753–1776)

Wang Ts'ai-wei (*Yü-ying, Wei-yü*), a native of Wu-chin, Kiangsu province, was the fourth daughter of Wang Kuang-hsieh (1711–1779), a district magistrate. According to her father, she was very intelligent as a child and fond of reading, and she distinguished herself early as an excellent calligrapher. Her father, surprised by her precocity, often hid her poems, believing that the writing of poetry was unsuitable for young women. At the age of nineteen, she was given in marriage to the famous scholar and bibliophile Sun Hsing-yen (1753–1818), who lived with her family during the first few years of their marriage.[1] Wang Ts'ai-wei was very much attached to her own family and wrote a number of poems lamenting the deaths of her second and third sisters. Believing that, like her sisters, she would die young, she seems to have lost her will to live. Having suffered from poor health, she died at the age of twenty-four after giving birth to a daughter.

Wang Ts'ai-wei's fame as a poet (along with Sun's devotion to her after her death) was widespread. Yüan Mei (q.v.), the leading poet of her time, for instance, praised her works as being "melancholy and moving" and "possessing a ravishing beauty of a primitive sort." He further described her verses as being "resonant, pure, and untrammeled." Her surviving oeuvre, consisting of thirty-six poems and one *tz'u* composition, was printed in a slim volume entitled *Ch'ang-li ko chi* (which may be found appended to her husband's collected works, *Sun Yüan-ju shih-wen chi* in the SPTK edition).

(Pao Chia-lin)

---

1. Lien-che Tu, ECCP, 2:675.

Since You Went Away

Since you went away,
Both of us have grown thin, unrecognizable.
My heart flames like flowing cinnabar;
How could I hold it, offer it up to you?

(CLKC, 1:1a) *(Tr. Irving Lo)*

Written in the Mountains

How blurred and misty are the pines in the evening!
The moon is too small to take off.
I know someone is holding the zither;
Moonlight falls at the bottom of a green curtain.
Dewy air brightens the curving precipice,
The flowers' radiance glows in the empty night.
Everywhere are the sounds of white clouds;
The splashing waterfall tumbles down behind a veil of mist.

(CLKC, 1:1a) *(Tr. Pao Chia-lin)*

Tune: *Tsui hua-yin*: (Tipsy in the Flowers' Shade)
Title: Written in Response to [My Husband] Wei-yin's Rhymes

Shrilly, the returning geese warn of the seaon's passing;
In an inn, even my thoughts of home tarry.
My dream enters the dawn clouds in flight,
Everywhere it is green, to the very edge of the world;
I fail to recognize the willow at the gate.

Beneath the dewy shadows of peach trees, I'm no longer the same;
Spring, too, should find it hard to endure.
Wind and sun, then it's Ch'ing-ming time again:
Alone I face withered petals of red,
Solitary hangs the curtain all day long.

(CLKC, 1:14a) *(Tr. Irving Lo)*

SUNG HSIANG
(1756?–1826)

Sung Hsiang (*Huan-hsiang, Chih-wan*), a native of Chia-ying, Kwangtung, belonged to no clique or school and achieved only regional fame in his lifetime as one of the leading poets of Kwangtung. In fact, his brief biography in the standard Ch'ing history makes prominent mention only of his reputation as a magistrate and his success in pacifying local uprisings. Yet, despite the relatively small corpus of his output, his poetry won the praise of modern critics, including Ch'en Yen (1856–1937), for its affinity with the style of the great T'ang poet Tu Fu. Later his works exercised a decided influence upon the poetry of his fellow townsman, Huang Tsun-hsien (q.v.)

Born either in 1756 or (according to another source) 1748, Sung passed his *chin-shih* examination in 1779 and, after a brief stint as a compiler in the Hanlin Academy, took up posts in the remote provinces of Szechwan, Kweichow, and Yunnan, either as examiner or as magistrate. He left six collections of his poetry, separately titled, and he also wrote prefaces to the various collections. His earliest collection, known as the *Pu-yi-chü chai chi* (Collection from the Studio of Not-So-Easy Living), derived its title from the name of another T'ang poet, Po Chü-yi, who frequently expressed his frustrations as an official in exile and over the plight of the common people. As is true of many of Po Chü-yi's poems, Sung's work is predominated by landscape poetry; he also prefers simple diction and often adopts an allegorical style. In his passionate defense of originality and spontaneity, however, he goes even farther than Yüan Mei (q.v.). He also shows greater daring in innovation with diction and prosody. His critical remarks on poetry include such unorthodox comments as, "Most people like what they like. Those who drink honey don't think of it as [overly] sweet; those who chew on the sugar cane don't prize its beauty. But honey will not lose its sweetness because some people don't like it, and neither will sugar cane lose its beauty because some people don't like it." Also to his credit, he is one of the few critics who openly expressed his admiration for the quatrains of Tu Fu (which traditionalists did not value as highly because of their prosodic irregularities), for Tu Fu (he wrote) "dares to be different."

(Irving Lo)

First Rain: Sent to Magistrate [Yi] Mo-ch'ing[1]

Shadows of bamboo hats beyond thousands of dikes,
Sounds of orioles all along the road—
The grasses' greening starts from today;
Flowers are again as red as the year before.
Tenderly, the farmers' hands on the plow handle,
Carefully, they skim off the water bugs.
Their constant worrying gives way to exhaustion;
Feebly, I offer consolation to my neighbor, the old man.

(No. 3 from a series of 4; HHSFYK, pp. 55–56) *(Tr. Irving Lo)*

Written on the Wall of the Flying Cloud Cave in Kweichow

The green mountain and I are old acquaintances;
Shouldn't the green mountain be able to recognize an old friend?
Just another October: autumn's crimson leaves;
Twice three years gone: a wanderer's white head.
Heaven's purple clouds[2] are only an illusion;
The roadside rill is also pure stream.
Never mind who said "[clouds] aimlessly rise from the peak,"[3]
The monk goes on striking the bell in a wind-swept tower.

(HHSFYK, p. 110) *(Tr. Irving Lo)*

On Poetry

I

Did every one of the three hundred poets[4] have a teacher?
Yet their unrivaled songs live in our minds and hearts.

People today never talk of water at the fountainhead;
Instead, they just ask: which current trend starts with whom.

II

Emulate Han, emulate Tu, emulate the bearded Su—[5]
Each commands a stage unlike any others.
Should someone be found wanting a song of his own,
Bells, drums, and pipes will all be for naught.

III

True, one must read ten thousand volumes until threadbare;[6]
A thousand chants of Buddha's name come down to emptiness.
How many aspiring brave men are there who must weep
That they are wearing out their lives, strangled by a brush?

Nos. 1, 5, and 8 from a series of 8; HHSFSC:TYK; p. 126) *(Tr. Irving Y. Lo)*

Upon Reading the Works of Tu Fu

He pledged himself to live with poetry until old age,
Assured that his words would spread long after he died.
His books, his sword followed him to every mountain and stream;
His singing, his weeping stopped the sun and the stars.
Could wind and dust alone have turned his head all white?
His heart poured out even for stragglers on the road.[7]
For a thousand autumns the moon above the surging river will
shine,
Utterly alone but also exquisitely beautiful.

No. 4 from a series of 4; HHSFYK, p. 5) *(Tr. Irving Lo)*

NOTES

1. The noted calligrapher-scholar-official Yi Ping-shou (1751–1815).
2. Most probably referring to success at the Palace Examination.
3. Alluding to the famous line about clouds by T'ao Ch'ien: *yün wu-hsin yi ch'u hsiu,* from the rhyme prose composition "The Return," translated by James Robert Hightower, in his *The Poetry of T'ao Ch'ien* (Oxford: Clarendon Press, 1970), p. 269.
4. I.e., *Shih-ching,* the earliest anthology of Chinese poetry, containing 305 poems, most of which are anonymous.

5. The T'ang poets Han Yü and Tu Fu and the Sung poet Su Shih.
6. Alluding to the famous couplet by Tu Fu:

> *Tu shu p'o wan chüan*
> *Hsia pi ju yu shen*
> (Only after you've read ten thousand volumes until theadbare,
> Then you can feel truly inspired when you write.)

7. Alluding to a famous poem of Tu Fu's, "Ai wang-sun" (The Unfortunate Prince), written in the autumn of 756, in which the poet recorded his encounter on the road with a royal prince, who had been abandoned by the fleeing court after the An Lu-shan Rebellion and the sack of the capital Ch'ang-an. Cf. David Hawkes, *A Little Primer of Tu Fu* (Oxford: Clarendon Press, 1967), pp. 33–44.

CHANG HUI-YEN
(1761–11 JULY 1802)[1]

Chang Hui-yen (*Kao-wen*), scholar, calligrapher, teacher, and poet, was a native of Wu-chin, Kiangsu province. Orphaned at the age of three, he was supported by his mother and an uncle in pursuing a classical education. He proved to be a child prodigy, and he began to teach at the age of thirteen. He received the *chü-jen* degree in 1786. The next year he became a tutor in a school for the nobility. Later, the death of his mother, which required his returning home to attend to her funeral arrangements, interrupted his career; and for a time he was associated with his fellow townsman Yün Ching (1757–1817), a master prose essayist. Together with Yün, Chang was known as a cofounder of the Yang-hu School of prose writing, rivaling the claims of the T'ung-ch'eng School under Yao Nai (q.v.), with a greater display of breadth of learning. Chang returned to Peking in 1799 to pass the *chin-shih* examination, and was later appointed as a compiler in the Hanlin Academy, after holding other minor posts. His life and career were cut short when he died of plague in 1802.

In addition to calligraphy, classical scholarship, and his reputation as a prose essayist, Chang is best known for his contributions to the study and composition of lyric poetry. Acclaimed for his archaic "seal" (*chüan*) style of calligraphy, Chang also wrote no less than twelve works of interpretation on the *Yi-ching*, exemplifying the approach taken by the Han dynasty scholars, in addition to other studies of the *Yi-li* (Decorum Ritual) and of the philosophical writings of Mo Tzu (fl. 479–438 B.C.). His most influential work, however, is the slim volume *Tz'u-hsüan* (Selected lyrics), printed in 1797, which he co-edited with his brother Chang Ch'i (1765–1833). A supplement to this anthology,

1. Man-kuei Li, ECCP, 1:42–43.

known as the *Hsü tz'u-hsüan,* was issued in 1830, with a preface by Chang Ch'i. The lyrics in these compilations were so selected as to illustrate the doctrines Chang and his brother advocated for *tz'u* writing; hence, this school came to be known as the Ch'ang-chou school.

The Ch'ang-chou school of lyric poetry insisted that the *tz'u* should primarily embody a serious social purpose—an allegorical meaning beyond the surface meaning of words—while expressing delicate, sensitive, deeply felt, and honest emotions. Chang frequently talks about *feng, sao, pi,* and *hsing,* the purpose of which is clearly to elevate the status of *tz'u* writing; and one quality he advocated for lyric poetry above all others is *han-hsü,* which may be translated as "decorum" or "restraint." Among the precursors of *tz'u,* for example, Chang had the greatest admiration for the T'ang poets Wen T'ing-yün (813?–870) and Wei Chuang (836–910); but he frequently errs by reading into some of their simple love lyrics a profound allegorical meaning. Despite this bias, however, many contemporary and later writers listened to his call for a more serious attitude toward lyric poetry as a result. His own reputation as a master of this form rests on a small collection entitled *Ming-k'o tz'u,* published in 1822. The best of his lyrics convey a lightness of touch and a certain freshness and delicacy, and they may well be cited to exemplify his critical theories.

(Michael Duke)

Tune: *Hsiang-chien huan* (Joy at Meeting)

I

Year after year, I've missed the season of flowers,
When springtime's past.
The only thing to do: sort out grief and bid spring farewell.

The snow of plum flowers,
Pear blossoms under the moon:
The same thoughts of longing.
So it is that no one senses spring's coming, only its leaving.

(No. 1 from a series of 4; MKT, p. 7) *(Tr. Irving Lo)*

II

Young warbler crying through the Festival of Tombs[1]—
Who's there to listen?
Even less the dawn wind, the night moon, and the cuckoo's call.

Holding spring back,
Hurrying spring away,
As though full of feelings.
Try to change into a pair of butterflies, and wake up embracing flowers.

(No. 4 from a series of 4; MKT, p. 8) *(Tr. Michael Duke)*

Tune: *Huan hsi sha*

A royal air comes from the east: hundreds of hard battles—
Travelers point to stained spots among earth-hugging blooms,
Just beyond a hill of almond trees, and another of pine.

After a hundred years war horses still yearn for border grasses;
Marching men, eyes filled with tears, sing the Sword Ring song.[2]
Which one of them dares look back on the battlefield?

(MKT, pp. 13–14) *(Tr. Irving Lo)*

Tune: *Man-t'ing fang* (Courtyard Full of Fragrance)
Title: Boating on Feng Stream[3] on the Double Fifth[4]

Clouds darken, then disperse;
The rain lessens, finally stops.
Rapid waters, newly risen, rush and roil.
Bamboo poles, light and swift—
We cross the level rapids easily. 5
A few village huts among the trees—
Tea pots and wine cups warm, amid a profusion of laughter and talk.
Above the sound of the stream,
A swath of slanting sunlight—
Quite numberless these green hills. 10

A place to think back on my old home:
Green oars, kingfisher feathers,

Pipes of jade and red sandalwood.[5]
Sad for ten years at sky's end,
Old dreams all cut off. 15
Some say our prime years are like flowing water;
Then let my thoughts of return
Follow again this mighty torrent.
But it's quite impossible:
Feng Stream's thousand turnings 20
Will never reach White Cloud Cove.[6]

(MKT, pp. 8–9) *(Tr. Michael Duke)*

Tune: *Shui-tiao ko-t'ou* (Prelude to Water Music)
Title: Composed on a Spring Day and Shown to Yang Tzu-shan[7]

The spring breeze[8] is a loafer
Whose handiwork is to adorn myriad blossoms.
Idly surveying here and there the shadowed flowers,
There's only the hook of a moon aslant.
I, the master iron flautist south of the Yangtze,[9] 5
Must lean against a branch of fragrant snow
To blow a tune through Jade City's[10] auroral clouds.
But vauge and fleeting is the pure image,
And flying floss fills Heaven's rim.

Let's drift away, 10
You and me,
Floating on a cloud-borne raft.
The God of Spring will smile and say,
"In whose home will this fine sentiment lodge?"
Could it be that spring flowers will again open and fall, 15
That spring breeze will again come and go,
And thus send away the prime of youth?
Beyond the flowers lies the road spring comes along;
It has never been obscured by fragrant grasses.[11]

(No. 1 from a series of 5; MKT, p. 4) *(Tr. An-yan Tang)*

NOTES

1. The Ch'ing-ming festival.
2. *Tao-huan* (the curved blade of a sword) may refer to a *yüeh-fu* folksong title, "Shih tao-huan ko," preserved in *chüan* 94 of the *Yüeh-fu shih-chi*. Or,

it could allude to some other familiar marching song. Etymologically, *tao-huan* is the name of an insect, its body made up of many rings, which lies on its side when it dies, therefore resembling the curved blade of a sword.

3. In Anhwei province where Chang was a teacher from 1796 to 1799.

4. The day of the Dragon Boat Festival.

5. All precious and elegant objects remembered from his home in Wu-chin, Kiangsu.

6. *Po-yün wan* may be either an actual place in the poet's home district or an image for a place of transcendent seclusion.

7. Probably a pupil of the poet. Otherwise unidentifiable.

8. The text reads *Tung-feng* (east wind), which is the prevailing wind in springtime.

9. The Master Iron Flautist refers to a recluse named Liu, of Wu-yi Mountain in northern Fukien, who is celebrated in a poem by the Sung Neo-Confucianist philosopher Chu Hsi (1130–1200). In the preface to the poem entitled "Iron Flute Pavilion," Chu mentioned that Liu was a frequent companion of a friend of his, Hu Ming-chung; and one day, with Hu and several other friends, he set out for the mountains to visit this musician. And before he arrived, he heard heavenly music from Liu's flute. During the Six Dynasties period, the appellation "Iron Flautist" was given to a man named Sun Shou-jung who was said to have gone blind at the age of six. He was later taught by a stranger, probably an immortal, the art of fortune-telling and, finally, of playing on an iron flute (before the teacher vanished).

10. The heavenly city of the Taoist Jade Emperor.

11. I.e., old friends.

CHANG WEN-T'AO

(26 JUNE 1764–1814)[1]

Chang Wen-t'ao (*Chung-yeh*; CH'UAN-SHAN), a native of Suining, Szechuan province, was born in Kuan-t'ao, Shantung, where his father was then serving as district magistrate. After winning the *chin-shih* degree in 1790, he held both local and national office. His outspoken manner eventually led to his resignation and retirement to Wu-hsien, Kiangsu.

Chang Wen-t'ao was acclaimed in his own times as an accomplished painter and calligrapher, and his contemporaries, such as the poet Yüan Mei and the scholar Hung Liang-chi (qq.v), spoke highly of his talents as a poet. In 1797, while employed in the Hanlin Academy, he requested leave to visit his family home in Szechuan, probably out of concern for the safety of his parents and family, for the White Lotus Rebellion had by then spread into that region. On his return trip, he recorded some of his thoughts on that massive uprising in a cycle of eighteen poems, which, according to the poet-scholar Chang Wei-p'ing (1780–1859), were widely praised. Somewhat obscure to the modern reader because of their topicality, these poems nonetheless reveal one dimension of the poet's mind—an interest in the problems of statecraft which were then coming under renewed scrutiny by the scholar-official class. Chang Wen-t'ao was a man of wide-ranging intellectual and artistic interests, and his poetic corpus, while not large by traditional standards, is many faceted. There are, of course, the usual occasional poems and set pieces; but there are also poems of a serious and thoughtful nature, those which are lighthearted and joyful in spirit, and still others which are movning and compassionate in tone.

---

1. J. C. Yang, ECCP, 1:59–60.

As a poet concerned with the larger problems of his art and craft, Chang Wen-t'ao manifested a desire, not altogether uncommon at the time, to free himself of the oppressive weight of traditional literary theories and practices. While acknowledging the valuable lessons to be learned from earlier masters and theorists, he nevertheless forthrightly declared, "I will employ my own methods,/Stand alone, reject all labels." In this respect, he added his voice to others of his time who were searching for a new poetics.

(William Schultz)

On Literature

I

To condone rotten rubbish is to deny the miraculous;
To seek a source for each and every word is bitterly tedious.
Can only sages fabricate lines like Master Tu?[1]
How I admire Pao Hsi[2] for that first stroke fashioned out of the blue!

II

A poem without a self is fit only to be excised;
Ten thousand volumes piled on a bed are of little worth.
Never imitate contemporaries who cover the wall with paintings,
And, when finished, talk of having copied the pictures of Ching and Kuan.[3]

(Nos. 1 and 7 from a series of 8; CCSTH; pp. 7b–8a) *(Tr. Irving Lo)*

Moving to the Cottage of Pines and Bamboo on the Third Day, Ninth Month of the *Keng-hsü* Year [10 October 1790], Two Poems.

I

Pure is the sandalwood incense—a good place to live,
But will the family furniture fill an entire cart?

I'll keep some material possessions, though a burden after I'm gone:
One shoulder basket of luggage, another of books.

II

This floating life—a grain of millet on a boundless sea!
And in the end, another village unlike my native place.
The chrysanthemums and me, together we wither and fall;
In divining a place to live, most suitable is the day of the Double Ninth.

(Nos. 1 and 2 from a series of 4; CSPCTP, 4:22b–23a) *(Tr. William Schultz)*

A Poem on Returning Home
[9 November 1792]

Five or six years ago I took a wife,
Planned to return home, but it could not be.
A boy was born, but suddenly he died;
A girl was born—now higher than my knee.

When I was granted temporary leave this winter, 5
Wife and daughter whooped as if crazy.
Hastily, carriage and horse were sought;
In an evening our luggage was packed.

In an evening our luggage was packed;
In five days' time we reached home. 10
Entering the gate, we saw the bamboo close by,
The bamboo close by made me rejoice.

Father and Mother, hearing their daughter-in-law had come,
Rejoiced as if their son had just taken a bride.
They comforted my wife and one another: 15
Next year they'd certainly have a grandson![4]

Sister-in-law, hearing that her niece had come,
Tied ribbons around pears and dates;
Took her niece to see Wan-jo;
Wan-jo was a beautiful child. 20

Younger brother, hearing that my wife had come,
Brought his wife to offer greetings:
"She can read *Admonitions for Women*,
And surely Elder Sister will be her teacher."

Elder brother's daughter, hearing her cousin had come, 25
Babbled on and on as if exchanging greetings:
Like an old scholar chatting about the *Golden Mean*,
But knowing nothing at all about the subject.

Female and male servants peeped in the door;
Chickens and dogs leapt upon the fence. 30
Guests beyond number, filling the gateway,
Honored me as if I had just been ennobled.

Honored me as if I had just been ennobled;
Drunk, I suddenly uttered a wild shout:
"I have an elder brother in the South Seas; 35
Should he return, wouldn't that be wonderful!"

The next day a letter arrived:
Elder brother had already passed Yü-chou.
The day after, a carriage arrived,
Wonderfully quick like a posted letter. 40

Flute and song filled the courtyard;
Elder brother had returned—the family was now complete!
The whole family, suddenly brought together.
Long ago parted, who knows how many years?

(CCSSH, 1:3b–4b) *(Tr. William Schultz)*

[On Calligraphy]

My script soars up, flies away, but I'm too drunk to know;
Dripping ink, the large graphs leap from the Heavenly Pool.[5]
Never mind the sun now rising from the eastern sea;
For eons and eons, divine light will illumine this verse.

(See illustration 6) *(Tr. William Schultz)*

NOTES

1. The common expression *tu chuan* meaning "fabrication" (still current today) refers to a legend about a poet named Tu Mo (though other versions of the story give the name of the poet as Tu T'ien or Tu Yüan) who wrote verses violating the strict rules of prosody.

2. Fu Hsi, the legendary inventor of the Chinese writing system.

3. "Ching" and "Kuan" refer to two famous painters, Ching Hao and his disciple Kuan T'ung, both of the Later Liang dynasty.

4. Author's note: "At this time they knew that my son had died only twenty-two days before."

5. Heavenly Pool (*T'ien-ch'ih*) alludes to a passage in the "Hsiao-yao yu" (Free and Easy Wandering) chapter in the *Chuang-tzu*, where it is mentioned as the habitat of the mythical fish called K'un. Compare Burton Watson's translation: "In the bald and barren north, there is a dark sea, the Lake of Heaven. In it is a fish which is several thousand li across, and no one knows how long. His name is K'un. . . ," in his *The Complete Works of Chuang Tzu* (New York: Columbia University Press, 1968), p. 31.

6. "On Calligraphy," by Chang Wen-t'ao. Courtesy of the Shanghai Museum, People's Republic of China.

SHU WEI

(1765–1816)[1]

Shu Wei (*Li-jen*; T'IEH-YÜN) was born in Soochow, Kiangsu province, although his father's ancestral home was in Ta-hsing, in Chihli province (around modern Peking). He first took the provincial examinations in 1782; however, he did not receive the *chü-jen* degree until 1788, and even after nine attempts he never succeeded at the *chin-shih* exams. He filled various lower-level bureaucratic and secretarial positions for the rest of his career.

Shu possessed great talent in a number of artistic endeavors. In addition to being a poet in the traditional *shih* mode, he wrote a series of *tsa-chü* (lyric dramas), six of which are extant. His interest in music extended to composition, and for some of his dramas he wrote both libretto and score, demonstrating a rare mastery of both forms. He himself played several musical instruments, and his poetry has been praised for its lyric quality. He also was a skilled painter and calligrapher.

Being a man of many parts, Shu had no great difficulty in finding employer-patrons. He was attached to the staff of Wang Chao-wu (*chin-shih* 1781) during a campaign (1797–1799) against the aboriginal Miao tribes in Kweichow. Later while in Peking he was introduced to Chao-lien (1780–1833), a Manchu imperial prince at whose mansion he staged some of his plays in collaboration with Pi Hua-chen. This relationship lasted three years, from 1809 to 1812. Shu died in the city of his birth in 1816 while in mourning for his mother.

Aside from the dramas mentioned above, Shu's works include over a thousand poems collected in the *P'ing-shui-chai shih-chi*. Among

---

1. Man-kuei Li, ECCP, 2:661–662.

these are a set of fifty-two poems with long descriptive annotations written in 1797 about the customs of the various Miao tribal peoples in Kweichow.

Shu wrote well in both the ancient- and recent-style verse forms. He used the ancient-style for serious reflections on his life, as in "Crossing P'o-yang Lake," and for poems in a humorous vein, as in "I Hate Mosquitoes." He seems to have used the ancient-style poetry also for poems on historical themes or events.

Shu excelled in the more lyrical recent-style poetry. A Japanese commentator has said that Shu's ancient-style poems are extravagant, but his recent-style verse is exquisite. Shu is particularly adept at evoking a mood within a landscape. A modern editor of Shu's works, Chiang Chien-jen, praises Shu by saying that he combines the surpassing talent of Li Po with the elegance of Tu Fu. Shu Wei is somewhat unconventional in relating the stories of the *Lun-yü* in verse form. In other poems, he manifests a skeptical turn of mind, and elsewhere he adopts a realistic, and occasionally a satirical manner in responding to contemporary events. Although profoundly aware of the greatness of the literary tradition which he had inherited, he refused to be bound by the past and sometimes reveals a flair for innovation.

(Barry L. Gartell)

Composed on a Moonlit Night Outing on Ancient West Lake [Lake T'ai],[1] Two Poems

I

The wind comes up, clouds depart, the moon just overhead;
The shore of Hsiao-hsia Bay is a link to white autumn.[2]
The same misty waves, and a night just the same—
Finally I am given a little skiff.

II

I neither trim the sail nor tend the mast;
Two oars delicately open frost blossoms on the water.
At midnight a cross wind blows without ceasing,
And green hills fly across Lake T'ai.

(Nos. 1 and 2 from a series of 5; PSCSC 11, 21a–b) *(Tr. Barry L. Gartell)*

Impressions of Things Encountered

My, my! My, oh my!
A hundred generations are but passing guests.
A hero prizes his word over yellow gold.
A moral man values himself more than a disc of white jade.
But should the white jade disc be flawed,
It's no better than tile or stone.
And though gold can be worn around one's finger,
It's only good when cut and sold inch by inch.
What is treasured is revealed in frost and snow:
How luxuriantly green stand the pine and cyprus trees.
If a white egret is not truly noble-minded,
Its feathers are pure and white for naught.

(No. 1 from a series of 4; PSCSC 1, 14b–15a) *(Tr. Barry L. Gartell)*

I Hate Mosquitoes

Mosquitoes come in stately rank,
Three by three or two by two.
Their needs I think are not too much,
But what care I for a little itch?
I don't begrudge their eating their fill, 5
I'm lucky they don't press close to my ear and buzz.
But, alas, they swarm and make their thunder!
Though already autumn, they still gang up.
Biting flies I chase away by day;
And frogs have made the nights hard to enjoy. 10
Yet you mosquitoes truly work in silence,
And gnaw at my flesh as if sacrifices were your due.
I'll repay your desire for warmth and food,
But please leave me to my own calm thoughts.
Slap! Slak! Why can't I swat you! 15
I too love my palms.

(PSCSC 7, 9a–10a) *(Tr. Barry L. Gartell)*

The Price of Rice, Two Poems

I

The price of rice this year is so dear,
A piece of silk vanishes like a goose in flight.

Steamed millet—a new dream rekindled;[3]
To abstain from rice, ancient recipes are few.
To beg for rice: there's Tsang Wen-chung;[4]
To corner the market: there's Lü Pu-wei.[5]
Myself but a single grain in the Royal Granary,
Dare I complain of hunger before the throne?

II

And so, wine and meat markets are proscribed,
But people still string nets to catch sparrows.
Is the meat of the roe deer really edible?[6]
After all, most everyone is sallow of cheek.
Perhaps only pigmies are fully fed;
And no one can rival the Ravenous Beast for gluttony.[7]
Do not despise the flavor of bamboo shoots and vegetables,
For with an empty belly, one can still sing long songs.

(Nos. 1 and 4 from a series of 7; PSCSC 16, 13a–b) *(Tr. Irving Lo)*

NOTES

1. Hsi Ku-hu, or Ancient West Lake, refers to T'ai-hu, which is associated with the life of Fan Li. See Wu Chia-chi, note 2.

2. Hsiao-hsia (Escape-from-summer) Cove, located in West Lake, is known as a place of refuge from summer heat.

3. Alluding to an ancient legend and the play *Huang-liang meng* (Yellow Millet Dream).

4. Also called Tsang-sun Ch'en (d. 617 B.C.), a statesman of the Warring States period, who served under four dukes of Lu and was known for his mercantile genius.

5. According to history, Ch'in Shih Huang-ti was the illegitimate son of Lü Pu-wei, a merchant who made his fortune in the marketplace.

6. The Chinese regarded venison as inedible.

7. *T'ao-t'ieh*: headless monsters who were always ravenous according to ancient legend, and as stylized figures, the common motif of Shang and Chou bronzes.

PART III

Poets of the Nineteenth Century

KUNG TZU-CHEN

(22 AUGUST 1792–26 SEPTEMBER 1841)[1]

Kung Tzu-chen (*Se-jen*; TING-AN), a native of Hangchow, has the distinction of being a leading poet and one of the most influential thinkers of his time. Much of this distinction he earned by virtue of his breadth of vision as a scholar and his extraordinary sensibility as a lyric poet.

The historical Kung Tzu-chen was a colorful personality and a man of many callings. Coming from an exceptionally learned family, he received a good foundation in the basics of traditional scholarship while still a young child. From his early teens on, he was steadily drawn into a variety of antiquarian pursuits, but soon found his most forceful voice as a social critic and political essayist. The rest of his career was divided between what he called "tending the flutelike heart" (poetry writing) and "wielding the sword" (political ambition). In his quest for a public career, however, he failed rather miserably. Through a string of ironies, including a handwriting that was not quite standard, he did not pass the *chin-shih* examination until 1829 (after five earlier attempts) and never rose beyond the position of a "minor official." In the early summer of 1839, after twenty years of residency in the capital and a series of inconsequential posts, he suddenly called a halt to the tedium and returned to his home in the south. To commemorate this "homecoming," he wrote during the subsequent months a total of 315 inter-echoing quatrains (*chüeh-chü*), in which he made a thorough review of his past career in the capital, the highlights in his intellectual life, the state of the nation on the eve of a major war, as well as his

1. Chao-ying Fang, ECCP, 1:431–434.

own state of mind as he was moving progressively from the past into the future. These quatrains, generally known under the title *Chi-hai tsa-shih* (Miscellaneous Poems of the Year Chi-hai), won instant acclaim for their stylistic novelty, depth of feeling, and concentrated range of reference; they have since remained the most widely read of Kung's poetic works. Two years later, shortly after the outbreak of the Opium War (1840–1842), Kung died in Tan-yang, near his native town Hangchow, leaving behind the prophecy that in realms of political thought and general scholarship, he would soon be remembered as a "starter of trends."

History did remember Kung Tzu-chen well and in more than one way. As a scholar, he is particularly known for his penetrating analysis of traditional society, and for his fervent advocacy of *pien* (change/reform) and *chih* (statecraft) as a countermeasure to the rapidly deteriorating social and political situation of his time. Both these ideas—*pien* and *chih*—have become cornerstones in modern Chinese thought; they have also inspired more than one generation of political activists, beginning with the late Ch'ing reformers. As a poet, he has many enthusiastic admirers, and has been alternately hailed as a synthesizer of the classical tradition and the harbinger of modern trends.

A critical appraisal of Kung Tzu-chen, however quick, will need to take into account three distinctive features. The most notable feature is his thematic concentration. In lieu of the disjointed moments of pure landscape modes, he reintroduced into Chinese poetry the relevance of biography by writing extensively about his immediate milieu and his own intellectual and emotional life, frequently dwelling on such intensely personal topics as childhood innocence, maternal love, Buddhism as an intellectual paradox, and Buddhism as a personal faith. This microscopic scrutiny of personal experience, when coupled with the recurrent use of private symbols, gives Kung's *shih* and *tz'u* an exceptionally dense range of reference as well as an orchestrated effect. Another feature is his fondness for conversational idiom and his subtle manipulation of speech rhythms within the confines of prescribed prosody. This is particularly noticeable in the *Chi-hai* quatrains, where the fluid rhythm and colloquial ease partially contribute to their charm as a spontaneous and continuous reflection on a life in motion. Finally, Kung Tzu-chen is also distinguished by his stylistic range and tonal complexity. At his finest moments, whether writing as a social critic or about personal experience, he is capable of fusing description with commentary, balancing thought against feeling, and moving freely along a tonal spectrum which ranges all the way from sardonic humor to tender sorrow. In the final analysis, it is this perennial tension between thought and feeling, this blending of tones and styles, that makes Kung Tzu-chen particularly attractive to the modern reader.

(Shirleen S. Wong)

In the City of Wu [Soochow], I Obtained a Record of Names [of Candidates] from the Civil Service Examinations Given in the Year *Wu-ch'en* [1628], during the Ch'ung-chen Reign of the Ming.[1] I Added This Regulated Verse at Its End as a Postscript.

When Heaven's about to withdraw its blessing, signs abound in examination halls.
In supporting scholars, fourteen Ming emperors played the patron.[2]
In times of turmoil, talents discoursed on grandiose topics,
A bundle of weedy writings became the only record of a historian!
Despite the nod of a red-robed judge,[3] none showed luster.
In a heap of faded black ink, seek a nation's rise and fall.
Before these men achieved their fame, the world had changed;
Half of them became martyrs, half became monks.[4]

(KTCCC, pp. 450–451) *(Tr. Shirleen S. Wong)*

Miscellaneous Poems of the Year *Chi-hai* [1839]

I

This trip shall take me through hills to the north and east.[5]
My image in the mirror looks passably young, still.
A white cloud floats along no fixed path:
Alone it visits the world, alone it drifts away.

II
I Saw a Professional Juggler by the Roadside and Presented Him with This Poem.[6]

You know this art well, but may I venture a thought
And offer you, Master of Illusion, an honest word.

Though the principle is hard to fathom, facts are plain to see:
Ten balls you've tossed up in the air, ten in all!

III

By chance I composed "Ascending the Clouds,"[7] by chance I grew tired of flying.
By chance I longed for leisure, and here I am in my layman's robe.
If by chance I meet a lady with a patterned Lute,[8]
I'll say: "It's for you and the spring I've returned."

IV

Tending a bare hill takes no small talent;
A poet's mind flows from a painter's eye.
Those low camelia close together, this soaring pine alone—
Remember, it was I who put them where they are.

V

View phenomena as void, view phenomena as appearance, such is the ultimate view.[9]
Buddha's words and the truth of the phenomenal world are not the same.
But human life does have past, future, and the now:
As I lie under an eave, listening to the flowers fall till autumn's half gone.

(Nos. 4, 19, 135, 202, and 226 from a series of 315; KTCCC, pp. 509–530)

(Tr. Shirleen S. Wong)

Tune: *Pu-suan tzu*

There is a tall tower by the river.
Is it as secluded as the tower by the lake?
Beyond that tower, gentle ripples spread, ring after ring,
Staying not even the shadow of a startled wild goose.

Duckweed leaves flirt with the slanting sunlight,
Orchid buds wilt in the bright mirror.
Nipping every autumnal bloom, the cold air hangs heavy,
And someone lies ill south of the river.

(KTCCC, p. 574) *(Tr. Shirleen S. Wong)*

NOTES

1. Only sixteen years before the fall of the Ming dynasty.

2. Of the sixteen Ming emperors, only fourteen were given imperial burial, thirteen near Peking.

3. The "red-robed judge" alludes to a legend which features the Sung scholar-statesman, Ou-yang Hsiu. It is said that one day when Ou-yang was grading a set of examination essays, he was vaguely aware of someone in a red robe standing behind him and offering him assistance. The man in red allegedly nodded his head from time to time; each time the nod sealed Ou-yang's favorable opinion of the essay he was reading.

4. The poet seems to be suggesting that, though these late-Ming scholars may be lowly in status and lacking in intellect, they at least had the moral sensibility not to capitulate to the alien conquerors as did some of the ranking Ming officials. Some descendants of the Ming royal house, such as the painter Chu Ta (ca. 1626–ca. 1705), as well as many late-Ming literati—e.g., Ch'ü Ta-ch'ün and the scholar-official Fang Yi-chih (d. 1671?)—also chose the route of monastic retreat instead of declaring their allegiance to the new dynasty.

5. "Hills to the north and east" (Tung shan and Pei shan) may allude to two poems in the *Shih-ching*—both of which lament the plight of soldiers and officials separated from their families. The two terms may also refer to the Tung Shan associated with the Tsin statesman-general Hsieh An and the fictitious Pei Shan immortalized by K'ung Chih-kuei's (448–501) *Pei-shan yi-wen* (Proclamation of the North Mountain). In that case, they suggest retirement and reclusion.

6. This is an example of how Kung Tzu-chen can turn a trivial incident, real or imagined, into an occasion for allegory. The "Master of Illusion" in the second line may allude to the Ch'ing government, whose act of balancing ten balls in the air vividly captures the precarious situation it was in at the time of the poet's departure from the capital in 1839, one year before the outbreak of the Opium War.

7. "Ascending the clouds" alludes to the *Ta Jen Fu* by Ssu-ma Hsiang-ju, written for the perusal of the author's royal patron, Emperor Wu of Han. The emperor allegedly was so entranced by the rhetoric of the composition that in his mind's eye he began to "take on wings and ascend to the clouds."

8. "A lady with a patterned lute" (*chin-se chia-jen*) echoes the last line of a poem by Tu Fu: *Ch'ü-chiang tui-yü* (Facing the Rain at Ch'ü-chiang).

9. This line sums up the doctrine of the T'ien-t'ai School of Buddhism, which stresses that the phenomenal world is both empty or void (*k'ung*) and apparent (*chia*), and that these two views of reality can exist in a single instant of thought.

WEI YÜAN

(23 APRIL 1794–7 APRIL 1857)[1]

Wei Yüan (*Han-shih; Mo-shen; Mo-sheng*) a native of Shao-yang, Hunan, was a versatile genius and something of a prophet of a new age. He wrote some of the finest landscape poetry in Chinese literature. "Nine-tenths of my poems deal with mountains and waters," he said, and he left about a thousand poems. Yet his fame as a poet has been sharply eclipsed by his accomplishments as a historian, geographer, exegete of Confucian classics (he belonged to the "Modern Text" school), essayist, and political economist, as well as a student of Buddhism later in life. To add to the mystery and wide range of his life's callings, he was also said by his contemporaries to have been the real author of a book of literary criticism, published under the name of his best friend and to which he had merely contributed a preface. The book, *Shih pi-hsing-ch'ien*, ostensibly by Ch'en Hang (1785–1826), was published in 1854.

Son of a minor Kiangsu official, Wei Yüan passed the *hsiu-ts'ai* examination at the age of fourteen, and so impressed his examiner when he passed the *chü-jen* examination, in 1822, along with the poet Kung Tzu-jen (q.v.), that the examiner wrote a poem in praise and recommendation of the two scholars. Yet Wei Yüan repeatedly failed the *chin-shih* examination; finally, in 1844, when he was fifty, he passed and was placed in the third class of graduates as the result of the Palace Examination a year later. But his lack of success on the official ladder was more than compensated by the appreciation he received from friends and peers for his literary and scholarly abilities. It was his distinction to contribute importantly to the revival of *Ching-shih* (Practical Affairs) studies in the nineteenth century. For example, soon after

1. Lien-che Tu, ECCP, 2:850–852.

1822, he was given the task of editing government documents on political and economic affairs, the *Huang-ch'ao ching-shih wen-pien,* a task he completed in 1826. In 1842, he finished writing a history of Ch'ing military operations up to the Tao-kuang era, which was published under the title *Sheng-wu chi.* He next undertook a major revision of the history of the Yüan dynasty, the *Yüan-shih hsin-pien,* which was completed in 1853 though not published until 1905. After the defeat of China by the British in the Opium War, Wei began compiling a geography of foreign nations, by consulting translations from Western periodicals, which was published under the title of *Hai-kuo t'u-chih,* (An Illustrated Gazetteer of Countries beyond the Sea) first in fifty *chüan* in 1844, and later twice augmented (1847 and 1852) to sixty and then one hundred *chüan.* Portions of the *Hai-huo t'u-chih* and the *Sheng-wu chi* were translated into English and Japanese during his lifetime. In between these larger undertakings, Wei had time to write more than a dozen exegetical treatises on the *Lao Tzu,* on various Buddhist sutras, and on the Confucian classics, which he began to study under the leading "Modern Text" scholar Liu Feng-lü (1776–1829) when he was a student in Peking in his early twenties. His collected poems, in ten *chüan,* were published in 1870 under the title *Ku-wei-t'ang shih chi* (Poems from the Hall of Ancient Antiquities).

(Irving Lo)

Song of Chiang-nan:[1] Two Selections

I

"Plant the flower farms,
Plant the flower farms!"
At Tiger Hill, for ten leagues around, all along the canal—
Roses bloom in the spring breeze, azaleas in the summer,
Jasmines in the hottest summer days, and lotus in early autumn; 5
Showers of crimson in the forest perfume the entire river.
"Picked in the morning, blooms by night;
Picked at night, blooms in the morning."
Flower gatherers come at the crack of dawn,
Flower peddlers' boats return by night. 10
"When you have your own fields, why not grow rice and grain?"
"The autumn harvest can't meet the double-tax payments.[2]
Foreign silver soars in price, and official measures grow larger.[3]

After meeting the official quota, what's left but dried stalks?
Rice fields have become so cheap no one wants them; 15
Turned into flower farms, they give me double profit.
The lower fields are too damp, unfit for flowers;
Some folk run away from debt, leaving water lily sprouts."
Alas! extravagance abounds in the city, more than in ancient Wei and Cheng;[4]
People outside the city toil harder than the ancients of T'ang and Wei. 20
Travelers know only to praise the elegance of Soochow folks;
Flower growers alone remain to weep for growers of rice.

II

Ah-fu-jung, ah-fu-jung![5]
A product of the West,
Shipped to the eastern lands—
I know not how many countries had smelled it in the wind
Before it came to titillate our men and women like strong liquor. 5
At night, they see no moon or stars;
Nor the bright sun at day—
They make for themselves a perpetual night, a Never-Never Land:[6]
A kingdom of enduring darkness,
A lake forever without grief,[7] 10
In a den of pleasure purchased with gold, the Universe is forgotten:
Where the Six Directions are merged,[8]
Where the Nine Districts become one;[9]
The nobility behind crimson gates,
The humble in their hovels— 15
They dull their senses to *addiction*, what's to be said?
But whose fault that the national wealth is squandered, defenses collapse?
Let me say to you: don't put all the blame on the *ah-fu-jung*!
Palpable, or vanishing in smoke—*addiction*[10] leads to the same result.
Border officials have their *addiction*: it's called "trafficking in poison"; 20
High ministers have their *addiction*: it's called the "Golden Mean."[11]
Scholar-officials are parrots who speak clever words by rote;
Finance ministers, like Yang the Tiger,[12] steal treasures from the state.

If only the court could cure the *addiction* of the great officials,
The smoking of opium would be instantly eradicated. 25

(Nos. 1 and 8 from a series of 10; WYC, 2:670–673) *(Tr. Irving Lo)*

On the Chia-ling River[13]

Evenings, I lodge with the evening mist,
At dawn, I sail with the dawn wind.
The sounds of the scull shatter my dream,
While boatmen talk beneath a waning moon.
Perching fowls fly up from shallow banks; 5
Last night's fog merges with the hill in front.
Thus a reed mat's width of water is made
To look as distant and faraway as Lake P'eng-li.
Abruptly turned about by the current in midstream,
I find myself cut off from a solitary island. 10
Dimly I begin to discern trees on the bank,
And then the sun emerges clearly on the river.
Longing to return home, yet I forget all thoughts of return:
The dawn clouds above the river distress a traveler's heart.

(No. 3 from a series of 3; WYC, 2:626) *(Tr. Irving Lo)*

Remembering the Past at Chin-ling[14]

Naught remains of the dying glow, past and present, on the waters of Ch'in-huai;
Many a hero ground to dust by Tsin's Stone Head Citadel.
Terrestrial spirits depart time and again with the vanishing of the royal aura;
The departed ones bequeath to future generations only grief.
Wu and Yüeh of the "Spring and Autumn" era: ramparts viewed in lamplight;
Kiosks and pavilions of Ch'i and Liang: children's songs heard in a mist.
Most melancholy and full of feeling is the moon in the sky:
Year after year, it lingers lovingly over Yeh city in autumn.[15]

(No. 2 from a series of 8; WYC; 2:803) *(Tr. Irving Lo)*

Sitting in Meditation at Night, Facing Hui-shan[16]

Everyone says the autumn moon is lovely—
Lovelier still when its light falls on a mountain stream.

Shadows of trees sink into the shadows of the cliffs;
Sounds of the stream are lost in the sounds of rain.
Only by degrees I sense the sky to be dawning;
I hardly notice the water's widening gleam.
Should visitors fail to disperse and leave,
Who's there to know the mountain air is pure?

(No. 3 from a series of 3; WYC; 2:777) *(Tr. Irving Lo)*

NOTES

1. This series of ten poems entitled "Chiang-nan yin" was also given a subtitle by the poet: "*Hsin Yüeh-fu* [New Music Bureau Songs], in Imitation of Po Hsiang-shan's [Po Chü-yi's] Style." By definition, a *hsin yüeh-fu* poem must deal with contemporary events, and the style involves the use of irregular meter and dialogue. Tiger Hill, or Hu-ch'iu (line 3), is a famous scenic spot seven *li* northwest of Soochow.

2. Starting in 1723, at the beginning of the Yung-cheng reign, Chinese farmers were taxed twice a year, in the spring and fall.

3. Between 1830 and 1838, because of the heavy flow of silver abroad to pay for the importation of opium, silver gained 60 percent in value against the native currency. "Official measures" refers to the standard used to measure grain when collected as tax by the government. During the same period, one *hu*, equivalent to ten pecks or piculs in former times, was decreed to be equal only to five pecks or piculs.

4. Cheng and Wei were two states in ancient China censured by Confucius for their alleged taste for lascivious music. T'ang and Wei, two states in Shensi province, were noted for their hardworking and frugal people.

5. *Ah-fu-jung* is the Chinese name for opium, so called because the flower of the opium poppy was said to resemble the hibiscus or *fu-jung*.

6. *Hsiao-yao kuo*; literally, "pleasure roaming" country, was probably coined from the Taoist phraseology *hsiao-yao yu*, or "free and easy wandering."

7. See Wang Shih-chen, note 17.

8. The traditional Chinese three-dimensional concept of spatial direction: East, West, North, South, up, and down.

9. The ancient division of China into Nine Districts.

10. A note supplied by the poet to this word reads: "The word *addiction* or *yin* [Morohashi, 7:22631] in the vulgate speech, referring to opium addiction, is not found in the dictionary. Hence, I borrow another word from the *Shuo-wen*, the word that means 'carbuncle or swelling' " (Morohashi, 9:29300; cf. *Shuo-wen chieh-tzu*, 5b:10a). Since this word may also be pronounced *yin*, it is possible to imagine that the poet intends a pun with the four words preceding it in this line, which read *yu-hsing* (literally, "having form," probably meaning "palpable to the touch") and *wu-hsing* (literally, "formless," i.e., "existing without shape or form").

11. The term used by the poet here is *chung-yung*, also the title of one of the "Four Books" in the Confucian canon. Literally meaning "showing no

partiality or bias," this concept had by the mid-nineteenth century been reduced to such trite expression that the poet considered it as the root cause of all of China's troubles.

12. The name used by the poet here is Yang-hu, alluding to the corrupt official of Lu, also called Yang Huo, mentioned in *Lun-Yü,* as a dishonest officer who served the Chi family. He once stole the precious jade-studded bow, a treasure of the state of Lu.

13. A river in Szechwan that flows into the Yangtze, near Pa Hsien.

14. The modern-day city of Nanking is also known as the Stone Head Citadel. The Ch'in-huai River once flowed through the capital's most prosperous district. See Ch'ien Ch'ien-yi, note 4.

15. The city derives its name from a hill west of Chiang-ning county in Kiangsu, originally the smelting center of the Kingdom of Wu. Later a Taoist temple was built there, and visited often by men of lofty mind and principle, such as the famous calligrapher Wang Hsi-chih (320–379) and Hsieh An, who were said to have climbed the hill together.

16. A famous mountain near Wusih, Kiangsu province.

HSIANG HUNG-TSO

(1798–1835)

Hsiang Hung-tso (*Lien-sheng*) is also known by the name Hsiang T'ing-chi (his earlier name was Hsiang Chi-chang). A native of Hangchow, Chekiang, he was born into a wealthy salt merchant's family which was, however, beginning to decline. He lost his father early in life, and became known as a reclusive and somewhat eccentric individual. He passed the provincial examination in 1832, earning his *chü-jen* degree. He made a journey north by boat, during which time the boat capsized and his mother and a nephew drowned. This tragedy, coupled with his subsequent failure at the *chin-shih* examination, might account for the deeply melancholy mood of his poetry. His collection of lyrics, the *Yi-yün-lou tz'u* (Remembering Clouds Lyrics), published in 1835, and consisting of four series, chronologically arranged, won wide fame among his contemporaries. Although many of his lyrics are stylized and derivative, some contain striking imagery and flashes of insight.

(Irving Lo)

Tune: *Yeh Chin-men*

Title: In Imitation of Sun Kuang-hsien's [Style][1]

I can't keep you here:
E'en if I could, it would be just for today.
Today your taut sail lies a few feet from me;
Tomorrow where can it be found?

On the river the tide is not yet in, though the wind is blowing hard,

Drowning the fading strains of a flute.
A desolate chill seizes me as I lean against the railing;
Black night robs me of sleep as the lamp wick gives out.

(YYT, p. 59) *(Tr. Irving Lo)*

Tune: *Ts'ai-sang tzu* (A Mulberry-Gathering Song)
Title: Sent to Wu Tzu-lü[2] Who Wished to See My Recent Lyrics

A tree reddens in the frost; the setting sun chills;
Falling leaves startle away the cicada;
Withered grasses indistinguishable from mist.
For a tired man, coping with autumn, only unfinished dreams come to his pillow.

For flitting fame, versifying has played me false—
Indulging myself in wine and song.
My affinity with the flowers and the moon,
When etched on lined paper, can only plead for human tears.

(YYT, p. 10) *(Tr. Irving Lo)*

Tune: *Huan hsi sha*

Wind-tossed catkins fly past a silken blanket of green;
Willow strands too weak to snare the dying spring into staying—
The same weather last year, but not the same people.

In secret, a cicada-embossed letter
wipes out my tears falling on paired pillows;
In grief, my message for the wild geese
is locked in the strings of a dust-covered lute:
Just forgetting the past is a kind of torture.

(YYT, p. 4) *(Tr. Irving Lo)*

NOTES

1. Sun Kuang-hsien (?-968), a prominent lyric poet whose sixty *tz'u* are included in the *Hua-chien chi* (Among-the-flowers Collection), the earliest *tz'u* anthology noted for its boudoir poetry. The original lyric by Sun, with the same tune title, goes as follows:

I can't keep you here:
E'en if I could, it would be of no use.
His springtime gown of white gauze is the color of snow
On the day he sets off for Yangchow.
He makes light of parting, delights in abandoning me.
On the river, the full sail is blown by a swift wind.
How much I admire those parti-colored mallards, all thirty-six of them!
A single female phoenix is all alone.
[*Hua-chien chi,* 8:9b]

2. An unidentified friend of the poet.

HO SHAO-CHI

(1799–11 SEPTEMBER 1873)[1]

Ho Shao-chi (*Tzu-chen;* TUNG-CHOU, YÜAN-SOU) was a native of Tao-chou, Hunan province. After he received his *chin-shih* degree in 1836, Ho pursued an official career, serving as a member of the Hanlin Academy and in numerous local government positions all over south China. In 1852 while serving in Szechwan province, Ho was removed from his post for criticizing the central government. He spent the rest of his life teaching in local academies and eventually settled in the city of Soochow, where he supervised a publishing firm and edited the *Thirteen Classics*. During his own lifetime, Ho was perhaps even more famous as a calligrapher than a poet (he and three brothers were all famed for their mastery of this art form), and today he is considered one of the greatest nineteenth-century calligraphers with a highly original style derived from intensive study of Wei and T'ang dynasty inscriptions.

Ho Shao-chi was a major figure in the nineteenth-century revival of interest in Sung dynasty *shih* poetry, and the influence of the great Sung masters is evident in the spontaneity and *joi de vivre* of Ho's verse. Although his poetry covers a wide range, his most delightful poems are surely his descriptions of the Chinese landscape, written during his extensive travels. Unlike some of the more innovative nineteenth-century poets, Ho's works, collected under the title *Tung-chou ts'ao-t'ang shih-ch'ao* for *shih* style poems and *Tung-chou ts'ao-t'ang shih-yü* for *tz'u* poems, seldom touch on social or political themes, but his warm sense of humor makes up for any apparent deficiencies in this area. In the preface to his complete poetic works, Ho wrote: "I neither enjoy nor presume to write heroic, ornamented, or critical lines."

---

1. Man-kuei Li, ECCP, 1:287–288.

Although he has been somewhat unfairly taken to task by contemporary critics for his lack of social criticism, the naturalness and simplicity of Ho Shao-chi's verse is difficult to resist.

(J.D. Schmidt)

I Love Mountains

This poet loves mountains like his own flesh and blood;
All day he opens his door to gaze, can't get his fill.
There were originally no poems in this poet's belly,
So every day he reads green mountains just like a book.
I've been north of the Hsiang River for half a year; 5
Peaks twist, crags bow, leaning on each other.
Mountain mists, turquoise hues, captivating as rain,
Fly to me and drench my traveler's robes.
Then I recall jet-black worldly dust deep as the sea,
Totally absent from thoughts of mountains and water. 10
I know too well my face and eyes are dirty, defiled,
So, facing these green mountains, I'm ashamed of myself.
When a poet who loves mountains doesn't live in the mountains,
He doesn't understand mountain thoughts; how churlish!
White clouds send this traveler across the river, 15
While the green mountains stand eternally, looking compassionate.

(Chen, pp. 77–78) *(Tr. J.D. Schmidt)*

Mountain Rain

In my bamboo rainhat, I avoid tree branches dripping with dew;
The first cool weather, just right for a country excursion.
Mountain torrent clouds gather everywhere by themselves,
And mountain rain arrives suddenly before you know it.
Riding on horseback, I let my hat and robe get drenched;
Melons and beans by the village side are scattered, scraggly.
The weather clears, peaks and crags emerge;
Myriad waterfalls fly in unison, just one more miracle!

(Chen, p. 86) *(Tr. J.D. Schmidt)*

A Contrary Wind

A cold rain beats the river, the wind's contrary, too;
The boatmen get mad at me for constantly opening the door:
"Listen, if it weren't for the green mountain hues,
Why would *I* be bouncing around midst the white waves?!"

(Chen, p. 111) *(Tr. J.D. Schmidt)*

Samantabhadra Facing Westward[1]

Can this night be tonight?
Can this village be real?
Once we reach the top of Mount Omei,
We can feel perplexed to no end.

To the east we gaze at Honan and Shantung, to the west tribal land; 5
To the north we behold Shensi and Shansi, to the south Hunan and Hupeh.
But, for upwards of five years, in my reckoning,
All these places have been turned into battlefields.
All I can see: cities in ruins, subjects maimed;
Brave generals killed, weakling ministers fleeing; 10
Yamens and temples turned into scorched earth;
Women, children driven hither and yon like sheep!
People's wealth commandeered into the treasury!
Broiling one's own flesh will not cure an ulcer.
Calamities not averted, how can you be the King of Spirituality?[2] 15
Bandits not slaughtered, how can you be the true Vajra?[3]
Of late, the greater barbarians wriggle and plot,
Coveting our stronghold, encroaching upon our territory.
Why can't you put them to the torch with your Wisdom's Flame?
Why can't you wave your shining Sword of Intelligence? 20
Control, subdue them with the strength of a true and brave Vajra?
Soften, transform them with mercy and compassion?
And yet you've claimed for your own this clean, quiet place;
Keeping quiet, looking down on the hurly-burly of mankind below!

At the foot of the mountain, thousands and tens of thousands, 25
All year long come to burn incense before their Buddha.
Children follow on grandfathers' and grandmothers' heels;
They spend the night in cold corridors, under rain;
They sell off grain or silk for money,

To provide meals to feed the monks. 30
Greater hardships are in store for travelers to foreign lands;
For myriads of miles, they walk through rain and frost.

My heart's in turmoil, there's no recourse;
Coming here to complain to Buddha, isn't it preposterous?
The bodhisattva, too, is deserving of pity; 35
His radiance long gone, he sits ashen-faced.
Glum like wood, sorrowing, and facing west,
He dares not turn his head to look eastward;
For ten thousand years, stiffly sitting, watching the sunset.

(Ch'en, p. 99) *(Tr. Irving Lo)*

NOTES

1. I.e., P'u-hsien, the Chinese name for Samantabhadra Visvabhadra, Lord of the Fundamental Law of Buddhism. He and Manjusri are the right- and left-hand assistants of Buddha, respectively representing Law and Wisdom. He rides on a white elephant and is the patron of the Lotus Sutra and its devotees. His region is in the east, and he is usually represented with a sword, indicative of the Law as the basis of Wisdom. The temple to P'u-hsien, who is seated on a huge white elephant, is located in Wan-nien Monastery on Omei Mountain in Szechwan. It is still visited by worshippers today, and it is also a mecca for foreign tourists.

2. The text reads *k'ung-wang*, which, in Buddhism, refers to the king of immateriality or spirituality—Buddha, who is lord of all things.

3. The text reads *chin-kang*, Vajra or Thunderbolt, or any one of the beings represented with the Vajra, employed by the esoteric sects as a symbol of wisdom and power over illusion and evil spirits.

KU T'AI-CH'ING

(1799–1876?)

K'u T'ai-ch'ing (*Tzu-ch'un;* YÜN-CH'A WAI-SHIH), a Chinese bannerman in ancestry, is also known by her Manchu name of T'ai-ch'ing Ch'un. As a favorite concubine of the Manchu prince Yi-hui (1799–1838), who was also a poet, she shared with him a life of travel and literature and the arts.[1] After his death, she and her children were expelled from the family mansion by one of his sons by an earlier wife, who had inherited his father's title as Prince Jung. Suddenly fallen into poverty, she had a difficult time but managed successfully to raise her seven children, all of whom she married off to noble families. In 1875 she went blind. The suffering she endured in her late years can be detected in her verse, some of which contain Buddhist overtones.

Ku T'ai-ch'ing is said to have left seven *chüan* of *shih* poetry, entitled *T'ien-yu-ko shih-chi* (Poems from the Heavenly Wandering Studio), and four *chüan* of lyrics, entitled *Tung-hai yü-ko* (Fisherman's Songs from the Eastern Sea). The Japanese scholar Suzuki Torao records that he saw the entire collection, and the manuscript may still be in Japan. Chinese printed sources, however, have preserved less than half of her oeuvre. As a *tz'u* writer, Ku is sometimes considered the equal of Singde (q.v.) and a worthy successor of the Sung poet Chou Pang-yen (1056–1121). Stylistically, her poetry, both *shih* and *tz'u,* departs from the ornately allusive manner and favors the natural rhythms of simple speech and direct expression.

(Pao Chia-lin)

---

1. Chao-ying Fang, ECCP, 1:386–387.

Sitting in Meditation: A Random Thought

One more round of trials, another ordeal endured—
Aware that there's only Nonbeing, my mind is composed.
Talk of finding the true source of wisdom?
Tangled branches, o'er-reaching leaves must all be cut down.

(Hsu, 188:5a) *(Tr. Pao Chia-lin)*

Tune: *Huan hsi sha*
Title: Sitting Up at Night

Bamboos cast blurred shadows, the shadows of trees lengthen;
A pale, thin mist and the moon at yellowing dusk—
In the autumn courtyard, the confused chirping of cicadas.

A few dots of glowworm's lights—tiny, brilliant;
Beneath a sky of wind and dew, bean blossoms stay cool.
Night advances, flying squirrels climb up palace walls.

(THYK/THCK, 2:158) *(Tr. Pao Chia-lin)*

Tune: *Lang t'ao sha* (Waves Washing Sand)
Title: In a dream, I visited a place called the Monastery of Heavenly Music, and I saw the text of a lyric on the wall [of a room]. Upon awakening, I tried to recall the words and to write them down. It was written, "To the Tune of *Lang t'ao sha*," and I have now completed it.

Outside the pavilion, the rain just cleared;
I lean against the mica screen
Moonlight floods the room, shining on the singing mouth organ;
Half of my arm catches the chill of the meddling night air,[1]
So callous, too, is spring.

The dying candle is still aglow,
As I awake from my pleasant dream.
Dawn's colors at the window, it is already daylight;
Heavenly music comes from a monastery I know not where—
Just a scene of an unreal encounter.

(THYK/THCK, 1.2, p. 160) *(Tr. Irving Lo)*

NOTE

1. Alluding to a line from Tu Fu's poem "Moon Night," written while the poet was separated from his wife. Tu Fu's couplet, in which the poet visualizes his wife watching the moon from her bedroom at home, reads (in a translation by David Lattimore): "In the sweet mist her hair-clouds moisten/In the pure glitter her jade arms are chill."

WU TSAO

(FL. 1840)

Wu Tsao (*P'in-hsiang*; YÜ-CH'EN-TZU), a native of Jen-ho (present-day Hangchow), Chekiang province, published two volumes of *tz'u* in her lifetime: *Hua-lien tz'u* (Flowered Curtain Lyrics) and *Hsiang-nan hsüeh-pei tz'u* (Lyrics from the Fragrant South and the Snowy North). She also wrote some song poems (*ch'ü*). Her lyrics, frequently set to music and widely sung, were popular among literate women, courtesans, and performers of the time.

Not much is known about her life. She grew up in a merchant family, married a Mr. Huang, and kept her own name. Because no exchanges of poems of theirs exist, and because there is no mention of him in her poems, it is presumed he was a merchant and that the marriage may have been unhappy.

Sometime between the publication of her first collection, before she was thirty, and her second, after she was forty, her circumstances declined radically. She moved south, probably alone. In the preface to her second collection of lyrics, she writes of ten years of "sorrows and burdens" that were overwhelming. She declines to enumerate them, however, but one gathers from the poems that illness may have been one cause of her depression. In any event, as a result of these reverses, she cast off hope for this life, became a devout Buddhist, and followed the Way of the Pure Land sect. "As for poetry," she writes, "I gave up writing it." Poetry was for Wu Tsao a karma, tying her to this world. She never wrote again. Neither the date nor the circumstances of her death are known.

Wu Tsao is admired for a style that is not typically feminine. She is particularly adept at using a vernacular vocabulary and an easy colloquial style to delineate true emotions; her stance is direct and bold rather than languid or contrived. She seems to have identified herself to some degree with the Sung poet Li Ch'ing-chao (1085?–*ca.* 1151), also a woman, and to have captured some of Li's most-admired qualities: delicacy, honesty, and grace.

(Julie Landau)

Tune: *Ju-meng ling* (As in a Dream: A Song)
Title: Swallows

Not all the swallows have left with the spring:
One flies past embroidered curtains into my inner room.
Softly, endlessly, it murmurs;
Could it be saying, "May I stay with you?"
Waiting for an answer,
Waiting for an answer,
With a smile, I reply, "No, you mustn't."

(WTT, p. 24) *(Tr. Irving Y. Lo)*

Tune: *Man chiang hung* (Full River Red)

Shut the door against the setting sun
The yard is full of broken flowers, faded grass!
Sparse shades rolled up, the wind blows taut the paper window
Smoke curls from the incense burner
From the sky's end cry the migrating geese that have passed 5
From the edge of the forest caw a few spots of disappearing crows

. . .

There is no one—softly, leaves fall on the cold empty step—
Who swept away the petals?

I set down endlessly
The draft of a broken heart 10
Words don't keep pace
With idle sorrow
Whatever I see
Adds to the stuff of poetry.
Even my own shadow pities me—thin sleeves, 15
Sick soul already three autumns old—

Wait! Inspect the eaves! Absurd—but ask the freezing plum:
Is it still too soon for spring?

(WTT, p. 18) *(Tr. Julie Landau)*

Tune: *Hsing-hsiang tzu* (Fragrant Wandering: A Song)

The night seems endless
Leaves whisper as they fall
The wind oppresses the paper window nonstop.
Steam from the tea grows cold
The stove is dark, the incense finished, 5
Empty as the small yard.
I close the doors,
Raise the wick.

Sorrow is as hard to shake off
As dreams are difficult to summon. 10
And to sleep in the embrace of a cold quilt—no!
This night is one long cold misery.
The dregs of time seep through the clepsydra
The grim sound of a bell
The shrill cry of the geese. 15

(WTT, pp. 18–19) *(Tr. Julie Landau)*

Tune: *K'u hsiang-ssu* (Bitter Longing)

Dusk in the still yard, cut from the same pattern
The phrases of sorrow, still the same
The blend of dreams and autumn lamplight too, the same
Last night the raging of the wind and rain
Tonight again the sound of driving rain

It spatters on and on 'til dawn—
If only there were fewer plantains!
I wonder, how many cold crickets chatter on the steps?
Outside the window too I hear them crick, one by one,
And beyond the wall, sound after sound

(WTT, pp. 24–25) *(Tr. Julie Landau)*

CHENG CHEN

(28 APRIL 1806–17 OCTOBER 1864)[1]

Cheng Chen (*Tzu-yin;* TZU-WENG, WU-CH'IH TAO-JEN), a native of Tsun-yi, Kweichow province, was a poet, scholar, painter, calligrapher, and minor education official. His grandfather and father were both physicians, but Cheng Chen studied for the civil service examinations, in which he successfully completed the first and second degrees. After failing in the metropolitan, or *chin-shih,* examination, he applied for appointment to the civil service and was subsequently named a subdirector of schools. He served in that capacity in several different districts in his native province, and later taught in the Hsiang-ch'uan Academy in Tsun-yi. Just before his death in 1864, he was notified of a new appointment by the eminent statesman Tseng Kuo-fan (1811–1872).

His scholarly interests resulted in several philological studies, a work on sericulture, and an anthology of poems by men of his native district. He also compiled the local gazeteer of Tsun-yi with the help of his friend Mo Yu-chih (1811–1871), who was a noted bibliophile and also a poet of some repute.

Along with Chin Ho and Huang Tsun-hsien (qq.v.), Cheng Chen is regarded by some Chinese critics as one of the best *shih* poets of the middle and late nineteenth century. He manifested no interest in the decorative or highly allusive styles, but instead preferred a simple, unencumbered diction and a realistic manner. Those poems written before the outbreak of violence in Kweichow, which are characteristic of the *Ch'ao-ching-ch'ao shih-chi* (Nesting in the Nest of the Classics Poetry Collection), mainly reflect a subdued, quiet lyricism untouched by classical aestheticism. On the other hand, the poems of the last

1. Chao-ying Fang, ECCP, 1:107–108.

decade of his life, when local banditry, Miao uprisings, and the invasion of Kweichow, Szechwan, and neighboring provinces by the Taiping leader Shih Ta-k'ai (1821?–1863) caused widespread destruction and human suffering for his fellow provincials, reflect a distinct change of mood and manner. Those momentous events became the subject matter or the background for many of the poems collected under the titles *Ch'ao-ching-ch'ao shih hou-chi* and *Ch'ao-ching-ch'ao i-shih*. As both a witness to and a victim of troubled times, Cheng Chen recorded those events in richly descriptive detail, including several long narrative poems which tell of family and friends having to flee from rebel raids on his home town. Objectively realistic in manner, sometimes sharply critical in tone, his war poems are richly evocative of the harrowing uncertainties of life in a world ravaged by civil strife and rebellion.

(William Schultz)

Evening Prospect

Toward evening on an ancient plain,
Far, far away is the spring of antiquity.
Dark clouds gather up the departing birds;
Travelers emerge from jasper stalks of grain.
Before autumn, the hue of the water is undisturbed;
After a rain, the face of the mountain is cleansed.
I only regret that on either side of the creek,
Nine families out of ten are destitute.

(CCCSC, 2:5a) *(Tr. Chang Yin-nan)*

Miscellaneous Poems Composed While Drinking Wine in the Hsia Mountains

I

Tall willows canopy the thrashing ground with their shade;
White water lilies, green bamboo, and the same old pond.
Past events of the last ten years, no one remembers;
Alone, I watch the yellow chicks pecking at the sunset.

II

Butterflies and dragonflies come in succession,
Yet nothing surpasses this cup in hand to rejoice my heart.
It's half a year ago I paid the price for a hill.
Just ask yourself: How many times have you been there?

(Nos. 4 and 10 from a series of 12; CCCSC, 5:8b) *(Tr. Irving Lo)*

Responding to [T'ao] Yüan-ming's "Drinking Wine" Poems

In the seventh month of the *jen-yin* year [1842], I returned home tired from the district office and did not wish to go out. Every time I drank several cups of wine, I would feel inspired to write something to respond to the poems by T'ao [Ch'ien]. By the tenth month, I had accumulated many, many poems. I have now discarded what was merely repetitious and saved enough to express my feelings.

I

Sad, sad is the bird in a cage:
All its life, it chases the four corners.
Man is the quintessence of all things,
And yet he's confined to No Exit.
How does he compare with horses and oxen?
Driven alike by fame and profit.
Alas, he dies halfway on his journey home,
Without a single thing to call his own.
Is it that his mansion is not commodious?
It's only that none can live there forever.

II

Born to cling to this human road,
Who can deviate from its path?
Twisting, turning, there's no other way.
Alas, both the Buddha and Lao Tzu
Exhausted all their ideas,
Only one day to stiffen and die.
Since dying for naught benefits no one,
Isn't it best to submit to life?
A pot of wine in front of you—

Is truly a priceless treasure.
Let me place myself always in the crowd
And watch you climb to the pinnacle.

(Nos. 10 and 11 from a series of 20; CCCSC, 6:4a) *(Tr. Irving Lo)*

Reading beside Ox Rail River[1]

I

I read books beside Ox Rail River,
I cook food next to Ox Rail River.
Both of these things are acts of purity,
But how do I deserve this situation!
By reading, I seek only to please my mind;
By eating, I seek only to fill my belly.
What has this to do with heaps of dung,
Or with questions of good and bad fortune?

II

Dim, dim the light from the small window;
Bright, bright the charcoal fire.
Huffing, puffing, this mustachioed old man
Sits the whole day long, turning pages.
For ten days or more the rain has fallen,
Thus making me aware of my lame back and knees.
When I arrived, the apricot was coming into bloom;
Getting up to look, I see they've already fallen.

(Nos. 1 and 2 from a series of 3; CCCSHC, 4:8a) *(Tr. William Schultz)*

A Discussion of Poetry to Demonstrate to the Students the Coming of a New Age

I really can't write poetry,
But perhaps I understand its meaning:
The language must be one's own language,
Though the words are the ancients' words.
It is indeed proper to read many books, 5
Even more to nourish and honor the spirit.
When the spirit is correct, then the self exists;

When the study is sufficient, they are mutually helpful.
Li Po and Tu Fu, Wang Wei and Meng Hao-jan—
In talent, each is like the other. 10
A sheep in essence, a tiger only in appearance,
Tho' cleverly deceptive, it's still a fake.
From of old those who are established in words
Are never those who follow the vulgar mode.
Please consider those flowers admitted to first rank: 15
Their branches and stems must first be different.
And consider that when bees make honey
All stamens share a single flavor.
Pattern and essence must truly harmonize;
The writing of poetry is surely a secondary thing.[2] 20
Human talent has always been hard to come by;
Treasure your talent, never stop halfway.
Aging and ridden with illnesses,
Scruffy and stale, unfit for this world,
I return to a different landscape. 25
When will I see you gentlemen again?
In your thoughts, please ponder my words;
When you chance upon something, always drop me a line.

(CCCSC, 7:12b) *(Tr. William Schultz)*

On Hearing that the Market Outside the East Gate of the City Has Been Burned Down

From Lord Wu's Bridge, by Master Sung's Hollow, to Mu-lai Gate—
One long market crowded shoulder to shoulder for seven *li*.
For over two hundred years a thriving city;
Several thousand Long-hair rebels[3] have emptied its walls.
It is as if Heaven wished to punish the immoral and crafty,
Otherwise, how can these rebel flames indulge their sly
stubbornness?
Day after day we've seen the murderous crowd slaughtered,
But who knows when the people's innate vitality can be restored?

(CCCSHC, 1:9b) *(Tr. William Schultz)*

On Hearing that on the Sixteenth Day of the Tenth Month the Magistrate of Li-po, Chiang Hsiao-yün, *tzu* Chia-ku, of Shao-hsing [Chekiang province] Attacked the Rebels at Shui-ts'o River Forty *li* East of the City: They Overwhelmed His Forces and Killed Him

The Cold Miao, the Savage Miao, rose up in revolt,[4]
For two months we've relied on three hundred home guards.
Our granaries smashed, cellars emptied, we've nothing left,
And if we can't hold out, we'll die in battle.
Alas! The great officials sit and watch, as if unaware;
When one magistrate dies, it's like a chicken being slaughtered.
Heaven made their kind to destroy our Kweichow land;
Your duty has been fulfilled, so of what use are tears!

(CCCSHC, 2:9a) *(Tr. William Schultz)*

A Lament for Those Who Hanged Themselves

Before the tigerish soldiers leave, tigerish bailiffs arrive
To press for payments of late taxes, their voices like thunder.
Their thunderous voices still audible, the sounds of crying arise;
A man comes forward to report that his father has already died.
The senior official grinds his teeth, his eyes flashing angrily: 5
"I don't want your life; I only want your money,
But if you think by becoming a ghost, I'll kindly reduce the charge,
Perhaps not a single person in the district will survive!"
He ordered that the man be seized
And given one hundred lashes. 10
"To give your father a bad reputation is the most heinous of crimes;
If you'd solve your father's dilemma, hurry off for a hundred cash."
Alas! A house was sold in Northgate and even the insects fled;
In Westgate there're also reports of people hanging themselves, three or five.

(CCCSHC, 4:11b) *(Tr. William Schultz)*

NOTES

1. A river which rises in Yunnan Province and flows north to join the Chin-sha River, a major tributary of the Yangtze River.

2. An allusion to Confucius's view of literature, which often places literature (*wen*) below moral conduct (*hsing*) or learning in importance. In line eleven of the poem, the poet quotes directly from the *Lun-yü*.

3. I.e., the army of the Taiping leader Shih Ta-k'ai.

4. The Chinese records often designate different Miao tribes according to the dominant color of their traditional tribal dress, but in some instances the origin of a specific designation is less readily apparent, as in the case of the Cold (Ping) Miao, which one source explains as indicating the ability of that tribe to endure cold weather.

CHIANG CH'UN-LIN
(1818–1868)

Chiang Ch'un-lin (*Lu-t'an*), a native of Chiang-yin, Kiangsu, led a rather undistinguished life, but won recognition as a leading lyric poet of his time.

Son of a minor government official who died early, Chiang grew up in destitute circumstances and early gave up hope for a career through the civil service examination, despite promises of poetic talent which he showed as a boy. In 1852, however, he was given an appointment in the Salt Administration of Fu-an District of Kiangsu, but he resigned his post five years later on account of the death of his mother. His last ten years were spent in retirement in Yangchow, where he witnessed much of the devastation caused by the Taiping Rebellion. His later life was also dogged by unhappiness and tragedy. According to one contemporary account, he had married a young wife named Chang Wan-chün, who did not return his affection. He sought out the company of Hsiao-fang (Little Boat), a singsong girl, in Soochow. Later, apparently because of a misunderstanding, he took poison and died in a boat leaving a suicide note. Upon hearing the news, his wife Chang also committed suicide.

Early in his career, Chiang wrote some realistic poems (in the traditional *shih* form) about the life of salt farmers. But he soon recognized his forte lay in the composition of *tz'u* and gave up the writing of *shih*. He regarded *tz'u*, however, as more akin to the *yüeh-fu* (Music Bureau) poetry, though sharing the same origin as *shih*—both attempting to express ideas through a blending of emotion (*ch'ing*) and tone (*yün*).

Modern critics and scholars from T'an Hsien (q.v.) to T'ang Kuei-chang (b. 1899) generally regard Chiang, along with Singde and Hsiang Hung-cho (qq.v.), as the three most accomplished lyric poets of the

Ch'ing dynasty. It is, therefore, perhaps more than accidental that he chose to entitle his slim collection of 106 lyrics (he had deliberately removed a larger number which he did not want preserved) *Shui-yün-lou tz'u* (Lyrics from the Water-and-Cloud Pavilion): Singde's lyrics had been published under the title *Yin-shui tz'u* (Drinking Water Lyrics), and Hsiang's, that of *Yi-yün tz'u* (Remembering Cloud Lyrics). Chiang, however, has never been considered a follower of any school. Rather, his style is highly eclectic, has many moods, and excels in both description (*fu*) and the use of metaphors (*pi*). He often evokes the best of the Southern Sung lyric tradition, and the poet to whom he is most often compared is Chang Yen (1248–ca. 1320).

(Irving Lo)

Tune: *T'a so hsing*
Title: A Descriptive Piece for April, 1853

On jagged steps moss grows deep;
Shading the windows, dense pines—
A courtyard empty of people and the tiniest trace of dust.
In the setting sun a pair of swallows wish to come home;
Rolling up the curtain, I let in the willow catkins by mistake.

Butterflies mourn the weak scent of flowers;
Orioles chafe at their own insipid chatter.
Aging red petals blown clean, spring has grown powerless.
The east wind in one night whirls up from the level knoll.
What a pity, grief overspreads the northern and southern reaches of the river!

(SYLT, p. 9) *(Tr. Irving Lo)*

Tune: *Yü mei-jen*
Title: The [New] Moon on the Night of the Third of the Month

An icy scar in the afterglow sends off the setting sun;
A hook so tiny as to startle fishes from their dreams.
Passionate souls would still say it's perfect and round;

Just the barest hint of a woman's brow
And suddenly it's the Goddess of the Moon!

Enveloping the steps, the night air as thin as mist;
Flowers' shadows lightly traced on the curtain.
I lean against the railing, no need to sleep late.
Just gazing into the yellow dusk—
One glimpse of her overwhelms me with longing.

(SYLT, p. 13) *(Tr. Irving Lo)*

Tune: *Yü mei-jen*

Crystal curtains rolled-up have cleared the dense mist;
In the still night, coolness oozes out from trees.
Since my illness, my body is like the lean paulownia:
I feel my every limb,
Every leaf, is dreading the autumn wind.

From the Milky Way when will this warlike aura subside?
And swords point at wintry stars causing them to shatter?
From afar, I follow the Southern Dipper to look at the capital;
Oblivious that I was
Dew-covered, at the edge of the world.

(SYLT, pp. 20–21) *(Tr. Irving Lo)*

Tune: *Yang-chou man* (A Slow Song of Yangchow)
Title: On 19 December 1853, the [Taiping] Rebels Are Approaching the Capital. Upon Hearing of the Recovery of Yangchow by Government Troops

Crows nesting in abandoned tents,
Magpies jabbering on flagpoles,[1]
Broken notes of reed pipes from the watchtower—
One moment gone by in a vast sea change;[2]
Again the leveled towns of yesteryear! 5
I fear the paired swallows
Will lament their returning late.
A tumbledown pavilion in the setting sun:

I can't bear climbing up again.
Only a red-railed bridge in wind and rain, 10
And plum trees past blooming in an empty camp!

Where the ashes remain from the kalpa fire,
A familiar sight to many,
Even they are struck with terror.
Ask for a long fan[3] to ward off the dust, 15
Or a game of chess with castles for the stake;
But what avails the common folk?
Under a dark moon, fireflies are drifting aimlessly;
The west wind sobs
Amidst ghost fires[4] here and there. 20
But it hurts even more as I look toward the south:
Across the river, innumerable green-peaked hills!

(SYLT, p. 13) *(Tr. Irving Lo)*

NOTES

1. Popular superstition in China holds that hearing magpies singing foretells good news, such as the return of an absent lover.
2. A free translation of *ts'ang-sang*. See Cha Shen-hsing, note 1.
3. As a gesture of a heroic temperament, following an association that can be dated to Han times.
4. Will-o'-the-wisps.

CHIN HO

(17 JULY 1819–1885)[1]

Chin Ho (*Kung-shu*; YA-P'AO) was born in Ch'üan-chiao, Anhwei province, and was distantly related on his mother's side to the famous eighteenth-century novelist Wu Ching-tzu (1701–1754). He spent the greater part of his carefree youth in Nanking where he and his family were trapped when the Taiping rebels captured the city in March, 1853. When government troops arrived outside Nanking, Chin began plotting with his friends to stage an uprising within the city to coordinate with an attack from without, and Chin himself escaped to the government camp to inform the general in charge, Hsiang Jung (d. 1856), about his plot. Hsiang did not have confidence in Chin's stratagem, and after his wife and other relatives managed to escape, Chin left Nanking in disgust to return to Ch'üan-chiao. In the meantime the plot was discovered, and many of Chin's friends were executed by the Taiping rebels.

By 1856 Chin was employed as a clerk to collect the new *likin* tax, and in 1859 he failed the provincial examinations in Hangchow. As the territory of the Taiping rebels expanded, he was forced to flee to Shanghai in 1860. Later he spent approximately six years in Kwangtung province serving in various minor secretarial posts, but by 1867 he was back in Nanking, which had been recovered from the Taipings in 1864. After residing in a number of southern Chinese cities, he passed away at Shanghai in 1885. Although his poems were widely read in manuscript during his life, they were not printed until 1892, when a collection was published under the title *Lai-yün-ko shih-kao* (Poems from the Pavilion of Advancing Clouds). A definitive edition under the title *Ch'iu-hui yin-kuan shih-ch'ao* (Poems from the Hall of Humming Au-

1. Chao-ying Fang, ECCP, 1:163–164.

tumn Cicada) did not come out until 1914. Even so, most of Chin Ho's earlier works have been lost.

Chin Ho was one of the most daring innovators of mid-nineteenth century China, writing in a highly colloquial style strongly indebted to the folk ballad tradition. Chin himself wrote:

> Although what I write is not the purest of the pure;
> In short, every word is natural and true to life.
> No contemporary man is capable of this;
> And I can't be called an ancient either!

In addition to injecting much more colloquial language into his verse than other nineteenth century *shih* poets, Chin's style is quite prosy and breaks practically all of the traditional rules of line length and rhyme. His works are distinguished by his long narrative poems, a form relatively uncommon in the Chinese poetic tradition. Some of his finest poems relate his harrowing experiences during the Taiping Rebellion or satirize the corruption and ineptness of the government forces with a scathing, mordant humor.

Liang Ch'i-ch'ao (q.v.), one of the major political and intellectual figures of late Ch'ing China, considered Chin Ho and Huang Tsun-hsien (q.v.) to be the two major poets of the nineteenth century, and Hu Shih (1891–1962), one of the leaders of the early twentieth century vernacular literature movement, ranked him in the same class as the T'ang giants Tu Fu and Po Ch'ü-yi. Since the Communist Revolution in 1949 Chin Ho's verse has been largely ignored, possibly because of his hatred for the Taiping rebels, whom the Communists consider their spiritual ancestors. In any case, Chin Ho had a major impact on Huang Tsun-hsien and other late nineteenth-century poets.

(J.D. Schmidt)

Strolling in Simplicity Garden for the First Time

All of spring's colors are found inside a brushwood gate;
How I regret sticking my feet in this Red Dust[1] by mistake.
A burst of bird songs is enough to urge us to our drinking;
Round about, flower scents make do to perfume our clothes.
A few ill-shaped rocks are brought in; the mountains look more seductive;
Newly covered with sparse duckweed, the water serves to fatten the soil.

It's not that your host is known for hospitality:
I just wait for the night to deepen, so I can return by moonlight!
(Ch'en, p. 450) *(Tr. J.D. Schmidt)*

Ballad of the Girl from Lan-ling

Soon as the general broke Hsüan-chou's seige,
He traveled swift as a bird, cymbals clanging all the way.
Marching, marching, east to the River Lai,
And built a gold house fixed with jade gates.
Ten-layered screens, covered with silk and gauze; 5
Hundreds of hanging tassels, heavy with pearls.
Sea monsters, purple phoenixes stitched on his carpets;
Corals, jade trees flash beneath his lamps.
Magic tortoise trays, huge conch shell cups;
Pepper flowers ferment, lambs fatten. 10
At his table, sable, brocade, the age's nobility for the time;
Before his eyes, pomp, luxury, rare in our world.
They say the general consummates his wedding today;
The noble lady comes to marry, previously betrothed.
Far, the road to Lan-ling, matchmakers gone thither; 15
Along the vernal river, boats of Wu travel by his command.

On this auspicious occasion, wind and sun, fresh, charming;
Snow melts, sands warm, waves sparkle in the clear weather.
The children on Double Bridge vie in their joyous shouting;
New Year plums and willows intoxicated in spring feelings. 20
At high noon the clamor of drums and horns is heard afar;
From upriver Milady's approach already reported.
The general smiles and descends his stairway;
His guests surround him, waiting in silence.

Just as the gay boat docks by the general's gate, 25
A girl swoops out like a hawk, running fast as an ape.
Her dress is elegant yet plain, avoids decoration and ornament;
Her manner meek and modest, honored in heaven and earth.
If she isn't a fairy princess attending Jasper Pool's heavenly chariot,[2]
She must be the immortal who weaves in Jade Palace at night.[3] 30
Her tall frame stands firm and erect;
Her jade countenance grieved, not warm.
She straightens her sleeves to address the guests:
"All you present in this hall ride in tall carriages;
I, too, am not without culture. 35

Listen as I tell everything from the very beginning;
I am the daughter of an official family of Lan-ling;
In this disorderly age, most people are crafty by nature.
I have but one mother and two elder brothers;
We live in the country, at an isolated spot. 40
One day I watered vegetables in our icy plots;
When the general passed by and stopped to stare.
I carried my bucket home, quickly barring the door;
I didn't even give him the time of day.
Yesterday came two of his officers, 45
Baskets brimming over with gold coins.
They said our marriage had been made in heaven,
And my mother had previously given assent.
Now they've come by boat to take me;
The wedding is soon, better not delay. 50
When my brother asked them who they were,
Their loud roar shook our house to its foundation.
Several dozen men drew their swords,
Standing in a pack like wolves and tigers.
With one shout they quickly surrounded our house, 55
Terrifying all passersby outside.
Their manner was exceedingly violent
And there was no place for us to fly from them.
If I would not go with them now,
My frightened family knew we were finished. 60
Now that they have brought me here,
I ask the general what he means by this."

The words burst from her heart, sentence by sentence;
Suddenly her arm shot out, she grabbed the general.
In her other hand, a sword, still unsheathed, ready for action. 65
"Is what I have said true or not?
General, have you heard what I said?
I want only to drag you to Soochow,
Accuse you in the governor's court;
Request him to appeal to the emperor for me; 70
From ancient times famed generals' deeds were inscribed on bronze;
They were given titles, land, money, silk, all rewards by the nation,
But when could they kidnap women of good family to repay their
valor?
When an imperial command comes from the five-layered clouds,
If the emperor commands me to marry you, 75
Wouldn't you be satisfied then?

But if you don't have the emperor's decree,
Our dispute will never be settled.
If you are angry then kill me!
Just like crushing tiny fleas and mosquitoes on a pile of manure. 80
Otherwise, I'm taking *your* life with my sword;
Blood gushing from your throat will spatter these blue silk dresses for five full paces.
Outside your gate on the long dike are plenty of wild crabapple trees,
With enough space to bury a lecherous general tomorrow.
Quickly decide if you want to live or die; 85
What use lowering your head, speechless, politely embarrassed?"

The general usually bawled and cursed with a thunderous roar;
His arms could easily hoist a thousand-pound stone.
But now his face and eyes were dead as ashes;
Flushed as if drunk, his expression tipsy. 90
The toughs under his command fumed with anger;
Clenched fists, fingernails biting flesh, teeth grinding.
Now their general was in someone else's hands,
Suddenly there was nothing they could do.
When you strike a rat, you fear smashing the furniture; 95
There's no way for them to make use of their weapons.
The general waved his troops to back off;
His eyes stared at the guests, pleading with them to say a good word.

Soon as the guests had recovered from fright,
They came and bowed before the girl. 100
"After hearing Milady's speech,
Our hair stands straight with indignation.
In short, the general's idea,
Was not that things should come to this.
Of course, he asked your hand in marriage. 105
But he wouldn't dare be so unreasonable as to force you.
Rash and rude, they didn't understand what they were doing;
The fault was entirely with the messengers.
As for those two officers of his,
If they've disobeyed his command, they will be soundly thrashed. 110
And today, without further ado,
You'll be sent back to your village home.
The general himself will walk you to your gate,
Bare to the waist, to beg a thousand pardons.

He will respectfully present a humble gift, 115
To help you care for your elders.
This matter will pass like clouds and mist,
The sky return to its pristine purity.
Let us send the boat back right now,
And God forbid we should break our word!" 120

The girl observed the guests, smiled, then frowned;
"Gentlemen, you take me for a rosy cheeked babe!
Your general has been foiled today,
Will his vicious temper now be tamed?
Like a mountain demon, he'll seek vengeance; 125
The more he fumes, the crueler he'll become.
Alas! Since the army was sent into action,
Everywhere soldiers murder the people.
They murder people as if *they* were the bandits,[4]
This vicious poison spreading far and wide. 130
On the official road near my Lan-ling,
You people constantly march to and fro;
Sometimes on frost-laden evenings,
Sometimes on mornings of rain.
The few rooms in my lowly house, 135
Would burn crackling like firewood on the plain.
There are only a few souls in my home,
Now anxious as fish in a cooking pot.
If in a moment trouble broke out,
We'd be instantly turned to ashes and dust. 140
Who wants to cultivate future disasters,
And become an avenging ghost in the end?
Who knows there really *is* a King of the Dead,
To whom we can appeal for vengeance in Hades?
Why shouldn't I shout to the ninth heaven above, 145
The celestial emperor must remain impartial.
I think I'll carry through this violent deed,
For public opinion will approve my right.
I clearly knew that in coming here,
I was like a praying mantis boxing with a wheel. 150
I have no wish to live in shame;
What do I care for this frail body of mine?
Gentlemen, all these compromises of yours,
Are far from the mark, I won't give in!"

The guests all came forward bowing; 155
"Don't let your face glare with such anger!

The general is famed for his great virtue,
For he has always treasured his reputation.
He's single-minded in devotion to the scholar's etiquette,
Especially dignified and trustworthy. 160
He was certainly wrong in his actions,
And when news of this gets out,
Everyone will complain of his unfairness.
You can imagine how people will curse him;
His bad reputation won't be without reason. 165
He will be hard pressed to speak in his defense,
Like a white jade that has soiled itself.
His name won't be worth a copper penny;
He won't have enough time to repent his errors.
If the elders east of the river see him, 170
They will be mortified to recognize him.
How would he dare arouse the masses' wrath,
Using military force to take a wife?
After breaking all the Confucian proprieties,
He wouldn't be thought a human being. 175
Our general is not your ordinary fellow;
He's suffered hardship battling bandits everywhere.
He may not be a great talent like Kuan Chung or Lo Yi,[5]
But his heroism *is* equal to Chao She or Lien P'o.[6]
Milady is the descendant of a noble stock; 180
We hope for the court's sake you'll forgive its brave soldier.
As for the future, we solemnly guarantee your safety,
Some of us are government officials, some local gentry.
Together we deeply bow, begging for our general's life;
Oh! Milady! Be compassionate as immortals, Buddhas, gods!" 185
The girl knew they'd be hard to defy,
And replied: "I'll give in a bit.
What you just said, let's ignore for a while;
I only want to borrow something from you.
I've heard the general has a fine steed named White Fish, 190
Galloping slowly, he can run a thousand miles a day.
Since I left my village Lan-ling,
My family has waited more than four days.
My old mother leans against our gate, crying bitterly;
My two brothers, fists clenched, stand in the courtyard, sighing. 195
If I ride this horse back home,
I can arrive today before sunset.
From now on I'll abandon my lowly house,

And seek a dwelling with men of Ch'in times.[7]
In their Peach Blossom Grove I'll serve Mother; 200
With my brothers I'll read the books of Hermit Huang;[8]
Isolated in Wu-ling even foolish fishermen won't find us.
Within three or five days,
I'll move from our old house.
At Chiang Tzu-wen's[9] Temple in Mo-ling, 205
I'll return the horse, all right?"

The general's horse was rarely ridden;
All they wanted was the girl to leave.
They quickly ordered soldiers to lead the horse forward,
Its four feet, white as frost, two ears, cotton strands. 210
Soon as the girl set eyes on the horse,
Her brow beamed with radiant joy.
Her hand let go of the general's robe,
And with one leap she mounted the saddle.
She bade farewell, seemed to dash into the sky; 215
A flash of light, a meteor, she vanished.

Several days after the girl left, the army settled down;
The general marshaled his ranks, his bravery recovering.
By the side of the Bell Mountain he built barracks around;
Guests, underlings visited, congratulating his efforts. 220
They urged him to sip ladles of new grape wine;
Gongs and horns mixed together roared with joy.
From beyond the clouds came a dusty horse, neighing loudly;
Of the same pure radiance, galloping with flowing gait.
Her word good as gold, more reliable than cash; 225
The general met his horse, led it back to its trough.
The horse sweated blood, neighed without stop.
On its back something tied up, bunched together, nearly three feet tall:
The betrothal gifts presented by the officers on the day before his wedding!
Returned sealed, not a hair lost; 230
Beneath the gifts as they were being untied,
A single knife, sharp as the leek's leaf, appeared.
The knife sparkled, sparkled, blade razor-sharp;
And for the next few nights, the general lost sleep!!

(Ch'en, pp. 470–472) *(Tr. J.D. Schmidt)*

NOTES

1. A term used to describe the mundane world. (It is possible that the word *red* also refers to flower blossoms lying on the ground, hence, turning to dust.)

2. I.e., an attendant of Hsi-wang-mu, the Queen Mother of the West, a fairy queen who resided to the west of China according to popular mythology.

3. A reference to the Chih-nü or Weaving Girl, an immortal who weaves in the constellation Lyra.

4. I.e., the Taiping rebels.

5. Kuan Chung was a famous prime minister of the Spring and Autumn period, Lo Yi, a great general of the Warring States period.

6. Chao She and Lien P'o were both well known generals of the Warring States period.

7. The references to men of Ch'in times, Peach Blossom Grove, and Wuling are all allusions to the poet T'ao Ch'ien's well known preface and poem on the Peach Blossom Grove, which describe a fisherman who stumbles upon a paradise inhabited by men who deserted the Chinese empire during the Ch'in dynasty to escape political disorders of that period. The fisherman foolishly left the paradise to tell the outside world of its existence but could not find it when he attempted to return.

8. Hermit Huang or Huang-shih-chün (Man of Yellow Stone) was a recluse of late Ch'in times who wrote a book on military strategy supposedly used by Chang Liang to assist Liu Pang in founding the Han dynasty. See Wu Weiyeh, note 26.

9. Chiang Tzu-wen was a general of the Three Kingdoms period.

CHIANG SHIH

(FL. CA. 1861)

Chiang Shih (*T'ao-shu*), a native of Ch'ang-chou, Kiangsu province, was a man of obscure origin and of practically no known accomplishment except for his skill as a poet. Nothing is known of his life save that he was active at the end of the Hsien-feng era (1851–1861) and, after becoming a licentiate, was an alternate candidate for appointment to a magistracy. He probably earned his living as a tutor. He lived for some time in Fukien province, and he died after he reached the age of forty-five. No date of birth or death is given in any of the sources on him or his works. Chiang's poetry, however, had many admirers among his contemporaries. It was approved chiefly for its lean, or sparse, and plain style, somewhat reminiscent of such T'ang poets as Han Yü and Meng Chiao, or the Sung poet Huang T'ing-chien. Often writing about loneliness and frustration, he was capable of some striking and original imagery, as in the following couplet:

> Remorse I have: cloudy vapors that thunder against heaven;
> My tears are like resounding tidal waves coming from the sea.

(*yüan yu ho-t'ien jo-yün-ch'i/lei ju tao-hai tso-ch'ao-sheng*; with the third word *ho* in the first line meaning "to reprimand" or "breathe upon.") His collected works, entitled *Fu-yü-t'ang shih-lu* (Poems From the Studio of A Submerged Ancient Musical Instrument), were printed in *T'ung-jen-chi* (An Anthology of Contemporary Poets), edited by Wang Ch'ing-hsiung.

(Irving Lo)

Crossing Several Mountain Ridges on My Way to P'u-ch'eng from Chiang-shan'[1] after a Snowfall

For nights on end, I've been pursued by rain and sleet;
Now inside a sedan-chair, I long for sunny sky at dusk.
Myriad bamboos are without a sound only when snow is falling;
Jumbled hills are like my dream: forever cloud-capped.

(Ch'en, p. 416) *(Tr. Irving Lo)*

Getting Up Early at Lakeside Pavilion: Two Poems

I

Morning light floods my room overlooking the lake;
Last night's dream, so vivid before, quickly fades as I get up.
I recall only the dawn bells from two temples:
The sound of one bell short and the other long.

II

Vapor rises from the water's surface at dawn;
Coldly forbidding: the color of the cliff to the south.
Look, a tiny raft heads for haven on the Western Shore;[2]
It carries three people, two of them are monks.

(Ch'en, pp. 429–430) *(Tr. Irving Lo)*

Night at an Inn: Written in the Style of Meng Chiao

A hundred griefs are like a hundred arrows;
I lack a bow to control my mind.[3]
But once let go, they return and pierce my heart;
So miraculous is the arrow of grief that it never misses.
Alas, the lonely eccentric
Shares his shadow only with the lamp!
His guts twist with every turn of the cart wheel;
His broken dreams cannot be mended for want of gum rubber.
Hungry rats scurrying stir up the dust—
How can they make reply to my short satire?

(No. 1 from a series of 4; Hsu, 159:9a) *(Tr. Irving Lo)*

NOTES

1. Also called Chiang-lang Shan, in Chekiang province, south of Chiang-shan county. P'u-ch'eng refers to Chien-ning in northern Fukien.

2. In Buddhist terminology, the "Western Shore" implies salvation.

3. "Mind" or "heart"—actually the same word as the last word of the next line, since the Chinese consider *hsin* to be the seat of both emotion and the intellect.

LI TZ'U-MING

(21 JANUARY 1830–20 DECEMBER 1894)[1]

Li Tz'u-ming (*Ai-po* and *Shih-hou;* SHUN-K'O and YÜEH-MAN), official, scholar, and man of letters, was a native of K'uai-chi (Shao-hsing), Chekiang province. He entered the civil service by purchasing an office in the Board of Works, but he passed the *chü-jen* examination in 1870 and obtained his *chin-shih* degree ten years later. When he was later posted to the censorate, his frank and outspoken manner earned him the enmity of many people in government. Unhappy in his work and despondent over the outbreak of war with Japan, he fell ill and died.

Li Tz'u-ming left a large collection of writings on history which was published after his death. His best known, and perhaps his most important work, is however the *Yüeh-man t'ang jih-chi,* a voluminous diary covering the years 1863–1868 (a supplement covers the years 1854–1863), which contains Li's comments on the classics and histories, reading notes, personal observations on leading personalities of the time, as well as poems and essays. He was also the author of one play, but he was most admired as a master of the literary prose style and a poet of considerable wit and erudition.

(William Schultz)

---

1. H. S. Tseng, ECCP, 1:493.

On a Rainy Evening: Written in Playful Imitation of [Li] Yi-shan's[1] "Untitled Poems"

A brief meeting, the East Wind has no will of its own;
A scented carriage with polished panels is detained for just a word.
None could forget the smile of jade fingers rolling up the blinds;
Who made those moth eyebrows drown a mirror in grief?
Orioles chat on the painted screen as someone leans over her lute;
Through fragile curtains of cobweb silk, the moon shines down on
her room.
The Silver River to keep its faith—who will wait for that?
It spills forth chill and forlorn in an autumn evening rain.

(Hsü, 173: 13a–13b) *(Tr. Daniel Bryant)*

While on an Evening Stroll Outside the Gates, I Stood Alone Looking Out on the Water, a Vast Panorama of Wind and Waves, and, Full of Reflections on Rivers and Lakes, Wrote this Five-word Poem

A distant wind blows as I stand alone;
From the azure heaven descends frontier sorrow.
The hills dusky, weighing down on a lonely village;
The walls autumnal, slapped by turbid waves.
Direly poor, I meet with trouble and hardship;
Often ill, I miss out on favor and spite.
Thoughts of the mountains and rivers that fill my view—
In equal portion, I'll share them with the untrammeled gulls.

(Hsü, 173–11a) *(Tr. Daniel Bryant)*

Written at Night, after Dreaming That I Had Returned to My Old Home

What have I dreamt of, all this night?
I dreamed of returning to my old hut in the hills.
Beyond the western suburb of Shan-yin Town,[2]
My clan has gathered to dwell across the river.
Behind the houses, a plot of several acres; 5
With a view to the side of government ditches and ponds.

Bamboo gardens open one after another,
Broadly extended for more than half a league.
House by house, each with a tall pavilion,
Scarlet and emerald linked and entwined together. 10
My house stands on its own tidy lot,
Facing the town and open to village and hamlet.
In back there is a five-room pavilion,
With green moss spreading out to dim the gold.
On seasonal festivals I sometimes climb to the top, 15
Lean on the railing and look down on hunters and fishermen.
When the light on the lake has not entirely vanished,
Level meadows are linked to tangled coves.
Scattered sails pass by like leaves;
Men working the sculls call out from time to time. 20
Fishing cormorants are arrayed on boats in a line;
Flying up in alarm beyond sea gulls and ducks.
A weir made of twigs suddenly breaks in the center;
Appearing in the interval, pink lotus flowers.
I have this scene always before my eyes; 25
On endless travels I can only heave a sigh.
One morning, I let my hand drop down,
And traced a map with the tip of my finger.
Green hills lined up at the end of my lashes;
The light of the sky appeared on my robe and collar. 30
To left and right I hold a bright mirror,
Glass lets in the sky at the window.
If I did not awaken after seven days,
What need would I have for a trip to Hua-hsü Land?[3]

(Hsü, 173:3b) *(Tr. Daniel Bryant)*

NOTES

1. I.e., Li Shang-yin. Allusions to the T'ang poet Li Shang-yin's love poems, most carrying the title "Without Title," are many and taken from several different poems. Readers who are not familiar with Li Shang-yin's verse would do well to consult James J. Y. Liu, *The Poetry of Li Shang-yin: Ninth-Century Baroque Chinese Poet* (poems 4–5, 17–18, and 28 in particular).

2. Shan-yin is adjacent to Shao-hsing, Chekiang Province.

3. According to an account in the *Lieh-tzu*, Hua-hsü was a utopian land visited by the Yellow Emperor in a dream. The country there observed no hierarchy of officials or leaders, and the people lived a simple, carefree life. When awakened from the dream, the Yellow Emperor was able to bring peace to his people.

WANG K'AI-YÜN

(19 JANUARY 1833–20 OCTOBER 1916)

Wang K'ai-yün (*Jen-ch'iu*; HSIANG-CH'I) was a native of Hsiang-t'an, Hunan province. He became a *chü-jen* at the early age of twenty-two and worked as an advisor to a government official for a while, but quit when he had a disagreement with his superior. Thereafter, he spent some time in Chengtu, Szechwan province, as president of the Tsun-ching Academy (of Classical Studies). Later he returned to his home province of Hunan, where he presided over the Ssu-hsien Academy at Changsha, and the Ch'uan-shan Academy at Heng-chou. In 1903 he was named a lecturer at the Nanchang School of Higher Learning. Later, he left this position and returned home, where he began receiving students in his own Hsiang-ch'i Study. His reputation for scholarship and personal conduct later earned him a position in the Hanlin Academy. In 1914, he was made director of the National Historical Archives, and a member of the National Senate (Ts'an-yi-yüan). With the eruption of the debate over Restoration, he resigned and retired to his home in Hunan, where he spent the remaining years of his life at ease. As a classicist, he specialized in the study of the *Kung-yang chüan* (Kung-yang Commentary) to the *Ch'un-ch'iu* (Spring and Autumn Annals). In addition to the *Hsiang-yi-lou shih-chi* (Poetry Collection of the Hsiang-yi Pavilion), his numerous publications include the *Pa-tai shih-hsüan* (Selected Poems of the Eight Dynasties [from Han to Sui]), the *T'ang ch'i-yen shih* (An Anthology of the Heptasyllabic Poetry of T'ang), two collections of essays and memoranda as well as commentaries on the classics.

While other major poets of the late Ch'ing period tended toward the style of the Sung masters and wrote a good deal of poetry reflecting the issues of their time, Wang K'ai-yün imitated the style of the Han, Wei, and Six Dynasties periods for his old-style verse, and that of the

High T'ang for his regulated poems. He is said to have removed from his collected works all the "new-style" quatrains which he had ever written. Some of his poems reflected and documented the turbulence and concerns of late Ch'ing society, such as the "Twenty-two Poems on Setting Out from Ch'i-men," which were written between 1860 and 1862, when there was much fighting in Anhwei province during the Taiping Rebellion, and the long popular poem "Song of Full Splendor Park," which describes the destruction of the Yüan-ming Yüan by British and French soldiers in 1860.

Most of these poems, however, are so carefully framed in the style of ancient poets that they could easily pass for ancient works themselves. In fact, the modern critic Ch'en Yen has said of him, "If you mix his verses together with a collection of poems by ancient authors, you could not distinguish his from theirs, and because they are indistinguishable, there is no rationale for their being the poetry of Wang K'ai-yün."

(Jan W. Walls)

Spring Sun

Spring sun shines on springtime dress,
But the spring heart does not know.
Why claim the pain you feel inside
Is not the longing for your love?
"Longing? Surely no such thing!
My feelings are for no one!"
But as you sit with your shadow, an accidental mate,
Dawn has turned to dusk.

(HCLSC, p. 26) *(Tr. Jan and Yvonne Walls)*

Since You Went Away

Since you went away
The face in my shining mirror has lost its glow.
My longing for you is like my rouge,
The fragrance fades away with the years.

(HCLSC, p. 34) *(Tr. Jan and Yvonne Walls)*

7. Peking's Yüan-ming yüan (Full Splendor Park), summer, 1983.

The Sighting of a Boat

We awaited fair winds at the ford.
I came at dawn to send off your boat.
Spring waves tossed without end,
And my feelings flowed with them.
Sadly I snap a willow twig, and listen to the lonesome flute;
Wearily I hold a mulberry branch and dangle a waiting hook.
Today the ferry takes you across the river;
But when I come to greet you, will you be here?

(HCLSC, p. 28) *(Tr. Jan and Yvonne Walls)*

Song of the Full Splendor Park[1]

As in Ch'in's imperial Park of Auspicious Spring,[2] fleeting are the fireflies;
As in Han's Palace of Eternal Happiness,[3] willows have grown ten times in girth.
Summer palaces, from the earliest ages, were used for pleasure only;
How, then did this—outside the capital—become a royal seat?

Clear and blue is the old lake that flows from Yen and Chi,[4] 5
Through Hsi-ma campground, into the Kao-liang River, and across
grazing land.[5]
The Northern Lords once brought peace to this ancient Mongol
capital;
From within Western Hill's folds, the imperial aura reigned
supreme.
Then from the nine broad avenues, dust rose, reached the skies,
For the Polestar, too long absent from the Dipper,[6] had
withdrawn. 10
Once field ditches, like dried inlets, were all caked with mud,
What used to mirror the courtly grandeur: the mere trickles of a
stream!
A pool, dark and deep, could only dimly be seen on the banks of
Cinnabar Square,[7]
Where, on these rolling lands, the first to rise was the Garden of
Springtime Rapture.[8]
Springtime Rapture's scenery rivaled that of the Southern Park;[9] 15
Here his phoenix canopy, flying rainbow flags, came often for the
fetes.
Even the Earth Spirit did not begrudge the making of Urn Hill
Lake.[10]
The Son of Heaven himself christened it the Hall of Full Splendor.
Full Splendor was first bequeathed to the Submerged Dragon[11]
Who turned this suburban palace into a royal residence, 20
With eighteen gates and locks[12] that hugged a winding stream,
With a seven-pillared Great Hall[13] aloft among the pines,
And forty shoreline pavilions, each with its own view.[14]
Facing zigzagging garden rocks, where breezes seemed to rise.
Carts stopped here as at Sweet Dew,[15] to seek relief from summer's
heat; 25
And imperial palace guards could store away their bows in their
cases.

Emperor Ch'un,[16] succeeding to the throne, surely attained the
fullest glory;
No waves disturbed the bays or seas, awaiting his royal tours.
Along his journey where he stopped, four gardens he especially
esteemed;[17]
Those scenes the master painters sketched were replicated true to
form. 30
Who can say that fine scenery is found only South of the River?
To shift heaven around or shrink the earth is all within a
sovereign's power.

At first 'twas only to replicate King Wen's animal park,[18] from the time of Chou;
Who ever counted the meager cost for a Dew Terrace, as did Emperor Wen of Han?[19]
Earnestly he studied the words of the Duke of Chou[20] on curbing extravagance. 35
But who would have thought his descendents[21] could forget thrift and reverence?
Suddenly the *chuck-chuck*[22] cries were silenced at the deer enclosure in Jehol,
And evil forebodings spread unseen from the south to the north.[23]
Officials grew more callous, and people in anguish groaned.
Long whales[24] came plowing through the waves, against a ravaged shore. 40
Only then the treasurer began to grieve for the nation's wealth,
And sought to sell provincial royal residences for ordinance.

Lost in thought, I mull over the affairs of half a century,
When the times were like brushwood piled high near a house ablaze.
Could any have dared to raise bamboo poles against the Ah-fang Palace?[25] 45
Many a black ball for the crossbow[26] aimed at striking down civilian officials!
Now our late emperor[27] first sensed the danger, dark and imminent,
And decreed that three commanders[28] be chosen for the field.
But the seat for the worthy was left vacant[29] in Emperor Wen's court;
The Heavenly Altar overflowed with remorse as people bemoaned their fate. 50

Year after year, he saw new grasses spring up by the carriage road,
Here, and then there, he looked on flowers and birds with a grieving heart.
With palace girls he played at pot games to force himself to laugh
And sing as he exchanged wine cups of gold from dusk 'til dawn.
Through all four seasons, he loved the views from the country estate; 55
In winter's depth, from inside the palace, he longed for spring to come.
Tremulously, the Four Springtime Maids[30] trailed his phoenix carriage;
Furtively, through five night watches, the copper-fish[31] was passed from hand to hand.

Court ladies were schooled to coiff their hair in the style of the Ts'ui family;[32]
As admonition, many would have removed earrings to emulate Empress Chiang.[33] 60
Soon the Royal Boulevard[34] came to mourn the creakings of an imperial coach;
At Golden Phoenix Palace, none cared to talk about affairs after dark.
From Tripod Lake,[35] bowmen and soldiers returned heavy with grief;
The country fort, put to a torch, vanished in wind and smoke.
Jeweled Spring sobs and grieves; Kunming Pool is choked. 65
Alone the bronze rhinoceros stands guard among the thorns;
About Blue Magic-Mushroom Cavern,[36] foxes cry as night comes on.
Beneath Brocade Ripples Bridge,[37] fishes still weep in vain.

Ah, who is this aged eunuch, guarding the gate of the Garden of the Blest?[38]
Once among the nobles and ministers, he served the Most Exalted One. 70
In those days long past, he loathed the clamorous courtiers;
In these days of solitude, he greets all visitors with glee.
How unlike the clamorous courtiers are the lonely sightseers!
Guests come rarely now, none deemed worthy of admittance.

The Gate of the Good and Worthy[39] is shut; scattered lie its broken tiles. 75
Luminous Splendor Hall[40] now gutted, one must search out its ruined walls.
Here stood the Hall of Clear Light, newly built by Emperor Wen,[41]
Close by the shoreline of the lake, to catch the light of dawn,
Where a forest deity, in an ominous dream, declined the royal offer of courtly rank;[42]
And scattered, too, lies a replica of Sravasti Castle, the Buddha's seat.[43] 80
Rank and tall grow millet and cattails in the lake;
Before the steps, reeds and mugwort rustle with the wind.
Men steal new growth from withered trees for firewood;
Joyous fish leap up in play, and are startled by fishermen's nets.

Beside all this, there stood the Terraces of Open Cloud and the Ornamented Moon[44] 85
Where once, in a world at peace, three sage emperors[45] met together.

Could they foresee how scattered bamboo shoots would break through the moss?
Or how we still see spring blooms weep with dewdrops in full flower?
From Level Lake westward, we see the remains of kiosks and pavilions,
And calligraphic specimens on walls resembling silver hooks or bent leeks. 90
On gold-tiered steps, pair by pair, the lily feet of palace girls;
On papered windows here and there, traces of mascara still remain.

When the British came, the ruler fled in haste on bell-bedecked camels;
Left behind to guard the palace were the painted women who served him at night.
Low notes sounded from reed pipes as he followed the autumn moon; 95
Starving, without even rice and bean gruel to eat, he fixed his gaze on Jehol.[46]
The Upper Gate was opened to let the barbarians pass through;
To receive them, the lords and princes lined the left side of the palace road.
Before the enemy troops torched the maize about Yung Gate,[47]
The herdsmen had already seen the beacon fires lit atop Mount Li.[48] 100

How piteous the one loyal minister who perished alone on the Magic Isle,[49]
To uphold his moral principles, worthy of the ancient Ling-chün![50]
While ministers shunned the foe to survive under a white flag,
Commoners fought the brigands to the death, guarding the gate.
Now the rancour of the Sea of the Blest is as deep as the ocean, 105
Who can believe that from the Sacred Isle[51] the deities have not departed?

From success to ruin in a hundred years, how swift and sudden!
In all directions, wasted remains spread before our eyes.
To the Purple Forbidden City with its crimson gates, the court can still return;
But has anyone heard of river swallows nesting among trees in the forest? 110
Look well on these ruined roofs, these felled foundation stones!
Hardships and dangers teach that rebuilding a nation is hard.

The Censors already rebuked for prattling about repairs,
Stop the officials from amassing silks and rich brocades!

Silks and brocades squander in vain revenues from South of the
River, 115
With designs, new and old, of mandarin ducks and dragon's claws!
Let the grand palace gates be overhung with gorgeous hangings,
How could they hope to surpass the West Lake Boulevard of days
long past?
The land around West Lake is too thin to compare with Hsün-
hsia's;[52]
Even the mansion of the Marquis of Wu-ch'ing has only a short
lease,[53] 120
Just make the grain and fishes sufficient for the people's use;
Never allow the warblers in the willows to vie with palace blooms.

How can a modern lyricist understand the discourse "On the Merits
of A Capital"?[54]
A cart pushed by hand can never alter the royal course.[55]
The poet Hsiang-ju could claim the fame of eulogizing an imperial
park,[56] 125
Born to such hapless times, I mourn this sorrow here in vain.

(HYLSC, pp. 336–340) *(Tr. Irving Lo and Kenneth Yasuda)*

NOTES

1. The countryside around Hai-tien, northwest of Peking, was known for its scenic beauty even before there was a capital. Both under the Liao and Chin dynasties, during the eleventh and twelfth centuries, and under the Ming, the area had served as the site of imperial hunting grounds and summer lodges. The first ruler of Ch'ing, Emperor Shun-chih, had the place refurbished as a hunting park, which was known as the Southern Park (Nan-yüan). But it was Emperor K'ang-hsi (q.v.) who started the building program of what was later known as the Yüan-ming yüan, here translated as the "Full Splendor Park." It was he who enlarged the park by incorporating into it the mansion and grounds occupied by the family of Li Wei, the Marquis of Wu-ch'ing, who was the father-in-law of the Ming Emperor Ch'ung-chen (see line 120 of the poem). The first palace constructed by Emperor K'ang-hsi was named Ch'ang-ch'un Yüan, or the Garden of Springtime Rapture.

Real large-scale expansion of the Yüan-ming Yüan, however, did not start until after 1701, under the reign of Emperor Yung-cheng. Emperor Ch'ien-lung (q.v.), an eclectic architectural genius, added greater opulence to the site by elaborately replicating the sceneries of famous gardens he had visited in the south during his many tours of the provinces. He also had the service of the sinicized Italian painter J. Castiglione (Lang Shih-ning, his Chinese name,

1688–1766) and a Frenchman, P. Michel Benoist (Chiang Yu-jen, 1715–1744) to supervise the construction of a few Baroque-style European buildings. Toward the end of the Ch'ien-lung era, in 1793, Sir John Barrow was one of the first Westerners invited to stay in the park, as a member of Lord Macartney's mission to China; in his *Travels in China*, published in 1804, he described the general appearance of the summer palace: "The grounds of *Yuen-min-yuen* [i.e., Yüan-ming Yüan] are calculated to comprehend an extent of at least ten English miles in diameter, or about sixty thousand acres, a great part of which, however, is wastes and woodland" (p. 122).

As a result of the abrogation of the Treaty of Tientsin by the Chinese in 1859, France and England declared war on the Ch'ing government. Led by Lord Elgin and Baron Gros, an expeditionary force of 6,300 French troops and 10,500 English soldiers was dispatched to China, with the naval force consisting of over sixty French ships and 146 British transports. An extraordinary event of this war was the total destruction of the Summer Palace, which burned for two days, 18–19 October 1860, and which was preceded by days of plundering. These events were recorded by an eyewitness, Lieutenant-Colonel Garnet J. Wolseley, writing in his *Narrative of the War With China in 1860* (published in 1862):

> Sir Hope Grant, accompanied by Lord Elgin, rode thither . . . [and joined by General Mountauban] . . . proceeded together until they reached the large village of Hai-teen (Hai-tien). . . . About twenty badly-armed eunuchs made some pretence of resistance, but were quickly disposed of, and the doors burst open, disclosing the sacred precincts of his Majesty's residence. . . . A mine of wealth and of everything curious in the empire lay as a prey before our French allies. . . . Indiscriminate plunder and wanton destruction of all articles too heavy for removal commenced at once. . . . Officers and men seemed to have been seized with a temporary insanity; in body and soul they were absorbed in one pursuit, which was plunder, plunder. [pp. 224–227]
>
> Upon the 18th [of] October, the 1st division, under the command of Major-General Sir John Michel, marched from our camp near Pekin to Yüan-ming-yuen, and set fire to all the royal palaces. . . . Throughout the whole of the day and the day following, a dense cloud of black and heavy smoke hung over those scenes of former magnificence. . . . [U]pon both of those days, the light was so subdued by the overhanging clouds of smoke, that it seemed as if the sun was undergoing a lengthened eclipse. . . . [pp. 278–279]
>
> It was averred the complete destruction of the palaces would be a Gothlike act of barbarism. It seems strange that this idea did not occur to the generally quick perceptions of our Gallic allies before they had shorn the place of all its beauty and ornament, by the removal or reckless destruction of everything that was valuable within its precincts, leaving us, indeed, little more than the bare shell of the building to wreak our vengeance for the cruelties practised therein upon our ill-fated countrymen.
>
> By the evening of the 19th October, the summer palaces had ceased to exist, and in their immediate vicinity, the very face of nature seemed changed: some blackened gables and piles of burnt timbers alone indicating where the royal palaces had stood. In many places the inflammable pine trees near the buildings had been consumed with them, leaving nothing but their charred trunks to mark the site. When we first entered the gardens they reminded one of those magic grounds described in fairy tales; we marched from them upon the 19th October, leaving them a dreary waste of ruined nothings. [pp. 279–280]

This poem is here translated from Wang Kai-yün's collected works, where it was printed without a prose preface. A prose preface to this song written by the poet's contemporary, a fellow Hunanese, Hsü Shu-chün, appears in some editions, as it does in Ch'en Yen's *Chin-tai shih-ch'ao* (I:343–347). Because of its length and the fact that it was not written by Wang, we have omitted it. However, many of the historical facts mentioned therein and useful for the elucidation of the poem have been incorporated into our notes.

2. Yi-ch'un Yüan, the name of the imperial park of the Ch'in dynasty. In both this line and the next, the poet attempts to evoke the lesson of history by these allusions.

3. Chien-chang and Ch'ang-lo (Eternal Happiness) are both names of Han palaces.

4. Yen is the name of the area around Peking at the time of the Chou dynasty; Chi-hsien was the name given to the place known as Ta-hsing under the Chin, in the eleventh century.

5. The place called Hsi-ma-lin-pao, with its forest and fortress, is located 70 *li* northwest of Wan-ch'üan *hsien* in present-day Hopei province and only 20 *li* from the border; it had served as a cavalry training ground since Yüan times. The Kao-liang River is an upper tributary of the Jeweled River (Yü-ho), west of Wan-p'ing *hsien,* close by Jeweled Spring Hill (Yü-ch'üan Shan).

6. This line contains the names of two stars: *ch'en-chi,* the Polestar, which since Han times has often been used by poets to symbolize the emperor; and *Pei-tou,* or the Dipper, which could represent the capital (as it does in many of Tu Fu's poems). This line probably means that the emperor had taken flight from the capital.

7. The poet indicates his presence with this line. On Sunday, 28 May 1871, Wang K'ai-yün visited the Park in the company of two friends—Chang San (whose courtesy-name was Tzu-yü), and Hsü Shu-chün, probably the brother of the poet Hsü Shu-ming (?–1900)]—and toured the site with the Park's Superintendant Commander Liao Ch'eng-en. Hsü's prose preface to this poem is dated "Autumn, 1871." This poem, then, must have been written between May 28 and September or October of the same year. Tan-lin is the name of the river, upon the banks of which Emperor K'ang-hsi built his Ch'ang-ch'un Yüan on the property once belonging to the Marquis of Wu-ch'ing.

8. Ch'ang-ch'un Yüan, completed in the last decade of the seventeenth century.

9. Nan-yüan, referring to Emperor Shun-chih's hunting park.

10. In 1751, to celebrate his mother's sixtieth birthday, a lake was made by Emperor Ch'ien-lung at the foot of Weng-shan; hence, the hill is also known as Wan-shou Shan (Longevity Hill). The lake is K'un-ming Lake.

11. The Hall of Full Splendor (Yüan-ming Tien) was completed in 1709; before succeeding to the throne, Emperor Yung-cheng lived in a palace called Lung-ch'ien Shih-shih, meaning "A Dragon Submerged [and] Timely Bestowed" Garden.

12. The park has eighteen gates, some made of bamboo and some made of iron, including sluice gates for the water control system.

13. The largest of the three main halls is called the *Cheng-ta kuang-ming tien* (The Hall of Great Uprightness and Luminous Splendor), the Hall of Audience mentioned in the accounts of Westerners. Sir John Barrow described it as being "110 feet in length by forty-two feet in width, and twenty feet in height, with a floor paved with grey marble flag stones laid chequer-wise" (Barrow, *Travels in China,* p. 125).

14. The Summer Palace was celebrated for its "Forty Magnificent Views." Compare *Yü-chih Yüan-ming yüan shih* (Poems on the Yüan-ming Yüan by

Imperial Command) compiled under Ch'ien-lung's reign—a small anthology of forty poems, each written on a specific scene.

15. *Kan-lu* (Sweet Dew) is the name of the summer palace of Emperor Wu of Han (*reg.* 141–87 B.C.).

16. "Kao-tsung Ch'un Huang-ti" is the temple name of the Ch'ien-lung Emperor.

17. Referring to the An-lan Garden of Hai-ning and the Hsiao-yü-t'ien Garden, both of Ch'ien-t'ang (near Hangchow); the Chan Garden of Chiang-ning (Nanking); and the Shih-tzu (Lions) Garden of Soochow. Emperor K'ang-hsi made six southern tours during his reign, in 1684, 1689, 1699, 1703, 1705, and 1707.

18. *Ling-yu* alludes to probably the earliest animal park mentioned in Chinese literature, the "Ling-t'ai" of King Wen of Chou, celebrated in Ode 242 of the *Shih-ching* (Arthur Waley's "Magic Tower," in *The Book of Songs*, pp. 259–260; *Sunflower Splendor*, pp. 14–15)

19. This alludes to the story about Emperor Wen of Han (*reg.* 180–157 B.C.) who inquired about the cost of building a "Dew Terrace" (*lu-t'ai*). He gave up the idea when he learned that it would cost 100 gold pieces, which (the emperor said) would equal the wealth of ten middle-income families.

20. The text reads *Wu-yi*, a chapter in the *Shang-shu*, which contains the words of the Duke of Chou to King Ch'eng on the difficulties of farming and on the importance of thrift.

21. Referring to the two succeeding emperors: Chia-ch'ing (*reg.* 1796–1820) and Tao-kuang (*reg.* 1821–1850).

22. The text reads *mu-lan*, which, in the Manchu language, indicates a kind of whistling sound used to call deer. This refers to the annual autumn hunt which took place at the royal family's Summer Palace in Jehol Province, the famous *Pi-shu Shan-chuang* (in modern-day Ch'eng-te, just a short distance outside the Great Wall).

23. The text reads *li* and *k'an*, from the *Yi-ching*, representing respectively "the South" and "the North," which refer to the White Lotus Rebellion (1796–1804), which ravaged northwest China, and the Opium War (1840–1842) and Taiping Rebellion (1850–1864), which ravaged the South.

24. *Ch'ang-ching* (long whales): a euphemism for British gunboats.

25. Ah-fang is the name of the extensive palace built by Ch'in Shih Huang-ti. The dynasty was overthrown in 206 B.C. by peasant rebellions, and one of the leaders, Ch'en She, was said to have used only weapons improvised from hoes and tree branches.

26. This alludes to a story in the "Biographies of Harsh Officials" in the *Hou-Han-shu*, *chüan* 90: In an uprising against the harsh official Yi Shang, a band of young people gathered and decided to draw lots to determine the responsibilities of each person. Those who drew red balls from a bag were to kill military officials; those drawing black balls, the civilian officials; those drawing white balls were to keep a record of the funerals.

27. Emperor Wen, whose reign title was Hsien-feng (*reg.* 1851–1861).

28. The three commanders were the Manchu noble Sheng-pao (d. 1863), who had been successful in the suppression of the Nien Rebellion, and who later sustained a mortal injury at T'ung-chou, fighting the British and the French (cf. *Ch'ing-shih-kao*, *chüan* 403); Tseng Kuo-fan, the founder of the Hunan Army, which resisted Taiping rebels; and Yüan Chia-san (1806–1863).

29. Referring to the tragic story of Chia Yi who was first favored by Emperor Wen of Han as an honored guest and then maligned and exiled to Chang-sha where he died at age thirty-two.

30. The four favorite concubines of Emperor Hsien-feng all had names ending with the word *ch'un* (springtime); they were: Almond Blossom Springtime (*hsing-hua ch'un*), Wu-ling Springtime, Mu-tan (Peony) Springtime, and Hai-t'ang (Crabapple) Springtime.

31. Copper-fish was a kind of tally used to identify visitors to the living quarters of the palace.

32. An as yet unidentifiable fashion for a palace hairdo then favored by the emperor.

33. Empress Hsiao-chen (d. 1881), whose title was conferred on her in 1860, was known to be virtuous and upright. She once removed her hairpin, as a sign of admonition to the emperor for his dissolute life. The allusion is to the story in the *Lieh-nü chüan* about King Hsüan of Chou who had the habit of getting up late. Empress Chiang removed her hairpin and stood in an alley to confess that it was all her fault. The king then admitted his own failings and began to apply himself diligently to the affairs of state and became responsible for the reinvigoration of the dynasty.

34. The text reads: *yü-lu* (literally "jade road") referring to the boulevard that led from the West Gate (Hsi-chih men) to Hai-tien. The construction of this road impressed more than one Western observer. According to G. J. Wolseley, it was ". . . a well-made road, constructed after the most approved method, being slightly raised in the centre and having good drains upon either side. Were it not that it is unmetalled, one might fancy it an English thoroughfare. It is the only one of the sort I have ever seen in China." (Wolseley, p. 228)

35. Alluding to the death of Emperor Hsien-feng in 1861. See Wu Weiyeh, note 1.

36. The text reads *Ch'ing-chih hsiu*, referring to the three characters in Emperor Ch'ien-lung's calligraphy inscribed on a tablet.

37. A bridge south of the Wen-ch'ang Pavilion.

38. An old eunuch, with the surname of Tung, said to be over seventy, whom the poet interviewed in the late spring of 1871, when this poem was written.

39. The southern gate of the park is called the Hsien-liang Men.

40. See note 13 above.

41. Ch'ing-hui T'ang, built by Emperor Hsien-feng.

42. According to the preface to this poem, written by Hsü Shu-chün, one year before the burning of the Summer Palace, Emperor Hsien-feng had a dream in which a white-haired old man identified himself as the Park Deity. The emperor in his dream offered the deity the title of Second Rank, but the deity bade the emperor farewell and left.

43. The city of Che-wei refers to Sravasti, "the city of famous things," said to be a favorite resort of Sakyamuni, the Jetvana garden being located there.

44. K'ai-yün (Open Cloud) and Lou-yüeh (Ornamented Moon) Terraces were two of the forty famous scenes of the park.

45. According to the account given to the poet, in 1721, when the future emperor Ch'ien-lung, then aged eleven (twelve *sui*), was brought into the presence of his father, the future emperor Yung-cheng, Emperor K'ang-hsi was also there for the occasion.

46. Before the allied troops entered Peking, the royal party fled to their Summer Palace in Jehol, where the emperor died the next year.

47. This alludes to a story in the *Tso-chuan* (Eighteenth Year of Duke Hsiang; or 554 B.C.). When the state of Ch'i was attacked by the combined

forces of Tsin and Lu—the Marquis of Ch'i loved music and was an irresolute ruler—the enemy forces approached Yung Gate and cut down the fields of southernwood about the gate and put them to the torch.

48. Alluding to the practice of lighting beacon fires atop Li-shan in ancient times when China's capital was located near present-day Sian.

49. P'eng Isle was located in the center of the Sea of the Blest (*Fu-hai*), the largest lake in the park. Wen-feng, the official who committed suicide by drowning in the lake, rather than surrender, was a Han Chinese originally named Tung, who in 1854 was made Grand Councilor of the Imperial Household (*nei-wu-fu*). Wen-feng, who had previously served as Textile Commissioner in both Hangchow and Soochow and participated in negotiations with the British over the governance of Treaty Ports in 1843, was promoted to become Superintendent of Yüan-ming Yüan in 1858. He was also placed in charge of the imperial dispensary and hospital (*Ch'ing-shih-kao, chüan* 494).

50. It is, of course, poetic license to compare Wen-feng to the ancient poet Ch'ü Yüan, the author of *Li Sao*, who drowned himself in 278 B.C. (Ling-chün was the poet's courtesy-name).

51. The text reads *Shen-chou*, which stands for China.

52. This alludes to a story in the *Tso-chuan* (Sixth Year of Duke Ch'eng; or 584 B.C.). The statesman Han Hsien-tzu persuaded the duke to abandon the proposal to move the capital to the land of Hsün-hsia, an area near salt marshes, which he described as "thin in soil and shallow in water." His other advice to the duke was: "Mountains, marshes, forests, and salt-grounds are indeed most precious to a state, but when the country is rich and fruitful, the people grow proud and lazy." (James Legge, *Chinese Classics*, volume 5, page 360.)

53. See note 1 above.

54. The text reads *Lün-tu-fu*, alluding to the story about Tu Tu in the *Hou-Han-shu* (*chüan* 80A), who persuaded Han Kao-tsu *not* to consider moving the capital to Loyang.

55. Alluding to the story about Liu Ching (or Lou Ching) in the *Shih-chi* (*chüan* 99), who stopped the carriage of a general in order to plead for a chance to speak to Emperor Kao of Han. Lou Ching also advised the emperor against moving the capital to Loyang. Here the allusion seems to have been directed at the repeated attempts by many scholar-officials to remonstrate with the throne, during the seventies, against the plan of rebuilding the Summer Palace.

56. Ssu-ma Hsiang-ju, the celebrated poet of the Han dynasty, is the author of the "Shang-lin fu," a rhyme prose composition on the grandeur of the imperial park. Cf. Burton Watson, *Early Chinese Literature* (New York: Columbia University Press, 1952), pp. 273–284.

CHUANG YÜ

(?–1878)

Chuang Yü (*Chung-Pai*), a native of Tan-t'u, Kiangsu, was a classicist by training and *tz'u* poet of considerable repute. He came from a declining merchant family with no visible connections with the Ch'ing bureaucracy. Despite a fine reputation as an *Yi-ching* and *Ch'un-ch'iu* specialist, he was unable to find regular employment until late in his life, when the statesman-general Tseng Kuo-fan recognized his merits and placed him as a collator at the government printing offices in the Yangtze region.

Though not a prolific poet by traditional standards (his extant works consist of about 130 *tz'u*), Chuang Yü was easily the most accomplished of those who wrote under the inspiration of the Ch'ang-chou school of aesthetics. Like Chang Hui-yen (q.v.), the titular founder of the Ch'ang-chou school of *tz'u*, Chuang Yü rejected the early part of Ch'ing *tz'u* as excessively imitative in technique, and set out to restructure *tz'u* writing around two time-honored principles: *yi* (moral import) and *pi-hsing* (comparison and analogy). In his hands, both the *hsiao-ling* (short songs) and the *ch'ang-tiao* (long tunes) are infused with an emotional depth and a technical subtlety that give the *tz'u* poetry its distinct character. His treatment of boudoir themes in particular won him unreserved praise from both T'an Hsien (1832–1901) and Ch'en T'ing-cho (1853–1892), two of the most astute critics of his time.

(Shirleen S. Wong)

Tune: *Tieh lien hua*

I

The slanting sun across the city wall clings to green trees.
On a piebald horse he passes,
Looking back repeatedly.
The jade bridle, bejeweled whip, where will they pause?
I turn about, not realizing dusk is about to fall.

In the wind all the flowers have drifted away—
Once apart, I wonder,
Will they ever meet again?
If I gazed at you hard and long—please don't misunderstand—
There were so many secret thoughts only you can share.

II

Gossamer threads trail endlessly in the courtyard.
By the doorway,
Suddenly the face of my man[1]—
I try to turn back, but my hairpin trembles so;
Thank heavens, there is no one around.

A quick touch of hands, that's the only goodbye for now.
Mindful of spying eyes,
I keep turning my round, round fan.
How my heart trembles as I pull my hand away—
Please come back, and come back while young.

III

I was somewhere in a dream just a while ago;
Suddenly the east wind
Blew me back to Heng River's bend.
Send word not to bother with a date of return—
A dream unfinished will be a broken dream.

A faint green outside the window, fading are the hills.
So swift was our parting,
So little could I say.
The season of flowers has rushed by far too soon—
What now but to search the horizon till my eyes are sore?

(CPT, pp. 27–28) *(Tr. Shirleen S. Wong)*

NOTE

1. The text reads *Wei-lang* (Young Master Wei), most probably referring to the T'ang poet Wei Chuang, especially known for his lyrics to the tune *p'u-sa-man* that tell of the pangs of love.

FAN TSENG-HSIANG (1846–1931)

A native of En-shih county, Hupeh province, Fan Tseng-hsiang (*Chia-fu*; YÜN-MEN, FAN-SHAN) was a prolific poet. He passed the *chin-shih* examination in 1877 and later earned an excellent reputation as a magistrate in Shensi province. Although he did not play an important role in the political and cultural turmoil which marked his lifetime, he was nonetheless never far away from the center of these affairs. His political and literary association with the conservative reformer Chang Chih-tung (1837–1909) is consistent with the gentle but firm Confucian social concern which characterizes much of his best poetry in the *shih* form. His style is colorful and somewhat colloquial, while it is marked by not infrequent and often quite effective allusions to the classics. He left a collection of *shih* poetry containing over 30,000 poems, and he was also admired for his lyric poetry. Perhaps his most famous work is a long *ch'ü* narrating the life of the courtesan-entertainer Sai-chin-hua (1874–1936), sometime concubine of the scholar-diplomat Hung Chün (1840–1893). She later became well known as an entertainer and companion of the famous in the international community of Shanghai and is the real life model for the female protagonist in the novel *Nieh-hai hua* (Flower in an Ocean of Sin) by Tseng P'u (1872–1935). (For a partial translation of this lyric see *Literature East & West*, vol. 9, no. 4, winter 1965, pp. 334–336.) Fan's poetry shows an affinity of style with that of Chao Yi (q.v.) and the Sung poet Lu Yu.

(J.P. Seaton)

Written in a Cool Breeze

No light within the court, and moss climbs the stairs;
I move my couch, sit sprawled beneath the courtyard ash.
Cool clouds across the water, not likely it will rain;
Thin lightning leans against the mountain, no thunder yet.
In willows' shade I watch paired magpies settle;
To bamboos' depths from time to time come fireflies.
This great official feels drier than Hsiang-ju;[1]
To quench that thirst, would I be thinking only of a single cup of dew?

(Ch'en, p. 725) *(Tr. J.P. Seaton)*

Random Verses from a Boat

I

Within three days we've changed boats twice.
Now, they say, it's Hsi-ch'üan county.[2]
Smoke from kitchen fires is thick;[3]
The city walls, again in good repair.
We hear the yamen here's well run. 5
The common folk applaud the magistrate's decisions,
And on the eastern shore the grain grows glossy green.
A hundred coins will buy a peck of flour.
This same river burst its banks in Chengchow—
Groves and marshes are full of homeless geese.[4] 10
There, they're grounded, stranded fish,
And here secure as swallows nesting in the eaves.
These are both the people of Yü-chou:
But thirty miles divides calamity from joy.
Like fruits of the same grove, 15
Sweet and sour growing side by side.
Here many are at peace, at leisure;
There, the toilers, that eternal moan.

II

My good wife was born in the Capital:
She's never seen the finest of boats or oars.
Come South, to see the misty waters,

Her eyes, a sparkle like the eddying waves.
Water creatures, fishing gear— 5
One by one, she asks about their names.
A little afraid as the wind in the sails heels the boat,
But joyous to hear the soft music of the sculling oar.
Reed shoots supply a pretty dish;
Mallow leaves make a fragrant soup. 10
In the groves hard by, nets set in the sun to dry;
Along the dikes, occasional weirs,
At last I begin to understand the ancients' paintings
That depict the true joys of fishermen.
How I wish to sail off to the Five Lakes:[5] 15
In a boat light as a white gull.
Writing table, mirror stand,
All year long will be put away.
The brewing of tea is what I've long been accustomed to;
I would have no need to buy my own Fuelwood Green.[6]

III

Before dawn passing Chiang-k'ou town,[7]
Waters swift as arrows pass.
River of Stars astern on the right,
My boat passes it on the left.
Standing alone in the flow of the river, 5
Peak like a lotus, an elegant single flower.
And these little islets: green conch shells
Lying in a silver bowl.
Long ago I fell in love with Little Orphan,[8]
Sailed past, at least ten times. 10
That flowered islet hung amidst the flow,
Locked all about in misty waves.
This peak so much like that:
Call it a miniature, if you will! 15
It's five years since I left Kiukiang,
And now Heaven sends this gift.
Too bad there's no way to anchor;
Swift shallows rush the light barge down.
I turn, gaze back upon the coiffure of the mist,
At heaven's edge, its vast and supple grace!

(Nos. 2, 3, and 4 from a series of 7; Ch'en p. 722) *(Tr. J.P. Seaton)*

NOTES

1. Ssu-ma Hsiang-ju, a renowned master of the *fu*, or rhyme prose, was a diabetic, who required frequent large doses of water to quench his thirst.

2. Located in Nan-yang prefecture, Honan province (present-day Ju-nan), about seventy-five miles south of Chengchow (line 9), a large city south of the Yellow River.

3. I.e., the place is thickly populated.

4. People displaced by the flood, from an allusion to the *Shih-ching*.

5. Lake T'ai, in Kiangsu province, so called because it consists of a network of five lakes, alluding to the story of Fan Li of the Warring States period. See Wu Chia-chi, note 2.

6. Possibly concealing a pun on Fuelwood Green (Ch'iao-ch'ing) as a proper name. According to *T'ang-shu* (History of T'ang), the recluse-poet Chang Chih-ho (ca. 742–ca. 782) was once given a bondmaid and a boy servant by the emperor; and the poet made them husband and wife. He named the boy Yü-t'ung (Fisherman Boy) and the girl Ch'iao-ch'ing.

7. Chiang-k'ou: a key river station in Kiangsi province, located sixty *li* from Kan-hsien and south of Po-yang Lake.

8. Little Orphan, or Hsiao-ku, Shan is situated north of P'eng-tse county, Kiangsi province, which, together with P'eng-lang Jetty, near Kiukiang, commands the Yangtze traffic.

HUANG TSUN-HSIEN

(29 MAY 1848–28 MARCH 1905)[1]

Huang Tsun-hsien (*Kung-tu*) was born in Chia-ying-chou (modern Mei-hsien) of Kwangtung province to a reasonably well-off family of the Hakka minority. His family suffered from the depredations of the Taiping rebels, but Huang was able to pursue a youth of study and poetry writing. He had his first contact with non-Chinese culture when he visited Hong Kong in 1870 after failing the provincial examination for the second time. In 1876, he obtained the degree of provincial graduate (*chü-jen*) in Peking, wherupon he was appointed to accompany the new Chinese ambassador Ho Ju-chang (1838–1891) to his post in Tokyo. Huang was overwhelmed by the vitality of Japanese civilization after the westernizing reforms of the Meiji Restoration, and while in Japan wrote his *Jih-pen tsa-shih shih* (Miscellaneous Poems on Japan), which described the new Japan with great admiration and exhorted Chinese intellectuals to follow the Japanese example of reform. At the same time, he also started his highly influential *Jih-pen kuo-chih* (Monograph on the Japanese Nation), which was completed in 1887 and became a textbook for the reformers of late nineteenth-century China.

In 1882 Huang was appointed the Chinese consul-general to the United States in San Francisco and arrived shortly before Congress prohibited Chinese immigration to the United States. Huang was outraged by this insult to the Chinese government and the cruel abuse of the Chinese people that he witnessed in San Francisco. After returning from the United States, Huang spent four years in retirement before he was assigned a post in the Chinese embassy in London. His stay in London and travels on the continent allowed him to witness the

1. Chao-ying Fang, ECCP, 1:350–351.

power of the European countries at first hand, which only strengthened his desire for reform. Finally he served as Chinese consul-general in Singapore from 1892–1894.

The disastrous defeat of the Chinese in the Sino-Japanese War of 1894–1895 galvanized the reformers into action, and on his return to China, Huang began cooperating with Liang Ch'i-ch'ao and K'ang Yu-wei (qq.v.) in promoting reform through editing journals and making speeches; Huang was particularly active in the province of Hunan, which had become a hotbed of the reform movement.

In 1898, the famous "Hundred Days Reform" under the Kuang-hsü Emperor began, but Huang was unable to join his fellow reformers in Peking, because he had become seriously ill. His illness was fortunate, because the Empress Dowager Tz'u-hsi carried out a *coup d'etat*, seizing control of the government once again. Six of the reformers were beheaded, while Liang Ch'i-ch'ao and K'ang Yu-wei managed to escape to Japan. Huang's home in Shanghai was surrounded, but he was allowed to return to his native village. He remained active until the end, writing poetry and contributing articles on reform to overseas journals under a pen name. Huang Tsun-hsien died in his native village in 1905.

Huang Tsun-hsien was the major poet of the late Ch'ing "Poetic Revolution." Although the term "revolution" did not mean precisely the same as it does in China today, Huang's poetry marked a major innovation in the Chinese literary tradition. Even by his early twenties Huang was writing:

> My hand writes what my mouth says;
> How can antiquity inhibit me?

Huang constantly stressed the need for the poet to express his immediate experiences:

> There is really no such thing as ancient and modern in poetry. If one is able to take in immediately what the body experiences, the eyes see, and the ears hear, and write this into his poetry, then what need do we have of the ancients? Poetry is already present in my self. . . . The age which I experience today, the environment which I perceive, no matter when, I am always present. I gaze upon the ancients who came before me and look to those who are to follow me in the future, and none of them can contend with *me*.

The result of such a theory of literature is that much of Huang's finest verse is characterized by a vividness and immediacy rare even in China.

Huang felt that one of the most important missions of the poet was to regenerate Chinese culture, and so much of his verse attacks the ineptness of the Ch'ing government in dealing with foreign imperialism and the failure of the Chinese people to reform a society wracked with corruption, ignorance, and poverty. Therefore, his poetry paints a vivid picture of a China constantly humiliated by foreign armies and enslaved by smug conservatism, autocratic government, oppression of women, and superstitious religions. Although Huang wished to imitate the finer points of Western culture, he was appalled by the rabid racism and internecine warfare of the West.

Generally speaking, Huang Tsun-hsien felt that the most effective way to realize his goals was to instill new thought into the old form of classical verse. This did not prevent him from occasionally infusing his poems with vernacular language, and by his old age he was calling for the abandonment of classical Chinese and the adoption of the vernacular for the sake of educating the masses. More important than his use of the colloquial was the freedom with which he introduced foreign terms and new concepts into his verse, and his description of the new technology within the form of classical Chinese verse is almost as startling today as it was in the late nineteenth century.

Huang's contemporaries such as Liang Ch'i-ch'ao considered him the greatest Chinese poet of the late nineteenth century, and at least until the beginning of the Cultural Revolution in 1966 his reputation was still untarnished in China.

(J.D. Schmidt)

The Ballad of Ch'ao-chou[1]

When men are born in disorderly times,
Their plans frequently go awry.
One evening we moved three times,
Our footprints without fixed abode.

Coming to live at Three Rivers,[2] 5
We name it our Promised Land.
It is not man's nature to pity the unfortunate
And disasters assail us without mercy.

Chirp, chirp, the yellow bird sings:
"You cannot stay long in this land." 10

A single river stretches to Ch'ao-chou,
Where we must go to live now.

This time the north wind was frigid;
Our smooth oars agitated the level river.
On and on, about to reach the city, 15
Where hearth fire smoke was dense as threads.

Suddenly our boat did not advance;
Bandits hiding in the forest scrub!
We raise the alarm, the thieves upon us;
Their fast oars flying like raindrops. 20

Our boatmen quickly make fast our boats;
Flailing pikes fend them off left and right.
Suddenly we fear we are not their equal;
We may end up provoking their wrath instead.

Striking the boat's sides, we frantically shout: 25
"Better let them take what they want!"
Drifting aimlessly, midst calamity and disaster,
Practically nothing in our traveling cases.

At least it will fill the bandits' sacks,
And we will escape kidnap or slaughter. 30
With a roar, the thunder of cannon!
"Kill the bandits!" the bandits flee.

Our lives delivered from the tiger's mouth;
So happy, we cry as we talk.
I look back at my little brothers and sisters, 35
Lying on their bellies like a pack of rats.

"Get up! Get up!" We call them to sit straight,
And try to comfort them with kind words.
Leaning on the bed with ashen faces,
They lie, claiming they weren't really scared. 40

Alas! Midst calamities and disasters,
We have suffered every possible pain.
Soon we will arrive in Ch'ao-chou
Where we must quickly find help.
Then we will cut spirit banners to summon back our souls, 45
To summon back our souls by the river's bank.[3]

(JCL, p. 19) *(Tr. J.D. Schmidt)*

Song of the Exile

Chinese started to travel to America during the Tao-kuang and Hsien-feng reigns, at first because of the demand for workers. Those who followed in their footsteps increased in number, eventually reaching two hundred thousand. Since the local people began competing with the Chinese for a livelihood, they noisily discussed expelling the Chinese, and in the sixth year of Kuang-hsü (1880), the American Republic sent three representatives to China to negotiate a treaty limiting the immigration of Chinese workers. After the treaty had been signed, in the third month of the eighth year of Kuang-hsü (1882), Congress used the treaty as a pretext to pass a law prohibiting the immigration of Chinese workers. I wrote the following to give vent to my feelings.

Alas! What crime have our people committed,
That they suffer this calamity in our nation's fortunes?
Five thousand years since the Yellow Emperor,
Our country today is exceedingly weak.
Demons and ghouls are hard to fathom; 5
Even worse than the woodland monsters.
Who can say our fellow men have not met an inhuman fate,
In the end oppressed by another race?
Within the vastness of the six directions,
Where can our people find asylum? 10

When the Chinese first crossed the ocean,
They were the same as pioneers.
They lived in straw hovels, cramped as snail shells;
For protection gradually built bamboo fences.
Dressed in tatters, they cleared mountain forests; 15
Wilderness and waste turned into towns and villages.
Mountains of gold towered on high,
Which men could grab with their hands left and right.
Eureka! They return with a load full of gold,
All bragging this land is paradise. 20
They beckon and beg their families to come;
Legs in the rear file behind legs in the front.
Wearing short coats, they braid their queues;
Men carry bamboo rainhats, wear straw sandals.
Bartenders lead along cooks; 25
Some hold tailors' needles, others workmen's axes.
They clap with excitement, traveling overseas;
Everyone surnamed Wong creates confusion.

Later when the red-turbanned rebels rose up,
Lists were drawn of wanted rebels.[4] 30
Pursued criminals fled to American asylums,
Gliding like snakes into their holes.
They brandished daggers in the same house;
Entered markets, knife blades clashing.
This was abetted by the law's looseness, 35
And daily their customs became more evil.

Gradually the natives turned jealous.
Time to time spreading false rumors,
They say these Chinese paupers
Only wish to fill their money bags. 40
Soon as their feet touch the ground,
All the gold leaps out of the earth.
They hang ten thousand cash on their waists,
And catch the next boat back to China.
Which of them is willing to loosen his queue, 45
And do some hard labor for us?
Some say the Chinese are shiftless;
They first came with bare arms.
When happy, they are like insects milling about;
Angry, like beasts, biting and fighting. 50
Wild, barbaric, they love to kill by nature;
For no reason, blood soaks their knives.
This land is not a hateful river;
Must it hold these man-eating crocodiles?
Others say the Chinese are a bunch of hoodlums, 55
By nature all filthy and unclean.
Their houses are as dirty as dogs';
Their food even worse than pigs'.
All they need is a dollar a day;
Who is as scrawny as they are? 60
If we allow this cheap labor of theirs,
Then all of us are finished.
We see our own brothers being injured;
Who can stand these venomous vermin?

Thus, a thousand mouths keep up their clamor, 65
Ten thousand eyes, glare, burning with hate.
Signing names, the Americans send up a dozen petitions;
Begging their rulers to reconsider.
Suddenly the order of exile comes down,
Though I fear this breaks our treaties. 70

The myriad nations all trade with each other;
So how can the Chinese be refused?
They send off a delegation to China,
To avoid the attacks of public opinion.
A dicer can sometimes throw a six after a one; 75
They have decided to try their luck with this gamble.
Who could have imagined such stupidity,
That we would agree to this in public, eyes closed?
With all of the iron in the six continents,
Who could have cast such a big mess? 80
From now on they set up a strict ban,
Establishing customs posts everywhere.
They have sealed all the gates tightly,
Door after door with guards beating alarms.
Chinese who leave are like magpies circling a tree, 85
Those staying like swallows nesting on curtains.
Customs interrogations extend to Chinese tourists;
Transients and even students are not spared.
The nation's laws and international relations
Are all abandoned in some high tower. 90
As I gaze east, the sea is boundless, vast;
More remote, huge deserts to be crossed.
The boatman cries, "I await you";
But the river guard shouts, "Don't cross!"
Those who do not carry passports 95
Are arrested as soon as they arrive.
Anyone with a yellow colored face
Is beaten even if guiltless.
I sadly recollect George Washington,
Who had the makings of a great ruler. 100
He proclaimed that in America,
There is a broad land to the west of the desert.
All kinds of foreigners and immigrants,
Are allowed to settle in these new lands.
The yellow, white, red, and black races 105
Are all equal with our native people.
Not even a hundred years till today,
But they are not ashamed to eat his words.
Alas! In the five great continents,
Each race is distinct and different. 110
We drive off foreigners and punish barbarians,
Hate one another, call each other names.
Today is not yet the Age of Great Unity;[5]

We only compete in cleverness and power.
The land of the red man is vast and remote; 115
I know you are eager to settle and open it.
The American eagle strides the heavens soaring,
With half of the globe clutched in his claw.
Although the Chinese arrived later,
Couldn't you leave them a little space? 120

If a nation does not care for its people,
They are like sparrows shot in a bush.
If the earth's four corners won't accept them,
Wandering in exile, where can they rest?
Heaven and earth are suddenly narrow, confining; 125
Men and demons chew and devour each other.
Great China and the race of Han
Have now become a joke to other races.
We are not as simple as the black slaves,
Numb and confused wherever they be. 130
Grave, dignified, I arrive with my dragon banners,
Knock on the custom's gate, hesitant, doubtful.[6]
Even if we emptied the water of four oceans,
It would be hard to wash this shame clean.
Other nations may imitate this evil; 135
No place left to hold our drifting subjects.
In my far travels I recall Ta-chang and Shu-hai;[7]
In my recent deeds, ashamed before Generals Wei and Huo.[8]
I ask about Sage Yü's travels, vast, limitless;[9]
When will China's territory expand again? 140

(JCL, pp. 350–365) *(Tr. J.D. Schmidt)*

My Small Daughter

We sit around the lamp talking, hating to leave;
Hidden deeply within curtains, the door not closed.
My small daughter grabs my beard, struggling to ask questions;
Her mother does not answer her, but she pulls mother's clothes.
"The sun must be really close to our heads;
Is the ocean as large as my two hands clasped together?"
I want to spread out a world map to show her everything;
A wind blows the curtain, night lamp, moths flutter around.

(JCL, p. 422) *(Tr. J.D. Schmidt)*

Ballad of the Great London Fog

The blue sky has died, the yellow sky rises;
Oceans churn, clouds reverse, spirits assemble.
Suddenly heaven appears drunk and God dreams in a stupor;
The whole country sinks into confusion at the loss of the sun.
Vast and boundless, the nation is confused, muddled; 5
Dark and hazy, like the black, sweet land of slumber.

I sat in my ladle-sized room several months,
Facing the wall, I worship *my* king, the lamp.
I cannot tell if it's morning or night;
I cannot distinguish north from south. 10
Flickering low, my wick turns green,
While everywhere fly Armageddon's black ashes.

I feel like crossing the desert's endless yellow sand,
Or probing a bottomless cavern too dark to measure.
Things transform into dust, and the dust is blackened; 15
I watch the air, but the air is ink.
No names can be given to these colors or shapes;
Our eyes and nose are all blocked up.
How could we find another creator P'an-ku
To come forward and reopen the skies?[10] 20
Could this have been the work of devils[11]
Stirring the sea and beating up the waters?
Suddenly we plunge into the boundless night of Avici Hell;[12]
Startled by this evil wind that drove our ship to Demon Land.
I go outdoors but cannot take more than one inch strides; 25
Everywhere on the boulevards is the sound of bells.
Carriages and horses disappear and hide like roosting chickens;
In this mirage of towers and pavilions, the air stinks.
Heaven's net is finely spread, yet a hole appears,
Where we see the sun's red wheel, colored like blood. 30
Dim, dim, not enough light to irritate the eyes;
Pallid and chill, it can't even warm my hands.

I have heard that the earth circles the sun, the moon circles the
earth;
Now the English colonies spread over five continents.
There is nowhere the red English sun does not shine; 35
Its glory extends far and wide to the horizon's end.
But who would have thought their capital can't see the sun?
And people here are worried the sky is going to fall!

I have also heard the earth's moisture evaporates to form rain;
And clever mathematicians can calculate the number of
raindrops. 40
This nation has always made its home on the water—
Not to mention the smoke from ten million hearths.
If you could add up all the fog within the Four Seas inch by inch,
It would still be less than the fog in London City!

(JCL, pp. 509–514) *(Tr. J.D. Schmidt)*

NOTES

1. The prefecture of Ch'ao-chou, in Kwangtung province, is located about 870 *li* east of the provincial capital Canton. This poem describes an encounter the Huang family had with river pirates when they were forced to escape the fighting during the Taiping Rebellion.

2. The town of Three Rivers (San-ho), 40 *li* west of Ta-p'u, was the scene of a major battle in 1865 between the Ch'ing army commanded by Tso Tsung-t'ang (1812–1885) and the Taiping forces. The poet's family took temporary refuge in the town before moving to Ch'ao-chou.

3. Although Huang is referring to the shamanistic practice of summoning a soul, he merely means that the family will be able to calm down in Ch'ao-chou. Spirit banners were used to summon the spirits of the dead. Here the poet was merely trying to express a longing for a calmer life once the family moved to Ch'ao-chou.

4. The Taiping rebels.

5. The Age of Great Unity was the final stage of social development in which all would live in equality and fraternity, according to the Confucian prescription in the classics.

6. Huang arrives on his mission to San Francisco.

7. According to the *Huai-nan tzu,* the sage emperor Yü traveled from Chang-hai in the east to Shu-hai in the north, a distance of two hundred and thirty thousand Chinese miles.

8. Wei Ch'ing and Huo Ch'u-ping were Han dynasty generals who drove off the barbarian Huns.

9. The sage emperor Yü rescued China from a vast flood, delimiting the area of the country during his extensive travels.

10. According to popular mythology, P'an-ku created the world by separating the sky from the earth.

11. Monsters in Buddhist terminology, or *asuras.*

12. In Indian Buddhism, Avici was the lowest level of Hell.

CH'EN PAO-SHEN (1848–1935)

Ch'en Pao-shen (*Po-ch'ien;* T'AO-AN), a native of Foochow, Fukien, was a scholar-official, poet, and calligrapher, who had the dubious distinction of being the last of a long line of tutors to Chinese emperors. He passed the *chin-shih* examination in 1868 and shortly thereafter won an appointment to the Hanlin Academy as a compiler, and later rose to become a grand councilor. During the seventies, Ch'en was known for his fearless criticism of corrupt officials and his attempts to reassert a high moral tone in the Ch'ing court. Along with Chang Chih-tung, Huang T'i-fang (1832–1899), and others, he belonged to a group of conservatives known as the "Pure Trend" (*ch'ing-liu*) party. Following the defeat of China in the Sino-French War, he was accused of ineptness in administration and demoted. For more than twenty years after 1891, he returned to his native town where he built his Riverside Charm Villa (Ts'ang-ch'ü lou) and found consolation in poetry. In 1909, he was restored to court favor and honored with appointment as Tutor (*t'ai-pao*) to the last emperor, Hsuan-t'ung, better known as the private citizen Henry P'u-yi (1906–1967) after the fall of the dynasty. A loyalist to the very end, Ch'en was able, however, to resist the temptation to follow the deposed emperor to Manchuria when Manchukuo was established under Japanese protection. Ch'en's poetry was considered by the critic Ch'en Yen to be indebted to Han Yü and Wang An-shih (1021–1086), but his style, on the whole, appears closer to the Sung style of poetry than to that of the T'ang.

(Irving Lo)

Inscription for My Evergreen Pavilion

Silk Shearing Lake[1] is half clogged by reeds and grass,
But this knoll tops others in reflective charm of water and trees.
The sun hangs the pagoda's shadow on the branches above a cliff;
For pleasure and contentment one needs only find a suitable place;
In choosing a house because of neighbors, shouldn't one show some care?
On Western Hill gardens and walls crowd each other;
But here a man finds the right way to nurture his moral self.

(Holograph) *(Tr. Yi-yu Cho Woo)*

Without Title: Two Quatrains

I

The three peaks beyond my pavilion show no human feelings:
In all four seasons, I look on them entranced as if by a mica screen.[2]
I have spend my whole life in mountain clogs[3]—
How can that match viewing the green hills through the branches?

II

Dare I dislike the green pond for the reflection of my unkempt hair?
This tree I planted in the courtyard has spread beyond the eaves.
Shading me from the arrogant sun, it yet obstructs the moon:
Now I know that nothing in human affairs can achieve total perfection.

(Nos. 1 and 5 from a series of 5; Chen, p. 527.) *(Tr. Irving Lo)*

On the Twenty-Second Night of the Seventh Month, Facing the Moon at Listening-to-the-Water Studio

Autumn air snatches me out of a solitary man's dream;
The moon at the window is as insubstantial as the mist.
The raging sounds of the endless water,
The still, solemn sky just before daybreak—
Dense shadows of trees are like magic symbols;
The low chirpings of insects are mystic notes.

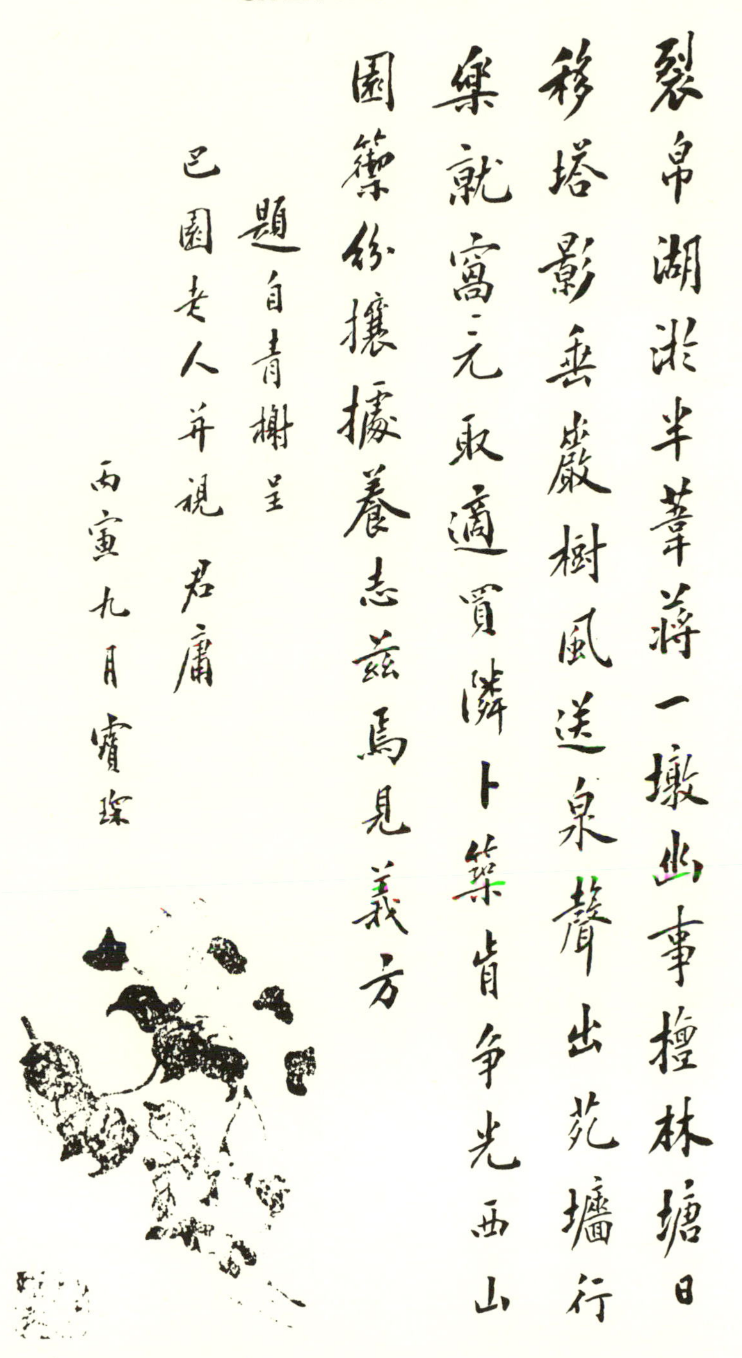

8. Calligraphy and text of the poem "Inscription for my Evergreen Pavilion" by Ch'en Pao-shen. From the collection of Catherine Yi-yu Cho Woo.

Pacing along the rail, I could burst into laughter—
Finding myself neither dead nor enlightened.

(Ch'en, p. 517) *(Tr. Irving Lo)*

NOTES

1. Lieh-po Lake probably derives its name from the sound of the waters, said to be similar to the noise produced by the shearing of a bolt of silk. The name given by the poet to his pavilion was Tzu-ch'ing hsieh, and his studio was called T'ing-shui lou (Listening-to-the-water Studio).

2. The last three words of this line: *ch'ang yün-ping* (literally, "open [up] the mica screen") is taken from a quatrain by the T'ang poet Li Shang-yin entitled "Dragon Pond" (*Lung-ch'ih*). The original poem is a political satire said to have been composed to describe Hsüan-tsung's attempt to convert a humble residence in Hsing-ch'ing Lane (*li*) into the Hsing-ch'ing Palace because of an alleged "dragon" or imperial air hovering over it. *Ch'ang* in another sense could mean "lost in thought" (cf. the compound *ch'ang-wang*).

3. Alluding to the poet Hsieh Ling-yün's famous mountain-climbing boots.

WANG P'ENG-YÜN

(1849–1904)

Wang P'eng-yün (*Yu-hsia;* PAN-T'ANG LAO-JEN, WU-WENG), a native of Kweilin, Kwangsi province, took the *chü-jen* degree in 1871 and was thereafter appointed to a number of posts in the provinces and the capital city, including that of censor.

Wang was a serious student of *tz'u* poetry, and he compiled a much admired edition of the *tz'u* of the Sung and Yüan periods. The modern critic Cheng Ch'ien (b. 1906) has observed that Wang played a key role in the late Ch'ing revival of the form. This late renaissance of the lyric is in part traceable to the emergence of the so-called Ch'ang-chou school in the late eighteenth century, and its insistence on the use of allegory and allusion in commenting on contemporary realities. Wang was on good terms with other poets, such as Cheng Wen-cho, K'uang Chou-yi, and Chu Hsiao-tsang (qq.v.), who were also involved in this movement.

Late in life, Wang edited his own collections of *tz'u* poetry, which he combined under the single title: *Pan-t'ang ting-kao*. Like many of his contemporaries, his poetry reveals a deep interest in current affairs, regret and sorrow for the declining political and military strength of the state at a time of internal disorder and external threat, and a lessening of the thematic gap between the *shih* and *tz'u* forms. Less experimental-minded than some of his peers, his poems are nonetheless richly allusive and evocative of the age in which he lived.

(William Schultz)

Tune: *Che-ku t'ien*
Title: Random Thoughts upon Reading History, Hastily Composed[1]

I

For thirty years the entire world has looked to *lung-men;*[2]
Who would expect a pedant scholar to be known for his mad fame?
In the private quaters of Wu-an, a festive toast was cut short,[3]
When, still in formal dress, he was bundled off on the road to Lin-ho.[4]

Startled by His Majesty's sudden disfavor,
Recalling those days of roaming through the classics.[5]
The edge of the world next day became for him a city of spring;
Before he could take leave of the Emperor, an edict was issued.
His hair now white, among rivers and lakes, he sobbed his way into a new life.

II

Brilliant minds were legion by the gate of the ancestral kingdom;
In the past, generosity belonged to the lord of P'ing-chin.[6]
At the crossroad, he alone shed tears for the people;[7]
Eight hundred "lost souls" were put to shame by this noble lord.[8]

Pour the parting toast,
No time to waste for the homeward boat.
My great ambition committed in vain to the wind and clouds;
Pitiful is the painted boat surging through the billows,
As I see with my own eyes the dust gathering over the P'eng-lai Isles.[9]

(PTTK, pp. 23–24) *(Tr. Kang-i Sun Chang)*

Tune: *Nien-nu chiao* (The Charm of Nien-nu)
Title: Climbing to the Peak of Yang-t'ai Mountain to View the Ming Tombs[10]

Ascending the mountain, I let my eyes roam,
Face rivers and plains embroidered intricately,
Like lapels and sleeves sewn together;

I point to shadows of trees on the thirteen royal tombs,
And T'ien-shou Mountain lurking low like a mound. 5
In a twinkling, the world has changed its course;
In the mountains all around, nothing but wind and rain,
And spirits of kings long mired in dissolution.
The swelling sound of the wind emerges from the mountain;
The ancient pines take it to be a dragon's roar. 10

There's nothing but the undefined grassland steppes,
And White Wolf River[11] running on forever,
Rushing in torrents along the frontier wall.
Even the old man in the wilds knows the world has changed,
But still he tells of mountain spirits and their sentry calls. 15
The forest stretches, cool and dark,
And confused clouds jostle one another.
I would make a libation to the gods, but the wine is nearly gone.
After emerging from the mountain, I turn back to look,
The slanting rays still linger lovingly on the mountain peak. 20

(PTTK, pp. 5–6) *(Tr. Kang-i Sun Chang)*

NOTES

1. This title is merely a pretext for expressing thoughts about a contemporary incident. The two songs relate to the dismissal of Weng T'ung-ho (1830–1904), the eminent tutor of the T'ung-chih (*reg.* 1862–1875) and Kuang-hsü (*reg.* 1875–1908) emperors, for supporting the latter in the Reform Movement of 1898. In the meantime, the author himself was also forced to resign from his post for similar reasons.

2. In Chinese mythology, *lung-men* (literally, "dragon gate") is where a carp turns into a dragon. Thus, the attainment of success is generally described as entering the "*lung-men*".

3. This alludes to an incident recorded in the *Shih-chi*. T'ien-fen, the Marquis of Wu-an of the Han dynasty, married the daughter of the king of Yen in 131 B.C. During the banquet toast at T'ien-fen's house, Kuan Fu boldly offended the tyrannical T'ien-fen, which action consequently brought death to Kuan Fu and his righteous friend Tou Ying, the Marquis of Wei-chi. This allusion emphasizes the fact that it was on Weng T'ung-ho's birthday that he was sent into exile.

4. Lin-ho Mountain is located on the border between Kwangtung, Kwangsi, and Hunan provinces. One must pass the mountain in order to reach the area south of the Five Ridges.

5. Before leaving the court, Weng T'ung-ho went to Yi-ho Garden to take leave of His Majesty. Yet much to his surprise and disappointment, the emperor, who was his longtime student, quickly passed him by in his sedan chair and completely ignored his presence. The truth was that the Kuang-hsü emperor, though himself aligned with the reform party, had already surrendered to the power of the Empress Dowager Tz'u-hsi, and had become a prisoner in the Forbidden City.

6. Kung-sun Hung of the Han dynasty was known for his ability to recruit the services of talented young men. He was also remembered for his generosity in giving all of his wealth to the needy.

7. Thousands of people thronged to see Weng T'ung-ho off the day he left the court. It is said that before his departure, a man suddenly cried out: "After you go, master, what can we commoners do?"

8. This alludes to the story of the T'ang official Li Te-ÿu (787–849). As a poet described it, "eight hundred lost souls" all shed tears when Li was banished to the south.

9. P'eng-lai is believed to be one of the three fairylands in the Yellow Sea, situated somewhere between Japan and China. This line probably refers metaphorically to the Sino-Japanese War of 1894.

10. Yang-t'ai Mountain is located in Wan-p'ing county, Hopei province. The tombs of thirteen Ming emperors were built near T'ien-shou Mountain.

11. The Po-lang (White Wolf) River originates in Po-lang Mountain in Jehol province.

CHING AN

(1851–1912)

Ching An (*Chi-ch'an*; PA-CHIH T'OU-T'O) was a Buddhist abbot. A native of Hsiang-t'an, Hunan, he was orphaned at an early age, and entered Fa-hua Monastery in his native town at the age of seventeen. It is said that even before he knew how to write, he was able to compose verses effortlessly, which other people had to write down for him. Later he took up the study of Buddhist sutras and the writing of poetry under well-known teachers. He also traveled extensively in eastern and central China, visiting famous monasteries. He earned the sobriquet of Pa-chih T'ou-t'o (The Eight-fingered Monk) after burning off two of his fingers as a sacrifice to the Buddha.

Also imbued with patriotism, Ching An made friends with many of the prominent literary figures of his time, such as Chang Ping-lin (1868–1936) and his fellow Hunanese poet Wang K'ai-yün (q.v.), and he took an active role in promoting the Buddhist faith. With the proclamation of the Republic, he journeyed to Peking to organize a Chinese Buddhist Association, where he died on 8 February 1912, in Fa-yüan Monastery. Before his death, he left word for his ashes to be buried in a stupa which he named the Pagoda of Cold Fragrance (*leng-hsiang t'a*), for which he wrote the following lines as his own epitaph:

> To transmit my mind, one bright moon,
> And bury my bones beneath ten thousand plum-blossoms.

Wang K'ai-yün wrote a preface to Ching An's collected works in which Wang praised him as more "craftsmanlike" (*kung*) than the T'ang poet Han Shan (?7th century). Wang considered him especially adept in the mastery of the five-word "regulated verse" (lü-shih) form and admired his poetry for its naturalness and simplicity, qualities which he associated with the style of another T'ang poet, Chia Tao.

(Irving Lo)

Inscribed on a Painting "Fishing in the Snow on a Wintry River:[1]

He drops his line east of a plank bridge;
Snow presses down on his straw rain cloak, chills.
The river is cold and the water, motionless;
The fishes nibble at plum blossoms' shadows.

(PCTTSC, 2:1a–1b) *(Tr. Irving Lo)*

Thoughts on Climbing the Swept-Leaves Pavilion on the Third Day before the Double-Ninth Festival

Toward evening whither shall I go?
Again I'm climbing a tall pavilion.
Winter sparrows chatter in the dark forest;
Among tangled clouds a faint moon rushes about.
Without even getting drunk on yellow chrysanthemum wine,
How could the heart of a white-haired man be told?
To myself I weep tears over our nation's fate;
In vain they dampen a hermit's lapel.

(PCTTSHC, 8:10b) *(Tr. Irving Lo)*

Mountain Dwelling

No one ever comes to this region of stillness;
The gate of my *Ch'an* cell is shut all day.
The white caps of the rising tide peep over my threshold;
The deepening green color of trees leaps across my wall.
Seen in meditation, mosses trace their patterns on stone;
Under the eaves, the breeze startles the temple bells chanting.
What need is there to snuff out sight or sound?
All things and I must both return to oblivion.

(No. 4 from a series of 4; PCTTSC, 7:1a) *(Tr. Irving Lo)*

Elegy for Myself[2]

Myriad affairs all end in silence and extinction;
In vain these green hills busily entice white clouds.
A frosty bell rings the moon's descent over streams and hills;
Only the plum blossoms exude their fragrance in the cold.

(PCTTSHC, 8:7a) *(Tr. Irving Lo)*

NOTES

1. The title of the painting is derived from the famous quatrain "River Snow" by the T'ang poet Liu Tsung-yüan.

2. Written in 1910, this is the last of twenty quatrains, all bearing the title "Reflection Upon Events—An Addenda to My Poem on Cold Fragrance Pagoda." The author's preface to the poem reads in part as follows:

> Since I wrote the two poems as inscriptions for my burial place, the Cold Fragrance Pagoda . . . I was startled upon hearing about the Russo-Japanese Treaty and Japan's annexation of Korea. I was grief-stricken by the fate of our nation, surrounded by strong neighbors and daily weakened by internal strife. I wrote these heptasyllabic quatrains as my last testimony. . . .

CH'EN SAN-LI

(23 OCTOBER 1852–14 SEPTEMBER 1937)[1]

Ch'en San-li (*Po-yen*, or *Po-yin*; SAN-YÜAN LAO-JEN), was a native of Yi-ning (modern-day Hsiu-shui), Kiangsi province. He grew up in a scholar's family, his father being the governor-general of Hunan, Ch'en Pao-chen (1831–1900), a leader of the Reformist faction and an associate of T'an Ssu-t'ung and K'ang Yu-wei (qq.v.), who planned on turning Hunan into a model, progressive province. Ch'en passed his *chin-shih* examination in 1886 and served as a second-class secretary in the Board of Civil Appointments. But the failure of the 1898 Reform Movement brought down on father and son the ire of the Empress Dowager Tz'u-hsi, who dismissed both of them from office. They took up residence in Nanchang after their dismissal, but after the death of his father, the poet moved to Nanking where he built for himself the San-yüan Studio and devoted himself to scholarship and the writing of poetry.

Along with Cheng Hsiao-hsü (q.v.) and Fan Tang-shih (1854–1904), Ch'en San-li was a leading exponent and advocate of the Sung school of poetry and especially that of Huang T'ing-chien. He also admired the poetry of Han Yü and, like him, he wished to effect a revolution in the poetic style of his time by demanding greater vigor. The attention he paid to craftsmanship and diction, avoiding both the elegant and the vulgar and familiar, was unrivaled—thus achieving an intensity of emotion without perhaps the quaintness or "tartness," that is sometimes identified with Huang T'ing-chien's verse. Ch'en San-li's poetic writings are found in the *San-yüan ching-she shih* (Poems from

---

1. BDRC, 1:225–238.

San-yüan's Studio), which has a modern edition published in 1922. Ch'en San-li was survived by several sons who distinguished themselves as scholars; the most prominent of them was Ch'en Yin-k'o, who enjoyed an international reputation as a Buddhist scholar and an authority on the institutional history of T'ang China.

(Irving Lo)

Strolling in the Moonlight

Bald trees neatly stand row upon row,
A deserted slope quietly beckons me.
Deepening the chill—the occasional sounds of a stone chime;
The moon in a haze—cliffsides seem to float in the air.
Rats gnaw at boulders at the base of a wall;
Crows' cries trail off near a boat on the creek.
Softly chanting poems beneath a faint moon,
This completes the picture of one night's grief.

(SYCSCHC, 3:6a) *(Tr. Irving Lo)*

View from the Pavilion on a Moonlit Night

Just now, when frost flies and the moon wears a halo,
Ten thousand hills stand still, and one pavilion, miraculous.
Pine branches shading roof tiles: a dragon leaving its claw marks;
Bamboo's rustle, sounding at the window: a mouse playing with its whiskers.
A melancholy landscape—tall grave mounds here and there;
The eternal principle of things—perceived in unstrained brew.
An idle night, my hair has been combed through by wind and dew,
Though fitting still for the howling pack of nature's demons to spy upon.

(SYCSS, 2:15b) *(Tr. Irving Lo)*

Prospect of the Wilds

Spring covers the mountains like the sea,
Every flight, every sound unconscious of itself.
Mixed flowers warmed by the sun's shadow.

Budding willows draw out skeins of mist.
By flooded paddy fields I hear the urgent croakings of frogs,
Wild geese fly past a poet's pavilion, crying mournfully.
The path where I come and go, staff in hand,
Inch by inch is fraught with traces of my tears.

(SYCSS, 1:12b) *(Tr. Irving Lo)*

A Night at My Lodge

Croaking, crying, the frogs form a kingdom;
Diving, bombing, mosquitos share my bed.
Desolate hills still disturb my thoughts,
A single candle faces the vast unknown.
My house eaves link up with the influence of the stars,
From beyond the bamboo blind are wafted the fragrances of plants.
This dying night, I listen as in a dream—
On the valley wind, the music of pipes and strings.

(SYCSSHC, 1:41b) *(Tr. Irving Lo)*

On the Night of the Fourteenth of the Eleventh Month Setting Out for Nanchang by Boat on a Moonlit Night

The dewy vapors are like tiny insects;
The waves' power is like a recumbent bull.
The bright moon is like a white silk cocoon,
Enveloping my boat on the river.

(No. 2 from a series of 4; SYCSS, 1:58a) *(Tr. Irving Lo)*

WEN T'ING-SHIH

(1856–1904)[1]

Wen T'ing-shih (*Tao-hsi*), a reform-minded official and scholar during the declining years of the dynasty, lived a relatively short but eventful life, observing and participating in the beginnings of the tumultuous changes which his country underwent. The son of an official, he spent his youth in the city of Canton rather than in his native P'ing-hsiang in Kiangsi. In 1882, he attained the *chü-jen* degree and, by 1890, became a *chin-shih*, finishing second in the palace examination. He was immediately appointed to the prestigious Hanlin Academy where he also received a quick promotion. His rapid rise, it is said, brought on the jealousy of some of his colleagues, and his progressive ideas and his easy access to the Emperor Kuang-hsü engendered further opposition among the conservatives. By 1896, under the direction of the powerful Empress Dowager Tz'u-hsi, he was denounced and stripped of his rank. When Tz'u-hsi took control of the government in 1898, Wen's life was threatened and he fled to Japan where he was aided by various Japanese scholars, especially Naitō Kōnan (1866–1934). He did return to China subsequently, but his fortunes never improved. In 1904, he died in his native P'ing-hsiang, not yet fifty years of age.

Wen's greatest contribution to scholarship was as a historian, especially of the Yüan or Mongol dynasty. As a poet, he is best known as a composer of lyric poems, for which he was acclaimed by his contemporaries. His quatrains translated here tend to juxtapose cap-

1. Hiromu Momose, ECCP, 2:855–856.

tivating worlds of natural beauty and a lingering concern with social affairs, thus reflecting the kind of life he led.

(Timothy C. Wong)

Miscellaneous Verses on Living in the Mountains

I

I diligently concoct my elixir in a crucible of Himalayan bamboo,
And freely scatter my gold in Jetavana Park.[1]
I have but a name untainted, and nothing to say.
The winds of heaven blow about my seat, thick with fallen flowers.

II

Out of the floodgate of stone, just closed, a three-foot cataract.
From the craggy ascent above dangle ancient vines.
Peering at my window and about to descend: an ape stealing fruit.
Crossing the brook and still looking back: a stork pecking ice.

(Nos. 1 and 2 from a series of 3; Hsü 177:19a–19b) *(Tr. Timothy C. Wong)*

Tune: *Lin-chiang hsien*
Title: Written on a Boat at Canton, 1882

Searching for spring beyond the Five Ridges,[2] I find spring's scenery strange:
Cotton plants blooming everywhere;
The sound of oars and human voices—an indistinguishable *yiya.*
Southern spirits residing among tamarisks and junipers;
Riverside market stocked with oysters and shrimp.

A song of the Recommended Scholar, a fine, skillful tune:[3]
I listen casually to the boat-girl's *p'i-p'a.*
A silken rain sliced by the wind sends off homing crows.
Lately I'm rather at odds with the world:
I weep no more at the "Song of the Jasmine Princess."[4]

(YCHT, pp. 23–24) *(Tr. Timothy C. Wong)*

Tune: *Che-ku t'ien*
Title: Impressions

The fires of kalpa: have they ever consumed one speck of dust?
Slipping into the human sea, I find myself renewed.
Idle I finger a little inkstone to grind smooth the affairs of the world;
Drunk, I pluck the flowering branches to mark off the passing of spring.

I listen to the nightwatch,
And the dawn cock's crowing;
Layer upon layer, last night's fog locks the city's double gate.
My platter is piled high with vegetables for the new year,
But I love only the red pepper's pungent taste.

(YCHT, pp. 20–21) *(Tr. Irving Lo)*

NOTES

1. Jetavana Park is said to be a favorite resort of the Buddha Sakyamuni, obtained for him by the elder Anathapindika from Prince Jeta. Unwilling at first to sell it, the prince, in jest, demanded as a purchase price enough gold to cover the park's entire grounds. To his astonishment, Anathapindika met his price, and the sale was thus concluded.

2. Canton lies to the south of five mountain ridges.

3. Author's note: "In the middle years of the Tao-kuang reign, Jung, a scholar recommended for office on the basis of his "filiality and uprightness,' composed a volume of the folksongs of Kwangtung, containing many lovely and mournful lyrics."

4. The song title derives from a place of that name south of Canton where, legend says, a palace girl named Su-hsing (White Jasmine) of the Southern Han dynasty (mid-ninth century) was buried. Another source says that the place was a burial ground for princesses, and that jasmine was widely planted there.

CHENG WEN-CHO

(1856–1918)

Cheng Wen-cho (*Chün-ch'en; HSIAO-P'O,* SHU-WEN, TA-HO SHAN-JEN) was a native of Kao-mi, Shantung province, whose father Ying-ch'i served as the governor of Honan and later Shensi provinces. Ying-ch'i was skilled in both poetry and painting, and these arts his son learned at home. Through his own efforts, Cheng Wen-cho also acquired a deep knowledge of such diverse subjects as traditional Chinese music and medicine and the ancient bronze and stone inscriptions. He received the *chü-jen* degree in 1875, but failed to secure a post in the regular bureaucracy. Until the fall of the dynasty in 1911, he lived in the lower Yangtze valley region, where he was employed as a *mu-fu,* or personal advisor to local and regional officials. Thereafter, he made his living as a painter and medical practitioner.

As a poet, Cheng Wen-cho wrote mainly in the *tz'u,* and in time he came to be recognized as one of the foremost exponents of this form in his day. It was because of his efforts, and those of such associates as Chu Hsiao-tsang (q.v.), that the *tz'u* form enjoyed a revival in the late nineteenth and early twentieth centuries. The poet Wang K'ai-yün (q.v.) remarked on the vigorous manner of his poetry, and the modern critic Cheng Ch'ien attributes to him this same quality, as well as those of rich detail and precise attention to the requirements of the form. His poetry is richly lyrical in tone, thus inviting comparison with some of the earlier masters of the form, and reflective of both private moods and the public events of the time. His personal reaction to the intervention of western armies in suppressing the Boxer uprising is seen, for instance, in the "Yeh chin-men" poems translated below.

(William Schultz)

Tune: *Yeh Chin-men*[1]

I

You cannot leave!
On the dark land, willows plucked in grief lie withering.
Frost crackling, the horses' hooves coldly clip-clopping,
Geese take wing under a darkening border moon.

Floating clouds in the northwest obscure my vision,
Yet I cannot bear to recall your visage.
Yesterday a host, today merely a guest
In these blue mountains, no longer our native land!

II

You cannot stay!
For the heart breaks to see ancient palaces in autumnal hues;
Jade pavilions and chalcedony towers cast long shadows on the waves;
In the evening sun, someone stands alone.

It is said Ch'ang-an is like a chessboard,[2]
But I cannot ask where you lodge.
River hostels, hill stations, none do I recognize,
So, if in dream I return, which do I explore?

III

You cannot return!
Tho' in one night the raven's head should turn white![3]
Where is this flute in mountain passes under a setting moon?
The horse nickers and turns northward.

Fish and geese[4] seek quiet depths in this rivered land;
I cannot endure news of your activities.
How hateful that I cannot soar upward on manifold wings;
Under jumbled clouds, grief hangs like a shroud!

(CFYF, p. 30) *(Tr. William Schultz)*

Tune: *Yang-liu chih* (Willow Branch)

Normally, who can explain the hurtful spring,
Or the wagering on steeds racing down catalpa lanes?

Silent, lonely is this empty city, the flying catkin gone,
The sounds of barbarian pipes now stirring up dust on its broad avenues.

(CFYF, p. 34) *(Tr. William Schultz)*

Tune: *Ch'ing ch'un-kung* (Celebration in the Spring Palace)
Title: Fellow Wanderers Gather for the Night in Late Autumn, and I Express My Inner Thoughts.

Frosty moonlight flows down the stairs;
Ragged mists envelop the imperial garden.
The sad notes of nomad pipes cross the tall citadel.
Vanishing geese over frontier passes,
Cold crickets at my door, 5
With broken hearts, we listen together to these sounds.
I circle the balustrade, taking bold steps;
Myriad leaves tremble; billowing winds arise in alarm
I mourn for the autumn season and my life;
But still I envy the drooping willow— 10
As if knowing it has already withered.

I walk and sing of my sorrows on leaving the capital[5]
My precious sword lies cold;
And candles weep their profuse tears.
Nearing old age on the Central Plain, 15
All I see is the frighted, dusty land.
Even the north wind is taken for frontier voices.
My dream sinks away into a sea of clouds;
Such lonely solitude, the fish and dragons have not wakened.[6]
A poet with a wounded heart 20
In this southern region
Will grieve until death still unknown.

(CFYF, p. 75) *(Tr. Kang-i Sun Chang)*

NOTES

1. As Cheng Ch'ien has pointed out, these three poems relate to the flight of the Empress Dowager Tz'u-hsi, the Kuang-hsü emperor, and other members of the court to Ch'ang-an during the occupation of Peking by the Allied Expeditionary Forces as a result of the Boxer Rebellion of 1900.

2. An allusion to the line by Tu Fu: "I've heard it said Ch'ang-an is like a chessboard."

3. An allusion to the famous story "Prince Tan of Yen," and to the miracles which preceded the prince's escape from captivity in the state of Ch'in.

4. I.e., letters or messages.

5. Cheng was born in Peking, but left for the south during his twenties.

6. It was believed that fish and dragons slept during the day in the autumn season. See Tu Fu's line: "While the fish and dragons sleep, the autumn river turns cold."

CHU HSIAO-TSANG

(1857–1931)

Chu Hsiao-tsang (*Kuo-sheng* and Ku-wei; OU-YIN and CH'IANG-TS'UN), also known as Chu Tsu-mou, official, scholar and poet, was a native of Kuei-an, in Hu-chou district (modern-day Wu-hsing), Chekiang province. He passed the metropolitan examination in 1883, placing first in the second rank, and was made a bachelor in the Hanlin Academy. After being promoted to compiler and then expositor in the Hanlin Academy, he was next assigned to the Grand Secretariat as a sub-chancellor, and still later made a vice-president in the Board of Ceremonies. When a belated attempt was made to reorganize and modernize the central bureaucracy in the waning years of the dynasty, he was selected for membership in the newly created Privy Council. When events soon overtook his political career, and when the Republic was born, his conservative views drove him into seclusion on the seacoast, where he remained until his death two decades later.

Chu Hsiao-tsang's scholarly interests were shaped by his literary preferences; namely, the *tz'u*, or lyric, tradition. Foremost among his contributions in this field is the much-admired *Ch'iang-ts'un ts'ung-shu*, in 259 *chüan*, the printing of which he supervised. This collectanea contains the carefully collated lyrics of 168 poets from the late T'ang to the end of the Yüan dynasty. Among his other publications is an annotated edition of the poems of Wu Wen-ying (?–ca. 1260), a popular anthology of 300 Sung lyrics, and an edition of the *yüeh-fu* poems of Su Shih.

As a young man, Chu Hsiao-tsang took up the writing of poetry in the traditional *shih* modes. He abandoned those forms after he was forty years of age, and began to cultivate the lyric form under the influence of Wang P'eng-yün and Cheng Wen-cho (qq.v.), with whom he had by then formed a close personal relationship. By temperament, he was attracted to the manner of the Southern Sung poet Wu Wen-ying, who has been said to combine a fanciful flight of the imagination with profundity of meaning. Later, he turned for inspiration to Su Shih and Hsin Ch'i-chi, both of whom, although very different as poets in many respects, are vigorous in manner and broad in scope. Chu's lyrics have been praised for their topicality, intricateness, and musicality. Wang Kuo-wei described him as being without peer in being able to forge a style that is "spontaneous and miraculously inspired."

(William Schultz)

Tune: *Che-ku t'ien*

Title: On the Ninth,[1] outside Feng-yi Gate, I Passed by P'ei-ts'un's[2] Country House.

Wild water and an arching bridge,
 left from another time:
I try to confess to the old gulls
 a heart full of sorrow.
Sad and confused in a southern suburb[3]
 I dropped my whip as I passed.
Toward the clear and bitter western range
 I peer from under my hat.[4]

These tears newly dried,
These poems set to ancient tunes.
Butterflies seldom come
 to the lonely house gates.
Red dogwood, white chrysanthemums
 have survived unharmed.
Only: before the wind there
 there is what I brood on.

(CTYY, p. 3) *(Tr. Li Chi and Michael Patrick O'Connor)*

Tune: *Che-ku t'ien*

Title: New Year's Eve in the Year *Keng-tzu* [1900]

A cup of wine as clear as water
 reflects my temples going white.
With such a cup, away from home

one easily grows old.
The prickly points of my drunken guts
are as terrible as a row of spears.
The poetry brush, icy and frosted,
sadly cannot bloom.

I throw away the pillow and sit up.
I roll up the book and sigh.
I don't mind
the screaming of the last roosting crow.
The red of candlewax flowers
changes the world where people live.
The green of mountain shining
brings back the home I dream of.

(CTYY, pp. 11–12) *(Tr. Li Chi and Michael Patrick O'Connor)*

Tune: *Huan hsi sha*

A solitary bird crashing into the waves wings off in joy;
Sundered sunset clouds are like dabs of carmine, the water's like a blank page.
But to whom shall I write endlessly of river and sky?

Over our twin pleasure boats, a moon rises at the plucking of the string;
Facing the window, coiffured hills entice the lingering clouds to stay.
The places where I've traveled alone aren't altogether desolate.

(CTYY, p. 22) *(Tr. Irving Lo)*

NOTES

1. On the ninth of the ninth month, when friends usually gather to climb the heights together.

2. Courtesy name of Liu Kuang-ti (1858–1898), a poet and one of the "Six Gentlemen" who met a martyr's death after the failure of the abortive 1898 Reform Movement.

3. Alluding to the letter, an apologia for his way of living, sent by the recluse Wang Seng-yu (?–ca. 493) to his cousin, containing the following lines:

> Your home is near the marketplace;
> Mine is at the southern suburb.
> Your home is crowded with guests;
> Mine is full of sparrows.

4. Alluding to the story about the handsome general Tu-ku Hsin (fl. 540) of the Tsin and Eastern Wei period, who one day came back into the city from hunting at dusk, wearing his hat aslant, thus unwittingly setting a fashion when his admirers in the city on the next day all wore their hats the same way.

K'ANG YU-WEI

(19 MARCH 1858–31 MARCH 1927)[1]

K'ang Yu-wei (*Kuang-hsia;* CH'ANG-SU, KENG-SHENG; also known by his earlier name of Tsu-yi), a scholar of the classics, teacher, an original thinker, leader of the 1898 reform movement, calligrapher, and poet, was a native of Nan-hai, Kwangtung province. Born into a scholar's family, he took up the study of the Confucian classics at an early age, read widely in Buddhism and Taoism, and later became a staunch admirer of Western civilization. In his youth, he repeatedly tried and failed the civil service examinations. In 1895 he passed the *chin-shih* examination which earned him, however, an appointment only as a second-class secretary with the Board of Works. Nonetheless, he left a heavy imprint on the intellectual life of the late Ch'ing with his contributions in almost every field from art to politics.

In the realm of Confucian scholarship, K'ang vehemently opposed the teachings of the Sung Neo-Confucianists and championed the study of the *Kung-yang Commentary*, and the "New Text" teachings of the Han dynasty. He contended that the texts of the "Old Text" school were forgeries, and he presented Confucius as a defender of social change. K'ang opened a school in Canton as early as 1891 and revolutionized its curriculum to include, for example, public speaking and physical education, along with the more traditional subjects of belle lettres and moral philosophy. A prolific writer, K'ang began to advocate not only his new interpretations of the classics but also ideas for social change, including his opposition to the custom of foot-binding for women.

In 1894, K'ang went to Peking to take part in the metropolitan examination. Disillusioned by the series of diplomatic defeats inflicted

---

1. BDRC, 2:228–233.

on the Ch'ing government by Japan and the Western powers at the time, K'ang, as a commoner (*pu-yi*), organized in the spring of 1895 a successful attempt to submit a memorial directly to the throne in the name of over a thousand petitioners, including 603 examination candidates. They opposed the peace treaty with Japan and advocated institutional reforms and the removal of the capital to the safety of the interior. This led to an audience in February, 1898, with the Kuang-hsü emperor, who eventually was won over by K'ang. On June 10 the emperor handed down a series of measures to institute reform. Following the effective opposition of the Empress Dowager Tz'u-hsi, however, this movement, known as the "Hundred Days Reform," ended in defeat on September 20 with the arrest and imprisonment of the Emperor Kuang-hsü. The "Six Gentlemen" executed for their participation in this movement included a younger brother of the poet, K'ang Kuang-jen (1867–1898), and T'an Ssu-t'ung (q.v.). K'ang Yu-wei himself narrowly escaped from capture, along with his disciple Liang Ch'i-ch'ao (q.v.), with the help of foreign diplomats.

Soon after the debacle of the 1898 reform, K'ang began a long period of exile abroad, which ended only in the winter of 1913. In the fifteen years he lived abroad, he circled the globe four times and lived in Japan, Canada, the United States, India, Mexico, Singapore, and several European countries. During this time, he kept up his political activities by raising money and establishing schools and newspapers, sometimes in competition with other revolutionaries led by Dr. Sun Yat-sen (1866–1925). After his return to China, K'ang made his home in Shanghai, where he engaged in private teaching. He remained a monarchist at heart, allying himself briefly with Yüan Shih-k'ai (1859–1916) in the latter's attempt to establish a constitutional monarchy, and a visionary, believing that the world will progress through the three stages of chaos (*luan*), small peace (*hsiao-k'ang*) and universal peace (*ta-t'ung*), and that the Great Commonwealth preached by Confucius is ultimately attainable.

K'ang's poetry, found in thirteen separate collections, chronologically arranged, is frequently marked by vitality and original thought. Although K'ang was not a part of the "poetic revolution" started by Huang Tsung-hsien (q.v.), his poems may be said to belong to the school of Huang and Kung Tzu-chen (q.v.), both of whom were inclined to the belief that poetry should contain the untrammeled expression of the spirit. In the preface to his collected works, written in 1909, K'ang called attention to the two aspects of poetry he considered most important: *ch'ing* (emotion) and *hsing* (sensibility) on the one hand and *ching* (experience) and *shih* (events) on the other. "My poems," he wrote, "are meant to describe my life's circumstances, to express my hidden sentiments, given vent at random to sadness or joy, and sighing and singing without restraint"—again a typically Confucianist prescription, both in letter and spirit.

(Irving Lo)

In Lieu of a Preface to *The Great Commonwealth Book*[1]

All manifestations of life[2] are simply pain;
My coming into the world, just an accident of birth.
Prisoners in jail bemoan this corrupt generation;
Pity those who suffer from hunger and cold.
Many ancient sages prescribed sound remedies,
But vast heaven is callous beyond belief:
Ten thousand ages with no progress,
This great earth is doomed to sink into oblivion.

(KNHHSSC, 1:2) *(Tr. Irving Lo)*

Seeing Spring Off

All day long, I ache for spring, for spring's already gone.
The flowers left behind: who's around to savor their smell?
A yellow oriole, in the tangled leaves, warbles insistently;
A purple butterfly, searching for spring, flies off by itself.
Old time feeling: the flourishing capital is now a fantasy;
Seeing a friend off: all the more unsettled by the onrushing river.
O Prince of Friends, refrain from summoning the hermit with a song:
Back to the fresh flora in the mountain garden: this wish I will not deny.

(KNHHSSC, 1:48) *(Tr. Eugene C. Eoyang)*

Upon Leaving the Capital: A Farewell to My Several Friends[3]

He who mounts the Heavenly Dragon[4] has the following of myriad souls;
A sacred cliff stands alone as if transported there on magic wings.
A final clasp of your hand: I carry away all your noble sentiments;
My eyes gallop over the universe: only a dense fog closing in.

Before our eyes, warring nations engage in chasing the deer;[5]
Among the empire's talents, who is the Reclining Dragon?[6]
Fondling my sword, I can only shout, "let us go home":[7]
A thousand hills, in wind and rain, reverberate from this blue blade.

(KNHHSSC, 1:55) *(Tr. Irving Lo)*

Discussing Poetry with Shu-yüan,[8] and Sent to Jen-kung, Ju-po, and Man-hsüan[9]

My meaning, my experiences have nothing to do with Li Po or Tu Fu;
Then what use can I find for the poetry of Yüan and Ming?
Let my words soar upward, to stir up the wind and clouds,
Or appear so strange as to startle spirits and ghosts.
Sweep away all the new "Remarks on Poetry" books,
Then, indistinctly, the music of the spheres may still be heard.
This thing called poetry is both profound and subtle:
For a thousand ages it has aroused people with its miraculous sounds.

(No. 3 from a series of 3; KNHHSSC, 11:89) *(Tr. Irving Lo)*

Visiting Mount Vernon and Paying Homage at George Washington's Burial Vault

Swiftly flows the emerald Potomac River;
In front of Mount Vernon, lush grass and fragrant trees.
Fondling his sword and clothing, I admire this sage-hero;
From these lovely hills and streams, earth sprouts a young culture.
His modest cottage recalls for me the steps before the grave of Yao;[10]
The clouds from the Cave of Yü[11] hover over the grave where he rests.
Declining to be a monarch, he made known his abundant virtue;
Democracy for myriad ages will celebrate these Three Sacred Mounds.[12]

(KNHHSSC, 8:26) *(Tr. Chang-fang Chen)*

NOTES

1. The *Ta-t'ung shu*, a book outlining K'ang's vision of a universal utopia built in part on the idea of a revival of Confucian teaching. See Laurence G. Thompson's nearly complete translation and explication of this book, *Ta T'ung Shu: The One-world Philosophy of K'ang Yu-wei* (1958).

2. Literally *ch'ien-chieh* (a thousand realms or stages), a Buddhist term.

3. Written in 1889, after the failure of K'ang's first attempt to submit his memorial advocating reform to the throne.

4. Alluding to two passages in the *Ch'u Tz'u*: "Harness winged dragons to be my coursers" (*Li Sao*, line 170, in David Hawkes's translation) with *t'ien-lung* used by K'ang instead of *fei-lung* and "hundred spirits" (*pai-shen*) from Wang Yi's commentary to the "Yüan-yu" poem, modified by K'ang to *wan-ling* (ten thousand living souls).

5. See Yu T'ung, note 1.

6. *Wo-lung*, i.e., Chu-ke Liang, the sage minister of Liu Pei in the Three Kingdoms period.

7. An ironic reference to T'ao Ch'ien's rhyme prose composition "Kuei-ch'ü-lai tz'u" (Let Us Go Home).

8. The courtesy name of Ch'iu Wei-hsüan, a wealthy Chinese merchant in Singapore who befriended the poet during his exile years.

9. Jen-kung is the courtesy name of Liang Ch'i-ch'ao (q.v.) who was K'ang's favorite disciple and later his associate in the Reform Movement; Ju-po is the courtesy name of Mai Meng-hua (1875–1915), one of K'ang's loyal followers; Man-hsüan, the brother of the above, is the courtesy name of Mai Chung-hua (fl. 1880–1900), who married K'ang's eldest daughter T'ung-wei (b. 1878) and was the compiler of a collection of essays on reform by eighty authors, including K'ang, published in 1898, under the title *Huang-ch'ao ching-shih wen hsin pien*.

10. Emperor Yao, from the legendary period of ancient Chinese history, abdicated the throne in favor of his successor Shun. Shun later also abdicated and passed on the throne, not to his son, but to Yü, another ancient culture hero of China whose many accomplishments included the pacification of the floods. Yao, Shun, and Yü are three sage-kings in Chinese mythology, and their times were regarded by Confucius as the Golden Age of Chinese civilization.

11. The burial place of Emperor Yü.

12. *San-fen* commonly refers to the three most ancient texts, or treasure-houses, of Chinese culture which were supposed to contain the writings of Fu Hsi, Shen-nung, and Huang-ti (Yellow Emperor), all three being ancient Chinese culture heroes who invented respectively the writing system, agriculture, and statecraft. This title, however, is not included in the *Yi-wen* (literature) section of the *Han-shu*. Although, by the end of the eleventh century, a man by the name of Chang Shang-ying did produce a book with such a title, most Chinese bibliographers have rejected the book as a forgery because of its fantastical content. Hence, it is not very likely that K'ang (who generally showed no respect for forgeries of classics) would use this term in this sense. *Fen* also means "grave mound," and it is quite logical to suppose that, since the poet links George Washington to Emperors Yao and Yü in this poem, he is using *san-fen* not to refer to the so-called *Three Sacred Texts* of Confucianism (which exists only in title) but to refer to the three graves. Note also that an implied "trinity" of heaven, earth, and man does exist in this poem and that the cardinal number *three* is important to K'ang elsewhere in his philosophical writings.

YI SHUN-TING (1858–1920)

Yi Shun-ting (*Shih-fu*), native of Lung-yang in Hunan, is little known and little studied in modern times; but in his own day he was considered a poet of prodigious talent, and, by the time of his death, he left the world nearly ten thousand poems. During his lifetime, his works were known and acclaimed throughout China.

It is told of Yi that in 1875, the year he attained his *chü-jen* degree, he passed through Nanking on his way to the higher examinations in the northern capital. Riding a donkey, he visited the city's various historical spots in the snow and, deeply inspired, dashed off in a single day twenty poems in the heptasyllabic "regulated verse" form.

As a statesman, Yi's career was not marked with success, even though he held fairly high office. During the Sino-Japanese War (1895), he served unsuccessfully as a military advisor to Liu Yung-fu (1837–1917) in Taiwan; two decades later, he was a member of Yüan Shih-kai's government during the latter's abortive attempt to restore the monarchy. Yüan's downfall soured Yi's taste for public life, and he spent his remaining years in taverns and dance halls, losing himself in the pursuit of pleasure.

Yi was known as a learned man who was proud and confident of his own talents. He traveled widely throughout China and drew inspiration for his poetry from the sights he saw. For a time, his many collections were highly popular; but as the taste for literature changed from traditional to modern in twentieth-century China, both Yi and his works fell into relative obscurity. The poems translated here, however, should show that his former reputation was not entirely without substance—that, as a poet, he had a remarkable gift for painting verbal scenes and imbuing those scenes with emotion and philosophical insight.

(Timothy C. Wong)

Dawn Journey

The rustling of yellow leaves quickly wakens me from the wine;
And, taking my last look at the misty waters, I lose sight of the solitary sail.
The border mountains still elude the visitor swallow,
While the moon and stars seem to follow my horse eastward.
My lingering dream still clings to where the autumn grass is green;
My former companion is as yet trimming the night lamp's glowing wick.
Where the willows hang may not be the south bank of the Yangtze;
Where can I find a pleasure pavilion to sing in the dawn breeze?

(Ch'en, p. 665) *(Tr. Timothy C. Wong)*

Leaving the Mountains in the Rain from Yellow Dragon Temple

From the gurgling of the brook I cannot surmise whether it's the dragon's head or tail.
In the gloom among the pines the feathers of the cranes must be wet through.
A verdant rain from the four hills soaks the skyward greenery;
White clouds from one valley appear as in a surging sea.

(WCSSCSC, p. 107a) *(Tr. Timothy C. Wong)*

Passing the Bridge of Immortal Encounter Looking for the Sublime Ascent Temple[1]

From the sudden stilling of the mysterious breeze
I know the mountain is about to greet me.
The water resembles the color of emerald jade,
And the mountain a dark lotus blossom.
The huge boulder lies like a dragon: 5
A man can walk the dragon's back.

To the right, a pool, dark and deep,
Above which hangs an ancient ape.
The ape comes to drink from the stream,
Then gathers up fruit from between the crags. 10
I gaze downward: fishes are moving about,
I look up: vines are in gentle coils.
The name here is the "Bridge of Immortal Encounter";
So take care not to miss encountering a goddess.
For the way to the Temple of Sublime Ascent is yet far off: 15
And I fear it is enwrapped within the petals of the lotus.

(WCSSCSC, p. 99b) *(Tr. Timothy C. Wong)*

NOTE

1. Ch'ung-hsü or Sublime Ascent Temple could refer either to the temple of Lieh-tzu, the Taoist philosopher, or to one built in honor of the granddaughter of Sun Ch'üan, the founder of the Wu Kingdom during the Three Kingdoms period, said to have achieved immortality and ascended to heaven.

K'UANG CHOU-YI

(21 AUGUST 1859–1926)

K'uang Chou-yi (*K'uei-sheng* and *K'uei-sun*; YÜ-MOU TZ'U-JEN and HUI-FENG TZ'U-YIN), official, literary critic, and poet, was a native of Lin-kuei, Kwangsi province. A child prodigy, he was made a licentiate on account of his literary talents at the age of eight and a senior licentiate at seventeen. When he was thirteen years old, he was said to have composed a couplet which his elders thought too "despondent and sickly." (The couplet can be translated: "Weak wine couldn't have induced a three-day stupor,/Wintry plum branches, after all, were outside the window's gauze.") In 1879, he earned the *chü-jen* degree and was appointed to the Grand Secretariat. About this time, he married a woman (née Chao), a skilled musician, for whom he had a deep and lasting affection. Later he was named to a magistrate's post in Chekiang, and subsequently to the secretarial staff of Tuan-fang (1861–1911), when the latter was serving as the acting governor-general of Liang-Kiang. K'uang Chou-yi had long had an interest in the subject of epigraphy, and as a serious collector of art, Tuan-fang seems to have used K'uang as a consultant in that field. In his later years, K'uang lived in Shanghai under rather straitened circumstances.

Developed from childhood, K'uang's lifelong interest in lyric poetry resulted in numerous publications, both of his own verse and of his critical notes and remarks. He published four separate collections of his *tz'u*, which were later collected in one volume published in 1917 under the title *Hui-feng tz'u* (Orchid Breeze Lyrics). His *tz'u* criticism includes six titles of *tz'u-hua* (talks on lyric poetry) and *pi-chi* (random notes) and contains some astute observations on many of the Sung lyric poets and the art of *tz'u* writing. As a poet, K'uang's early works are somewhat frivolous, but after coming under the influence of Wang P'eng-yün (q.v.), a fellow townsman, he adopted a different attitude and began to evolve a new style. This new style, he remarked, must have the following three qualities: *cho* ("ruggedness," "simplicity," i.e., "great cleverness" in the sense this word was used by the Taoists, though its dictionary meaning is "clumsiness"), *ta* (comprehensiveness) and *chung* (sobriety or dignity). The modern scholar Ch'ien Chi-po (1887–1955) has described K'uang's verse as being rich in content, graceful and lucid in manner, and somewhat less broad in scope but more elegant in form than the verse of Chu Hsiao-tsang (q.v.). K'uang is also noted for his precise observance of the complex tonal and metrical rules which govern the form.

K'uang Chou-yi figured prominently in the late Ch'ing and early Republican era revival of lyric poetry; and his name is often linked in this respect with those of Chu Hsiao-tsang, Wang P'eng-yün, and Cheng Wen-cho (qq.v.). As followers and advocates of the Ch'ang-chou school of *tz'u* poetry, they generally subscribed to the principle enunciated by Chang Hui-yen (q.v.) and Chou Chi that the poet should employ allusion and allegory as devices to reflect contemporary realities in his verse. Contrary to the general view that *tz'u* poetry was suitable only for the depiction of love, K'uang maintained that there was no subject on earth that could not serve as grist for its mill. To become proficient in this form of poetry, K'uang insisted, a poet must be a person who is willing "to let his or her innate sensibility shine through" (*hsing-ling liu-lu*) and who is "steeped in and thoroughly familiar with past literature" (*shu-chüan yün-jang*). The term *hsing-ling*, advocated by Yüan Mei (q.v.) in the eighteenth century and by other individualist writers later, is thus revived by this lyric poet who sought to make the *tz'u* form of poetry relevant to the times.

(Irving Lo and William Schultz)

Tune: *Tieh lien hua*

Coolness creeping through the willows, rain upon the flowers:
 It's certain, spring is gone
 What other proof is needed?
Petal upon petal of falling flowers still circle the tree;
Duckweed roots never know catkins that arrived before spring's coming.

Past affairs are whispered by paired swallows on painted beams.
 Purples and reds, reds and purples,
 All labor to entice spring into staying.

In my dreams I travel to fragrant grasses along hill-screened roads;
Awake, I find no trace of them and I become despondent.

(HFT, p. 12) *(Tr. Irving Lo)*

Tune: *Hsi-chiang yüeh*
Title: I Awake Crying on My Birthday, the Twenty-fifth Day of the Seventh Month in the Year of *Yi-mao* [21 August 1915]

In a dream: ten years of shadowy events;
Since awakening: half a day of idle grief.
Lying next to a cold silken quilt, I sense the late autumn;
The taste of tears is more sour than wine.

My heart is torn ev'rywhere I look;
My only regret, this life still wears on.
Before my eyes just now, a red sun hangs from the curtain hook;
This time I listen to the rain, listen to the wind.

(HFT, p. 21) *(Tr. Irving Lo)*

Tune: *Chien-tzu huan hsi sha*
(Sand of Silk-Washing Stream, with Words Deleted)
Title: Thoughts upon Hearing a Singer

Slow to stir up the faded reds, tears soak my clothing;
In another life, let me not be fooled by too much loving:
Under this sky, there's no spot on earth for love to take root.

E'en if flowers do bloom again, it's not on last year's tree;
Clouds may momentarily linger,[1] but only in a mournful song—
No help toward consolation, it just adds to my grief.

(No. 2 from a series of 5; HFT, p. 30) *(Tr. Irving Lo)*

Tune: *Shui-lung yin*

One autumn night in *Chi-ch'ou* [1889], I wrote a *tz'u* poem about the sounds of the horns [of the Peking militia] to the tune of *Su Wu man* (The Tune of Su Wu). It was enthusiastically received by Pan-t'ang (Wang P'eng-yün). In the fourth month [early summer] of *Yi-wei* [1919], I moved to the fifth lane of Chiao-ch'ang [the Military Reviewing Grounds in Peking], an out-of-the-way place. The night alarm sounded taratarantara till dawn, sad enough to penetrate the heart and guts. I slowly picked this *tz'u*. It is not as good as the previous composition but, because of time and things that have happened, it is even sadder.

One sound after another
emerges south of the street.
The deep night
doesn't care that one is haggard.
Sadness and coolness blend.
The watches are long
and the drip of the clock is insistent
Enough to keep one from sleeping. 5
The lamp is guttering.
The flowers have faded.
The incense disperses,
The ashes grow cold.
I am scared as I rise silently,
Slip around the screens and look out.
The moon is only half a medallion; 10
And even worse it is lost
Beyond a misty forest.

Sorrow enters an array of clouds
on the horizon.
The overspent *shang* scale[2]
is shrill and sad for no reason. 15
I have scratched my hair sparse.
My high ambitions were wasted
On the great trackless desert.[3]
Don't dwell on the heart's wounds
When even the homeland 20
Is wreathed with cuckoo cries.
There is a cawing crow sees me
As I stand alone on the empty steps
Shedding tears on my blue robe.[4]

(HFT, pp. 10–11) *(Tr. Li Chi and Michael Patrick O'Connor)*

NOTES

1. The text reads *yün neng chan chu*, probably referring to either the title of the song being sung by the celebrated singer or the words of the song sung on that occasion.

2. The second of five Chinese musical scales, to which the horn is always tuned, is associated with sadness and autumn.

3. Literally, "Dragon Sand," a general designation for China's desert region in the northwest.

4. The garment of a scholar, alluding to a line from Po Chü-yi's "Song of the P'i-p'a."

CHENG HSIAO-HSÜ

(2 APRIL 1860–28 MARCH 1938)[1]

Cheng Hsiao-hsü (*Su-k'an, T'ai-yi;* HAI-TS'ANG), calligrapher and poet, was a native of Foochow, Fukien, and were it not for his monarchist principles and political ambitions, he would have endeared himself to more of his contemporaries during the Republican era. He earned first-place honors when he passed the *chü-jen* examination in 1882, the same year as his fellow townsman Lin Shu (1852–1924), who later distinguished himself by translating the works of Charles Dickens and Alexander Dumas *fils* and many other Western writers into literary Chinese. For several years, Cheng served in diplomatic posts in Japan where he became proficient in Japanese and befriended many Japanese men of letters.

Cheng remained loyal to the Manchu dynasty even after the establishment of the Republic in 1912. Upon the founding in 1932 of the Japanese-sponsored state of Manchukuo, embracing the three northeastern provinces of China, Cheng, who had played a key role in negotiations with the Japanese, was named prime minister in the court of the puppet emperor Henry P'u-yi. For this reason, he was widely regarded as a traitor to the Chinese people. Inevitably, his reputation as a poet also suffered. For example, the eminent poet and critic Ch'en Yen (1856–1937) once thought so highly of Cheng's poetry that he began his commentaries on various poets in his *Shih-yi-shih shih-hua* (Poetry Talks from the Studio of Shih-yi), a work composed in 1914–1915, with an entry on Cheng. And throughout this book, he frequently discussed the accomplishments of Cheng, whom he considered to be a worthy follower of Liu Tsung-yüan and Meng Chiao among the T'ang poets and of Mei Yao-ch'en and Wang An-shih among

1. BDRC, 1:271–275.

the Sung masters. But when Ch'en Yen published his massive *Chin-tai shih-ch'ao* (Anthology of Contemporary Poetry; preface dated 1937), a work that contain selections from the works of 369 poets beginning with Ch'i Chün-tsao (1793–1866) and ending with his contemporaries, not a single selection of Cheng Hsiao-hsü's works was included (although the poet's brother, Cheng Hsiao-ch'eng, was represented)! Such a dramatic reversal of judgment may be cited as clear evidence of how literary criticism in China is often beclouded by irrelevant issues, such as a writer's political sympathies or his personal character.

Cheng left thirteen *chüan* of verse, all chronologically arranged and published under the title *Hai-ts'ang-lou shih* (Poems from the Studio of [Someone] Hiding in the Sea [of Humanity]), taken from a line by Su Shih: "Alone in a sea of 10,000 people." Cheng as a poet is especially adept in the five-word meter, and his style bears some resemblance to the *yüeh-fu* poetry of the Han, Wei, and Six Dynasties periods. The modern critic Ch'ien Chi-po says the following about Cheng's verse: "His words may be plain and simple, but they evoke a distant spirit; they are lean in outward appearance but abundantly rich in the essence [of what poetry should be]," (*Hsien-tai Chung-kuo wen-hsüeh shih,* p. 235).

(Irving Lo)

Wu Family Thatched Hall

After rain, the fitful cries of wild geese fill the hall in autumn;
By water's edge a poet's sentiments drift into the chill sky!
For such moods and feelings, what better than a grove of maple
trees?
In one night the frost of Soochow mirrors their crimson shadows.

(HTLS, 1:1b) *(Tr. Irving Lo)*

Written on the Wall of Ku Tzu-p'eng's Studio[1]

A guest leaves; the window gleams in the twilight;
Walking and humming a verse, I've startled the wild birds.
A mountain peak stands peaceful in the setting sun;
After an autumn shower, the tarn water is only half clear.
By tea tables and mat, manuscripts are scattered around;
Nearby is the temple in honor of the Three Elders.

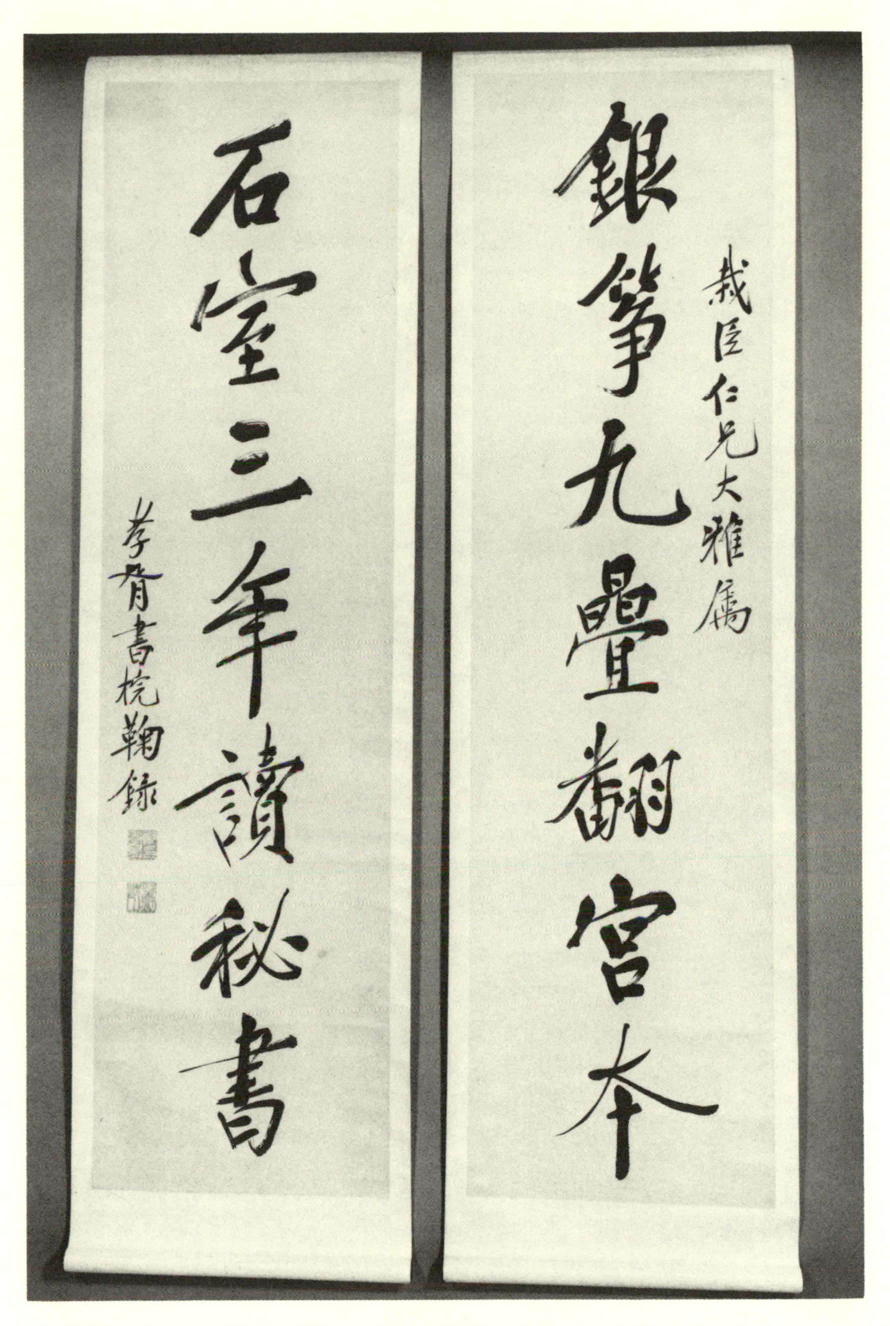

9. Hanging scrolls by Cheng Hsiao-hsü, originally written for and presented to Mr. Frank B. Dunn (1886–1949) of Shanghai, whose courtesy name appears in the upper colophon. From the collection of Irving and Lena Dunn Lo.

Returning to silence and quietude, this we all know,
Yet, always with feeling we set out on our trail.

(HTLS, 1:1b) *(Tr. Irving Lo)*

Night of the Full Moon

Not a thousand gold will make me part with the moon tonight;
All the kalpas I've lived through can't destroy my past affections.
Don't say that a man's life is not as pleasant as a dream:
Life *is* a dream. Saddest of all, it can't ever be found.

(HTLC, 13:11a) *(Tr. Irving Lo)*

A Random Poem

A moon, sinking, drops beside my pillow—
Pitying in vain this unworthy self.
Here I lie in the bright moonlight,
Only to be startled when the moon leaves me.
I would lift myself up and follow it,
But where can I find a pair of wings?
Mountains and rivers aren't hard to cross;
Troubles and woes can sometimes be overcome.
Better yet to fly away in an airplane,
But that would spread consternation among people.
It's hard to forget the world, even in a dream;
Bitter regrets drive me into lengthening shadows.

(No. 3 from a series of 4; HTLS, 12:11a) *(Tr. Irving Lo)*

Returning to Nanking

The north wind shakes my studio window,
Bitterly, the snow weighs down the spotted bamboo.[2]
Wayfarers return home late in the evening,
To a window glowing red and the bamboos still green.

(HTLS, 2:16b) *(Tr. Irving Lo)*

Upon Returning to the Capital in 1923[3]

Living useless to the world is more abhorrent than death;
Among these "bending ears of millet"[4] and brambles, I come back.

Here I search for faded dreams from a brass imperial carriage,
But the kalpa ashes of K'un-ming Pool[5] are too familiar an omen.
True, I've harbored the intent of swallowing coal or painting my body,[6]
But hurtling myself against mountains or chasing the sun is not in my bag of tricks.[7]
With the hollow name of a courtier under two dynasties,
My brittle bones could still be likened to those of Kuo Wei.[8]

(HLTS, 10:4b) *(Tr. Irving Lo)*

NOTES

1. The poet Ku Yün (1845–1906), whose courtesy name was Tzu-p'eng, was a native of Shang-yüan, Kiangsu, and Cheng Hsiao-hsü's best friend. The title of this poem is followed by a note of the author, indicating that the studio was located in Lung-p'an Alley, next to the temple built to the memory of Tseng [Kuo-fan], Shen [Pao-chen], and Tso [Tsung-t'ang]. All were eminent statesmen of the mid-nineteenth century. The area where this temple once stood is part of the compound of Peking's Tiao-yü-t'ai Guest House, which is used by the Chinese government to house distinguished visitors from abroad.

2. The spotted bamboo (*pan-chu*) was commonly believed to have been caused by the tears of the two sisters whom the mythical Emperor Shun married, the spots being the tear stains wept by the consorts upon the emperor's death.

3. The prose preface to this poem reads:

> I first left the capital in the ninth month of 1898, returning to it in the seventh month of 1910 after an absence of thirteen [inclusive] years—all recorded in my poems. I again was forced to leave the capital in the ninth month of 1912, and now I returned in the seventh month of 1923, again after an absence of thirteen years. Pondering my fate in this troubled world and my age and poverty, I wrote this poem.

4. Alluding to Ode 65 in the *Shih-ching*, traditionally taken as a lament for the removal of the capital in Eastern Chou.

5. Referring to the sack of the Yüan-ming Yüan (q.v.).

6. Alluding to the story of Yü Jan in the Warring States period who disguised his identity by turning himself into a deaf mute and a leper to carry out his revenge against his patron's enemy. (Cf. *Shih-chi, chüan* 86.)

7. The phrase "antagonizing mountains and chasing the sun" (*ch'u-mu chu-jih*) is a paraphrase of *ch'u-mu tao-jih*, taken from *Liang shu* (History of Liang). According to the biography of Liu Chün (462–521), he was a man of education who lived under three dynasties and was summoned for an audience with Emperor Wu of Liang because of his reputation. What he said at the interview offended the emperor and he was ultimately rejected. He submitted to his fate and wrote a discourse on fate, in which he said: "Fate is that which

thrives with heaven's mandate; even a force that antagonizes a mountain can't be resisted, and even a zeal for overturning the sun's course won't be effectual."

8. Referring to Kuo Wei in the Warring States period, a wise statesman of Yen who successfully sold himself to King Chao of Yen and was immediately recruited for the king's service. As a result, other wise statesmen gathered in the court, and the king was finally enabled to defeat the state of Ch'i.

T'AN SSU-T'UNG

(10 MARCH 1865–28 SEPTEMBER 1898)[1]

T'an Ssu-t'ung (*Fu-sheng;* CHUANG-FEI), a native of Liu-yang in Hunan, is noted much more as a patriot, a revolutionary martyr, and an eclectic philosopher than as a poet. Nevertheless, along with Huang Tsun-hsien, K'ang Yu-wei, and Liang Ch'i-ch'ao (qq.v.), his name has been included among those who, late in the Ch'ing dynasty, called for the development of a new poetry as part of the general changes needed to cope with the cataclysmic events, precipitated by foreign encroachment and civil war, which had shaken China's cultural confidence to the core.

While still a very young man, T'an traveled in many parts of China, as much for his own political education as to visit places of historical interest, to walk where heroic figures from China's glorious past had walked. The few of his poems translated here were written during this period and, even in their descriptions of scenery, show the heroic sentiments to which T'an was evidently inclined. In form, these poems are traditional and show that, like so many others who wished to reform things literary, T'an found it difficult to practice what he preached.

T'an's self-identification with great men of the past, his penchant for the heroic, is characteristic of his efforts to join forces with late nineteenth-century reformers who were desperate to come to terms with modern realities. When their impatient efforts brought about a conservative reaction—the removal of the reform-minded emperor Kuang-hsü from the throne on 21 September 1898, and the imminent arrest of the major perpetrators of reform—T'an had a chance to flee with other leaders and to regroup the movement in Japan. But, char-

1. Ssu-yü Teng, ECCP, 2:702–705.

acteristically, he refused, declaring his willingness to be among the first to shed blood for his cause. Along with five others, he was executed just seven days later, in the prime of a very dedicated and still promising life.

(Timothy C. Wong)

Parting Chant

The desert is full of powerful winds;
In every direction, a vast expanse.
The setting sun, descending to the level earth,
Lengthens our shadows in the desolate air.
Grasping my sword, I rise to pass the wine,
And with an elegiac song vent my defiant spirit.
Since I knotted my hair and set out on a distant journey,
I've fought battles everywhere.
If heaven and earth will endure,
Our reunion will come as surely as our parting.
The dust of my carriage has obliterated the interminable road,
But the road is interminable: how can I forget?

(TSTCC, p. 451) *(Tr. Timothy C. Wong)*

Fen-chou

Among crab apple and pear, birds summon the wind.
Alongside a trail, peach and plum are a mixture of white and pink.
Within a hundred *li*, spring is like a sea:
A city wall shines half hidden among ten thousand blossoms.

(TSTCC, p. 492) *(Tr. Timothy C. Wong)*

T'ung Pass

From high antiquity, lofty clouds have gathered at this city wall,
Where winds of autumn have scattered away the sounds of
  hoofbeats.
The river, even as it flows through the vast plain, decries its limits;

And the mountain, entering T'ung Pass, will never know about
leveling.

(TSTCC, p. 489) *(Tr. Timothy C. Wong)*

Written on an Autumn Day at the Garden of the Official Residence of the Governor of Kansu

On a small balcony, the shadow of someone leaning against the tall
sky;
In the distance, the sparse forest in twilight's glow.
Let me ask what the west wind is really doing:
To blow so gently, reddening the aramanth blossoms.[1]

(TSTCC, p. 493) *(Tr. Timothy C. Wong)*

Mooring at Night

The hawser tied against a stiff north wind,
A boat on a desolate shore at dawn,
The notes of a single horn from a garrison tower,
The longing for home in a strange land at year's end—
Beneath a hazy moon the mountains lie as if asleep;
In the frosty cold the river ceases to flow.
Forlorn, the ten thousand things are still.
Then what am I here to seek alone?

(TSTCC, p. 467) *(Tr. Irving Lo)*

Tao-wu Mountain[2]

A setting sun lingers lovingly among tall trees,
As dusk disappears into the blue peaks.
At the ancient monastery, clouds hover among cranes;
Above an empty pool, the moon shines on dragons.
Dust dissolves—by a ten-fathom waterfall;
My thoughts break off—at the single note of a bell.
The profound mind of Ch'an, where is it found?
"Chirp, chirp," sing the crickets beneath the steps.

(TSTCC, p. 466) *(Tr. Irving Lo)*

NOTES

1. *Yen-lai hung*: literally, "wild geese come red," or *Amaranthus tricolor*, with showy red flowers resembling the cockscomb. Because its flowering season is in late fall, it is also called *lao shao-nien* (youthful-looking old man) in the eastern part of China.

2. Located outside the city of Liu-yang, Hunan, where a pond is inhabited by lizards and is popularly thought to be a dragon's hiding place.

HSÜEH SHAO-HUI

(18 OCTOBER 1866–14 SEPTEMBER 1911)

Hsüeh Shao-hui (*Hsiu-yu, Nan-ssu*), a native of Foochow, Fukien, came from an impoverished scholar's family. A child prodigy, she was given instruction in embroidery, along with the flute and the singing of *K'un-ch'ü* (K'un-style opera). At thirteen, she startled the literary society of Foochow, which was known for its tradition of poetry contests, or *shih-chung* (literally, "poetry bell"), by winning prizes with her verses, submitted incognito at first (by using the name of her brother as a contestant). Soon she attracted the attention of a brilliant young graduate of the new Naval Academy, ten years her senior, Ch'en Shou-p'eng (1856–?), who admired her poetic genius and sent matchmakers to propose marriage. The wedding took place in 1880, when Hsüeh was only thirteen years old, and the occasion became a literary event celebrated by still another poetry-writing contest. The contest called for specimens to be judged—which were written in accordance with an announced topic and rhyme—to be placed in a box atop a stand from which a bell (*chung*) was hung, the clapper of which was attached by a piece of string to an incense stick. When the incense burned down, the bell struck and the lid of the box closed to further entries.

After marriage, Hsüeh continued her literary and artistic pursuits while keeping house for her husband who frequently was away, studying in Japan (1883) or traveling as an interpreter in England and France (1868–1889). Ch'en Shou-p'eng, a geographer, returned home with a large library of Western books and made his living by translating classics from abroad. Meanwhile, Hsüeh Shao-hui's reputation as a painter, poet, and a writer of Parallel Prose (*p'ien-wen*) continued to grow. Among Ch'en's works is a book of world geography entitled *Chiang-hai T'u-chih*, and the husband and wife jointly produced such works as *Wai-kuo lieh-nü chuan* (Biographies of Famous Women in Foreign Countries) and (*Pa-shih-jih yu-chi*) (Around the World in Eighty Days).

Despite her exposure to Western ideals and ideas, Hsüeh remained a product of strict traditional upbringing. For example, she was opposed to modern education for women, and she proclaimed Virtue, Speech, Arts and Crafts, and Beauty as the four desiderata of womanhood. She brought up her several children according to these beliefs. Her youngest daughter, in order to demonstrate her filial piety, committed suicide after forty days of mourning following her mother's death. A woman of weak constitution, Hsüeh contracted consumption at twenty; still she devoted herself tirelessly to her work and left a large corpus of writings, all published posthumously under the title *Tai-yün-lou yi-chi* (Posthumous Poems from the Pavilion of Brow-black Clouds), containing eight *chüan* of *shih*, two *chüan* of *tz'u*, and two *chüan* of Parallel Prose. She also edited the volume *Kuo-ch'ao kuei-hsiu chi* (Selected Lyrics by Women Poets of the Ch'ing Dynasty), in addition to completing the anthology *Kung kuei tz'u* (Lyrics by Palace Ladies), started by her sister-in-law. Although her poems sometimes contain references to foreign events, such as the assassination of the Japanese Premier, Itō Hirobumi (1841–1909), or the sale by auction of Empress Josephine's jewelry, the range of subject matter in her works is confined chiefly to family events, daily life, and occasional travels to cities like Shanghai or Peking. A note of perfect conjugal bliss runs throughout her poems and serves as a constant reminder of the close bond that always existed between living one's life and the writing of poetry in traditional China. Readers of Chinese poetry will recall the history of the Sung woman poet Li Ch'ing-chao and her husband, Chao Ming-ch'eng (1081–1129), an antiquarian scholar. Much of Li's poetry was inspired by her devotion to her husband. The same close bond between husband and wife existed in the poetic works of women poets until the very end of the imperial period in China.

(Irving Lo)

Ancient Sentiments

Wish to embroider a twin-budded flower?
First grow a pair of loving silk cocoons.
Unbroken is the thread of love
Which blunts the spring wind's cutting edge.

(No. 1 from a series of 4; TYLSC, 1:1b) *(Tr. Irving Lo)*

After Rain

What's to be done about the scorching heat after a rain?
Overflowing gullies seem like rivers.
A frayed carriage's like a steamer drawn by lean horses;
Broken bells capturing the wind, scabby camels approach.
Dozing dogs, in a daze, resemble lazy servants;
Buzzing, buzzing, flies outnumber the officials.
Under a wine-dark sky, all black dust is cleansed.
Let the Dragon King never be amused with a song!

(TYLSC, 3:19b–20a) *(Tr. Irving Lo)*

Emperor Wen[1]

Emperor Wen of his generation, trusting in reform,
Blindly cast to the ground a time-honored tradition.
Craving a nice posthumous title and history's praise,
None but he brought untold suffering to all the people!
Returning to a debt-ridden court without a single plan,
He naively invoked an ancient law to set up an infant ruler.
Pity, all the iron cast could not open a road to Szechwan;
He's left to hum: the "Song of Sorrow" by the River Hsiang.

(TYLSC, 4:8a) *(Tr. Irving Lo)*

In Honor of My Husband's Fiftieth Birthday

Faster than arrows race the rook and hare,[2]
And ruddy cheeks change unnoticed in the mirror.
Take pleasure where you can in this world:
A moment of bliss is better than taking the elixir.
I'll empty the goblet and drink deep the grape wine, 5
And arise to dance in honor of your birthday;
I wish you luck and good fortune for a million years,
That we may live together till our heads turn white.

You've enjoyed fifty springs and I forty;
Our allotted span has entered its ninety-first year. 10
The harvesting season is on, and a sunny day too,
And frolicking children all around our knees.
I recall the time when we exchanged marriage vows,

Your talents and expectations shone like the rays of the morning
  sun.
Even today your fame embraces north and south; 15
People of rank all yield to you, a commoner.

Have you not seen the pine trees of the Southern Mountain?
Beneath thick green canopies, their roots coiled like a dragon.
No carpenter's ax will tap them to make posts and beams;
By rocks and streams, they feed on rain and dew forever. 20
Have you not seen the cranes of the Southern Mountain?
Combing, ruffling their long white feathers at leisure?
Provided with no food, they know heaven and earth to be wide;
By flying high, they will never be caught by net or snare.
Both the pine and the crane live to a thousand years; 25
Abandoned and unknown, their destiny is secure.

Poor we are, but luckily we are rich in books;
The older we grow, the firmer set we are in virtue.
Our native hills may be thousands of miles away,
But birthdays celebrated far from home also bring joy. 30
Yonder Heaven quietly shows a tender love for good men:
It won't deny you an inkstone for an abundant life.
My only wish is that year after year it will stay the same:
With salt and rice, pestle and well water, I'll serve you.
At other times, we'll link our arms to pull a deer cart[3] 35
Or, stepping outside, view the peonies in bloom, all smiles.

(TYLSC, 3:10a–10b) *(Tr. Irving Lo)*

Tune: *Mu-fu-sha* (A Persian Song)[4]
Title: For My Husband Who Sent Me Several Rubbings of Ancient Egyptian Stone Tablets

  Every word a worm, a fish, an elephant;
Then, these strange images of spirits of snake or bull!
  I ask how letters come from the tracks of birds—
  Who, after all, was the chief inventor?
Unless the gods had yielded to each other, 5
How could anyone imitate this Kharosthi script?[5]
  Reputed to be the first beyond the western sea,
  They altered their shapes due to disputes among nations.
    Phonemes? Or pictograms?
    Su Che is long dead, 10

And so is Yang Hsiung.[6]
In vain will bamboo scripts hold the secret of ancient kings.[7]
Even though I may be another Ch'ing-chao,[8]
And you familiar with bronze and stone scripts,
The most learned must be baffled. 15

From ten thousand miles away, I watch the sea and the sky;
I see the vast and indistinct clouds and mist.
I laugh at the halberds and lances of the kingdoms of Man and Chu,[9]
A mirage of the ancients and the moderns:
A thousand years in an instant of time. 20
Left are fragments of inscriptions, chips of tablets.
Admiringly, I inquire into those former days:
Where did that heroic spirit go?
Might they not resemble the omens of dragons and phoenixes?
Only broken tiles and chipped bricks! 25
Neither Yin nor Hsia has left any record,
Who's to sacrifice to Chi and Tseng?[10]
Where once the wheat and barley grew, I face a scene of desolation.
How do those stone figures differ from our bronze camels
Still slumbering among briars and thorns? 30

(TYLTC, A:9b–10a) *(Tr. Irving Lo)*

NOTES

1. Literally, "the Literary Emperor," the posthumous title for Yi-chu, whose reign title was Hsien-feng. The last line of the poem alludes to the *Li Sao* by Ch'ü Yüan.

2. I.e., the sun and moon.

3. A deer cart is narrower and smaller than ordinary carts. The story refers to the wife of Pao Hsüan of the Han dynasty who once took off her jewelry, changed into a short tunic, and stepped down to help her husband pull such a cart out of a rut.

4. The tune *Mu-fu-sha* is a T'ang dynasty *Chiao-fang* or Music Academy title, originating from Persia. *Mu-fu* is a corrupt version of "Molkgu," or "Magu" in ancient Persian, meaning a priest of the Mani religion who flourished in the third century.

5. The text reads *Ch'ü-lu*, referring to Kharosthi, an ancient Aramaic script used between the fifth century B.C. and the third century A.D.

6. Su Che (?–after 300) and Yang Hsiung (52 B.C.–A.D. 18) were both distinguished Chinese phonologists.

7. The text reads *Li-wang,* the king of Li. Li is the name of a kingdom mentioned in the *Shan-hai-ching,* an ancient book of Chinese mythology.

8. The poetess Li Ch'ing-chao, whose husband was an authority on ancient bronze and stone scripts and an avid collector.

9. Mentioned by the Chinese Taoist philosopher Chuang-tzu in a parable purporting to narrate the battles between two kingdoms which occupied the space within a snail.

10. Yin and Hsia are the two oldest dynasties in Chinese history; Chi and Tseng and the two kingdoms conquered by the state of Ch'i (in modern Shantung) in the seventh century B.C. Bronze camels are symbols of royal power, usually erected in front of a palace gate.

LIANG CH'I-CH'AO

(23 FEBRUARY 1873–19 JANUARY 1929)[1]

Liang Ch'i-ch'ao (*Cho-ju, Jen-fu, Jen-kung*), a native of Hsin-hui, Kwangtung, was the most eloquent, impassioned, and influential spokesman among the intellectual leaders of China in the early part of this century.

His association with K'ang Yu-wei (q.v.) marked the beginning of his active life and brought him into the forefront of the ambitious but short-lived reform campaign, known as the Hundred Days Reform, for which he drew up a program for the translation of Western books and sought funds and personnel to establish the Translation Bureau.

Despite the failure of the campaign and the many political vicissitudes he subsequently endured, which involved such prominent figures as Yüan Shih-k'ai, Tuan Ch'i-jui (1855–1936), and Sun Yat-sen (1866–1925), he never abandoned his effort to achieve an intellectual and cultural regeneration through education. At the core of his philosophy of education was his firm belief that every individual should be free to develop his own thinking, unbound by any dogma, be it Confucianism or any other ism.

Through public lectures and prolific publications in the numerous periodicals he founded—the most famous and influential of which was *Hsin-min ts'ung-pao* (Journal of the New Citizen)—he sought to educate the young generation. The most comprehensive collection of his works is the *Yin-ping-shih ho-chi*, an impressive forty-volume work, the subject matter of which, embracing a wide variety of literary, scholarly, and political concerns, testifies to his stature as the foremost intellectual of his time.

---

1. BDRC, 2:346–351.

As a literary figure, he is most remembered for his powerful, lucid, and unique semicolloquial style, which he advocated as early as 1896, two decades before the literary revolution that marked the replacement of classical *wen-yen* by colloquial *pai-hua* as the popular standard for writing. It was, in his words, a *hsin wen-t'i* (new literary style), a mixture of colloquisms and even foreign expressions. But apart from these stylistic features, it was due to the lucidity of his thinking and the intensity of his feelings—the nib of his pen was often drenched with emotion, he wrote—not to mention his erudition, that he was able to touch the hearts of the countless young Chinese who later became the backbone of the New Literature movement. The eminent literary scholar Cheng Chen-to (1878–1958) described Liang's prose as having "toppled the drab and lifeless old style" and "enabled the youth to express themselves freely." Liang Shih-ch'iu (b. 1901), scholar, writer, and translator of Shakespeare, remarked that his oral delivery was even more moving than his prose. His passion for Chinese classical literature came through so powerfully, as he lectured on "The Expression of Emotion in Chinese Rhyme-prose," Liang Shih-ch'iu noted, that it literally swept the huge hall of Ts'ing-hua University. With his sonorous Cantonese accent, he chanted out loud not only the words in many of the poems he memorized as a child from the *Shih-ching* to the Ch'ing drama *T'ao-hua shan*, but also acted out the feelings, tears, and laughter contained therein as well.

While his heart was most intently set on the reformation of China through education and popularization of new ideas from the West, his love for traditional Chinese literature often moved him to compose poems in the classical style in order to record a sentiment or to vent a frustration, of which he certainly had a greater share than men of more ordinary capacities.

Strictly speaking, his verse expresses more of a literati's than a poet's sentiment, occasioned more by the twists and turns of his eventful life (see, for example, the poems translated below, "Autumn Thoughts" and "After the Rain") than by a sudden visit of creative imagination. It is in these classical poems that we find more of a traditionalist than a liberal spirit. He guarded the long tradition of Chinese lyrical poetry with gusto despite his interest in innovation in other areas of life and literature.

(Cecile Chu-chin Sun)

Random Thoughts on Autumn

Already heavy with grief is late autumn,
Sadder still that the season's better half lies squandered.
Bearing up under the rain, ten thousand lotus plants waste away;
Battling against the wind, a thousand leaves are tossed hither and
yon.
Outside this room of utter solitude,
Stars change and things move on relentlessly.
Many a heroic ambition I used to cherish,
But long have I been cut off from my raft to reach beyond the ocean
green.[1]
Grasping my knees I could only cry out my frustrations by chanting
"Hsi-shih,"[2]
Staring at the clouds I heave a long, lonely sigh.

(YPSHC, 16:43–44) *(Tr. Cecile Chu-chin Sun)*

After the Rain

Sunshine after rain, rain after sunshine,
Who can tell Heaven's will from its fickle ways?
The fine autumn is almost half spent;
A virtuous life is always dreary drifting.
Gazing upon streams and mountains yields a dim prospect:
Hesitating, pondering, musing, all to no avail[3]
Vexed still by fear of death, sadness of living—
It's far better to be like the river moving straight and deep.

(YPSHC, 16:25–26) *(Tr. Cecile Chu-chin Sun)*

Night of the First Full Moon

I wonder what kind of night is this night?
I force myself to sing and dance with the children.
Old dreams, like the shadow of a lamp, have long ago burnt out;
My own village, under the full moon, should be all the brighter
now.
Does the moon goddess, with her stolen elixir, know of our spring?
Alas, the Star Bridge[4] is locked in iron and the night is long.
High in the heavens there should be a god,
But can he bear to look upon hills and streams from the pearly
Dipper?

(YPSHC, 16:59) *(Tr. Cecile Chu-chin Sun)*

10. Calligraphy by Liang Ch'i-ch'ao. Text of a letter on *tz'u* poetry sent to Dr. Hu Shih. From the collection of the Hu family.

The Scarlet Red Tree

Scarlet red flowers burst into flame everywhere,
Fiery clouds hold forth a dazzling bright day.
How many rouge tears[5] might we gather together
To paint the azalea hills back home.

(YPSHC, 16:64) *(Tr. Cecile Chu-chin Sun)*

Tune: *Tieh lien hua*
Title: Thoughts at the End of Spring— A Farewell Poem for Someone Going Home

I

What is it that troubles you?
Even before middle age approaches,
Already so much bittersweet experience.
In the deserted courtyard spring is everywhere—
What does the crab apple know of our sorrow?

Suddenly the setting sun blends into the rain at dusk,
Such sunny wetness—how annoying!
Nor are the heavens to be trusted.
The flowers are silent and the orioles twitter aloud.
Alas, the heart knows more bitterness than the autumn lotus seed.

(YPSHC, 16:86) *(Tr. Cecile Chu-chin Sun)*

II

Trying to stay the departing spring is of no avail.
Again and again, the piercing cries of the cuckoo
Hurry one to go back home.[6]
Everywhere the catkins conceal the fragrant grass ford.
At the edge of the earth, can spring find its way back?

A nameless feeling, where to find an anchor?
The blackberry blossoms are all fallen,
Mixed with a few drops of Ch'ing-ming rain.
Don't sing the heart-rending words of Fang-hui[7]—
In all the world, affairs of the heart are hardest to tell.

(YPSHC, 16:86) *(Tr. Cecile Chu-chin Sun)*

NOTES

1. The raft and the green ocean suggest the legend of a fisherman who saw a raft floating out to sea every year in the eighth month, mounted it, and was wafted off to the Milky Way. Chang Ch'ien, the famous Han general, was reported to have had a similar experience when he was sent by Emperor Wu of Han to be the ambassador to Ta-hsia. Hence the line here seems to suggest that his ambition is thwarted and frustrated.

2. A poem in the *Ch'u-tz'u*, whose authorship is still unknown. Some attribute it to a contemporary of Yen Chi (188–105 B.C.) and Mei Sheng (?–141 B.C.); Wang Fu-chih (q.v.) was fairly certain that it was written by Chia Yi who was lamenting Ch'ü Yüan's treatment by the unworthy King Huai of Ch'u. Liang probably had Wang's interpretation in mind, for it seems that a parallel can be drawn here: like Ch'ü Yüan, Liang's faith in the young Emperor Kuang-hsü suffered a serious blow. His confidence in Kuang-hsü as a leader capable of executing a series of reforms met with great disappointment. This poem, although undated, was probably composed after the failure of the 1898 reform movement when Liang and his mentor K'ang Yu-wei barely managed to escape with their lives.

Poetically speaking, the imaginative description of air travel in "Hsi-shih" offers not only a beautiful parallel to the image of the green ocean of the previous line but is also subtly connected with the following line, in which the speaker gazes at the clouds up in the sky.

3. A more literal translation of the original would read: "Scratching one's head, clasping one's hands behind the back, musing aloud, all a waste."

4. The Milky Way.

5. Usually referring to the tears of a woman; here they could also mean the blood of the legendary cuckoo that stains the azaleas.

6. The cuckoo has strong associations with homesickness in Chinese poetry and its cry, *kuei*, is a homonym in Chinese for the word "return home."

7. Referring to the Sung poet Ho Chu's (ca. 1063–1120) famous *tz'u* to the tune *Ch'ing-yü-an*.

CH'IU CHIN

(15 NOVEMBER 1877–15 JULY 1907)[1]

Ch'iu Chin (*Hsüan-ch'ing, Ching-hsiung;* CHIEN-HU NÜ-HSIA), a native of Shao-hsing, Chekiang province, is widely known as a martyr of the anti-Manchu revolution, as well as a poet, writer, educator, orator, and feminist. She led a short but extraordinary life. The beloved daughter of a gentry family, she was taught to read and write as a child. As an adult, she took up fencing, riding, and drinking, thus revealing a flair for the romantic and sensational. An unconventional and strong-willed woman, shortly after the Boxer Rebellion she left her husband and children to study in Japan. There she became involved in revolutionary émigré politics. After returning to China in 1906, she taught school, published a woman's magazine, and assumed a leading role in the Restoration Society in her native province. While engaged in planning a local uprising, she and some fellow conspirators were arrested. While in prison she wrote the well-known single line poem: *Ch'iu-feng ch'iu-yü ch'ou-sha jen* (Amidst autumn winds and autumn rains, I am moved to profound sorrow), and shortly thereafter she was executed by decapitation.

Ch'iu Chin was a prolific and versatile writer. As a poet, she employed a wide range of metrical forms: the *shih*, the *tz'u*, various popular song patterns, and the *t'an-tz'u*. The freedom of form she demanded as a poet was accompanied by the choice of a strongly personal style. Her verse is expressed in a simple, vigorous, direct language, and it eschews the heavy weight of historical and literary allusions so common to traditionalist poetics. Feminism, heroism, and revolution are themes commonly encountered in her poetry, and the strong note of patriotism she sounds in many poems reveals a deep personal sense

1. Chao-ying Fang, ECCP, 1:169–171.

of mission and a determination to sacrifice herself to the revolutionary cause.

(Pao Chia-lin)

Random Feelings: Written in Japan

The sun and moon lusterless, heaven and earth grow dark;
Submerged womankind—who will rescue them?
Barrette and bracelet pawned to travel across the sea,
Parting from kith and kin, I left my homeland.
Freeing my bound feet, I washed away the poison of a thousand
  years,
And, with agitated heart, awakened the souls of all the flowers.
Alas, I have only a binding cloth woven of mermaid's silk,
Half stained with blood, half with tears.

(CCC, p. 85) *(Tr. Pao Chia-lin)*

Written on Board a Ship on the Yellow Sea, When a Japanese Friend Asked Me for a Poem, and When I Saw a Map of the Russo-Japanese War

Driven by a myriad-mile wind, I come and go;
Alone crossing the Eastern Sea, I bring with me the spring thunder.
How can I bear looking at a map with its colors altered?[1]
And consign rivers and hills to the fires of Kalpa?
Unstrained wine never quenches the tears of a patriot;
A country's salvation relies on exceptional genius.
I pledge the spilled blood from a hundred thousand skulls
To restore the universe with all our strength.

(CCC, p. 77) *(Tr. Pao Chia-lin)*

A Song: Promoting Women's Rights

Our generation yearns to be free;
To all who struggle: one more cup of the Wine of Freedom!
Male and female equality was by Heaven endowed,
So why should women lag behind?

Let's struggle to pull ourselves up,
To wash away the filth and shame of former days.
United we can work together,
And restore this land with our soft white hands.

Most humiliating is the old custom,
Of treating women no better than cows and horses.
When the light of dawn shines on our civilization,
We must rise to head the list.
Let's tear out the roots of servitude,
Gain knowledge, learning, and practice what we know;
Take responsibility on our shoulders,
Never to fail or disappoint, our citizen heroines!

(CCC, p. 113) *(Tr. Pao Chia-lin)*

A Song of the Precious Knife

The palaces of the House of Han lie in the setting sun;
Dead is this ancient country of five millenia.
Sunk deep in sleep these several hundred years,
No one recognizes the shame of being enslaved.
Remember our ancient ancestor Hsien-yüan[2] by name, 5
Who, born and raised in the K'un-lun Mountains,[3]
Expanded our domain to the Yellow and Yangtze rivers,
With great knives flashing conquered the Central Plain.

Then, a painful cry from Plum Mountain,[4] what could be done?
The imperial city filled with brambles, the bronze camels buried. 10
How often I've looked back on the capital's former glories;
The dirges of a fallen land bring copious tears.

Northward marched an allied army, eight nations strong,
And once more our territory was given away.
From the west came white devils to sound the warning bell, 15
To startle the Han Chinese from their slavish dreams.

My host bequeathed me this golden knife,
And now, possessing it, my heart is brave.
An "ism" of iron and blood is destined for our day;
One hundred million skulls we count as a mere feather. 20

Bathed by sun and moon, this radiant treasure,
Fit to be cherished by any death-defying man of stature.
I pledge to seek the road of life in the jaws of death,

For the peace of the world depends on force of arms.
Have you not seen Ching K'o[5] as a guest of Ch'in 25
Bare the foot-long dagger hidden in the map?

A single thrust at court, though it missed the mark,
Was so startling that it seized a tyrant's soul.
With my bare hands, I wish to save my fatherland,
Though this land of Emperor Yü[6] overflows with a degenerate
  breed. 30
When everyone's heart is dead, what can be done?
Seizing a pen, I write this "Song of the Precious Knife."

This "Song of the Precious Knife" strengthens one's resolve,
Awakens many a soul in this land of the dead.
With precious knife and valiant arm, what can compare? 35
Forget old friends and foes in this mortal realm!
Don't despise this foot of steel as of little worth;
The salvation of the nation depends on the miracle it will work!
Henceforth, I will take Heaven and Earth as my furnace,
The yin and yang as my fuel, 40
Gather iron ore from the six continents,
And cast thousands upon thousands of precious knives to cleanse
  this sacred land,
To renew the august name and power of our ancestor, the Yellow
  Emperor,
And scour clean from our national history, millennium upon
  millennium, this awful shame!

(CCC, p. 80) *(Tr. Pao Chia-lin)*

Tune: *Man chiang hung* (Full River Red)

In the capital for a short stay,
And again it is the splendid Mid-Autumn Festival.
Along the fence, chrysanthemums are everywhere in bloom;
The face of autumn shines as if wiped clean.
All around us our enemies sing of our defeat;
For eight years I have missed the flavor of my native land.
How I resent being taken for a reluctant female;
I hardly deserve that fame!

My sex disqualifies me
For the role of male,

But my heart
Is more heroic than a man's.
I guess I'm headstrong, full of daring,
One who warms up when people are around.
Among those of common mind, who can know me?
A heroine at road's end is bound to meet frustration.
In this vulgar world of red dust, where can I find someone
Who truly appreciates me?
Tears wet my dress.

(CCC, p. 97) *(Tr. Pao Chia-lin)*

NOTES

1. The ceding of territory is usually indicated on a Chinese map; the alteration of color results from redefining a nation's territorial limits.
2. The Yellow Emperor, the legendary founder of Chinese civilization.
3. The tallest mountain range known in ancient China, located west of Hsi-ning, Kansu province.
4. *Plum Mountain* is homophonous with *Coal Hill*, the place where the last emperor of Ming committed suicide.
5. See Ts'ao Chen-chi, notes 6–13.
6. The legendary sage-king who tamed the floods and founded the Hsia dynasty.

WANG KUO-WEI

(3 DECEMBER 1877–2 JUNE 1927)[1]

Wang Kuo-wei (*Ching-an* and *Po-yü;* LI-T'ANG, KUAN-T'ANG, and YUNG-KUAN), scholar, epigrapher, translator, literary critic, and poet, was a native of Hai-ning, Chekiang province. The heir to a family tradition of scholarship and patriotic public service, Wang Kuo-wei was tutored as a child in traditional learning in preparation for a career in government. In 1892, he succeeded in passing the lowest examination degree, but he failed in two successive attempts to secure the second, or *chü-jen* degree. Thereafter, he went to Shanghai to work on the newspaper *Shih-wu pao* (Contemporary Affairs Journal), and subsequently, by having come to the attention of the scholar Lo Chen-yü (1866–1940), with the Tung-wen hsüeh-she (Institute of Oriental Languages). With Lo's assistance, Wang began the study of English and Japanese, the sciences, and Western philosophy. Between 1904 and 1907, he concentrated his attention on Kant, Schopenhauer, and Nietzsche. His translations from the works of these philosophers were a pioneering venture; moreover, he was the first Chinese scholar to make serious use of Western ideas, particularly those of Schopenhauer, in the formulation of new critical concepts of literature, the subject to which he now turned his full attention. Over the next several years he produced some of his major scholarly works, particularly in the fields of literature and criticism, such as the pioneering *Sung Yüan hsi-ch'ü k'ao* (An Examination of Sung and Yüan Drama), the *T'ang Wu-tai Erh-shih-yi-chia tz'u-chi* (A Collection of the Lyrics of Twenty-one Poets of the T'ang and Five Dynasties), and the influential *Jen-chien tz'u-hua* (Talks on Lyric Poetry in the Human World). In the latter work he formulated a theory of poetry as a fusion of *ching* (external scene) and

---

1. BDRC, 3:388–391.

ch'ing (inner emotion), which in combination constitutes the "world," or *ching-chieh*, of the poem. (See the translation of the *Jen-chien tz'u-hua* by Adele Austin Rickett for a full exposition of this theory.)

After the overthrow of the Ch'ing dynasty by republican forces in 1911, Wang, along with his mentor and patron Lo Chen-yü, a political conservative like himself, sought refuge in Japan. This move also marked a turning point in his interests as a scholar, which now focused on the close textual analysis of the ancient classics and the recently discovered oracle bones. When he returned to China several years later, his reputation as a classical scholar was firmly established, thus leading to teaching appointments in Shanghai and later Peking, where he unexpectedly ended his own life by drowning in 1927.

Wang Kuo-wei's reputation as a poet rests on a rather slim corpus of poems in the *shih* and lyric forms, but it is only in the later genre that he achieved the greatest distinction. His lyrics, many of which date from the years when he was exploring the history and esthetics of that form, are widely admired today for their fresh and uncontrived expression of inner despair and the search for meaning in the human condition.

(William Schultz)

Random Thoughts

Thrust in life between heaven and earth, I can't but feel cramped.
And still far from reach is the ideal of a Taoist Spiritual Man![1]
The clouds seem aimless,[2] so they remain pure and free;
If the river isn't racing along, whence its mighty roar?
My heart embraces the Fu River and the T'iao Mountains;[3]
My mind is at home in the reigns of Wu-te and K'ai-yüan;[4]
Poets of all ages are indeed too frivolous:
They look to this world of dust in search of Paradise.

(WKTHSCC, 5: 1774) *(Tr. Irving Lo)*

Tune: *Ch'üeh-ch'iao hsien* (Immortal at Magpie Bridge)

The sentry drums boom.
The pent-up horses whinny.
I get up and find flowers
of frost everywhere.

Suddenly I remember when
I left her
The weather then was like
the weather today
at the road house.

Cart tracks travel north.
Homing dreams head south.
I know there's no way
to stop between.
In the human world not a thing
can be depended upon
Save and except the two words
"not depend."

(No. 2 from a series of 2; KTCTC, p. 13) *(Tr. Li Chi and Michael Patrick O'Connor)*

Tune: *Huan hsi sha*

A mountain temple dim and far away, its back against the setting sun—
No birds can reach that height far in the shade.
From above, at the single note of its chime, clouds pause in their passing.

When I try to climb the peak, to peer at the bright moon,
By chance I obtain the Eye of Heaven to look at the mundane world—
And I find in its revelation, alas, I am but a man.

(KTCTC, p. 12) *(Tr. Ching-i Tu)*

Tune: *Ts'ai-sang tzu*

The drum sounds from the high city wall as the lampwick burns out.
Asleep, yet awake;
Drunk, yet sober—
Suddenly I hear the two or three notes of a wild goose's lone cry.

Life is no more than willow catkins in the wind:
Joy in fragments,

Grief in fragments—
All turn to patches of duckweed spreading on the river.
(KTCTC, p. 8) *(Tr. Ching-i Tu)*

Tune: *Tieh lien hua*

I

How much has the light thickened outside the window, under the green bough?
Only the bright red cherries remain,
Still enticing the faded red petals[5] to linger.
All the fledgling orioles have grown old, in silence;
They come flying to pick the cherries before they fly away.

I sit and watch a pair of nursling swallows on the painted beam.
The swallows twitter softly
As if chiding someone for being tardy—
Surely a kind of longing. But how much do they know?
In the human world, only longing could have caused so much wrong.
(KTCTC, p. 5) *(Tr. Irving Lo)*

II

Who says that in the human world autumn has already gone?
Pale willows, strand upon strand,
Still play with their shadows of gosling yellow.
The setting sun upon a grove of thinning trees gleams brightly;
Never pass up the sight of dusk from a western window.

A myriad dots, the roosting crows; a chaotic, unsettled mass;
A glittering sea of golden waves
Again shrouds the tops of blue pines.
Where south of the Yangtze do you not find this scene?—
I'm distressed only because there's no one to savor it.
(KTCTC, p. 9) *(Tr. Irving Lo)*

NOTES

1. The text reads: *Ku-she shen-jen,* alluding to the Taoist concept of a "spiritual man" (translated as "Holy Man" in Burton Watson's translation of

the *Chuang Tzu*). Ku-she Mountain, first mentioned in the ancient *Shan-hai ching* is the Miao-ku-she Shan in the "Free and Easy Wandering" (*Hsiao-yao yu*) chapter of the *Chuang Tzu*, said to be inhabited by Beings who have attained spiritual perfection. According to the teachings of Taoism, there are three classes of Beings, with *Sheng-jen* (Sage) at the top, followed by *shen-jen* (Spiritual Man), and then by *chen-jen* (Perfect Man) at the bottom. The following passages from this chapter, in Watson's translation, may be relevant: ". . . there is a Holy Man living in faraway Ku-she Mountain, with skin like ice or snow, and gentle and shy like a young girl. He doesn't eat the five grains, but sucks the wind . . . rides a flying dragon, and wanders beyond the four seas. . . . [Emperor] Yao brought order to the people of the world and directed the government of all within the seas. But he went to see the Four Masters of the faraway Ku-she Mountain [and when he got home] north of the Fen River, he was dazed and had forgotten his kingdom there." (*The Complete Works of Chuang Tzu*, 1968, pp. 33–34)

2. Alluding to the two famous lines from Tu Fu:

> *shui liu hsin pu chin,*
> *yün tsai yi chü ch'ih*
> ("The water flows but my heart does not race with it,
> The clouds linger but my mind is the more sluggish")

from the "Chiang-t'ing" (River Pavilion) poem (Harvard-Yenching Concordance edition, pp. 356–357). The cloud image in Tu Fu's line is derived from T'ao Ch'ien's *yün wu hsin erh ch'u hsiu*, translated by James Robert Hightower as "The clouds aimlessly rise from the peaks" (*The Poetry of T'ao Ch'ien*, 1970, p. 269).

3. Fu-t'u (Land around Fu) is mentioned in the "Yü-kung" chapter of *Shu-ching*, referring to the land of China before it was divided into the "Nine Districts" by Emperor Yü. T'iao-shan, as a compound, is most probably derived from "T'iao-feng," the term found in the *Yi-ching* designating the auspicious wind from the northeast, which gives life to everything.

4. Respectively, the reign title of Kao-tsu (618–626), the founder of the T'ang dynasty, and that of Hsüan-tsung (713–741)—the two most splendid periods of the T'ang era.

5. A variant reading given in some other editions is *ts'an-ch'un* (residual spring).

SELECTED BIBLIOGRAPHY

ANTHOLOGIES AND GENERAL COLLECTIONS

Chinese

Chang, Ying-ch'ang, ed. *Kuo-ch'ao shih-to*, represented as *Ch'ing shih-to*. 2 vols. Peking: Chung-hua shu-chü, 1960.

Ch'en, Nai-ch'ien, ed. *Ch'ing ming-chia tz'u*. 10 vols. Hong Kong: T'ai-p'ing shu-chü, 1963.

Ch'en, Yen, ed. *Chin-tai shih-ch'ao*. 3 vols. Shanghai: Shang-wu yin-shu-kuan, 1923. Taiwan reprint, 1961.

Cheng, Ch'ien, ed. *Hsü tz'u hsüan*. Taipei: Chung-hua wen-hua ch'u-pan shih-yeh wei-yüan-hui, 1955.

Ch'ien, Chung-lien, ed. *Ch'ing shih san-pai-shou*. Shanghai: Han-wen cheng-k'ai yin-shu-chü. 1934. Revised and reissued in mimeograph form by Soochow Normal University [1982?].

Hsia, Ch'eng-t'ao, and Chang, Chang, eds. *Chin Yüan Ming Ch'ing tz'u-hsüan*. 2 vols. Peking: Jen-min wen-hsüeh ch'u-pan she, 1983. Volume Two is entirely given over to Ch'ing lyrics.

Hua, Kuang-sheng, ed. *Po-hsüeh yi-yin*. Shanghai: Chung-hua shu-chü, 1959.

Hsü, Shih-ch'ang, ed. *Wan-ch'ing yi Ch'ing shih-hui*. Tientsin, 1929. Taiwan reprint: *Ch'ing shih-hui*. 8 vols. Shih-chieh shu-chü, 1961.

Lung, Yü-sheng, ed. *Chin san-pai-nien ming-chia tz'u-hsüan*. Shanghai: Ku-tien wen-hsüeh ch'u-pan she, 1956.

P'u, Ch'uan, ed. *Ming Ch'ing min-ko hsüan*. Shanghai, 1956.

Shen, Te-ch'ien, ed. *Ch'ing shih pieh-ts'ai*. Reprinted in Taiwan reprint: 4 vols. Shang-wu yin-shu-kuan, 1956.

Wang, Ch'ang, ed. *Hu-hai shih-chuan*. Shanghai: Shang-wu yin-shu kuan, reprint of the 1803 edition in 2 vols., 1939. Taiwan reprint, 1958.

Wang, Chieh-t'ang, ed. *Ni-shang hsü-p'u*. 2 vols. In *Min-su ts'ung-shu*. Taipei: Tung-fang wen-hua shu-chü, n.d.

Wang, Wen-ju, ed. *Ch'ing shih p'ing-chu*. 3 vols. Shanghai: Wei-ming shu-chü, 1916. Taiwan reprint, 1978.

Wu, K'ai-sheng, ed. *Wan-Ch'ing shih-ssu-chia shih-ch'ao*. Taiwan reprint, 1970.

Wu, Tun-sheng, ed. *Ch'ing shih-hsüan*. Shanghai: Shang-wu yin-shu-kuan, 1935. Taiwan reprint, 1967.

Yeh, Kung-ch'o, ed. *Ch'üan Ch'ing tz'u-ch'ao*. 3 vols. Hong Kong: Chung-hua shu-chü, 1975.

Japanese

Kondō, Mitsuo, ed. *Shin shi sen*. Vol. 22 in *Hanshi taisei*. Tokyo: Shueisha, 1967.

Murayama, Yoshihiro, ed. *Shin shi*. Vol. 10 in *Chūgoku no meishi kanshō*. Tokyo: Meiji shoin, 1976.

Western

Birch, Cyril, ed. *Anthology of Chinese Literature*. Vol. 2. New York: Grove Press, 1972.
Demiéville, Paul, ed. *Anthologie de la poésie chinoise classique*. Paris: Gallimard, 1962.
Liu, Wu-chi, and Lo, Irving Yucheng, eds. *Sunflower Splendor: Three Thousand Years of Chinese Poetry*. Bloomington: Indiana University Press, 1975; New York: Doubleday Anchor, 1975, 1983.

BIOGRAPHICAL SOURCES

Chinese

Chao, Erh-hsün. *Ch'ing-shih kao*. 48 vols. Peking: Chung-hua shu-chü, 1977.
Cheng, Fang-k'un. *Pen-ch'ao ming-chia shih-ch'ao hsiao-chuan*, reprinted as *Ch'ing-ch'ao shih-jen hsiao-chuan*. Vol. 14 of *Ku-chin shih-hua ts'ung-pien*. Taipei: Kuang-wen shu-chü, 1980.
Ch'ing-shih lieh-chüan. Shanghai: Chung-hua shu-chü, 1928.
Teng, Chih-ch'eng. *Ch'ing-shih chi-shih ch'u-pien*. 2 vols. Shanghai: Chung-hua shu-chü, 1965.
Ts'ai, Kuan-lo, ed. *Ch'ing-tai ch'i-pai ming-jen chuan*. 3 vols. Taipei: Shih-chieh shu-chü, 1962.

Western

Boorman, Howard L., ed. *Biographical Dictionary of Republican China*. 5 vols. New York: Columbia University Press, 1967–1979.
Hummel, Arthur W., ed. *Eminent Chinese of the Ch'ing Period (1644–1912)*. 2 vols. Washington D.C.: United States Government Printing Office, 1943.

INDIVIDUAL WORKS

Cha, Shen-hsing. *Ching-yeh-t'ang shih-chi*. SPPY.
Chang, Hui-yen. *Ming-k'o tz'u*, CMCT. Vol. 6.
Chang, Wen-t'ao. *Ch'uan-shan shih-ts'ao hsüan*. In Shih-li-chü Huang-shih ts'ung-shu.
Chao, Chih-hsin. *Yi-shan shih-chi*. SPPY.
Chao, Yi. *Ou-pei shih-ch'ao*. KGCPTS.
Ch'en, Pao-shen. *Ts'ang-ch'ü-lou shih-chi*. CTCKSLTK, series 40.
Ch'en, San-li. *San-yüan ching-she shih* and *San-yüan ching-she shih hsü-chi*. Shanghai: Shang-wu yin-shu-kuan, 1922. Taiwan reprint, 1962.
Ch'en, Wei-sung. *Chia-ling tz'u ch'üan-chi*. SPTK.
Cheng, Chen. *Ch'ao-ching-ch'ao shih-chi*. SPPY.
Cheng, Hsiao-hsü. *Hai-ts'ang-lou shih*. Hong Kong: Tien-feng, n.d.
Cheng, Hsieh. *Cheng Pan-ch'iao chi*. Shanghai: Chung-hua shu-chü, 1962.
Cheng, Wen-cho. *Ch'iao-feng yüeh-fu*. CMCT, vol. 10.
Chiang, Ch'un-lin. *Shui-yün-lou tz'u*. CMCT, vol. 9.
Chiang, Shih. *Fu-yü-t'ang shih-lu*. In *T'ung-jen chi*, edited by Ch'ing-hsiung Wang, n.d.
Chiang, Shih-ch'üan. *Chung-ya-t'ang shih chi*. 1762.

Ch'ien, Ch'ien-yi. *Mu-chai ch'u-hsüeh chi* and *Mu-chai yu-hsüeh chi*. SPTK.
Chin, Ho. See Ch'en in List of Abbreviations.
Chin, Jen-jui. *Ch'en-yin-lou shih-hsüan*. Shanghai: Ku-chi ch'u-pan she, 1979.
Ching An. *Pa-chih t'ou-t'o shih-chi*. Taipei: Hsin wen-feng ch'u-pan kung-ssu, 1974.
Ch'iu Chin. *Ch'iu Chin chi*. Shanghai: Chung-hua shu-chü, 1960.
______. *Ch'iu Chin shih-wen hsüan*. Edited by Yen-li Kuo. Peking: Jen-min wen-hsüeh ch'u-pan she, 1982.
Chu, Hsiao-tsang. *Ch'iang-ts'un yü-yeh*. CMCT, vol. 10.
Chu, Yi-tsun. *P'u-shu-t'ing chi*. SPPY.
Ch'ü, Ta-chün. *Weng-shan shih-ch'ao* and *Weng-shan shih-wai*. Shanghai, 1909.
Chuang, Yü. *Chung-pai tz'u*. CMCT, vol. 10.
Ho, Shao-chi. See Ch'en in List of Abbreviations.
Hsiang, Hung-tso. *Yi-yün tz'u*. CMCT, vol. 8.
Hsü, Ts'an. *Cho-cheng-yüan shih-chi* and *Cho-cheng-yüan shih-yü*. In *Pai-ching-lou ts'ung-shu*.
Hsüan-yeh. *K'ang-hsi ti yü-chih wen-chi*. 4 vols. Taiwan reprint, 1966.
Hsüeh, Shao-hui. *Tai-yün-lou shih-chi* and *Tai-yün-lou tz'u-chi*. 1914.
Huang, Ching-jen. *Liang-tan-hsüan chi*. Shanghai: Ku-chi ch'u-pan she, 1983.
Huang, Tsun-hsien. *Jen-ching-lu shih-ts'ao ch'ien-chu*. 3 vols. Edited by Chung-lien Ch'ien. Shanghai: Ku-chi ch'u-pan she, 1981.
Huang, Tsung-hsi. *Nan-lei shih-li*. SPPY.
Hung, Liang-chi. *Hung Pei-chiang shih-wen chi*. KHCPTS.
Hung, Shen. *Pai-ch'i hsü-chi*. Shanghai: Ku-tien wen-hsüeh ch'u-pan she, 1957.
K'ang, Yu-wei. *K'ang Nan-hai hsien-sheng shih-chi*. CTCKSLTH, *hsü-pien*.
Ku, T'ai-ch'ing. *Tung-hai yü-ko*. In *Tz'u-hsüeh chi-k'an*. Vol. 1, no. 2 (1933).
Ku, Yen-wu. *Ku T'ing-lin shih-chi hui-chu*. 3 vols. Edited by Ch'u-ch'ang Wang. Shanghai: Ku-chi ch'u-pan she, 1983.
K'uang, Chou-yi. *Hui-feng tz'u*, CMCT. Vol. 10.
Kung, Tzu-chen. *Kung Tzu-chen chi-hai tsa-shih chu*. Edited by Yi-sheng Liu. Peking: Chung-hua shu-chü, 1980.
______. *Kung Tzu-chen ch'üan-chi*. 2 vols. Edited by P'ei-cheng Wang. Hong Kong: Chung-hua shu-chü, 1974.
Li, Chien. *Wu-pai-ssu-feng ts'ao-t'ang shih-chi*. 1796.
Li, E. *Fan-hsieh shan-fang chi* and *Fan-hsieh shan-fang hsü-chi*. SPPY.
Li, Tz'u-ming. See Hsü in List of Abbreviations.
Liang, Ch'i-ch'ao. *Yin-ping-shih ho-chi, ts'e* 16. Shanghai: Chung-hua shu-chü, 1936.
Liu, Shih. See Chou in List of Abbreviations.
P'eng, Sun-yü. *Sung-kuei-t'ang ch'üan-chi*. SKCSCP, series 3.
______. *Yen-lu tz'u*. CMCT, vol. 3.
Shen, Te-ch'ien. See Wu and Wang in List of Abbreviations.
Shih, Jun-chang. *Hsüeh-yü-t'ang shih-chi*. SKCSCP, series 3.
Shu, Wei. *P'ing-shui-chai shih-chi*. PPTSCC, *ts'e* 7462–7469.
Singde. *Na-lan tz'u*. SPPY.
______. *Yin-shui shih-chi*. In *Yüen-ya-t'ang ts'ung-shu*, series 7.
Sung, Hsiang. *Hung-hsing shan-fang yi-kao*. CTCKSLTK, series 63.
Sung, Wan. *An-ya-t'ang wei-k'o kao* and *An-ya-t'ang shih-chi*. SPPY.
T'an, Ssu-t'ung. *T'an Ssu-t'ung ch'üan-chi*. Peking: San-lien shu-tien, 1954.
Ts'ao, Chen-chi. *K'o-hsüeh tz'u*. CMCT, vol. 4.
Wang, Fu-chih. *Wang Ch'uan-shan shih-wen-chi*. 2 vols. Peking: Chung-hua shu-chü, 1962.

Wang, K'ai-yün. *Hsiang-yi-lou shih-chi.* CTCKSLTK, series 60.
Wang, Kuo-wei. *Wang Kuan-t'ang hsien-sheng ch'üan-chi.* 16 vols. Taipei: Wen-hua shu-chü, 1968.
Wang, P'eng-yün. *Pan-t'ang ting-kao.* CMCT, vol. 10.
Wang, Shih-chen. *Yü-yang shan-jen ching-hua lu.* SPPY.
Wang, Ts'ai-wei. *Ch'ang-li-ko chi.* In Sun, Yüan-ju, *Sun Yüan-ju chi,* SPTK.
Wei, Yüan. *Wei Yüan chi.* 2 vols. Peking: Chung-hua shu-chü, 1976.
Wen, T'ing-shih. *Wen T'ing-shih ch'üan-chi.* 10 vols. Taipei: Wen-hua shu-chü, 1969.
———. *Yün-ch'i-hsüan tz'u.* CMCT, vol. 10.
Wu, Chia-chi. *Wu Chia-chi shih ch'ien-chiao.* Edited by Chi-ch'ing Yang. Shanghai: Ku-chi ch'u-pan she, 1980.
Wu, Hsi-ch'i. *Yu-cheng-wei-chai tz'u.* CMCT, vol. 5.
Wu, Tsao. *Wu Tsao tz'u,* in *Tz'u-hsüeh hsiao ts'ung-shu.* Edited by Ch'iu-p'ing Hsieh, n.d.
Wu, Wei-yeh. *Wu-shih chi-lan.* SPPY.
Wu, Wen. *Lien-yang chi.* SPPY.
Yao, Nai. *Hsi-pao-hsüan shih-chi.* SPPY.
Yi, Shun-ting. See WCSSCSC.
Yu, T'ung. *Hsi-t'ang ch'iu-men lu* and *Hsi-t'ang hsiao-ts'ao.* In *Hsi-t'ang ch'üan-chi,* 1685.
Yüan, Mei. *Hsiao-ts'ang shan-fang shih-chi.* SPPY.
Yün, Shou-p'ing. *Ou-hsiang-kuan chi.* In *Ts'ung-shu chi-ch'eng,* series I. Shanghai: Shang-wu yin-shu-kuan, 1931.

STUDIES

Chinese

Ch'ien, Chi-po. *Hsien-tai Chung-kuo wen-hsüeh shih.* Hong Kong: Hua-lien t'u-shu kung-ssu, n.d.
Ch'ien, Chung-lien, ed. *Ming Ch'ing shih-wen yen-chiu ts'ung-k'an.* Vols. 1 (March, 1982) and 2 (December, 1982).
Ch'ien, Chung-shu. *T'an yi lu.* Shanghai: K'ai-ming shu-chü, 1937; Hong Kong: Lung-men shu-tien, 1965.
Chou, Fa-kao, ed. *Ch'ien Mu-chai, Liu Ju-shih yi-shih chi Liu Ju-shih yu-kuan tzu-liao.* Taipei, 1978.
Ho, Kuang-chung. *Lun Ch'ing tz'u.* Hong Kong: Tung-fang hsüeh-hui, 1948.
Liu, [James] Jo-yü, *Ch'ing-tai shih-shuo lun-yao.* In *Hsiang-kang ta-hsüeh wu-shih chou-nien chi-nien lun-wen chi.* Hong Kong, 1964.
Wu, Hung-yi. *Ch'ang-chou p'ai tz'u-hsüeh yen-chiu.* Taipei: Chia-hsin shui-ni kung-ssu, 1970.
———. *Ch'ing-tai shih-hsüeh ch'u-t'an.* Taipei: Mu-t'ung ch'u-pan she, 1977. Two appendices to this volume, pp. 285–333, contain extensive bibliographical data on theories of literature, criticism, and the collected works of major writers.

Japanese

Aoki, Masaru. *Shindai bungaku hyōron shi.* Tokyo: Iwanami Shoten, 1940. Chinese translation by Ch'en, Shu-nü, *Ch'ing-tai wen-hsüeh p'ing-lun shih.* Taipei: K'ai-ming shu-tien, 1969.

Western

Bryant, Daniel. "Syntax and Sentiment in Old Nanking: Wang Shih-chen's 'Miscellaneous Poems on the Ch'in-huai.' " Unpublished article.
Chang, Hao. *Liang Ch'i-ch'ao and Intellectual Transition in China, 1890–1911.* Cambridge: Harvard University Press, 1971.
Chao, Chia-ying Yeh. "The Ch'ang-chou School of *Tz'u* Criticism." In *Chinese Approaches to Literature from Confucius to Liang Ch'i-ch'ao,* edited by Adele Austin Rickett. Princeton: Princeton University Press, 1978.
Che, K. L. "Not Words But Feelings—Ch'ien Ch'ien-i (1582–1664) on Poetry." *Tamkang Review,* Vol. 6, no. 7 (April, 1975), pp. 55–71.
Chu, Madeline Men-li. "Ch'en Wei-sung, the *Tz'u* Poet." Unpublished doctoral dissertation, University of Arizona, 1978.
Doleželová-Velingerová, Milena. "The Origins of Modern Chinese Literature." In *Modern Chinese Literature in the May Fourth Era,* edited by Merle Goldman. Cambridge: Harvard University Press, 1977.
———, ed. *The Chinese Novel at the Turn of the Century.* Toronto: Toronto University Press, 1980. See introduction.
Hsia, C. T. "Yen Fu and Liang Ch'i-ch'ao as Advocates of New Fiction." In *Chinese Approaches to Literature,* edited by A. Rickett.
Hsiao, Kung-ch'üan. *A Modern China and a New World: K'ang Yu-wei, Reformer and Utopian, 1858–1927.* Seattle: University of Washington Press, 1975.
Kamachi, Noriko. *Reform in China: Huang Tsun-hsien and the Japanese Model.* Cambridge: Council on East Asian Studies, 1981.
Liu, James J. Y. *Chinese Theories of Literature.* Chicago: Chicago University Press, 1975.
Lynn, Richard John. "Orthodoxy and Enlightenment: Wang Shih-chen's Theory of Poetry and Its Antecedents." In *The Unfolding of Neo-Confucianism,* edited by Wm. Theodore de Bary. New York: Columbia University Press, 1975.
Martin, Helmut. "A Transitional Concept of Chinese Literature 1897–1917: Liang Ch'i-ch'ao on Poetry Reform, Historical Drama and the Political Novel." *Oriens Extremus* 20 (1973), pp. 175–217.
Nienhauser, William H. Jr., ed. *The Indiana Companion to Traditional Chinese Literature.* Bloomington: Indiana University Press, 1986. See articles on Ch'ing poets and books.
Rickett, Adele Austin. *Wang Kuo-wei's "Jen-chien tz'u-hua": A Study in Chinese Literary Criticism.* Hong Kong: Hong Kong University Press, 1977.
Schmidt, J. D. "Huang Tsun-hsien." An unpublished monographic study.
Schultz, William. "Sung Wan and the Narrative Poem." *Journal of the Chinese Language Teachers Association,* vol. 14, no. 2 (May, 1979), pp. 9–26.
Spence, Jonathan D. *Emperor of China: Self-Portrait of K'ang-hsi.* New York: Knopf, 1974.
———. *Ts'ao Yin and the K'ang-hsi Emperor: Bondservant and Master.* New Haven: Yale University Press, 1966.
Strassberg, Richard E. *The World of K'ung Shang-jen: A Man of Letters in Early Ch'ing China.* New York: Columbia University Press, 1983.
Wakeman, Frederic, Jr. "Romantics, Stoics, and Martyrs in Seventeenth-Century China." *Journal of Asian Studies,* vol. 43, no. 4 (August, 1984), 631–661.
Waley, Arthur. *Yüan Mei: Eighteenth Century Chinese Poet.* London: Allen & Unwin, 1956. Reprint edition: New York: Grove Press, n.d.

Wang, John Ching-yu. *Chin Sheng-t'an*. New York: Twayne Publishers, 1972.
Wilhelm, Hellmut. "The Poems from the Hall of Obscured Brightness." In *K'ang Yu-wei: A Biography and a Symposium,* edited by Jung-pang Lo. Tucson: University of Arizona Press, 1967.
Wong, Shirleen S. *Kung Tzu-chen*. Boston: Twayne Publishers, 1975.
______. "Ironic Reflections on History: Some *Yung-shih shih* of the Ch'ing Period." *Monumenta Serica,* vol. 34 (1979–80), pp. 371–388.
Wong, Siu-kit. "*Ch'ing* and *Ching* in the Critical Writings of Wang Fu-chih." In *Chinese Approaches to Literature,* edited by A. Rickett.
Woon, Ramon L. Y. and Lo, Irving Y. "Poets and Poetry of China's Last Empire." *Literature East & West,* vol. 9, no. 4 (December, 1965), pp. 331–361.

CONTRIBUTORS

FREDERICK P. BRANDAUER, Ph. D., Stanford University, teaches at the University of Washington. His research interests embrace Chinese literature and culture, and he is the author of a book on the seventeenth-century novelist Tung Yüeh.

DANIEL BRYANT, Ph. D., the University of British Columbia, teaches Chinese language and literature at the University of Victoria. His publications include scholarly articles, translations, and the book *Lyric Poets of the Southern T'ang.*

MARIE CHAN, Ph. D., the University of California at Berkeley, teaches Chinese language and comparative literature at the University of Arizona. Her special research interests relate to T'ang poetry, and she is the author of two books: *Kao Shih* and *Cen Shen.*

KANG-I SUN CHANG, Ph. D., Princeton University, teaches Chinese literature at Yale. Her scholarly publications include *The Evolution of Chinese Tz'u Poetry: From Late T'ang to Northern Sung* and *Six Dynasties Poetry..*

YIN-NAN CHANG, B. D., Nanking Theological Seminary, is a writer and translator now residing in Canada. His published writings include *Poems by Wang Wei* (with Lewis C. Walmsley) and translations in *Sunflower Splendor.*

CHANG-FANG CHEN, Ph. D., Indiana University, is a member of the Foreign Language and Literature faculty of National Taiwan University in Taiwan.

MADELINE CHU, Ph. D., the University of Arizona, teaches Chinese language and literature at Connecticut College. Her special research interest is classical Chinese literature.

JOHN C. COLEMAN, M. A. in Chinese language and literature; M. B. A., Indiana University, is a systems engineer, employed by Electronics Data Systems, with research interests in Chinese language and poetry.

MICHAEL S. DUKE, Ph. D., the University of California at Berkeley, teaches at the University of British Columbia. His publications include a monograph on the Sung poet Lu Yu and a book on contemporary Chinese literature.

EUGENE C. EOYANG, Ph. D., Indiana University, is a member of the Comparative Literature and East Asian Languages and Cultures faculty at Indiana. An editor, translator, and specialist in late T'ang popular literature, he has also edited and translated a volume of modern poetry by the poet Ai Qing.

BARRY L. GARTELL, M. A., the University of Arizona, is currently employed in the electronics field. His research interests are the poetry and literary criticism of the Six Dynasties era.

JAMES M. HARGETT, Ph. D., Indiana University, teaches Chinese language and literature at the University of Colorado. His primary research interest is the poetry and travel literature of the Sung dynasty.

COY L. HARMON, Ph. D., the University of Arizona, is Dean of Libraries and chairman of the Department of Library Science, Murray State University, Kentucky. He specializes in the classical fiction of the post-T'ang era.

HSIN-SHENG C. KAO, Ph. D., the University of Southern California, teaches at the University of La Verne. She is the author of *Li Ju-chen,* a nineteenth-century novelist and translator of the modern poetry of Chou Meng-tieh.

PAUL W. KROLL, Ph. D., the University of Michigan, is currently chairman of the Department of Oriental Languages and Literatures, the University of Colorado. His scholarly publications include a monograph on the T'ang poet Meng Hao-jan and a separate *Concordance to the Poems of Meng Hao-jan.*

JULIE LANDAU, A. B., Harvard University, is a professional writer. Her translations of classical Chinese poetry have appeared in various publications, including *Song Without Music: Chinese Tz'u Poetry,* edited by Stephen C. Soong.

LI CHI, B. Litt., Oxford University, is Professor Emeritus of Chinese at the University of British Columbia. She has translated Wordsworth's *Prelude* into Chinese, and Hsü Hsia-k'o's travel diaries into English.

IRVING YUCHENG LO, Ph. D., the University of Wisconsin, teaches at Indiana University. His major publications include a monograph on the Sung lyric poet Hsin Ch'i-chi and *Sunflower Splendor: Three Thousand Years of Chinese Poetry,* which he coedited with Wu-chi Liu.

RONALD C. MIAO, Ph. D., the University of California at Berkeley, teaches Chinese language and culture at the University of Arizona. He is the author of a book on the Han dynasty poet Wang Ts'an, and he has written extensively on T'ang and pre-T'ang poetry and criticism.

WILLIAM H. NIENHAUSER, JR., Ph. D., Indiana University, teaches Chinese language and literature at the University of Wisconsin. His scholarly publications include *P'i Jih-hsiu, Liu Tsung-yüan* (as coauthor), and the *Indiana Companion to Traditional Chinese Literature* (as chief editor).

MICHAEL PATRICK O'CONNOR, Ph. D., the University of Michigan, is the author of several books, including *Hebrew Verse Structure.*

CHIA-LIN PAO, Ph. D., Indiana University, has taught Chinese history at National Taiwan University and the University of Arizona. Her current research interests include a history of women in China and the life and works of Ch'iu Chin.

J. D. SCHMIDT, Ph. D., the University of British Columbia, teaches Chinese language and literature at the same institution. He is the author of a book on the Sung poet Yang Wan-li and is currently working on two Ch'ing poets: Huang Tsun-hsien and Chin Ho.

WILLIAM SCHULTZ, Ph. D., the University of Washington, teaches Chinese literature and history at the University of Arizona. He has contributed to various publications and edited the China volumes for Twayne's World Authors Series.

J. P. SEATON, Ph. D., Indiana University, teaches at the University of North Carolina, Chapel Hill. His publications include *The Wine of Endless Life, The View From Cold Mountain* (as coauthor); his translations from Chinese poetry have appeared in various journals and books, including *Sunflower Splendor* and *Chinese Poetic Writings.*

GLORIA HUNG-KUANG SHEN, M. A., SUNY at Binghamton, is presently working on her doctorate in Chinese language and literature at Indiana University. She has taught Chinese language at Middlebury College, Princeton University, and Indiana University.

JONATHAN D. SPENCE, Ph. D., Yale University, is George Burton Adams Professor of History at the same institution and presently the chairman of the history department there. He is the author of numerous scholarly works, his latest being *The Gate of Heavenly Peace* and *The Memory Palace of Matteo Ricci.*

LYNN STRUVE, Ph. D., the University of Michigan, teaches Chinese history at Indiana University. A specialist in seventeenth-century intellectual history, she has contributed to a forthcoming volume in the *Cambridge History of China* and is author of *The Southern Ming,* recently published by Yale University Press.

CECILE CHU-CHIN SUN, Ph. D., Indiana University, teaches Chinese and comparative literature at the University of Pittsburgh. She has also taught at the Chinese University of Hong Kong, Tsinghua University, Taiwan, and the University of Iowa.

AN-YAN TANG, Ph. D., Indiana University, wrote her dissertation on the poetics of Tu Fu. Presently she resides in Bloomington where she engages in private business.

CHING-I TU, Ph. D., the University of Washington, teaches at Rutgers University where he is Chair and Professor of Chinese. He is the translator of Wang Kuo-wei's *Poetic Remarks in the Human World* and frequently writes on Chinese literature and criticism.

JAN W. WALLS, Ph. D., Indiana University, is Vice President of the Canadian Pacific Cultural Foundation. He has collaborated with Yvonne L. Walls on several recent books, including *West Lake: A Collection of Folktales* and *Classical Chinese Myths.*

YVONNE L. WALLS, M. A., the University of Washington, teaches Chinese at the University of Victoria. She is coauthor (with Jan W. Walls) of several books on Chinese mythology and folklore.

JOHN E. WILLS, JR., Ph. D., Harvard University, teaches history at the University of Southern California. His publications include *Pepper, Guns, and Parleys: The Dutch East India Company and China, 1662–1681,* and *From Ming to Ch'ing: Conquest, Region, and Continuity in Seventeenth-Century China,* which he coedited with Jonathan D. Spence.

SHIRLEEN S. WONG, Ph. D., the University of Washington, teaches Chinese language and literature at the University of California at Los Angeles. A specialist in classical Chinese poetry, she is the author of *Kung Tzu-chen.*

TIMOTHY C. WONG, Ph. D., Stanford University, teaches Chinese language and literature at Ohio State University. A specialist in the fiction of Ch'ing era, his scholarly publications include a book on the Chinese novelist Wu Ching-tzu.

CATHERINE YI-YÜ CHO WOO, Ed., D., the University of San Francisco, teaches Chinese language and literature at San Diego State University. She is a painter, calligrapher, and translator and is coauthor (with the late Kai-yu Hsü) of the *Magic of the Brush.*

KENNETH KENICHIRO YASUDA, Ph. D., the University of Tokyo, is Professor Emeritus of Japanese at Indiana University. A specialist in *haiku* and the Noh drama, his major publications include *A Pepper Pod* and *Land of the Reed Plain.*

ANTHONY C. YU, Ph. D., the University of Chicago, teaches religion and comparative literature at the same institution. In addition to many articles and monographs, he has translated the classic novel *Hsi-yu chi* into English, published in four volumes under the title *The Journey to the West.*

INDEX OF NAMES

BOLD-FACED CAPITAL LETTERS are used to indicate Ch'ing authors whose poetry is included in this anthology.

INDEX OF TUNE TITLES

IRVING YUCHENG LO is Professor of East Asian Languages and Cultures at Indiana University. His major publications include a monograph on the Sung lyric poet Hsin Ch'i-chi and *Sunflower Splendor: Three Thousand Years of Chinese Poetry* which he coedited with Wu-chi Liu.

WILLIAM SCHULTZ is Professor of Oriental Studies at the University of Arizona and author of various articles on Chinese literature and history. He has also edited numerous books on Chinese literature.

Editor: Bob Furnish
Book designer: Sharon L. Sklar
Jacket designer: Sharon L. Sklar
Production coordinator: Harriet Curry
Typeface: Palatino
Typesetter: Impressions, Inc.
Printer: Braun-Brumfield